Armies and Wars of the French East India Companies 1664-1770

European, Asian and African Soldiers in India, Africa, the Far East and Louisiana

René Chartrand

Helion & Company

To William Y. Carman (1909-2003)
Curator, historian, friend, mentor

Helion & Company Limited
Unit 8 Amherst Business Centre
Budbrooke Road
Warwick
CV34 5WE
England
Tel. 01926 499619
Email: info@helion.co.uk
Website: www.helion.co.uk
Twitter: @helionbooks
Visit our blog at http://blog.helion.co.uk/

Published by Helion & Company 2024
Designed and typeset by Mach 3 Solutions (www.mach3solutions.co.uk)
Cover designed by Paul Hewitt, Battlefield Design (www.battlefield-design.co.uk)

Cover: A view of the shoreline of Pondicherry, circa 1750-1755. Painting by Eugène Lelièpvre. Musée des Troupes de la Marine, Fréjus, France.

ISBN 978-1-804513-40-8

British Library Cataloguing-in-Publication Data.
A catalogue record for this book is available from the British Library.

Contents

Preface and Acknowledgements

Rather surprisingly, the volume you are holding is the first book length study published concerning the military forces maintained by the French East India companies, be it in the English or French languages. There have been many excellent articles, publications of documents and biographies of leading personalities such as Dupleix, Bussy, La Bourdonnais and Lally with much valuable information on military aspects, but a specific volume devoted to the armed forces appears only now.

The author has always been intrigued by these troops, which were outside the royal army and navy establishments of metropolitan France and its territories in America. Yet, from the mid-seventeenth century, the commercial monopoly trading companies also needed soldiers for the security of their trading lodges operating in Africa, India and as far as Canton in China. Who were these troops that, even during the reigns of the Sun King and Louis XV, hardly never seem to have been mentioned in primary printed sources of those times except in passing?

Being devoted to the virtues of comparative research, the author simply noted what seemed like useful information on these troops when encountered. Having been a curator and thus never neglecting the crucial information brought by material culture, a sizeable amount of data was gathered concerned the weapons, uniforms and fortifications, some of which was most surprising. In all the above endeavours, encouragement always came from, in particular, William Y. Carman, the outstanding authority on the Indian Army at the time of the British Raj. We gratefully dedicate this work to his memory.

Another aspect was that, while the leaders and most European soldiers were natives of France, there were many more African and Asian auxiliaries also on the company's payrolls. From the mid-seventeenth century, they might form a third to half of the French garrisons in India until the advent of very large contingents of sepoys (Indian men-at-arms) were added to the establishment from the late 1730s, armed with European weapons and trained in linear tactics. By the early 1750s, there were four or five sepoys to one European soldier. These European-trained sepoys brigaded with French soldiers spelt the demise on battlefields of the huge traditional Indian armies. It was the troops of the French Compagnies des Indes that changed the history of India at Adyar in 1746 and later battles confirming the outstanding tactical superiority of European-trained units.

Organising these many wide-ranging topics into book chapters was a challenge and, while surely imperfect, we hope those presented cover the topic in its essential aspects. Chapters 1 to 14 inclusive are basically a narrative of events. Many battles were not against British opponents so that most are not covered in British military histories; we have of course given more attention to those and somewhat less to many others involving the British, such as Plassey, that have many sources. Our favourite overall British historians remain Sir John Forescue and Colonel Malleson, along with Martineau for the French, taking into account that they lived and published during an era when the now vanished colonial empires of their respective nations were at their peak. We humbly try to give a little more space to non-European soldiers and aspects in our study.

Chapters 15 to 20 inclusive are devoted to organisations, lifestyles, weapons, equipment and clothing, notably the very colourful uniforms in India, for both European and Asian soldiers. Chapter 21 concerns militias, especially those in Ile de France, Ile de Bourbon and Louisiana that had substantial European settlements.

We wish to acknowledge with considerable gratitude the assistance from many individuals and institutions over the last half century. We cite here Christian Ariès (Nantes, France), Geneviève Beauchesne (Lorient, France), Jean Boudriot (Paris), William Y. Carman (Sutton, UK), André Corvisier (Paris), Bruno Hélias (Britany, France), Randolph Jones (London), Marc Morillon (Les Arcs, France), Michel Pétard (Saint-Sébastien-sur-Loire, France), Stephen Wood (London), the kind staff of the Archives Nationales (Paris and Aix-en-Provence), the Bibliothèque Nationale de France (Paris), the Anne S.K. Brown Military Collection at the Brown University Library (Providence, USA), the Canadian War Museum (Ottawa), Library and Archives Canada (Ottawa), the Library of Congress (Washington), The National Archives (Kew), the Rijksmuseum (Amsterdam) are amongst the many persons and institutions that have kindly greeted us over the years.

We also wish to kindly thank Dr Andrew Bamford whose mastery of editorial as well as historical aspects has produced the attractive present publication with colleagues at Helion as well as Patrice Courcelle for his fine plates, all of which recreate accurately for the first time ever the visual aspect of those extraordinary soldiers. And definitely Dr Luce Vermette, historian of lifestyles and of fine art, who happens to be the author's beloved, encouraging and very patient spouse.

René Chartrand
August 2023

Notes on Spellings and Denominations

Almost each non-European event, place and individual's name mentioned in this study has several spellings from French and English language sources. Like any author, we must make a choice with the hope that it will not add to the ambient confusion.

French historian Alfred Martineau, who lived in India, made a short but helpful list of French spellings with English equivalents and we have mostly adopted it. Fortescue's history of the British Army has equally been used. They are far from having all the names, but at least do offer some uniformity.[1]

Another aspect is the English-language qualification of the French commercial companies as the 'French East India Company'. This is erroneous, especially from 1719 and we simply called it by its French name in our text: Compagnie des Indes.

The reason is that the Compagnie des Indes was one of European history's early and great multinational companies. Its activities were intense and very widespread during its relatively short existence (1719-1770). Its East India trade was most important. It also enjoyed trade monopolies in Africa, the Middle and Far East, Canada, had interests in the West Indies and actually governed Louisiana between 1719 and 1731. It further had an important role in the economy of metropolitan France.

The following abbreviations are employed in this work:

AC Archives des colonies at the Archives nationales d'outre-mer (ANOM) at Aix-en-Provence

AG Archives de la guerre (Vincennes, France)

AM Archives de la Marine at the Archives Nationale in Paris

ANF Archives Nationales de France

APL Archives du Port de Lorient (France)

AR Archives de Rochefort (France)

1 Jean Law de Lauriston (ed. Alfred Martineau), *Mémoire sur quelques affaires de l'Empire mogol, 1756-1761* (Paris: Société de l'Histoire des Colonies françaises, 1913), pp.LIII-LV.

BMG Bibliothèque du ministère de la guerre (Paris)[2]
BNF Bibliothèque Nationale de France
DFC Dépôt des Fortifications des Colonies at the ANOM
JSAHR *Journal of the Society for Army Historical Research*
TNA The National Archives (Kew, UK)
WO War Office (at TNA)

2 In which we conducted research: since closed, its collections transferred to the Service historique des Armées at Vincennes and the Musée de l'Armée in Paris.

Chronology of Main Events and Engagements

Fourteenth century – Arab navigator Dina Moghrabin lands at the 'western islands' (Ile de France/Mauritius and Ile de Bourbon/La Réunion) in the Indian Ocean.

1498 – Vasco de Gama reaches Calicut in India. In subsequent decades, the Portuguese establish fortified trading lodges of which Goa (1510) becomes the most extensive.
1526–1530 – Baber becomes first Mughal emperor in India.
1530 – Jean Parmentier arrives in France with information from a voyage in the Indian Ocean and present-day Indonesia.
1530–1556 – Reign of Humayun, Mughal emperor in India.
1556–1605 – Reign of Akbar, Mughal emperor in India.
1600 – British East India Company founded in London.
1602 – Dutch East India Company founded in Amsterdam.
1605–1627 – Reign of Jehangir, Mughal emperor in India.
1610–1643 – Reign of Louis XIII, King of France.
1627–1658 – Reign of Shah Jahan, Mughal emperor in India
1638 – French land as 'Mascarin' Island, official possession for France in 1642, named Ile de Bourbon 1649, first settlers arrive in 1643.
1639 – British found Madras (Fort St George).
1643–1715 – Reign of Louis XIV, King of France.
1643 – Fort Dauphin is established at Madagascar, to be both a colony and a base for French ships going to and from India and further East.
1651 – Hostilities in Madagascar between French and local warriors.
1658–1707 – Reign of Aurangzeb, Mughal emperor in India.
1659 – Saint-Louis is established in Senegal.
1664 – In May, Louis XIV through his minister Jean-Baptiste Colbert concedes monopoly power to the Compagnie des Indes Orientales (East Indies [or India] Company) to open trade and create lodges in the Orient.
1666 – In March, fleet of 10 ships under Marquis de Mondeverge sails to India, but reaches Fort Dauphin only a year later and Surat, India, on 13 February 1668. Nabob Aurangzeb allows the French to establish a lodge and trade at Surat and all his states.

1666 – Dutch fort of Arguin, Senegal, taken by the French on 29 August.

1667–1668 – Hostilities in Madagascar between French and local warriors.

1668 – First French lodge in India established by Caron at Surat for the Compagnie des Indes Orientales. A second lodge is established at Masulipatam in 1669.

1671 – French fortified lodge established at Ouidah, Guinea Coast.

1671 – 'Escadre de la Perse' (Persia Squadron) of nine ships under Jacob Blanquet de La Haye arrives at Surat on 18 October.

1672 – La Haye's squadron reaches Trincomalee, Ceylon (Sri-Lanka) on 22 March, chases away the few Dutch there, obtains trade agreement and Trincomalee from king of Kandi, builds a fort, leaves a small garrison and sails 9 July. Dutch arrive a few days later and take the fort.

1672 – La Haye's squadron takes Sao Tomé by assault on 25 July after incidents with local Indian official. Indian troops of the king of Golconde blockade the place.

1672 – News of war by France and Great Britain with the Dutch Republic reaches India in early September. Some Dutch join Indian troops in October outside Sao Tomé, but repulsed ending its siege.

1673 – Permission to the French Compagnie des Indes orientales to have a lodge at Pondicherry granted by Prince Chirkam Lodi to Bellanger de l'Espinau on 4 February.

1673 – Strong Dutch squadron with troops join Indian army outside Sao Tomé in July, and blockades and eventually besiege it from 18 September 1673; capitulates on 6 September 1674.

1674 – Fort Dauphin at Madagascar evacuated on 9 September after an attack by local warriors on 17 August. Survivors settle at Ile de Bourbon (La Réunion).

1676 – François Martin, chief of the Pondicherry lodge, trains with a few French soldiers some Indian allied soldiers of provincial governor Prince Chirkam Lodi that capture the fortress of Valdaour (24 September) of rival king of Gingee.

1677 – Dutch forts at Arguin and Gorée, Senegal, taken by a French squadron under d'Estrées in November.

1679 – End of Dutch war promotes trade of the Compagnie des Indes Orientales in years to come. Arguin and Gorée, Senegal, ceded to France. Establishment of Albreda on the Gambia River.

1682 – In April, Dutch expels French and British personnel at lodges in Bantam.

1686 – Chandernagor lodge established in Bengal.

1687 – French embassy lands in Bangkok, Siam with 500 soldiers in September.

1687 – Permission to build a fort at Pondicherry granted by Ram Raja.

1688 – Revolution in Siam. Sickly King Phra Narai dies. Anti French rebels led by Phra Petracha overwhelm the country in May and June. French troops besieged in Bangkok citadel until November when evacuated to Pondicherry.

1689 – News of War of the League of Augsburg reaches Pondicherry in July. Indian princes at Gingee and Tanjore lobby to expel the French. Martin skilfully negotiates customs taxes agreements.
1690 – British found Calcutta.
1690 – French squadron under Duquesne–Guitton arrives, bombards briefly Madras (25 August), returns to France.
1692 – Three French warships under *Capitaine de frégate* Dandennes cruise off Malabar coast (October to February 1693); two go back, one stays at Pondicherry and Bengal.
1693 – British from Gambia take and ravage Saint–Louis and Gorée.
1693 – Strong Dutch squadron lands troops near Pondicherry at end of August; small garrison resists until capitulation on 6 September. French commercial activity continues at lodges opened in Bengal since the mid–1680s.
1696 – Six ships under Serquigny d'Aché sent to India engage eight Dutch ships north of Goa on 7 March; inconclusive battle; squadron returns to France.
1696 – French squadron under the Comte de Gennes takes and blows up British Fort St James in Gambia.
1699 – Pondicherry evacuated by Dutch and returned to French on 3 September (by Treaty of Ryswick signed 21 September 1697). *Conseil Supérieur* (Superior Council) moved from Surat to Pondicherry.
1700 – Fort Saint–Joseph established in the interior of Senegal.
1701 – British attack on Saint–Louis, Senegal, repulsed in April.
1701 – Lodge at Surat closed. Its staff transferred Pondicherry making it the capital responsible for all French establishments in India (21 January); arrival of engineer de Nyon (17 July) to build Pondicherry's fortifications.
1702 – War of Spanish Succession breaks out in Europe.
1702 – Dutch attack on Saint–Louis, Senegal, repulsed in November.
1705 – French squadron under Baron de Pallières takes a Dutch ship off Negapatam (15 January) with Dutch East India commissioner Bernard Phoonen; he and Martin agree to a truce between Dutch and French on Coromandel coast (27 January).
1705 – French in Senegal and British in Gambia sign a local neutrality agreement.
1706 – Citadel built at Pondicherry inaugurated on 25 August. From a village in 1673, the city now had 60,000 inhabitants.
1707–1712 – Reign of Bahadur Shah I (Shah Alam I), Mughal emperor in India.
1712–1713 – Reign of Jahandar Shah, Mughal emperor in India.
1713–1719 – Reign of Farrukh–Siyar, Mughal emperor in India.
1715–1774 – Reign of Louis XV, King of France.
1718 – War of the Quadruple Alliance (of Austria, France, Great Britain and the Netherlands) declared against Spain on 2 August.
1719–1748 – Reign of Muhammad Shah, Mughal emperor in India.
1719 – The Compagnie des Indes Orientales (East India Company), the Compagnie d'Occident (Western Company), the Compagnie de la Chine (China Company) and the Compagnie du Sénégal (Senegal Company)

are merged together to form the Compagnie des Indes (Company of the Indies) in May.

1719 – Pensacola (Spanish Florida) captured by French in May, recaptured by Spanish in August, recaptured by French in September.

1720 – War of the Quadruple Alliance ends by Treaty of The Hague on 17 February.

1720 – Spanish expedition led by Villasur from Santa Fe (New Mexico) annihilated west of Illinois (French Louisiana) on 13 August by First Nations warriors with, most likely, some French/Canadian wilderness traders/adventurers.

1721–1724 – Hostilities in Fort Arguin area, Senegal, between French and local warriors and Dutch traders.

1721 – French lodge established at Mahé on the Malabar coast following agreement with local Indian ruler Bayanor.

1724 – The French lodge at Mahé on the Malabar coast ordered evacuated in April by Bayanor; on 29 November, a French squadron arrives at Mahé, attacked and scattered some 3.000 of Bayanor's troops, takes the fort and garrisons it.

1725 – French lodge established at Yanaon.

1737 – Successful punitive expedition by Compagnie des Indes ships and troops to Moka (Yemen, Arabia) in February.

1738 – Carical on the Coromandel coast granted to the Compagnie des Indes by the kingdom of Tanjore.

1740 – About 200,000 Marathas invade the Carnatic, defeat the army led by Nabob Dost Ali who is killed in battle. His wife and sons Sufder Ali, who succeeds as nabob, and Chunda Sahib obtain refuge in Pondicherry on 26 May thanks to Governor-General Dumas who also took into French service about 4,000 sepoys that were trained and armed in European fashion.

1741 – Carnatic prince Chunda Sahib leaves Pondicherry in later 1740 and raises troops, is besieged by Marathas in strategic fortress of Trichninopoly from 15 December to its surrender on 30 April 1741.

1746 – Naval battle between the French and British squadrons of La Bourdonnais and Commodore Peyton off the off Negapatam on the Coromandel coast on 6 July. Peyton withdraws leaving the British at Madras unprotected.

1746 – La Bourdonnais lands troops near Madras on 14 September, the city capitulates on 21 September.

1746 – On 4 November, Commandant Louis Paradis leading a small Indo-French force of 930 men utterly defeats a 10,000 men Indian army under Maphuze Khan sent by the nabob of the Carnatic to take possession of Madras. This engagement fought at Adyar near Sao Tomé is considered a turning point in Indian military history.

1747 – Dupleix signs a peace agreement with the nabob of the Carnatic.

1747 – French attempt to attack Fort St David foiled on 13 March by arrival of a British naval squadron.

1748–1754 – Reign of Ahmad Shah, Mughal emperor in India

1748 – British Rear Admiral Boscawen fails to take Ile de France in July.

1748 – Boscawen besieges Pondicherry from 9 September. Indo-French garrison led by Dupleix foils attackers; they withdraw on 15 October.

1748 – Death of Nizam-ul-Mulk, viceroy of the Deccan; grandsons Murzapher (or Muzaffer) Jung and his brother Nasir (or Nazer) Jung claim the throne and civil war ensues.

1749 – Devicotah ceded to British in July.

1749 – Outstanding Indo-French victory at Ambour on 3 August. The opposing numerous Indian army was largely crushed by the French corps.

1750 – Unsuccessful siege of Tanjore by Indo-French troops from January to March.

1750 – Mazilipatam, Trivady and Villapouram occupied by Indo-French forces in July.

1750 – Indian prince's attack on Trivady repulsed on 30 July by Indo-French troops.

1750 – The great fortress of Gingee taken by an Indo-French force led by Bussy on 11–12 September.

1750 – Nazer Jung killed in battle on 16 December near Gingee by an Indo-French army led by Muzaffar Jang and Commandant Latouche.

1751 – Commandant Bussy with 300 French and 2,000 sepoys sent by Dupleix march out of Pondicherry on 12 January to support Muzaffar Jang as ruling viceroy of Deccan.

1751 – Muzaffar Jang killed in battle on 14 February by opposing troops whose nabob leaders of Savanour and of Carmoul are also killed and their forces utterly defeated with assistance from Bussy's French corps. Salabat Jing succeed as ruler.

1751 – Arcot captured on 11 September by Indo-British troops led by Robert Clive. Besieged by Indo-French force from 5 October until 25 November when its assault was repulsed by Clive.

1751 – Maratha army of some 60,000 men under Balagirao is defeated and scattered by Salabat Jing's army at about the same strength and Bussy's Indo-French corps during a surprise attack on their camp in the early hours of 4 December. Bussy and his men are praised for their initiative and valour by allied Indian rulers for this victory.

1751 – On 10 December, Balagirao having rallied some of his Maratha army attacks a detachment of Salabat Jing's army of about 11,000 men that includes Bussy's French corps, whose artillery and firepower largely defeats the Marathas. A truce is agreed to during January 1752.

1752 – Indo-British force under Clive defeats an Indo-French force led by Commandant Véry at Covrepauk on 14 March.

1752 – Indo-French troops defeat Indo-British troops on 26 April at Simiaverum.

1752 – Trichninopoly captured on 12 June by Indo-British troops led by Stringer Lawrence. Chunda Sahib murdered by opponent Indian princes the same day.

1752 – Trivady and Villapouram taken by Indo-British troops in July.

1752 – Indo-British attack near Gingee repulsed and counter attacked at Vikravandi by Indo-French troops led by Commandant Kerjean on 7–9 August.

1752 – Ariancopang captured by Indo-British troops on 6 September (Carnatic).
1753 – Trivady taken by an Indo-French force on 7 May following the mutiny of its Indo-British garrison.
1753 – Abortive Indo-French siege of Trichninopoly held by Indo-British during August-September.
1753 – In October 1753, Bussy obtains the cession of the Four Sirkars (or Northern Sirkars) on the Orrissa coast to the Compagnie des Indes.
1754–1759 – Reign of Alamgir II, Mughal emperor in India.
1754 – Successful Indo-French raids on large Indo-British supply convoys on 15 February and 13 May near Trichninopoly.
1754 – Godeheu arrives at Pondicherry 1 September; replaces Dupleix as governor general.
1754 – Truce agreed on 29 September between British and French in India to be effective until 11 January 1755 at which date a formal agreement is signed.
1755 – Godeheu sails for France on 16 February, replaced by Duval de Leyrit as interim governor general.
1756 – Indo-French army under Salabat Jing and Bussy besieges Savanour, defended by Balagirao's Marathas troops, from 5 to 25 May when a peace agreement is made between Salabat Jing and Balagirao who renounces some of his claims.
1756 – Indian army led Nabob Surajah Dowlah occupies British Fort Cassimbazar on 9 May. Lays siege on 16 June to city of Calcutta held by British, evacuated from 19 June by most British residents and troops. The 146 remaining Europeans are locked up in the horrid and infamous Black Hole of Calcutta.
1756 – Salabat Jing and Balagirao partly unite their forces to rule central India without French or British allies in late April and early May. They interpret the recall of Duplex as disapproval from the King of France, Bussy is thanked for his services and asked to withdraw with his troops from Aurengabad, which he does.
1756 – Bussy's corps encounters Indian resistance at Hyderabad in June. A Maratha army blockades the city.
1756 – Indo-French reinforcement force led by Commandant Jacques-François Law beats a Maratha force at Mognapara on 11 August, arrives at Hyderabad on 14 August.
1756 – News reaches India on 6 October that war was officially declared between France and Great Britain on 9 June.
1757 – Calcutta taken on night of 4 and 5 February by Indo-British troops led by Clive.
1757 – Chandernagor taken by Indo-British forces on 14 March.
1757 – Lodges of Dacca and Cassimbazar in Bengal evacuated in April. Commandant Law de Lauriston forms a small column of Indo-French soldiers of their garrisons, marches east, reaches Delhi and visits imperial court in July. This was the first time a European force had gone so far.
1757 – Indo-French army crushed by Clive's Indo-British forces at Plassey on 13 June.

1757 – Vizagapatam taken by Indo–French force led by Bussy on 25 June.
1758 – Indo–French force led by Bussy captures the fortress of Dautalabad in February.
1758 – British attack Saint–Louis, Senegal, in April, which capitulates 1 May.
1758 – French withdraw from Maulipatam in February and loose the four Sirkars that are granted to the British by Salabet Jung on 14 May.
1758 – British squadron attacks Goree on 24 May and repulsed.
1758 – Comte de Lally arrives at Pondicherry on 28 April as Governor-General and commander in chief of all French forces in India.
1758 – Fort St David taken on 3 May by Indo–French troops under Lally.
1758 – Devicotah taken on 3 June by Indo–French troops under Lally.
1758 – British squadron attacks Goree again on 28 December which capitulates the next day.
1759–1760 – Reign of Shah Jahan III, Mughal emperor in India.
1759 – Masulipatam taken by assault by Indo–British troops led by Colonel Forde on 8 April.
1759 – City of Wandewash invested and taken by Colonel Coote 27–30 November.
1759 – Garangooly invested and taken by Colonel Coote 3–10 December.
1759–1760 – Naval raids on Muscat (Arabia), Bendar Abbas (Persia), Fort Natal and Bencoolen (Sumatra) from October 1759 to April 1760 by Comte d'Estaing.
1760–1806 – Reign of Shah Alam II, Mughal emperor in India.
1760 – On 22 January British force led by Coote decisively defeats French army under Lally at Wandewash.
1760 – On 5–10 February, Coote's British force besieges and takes Arcot.
1761 – Pondicherry, besieged since September 1760 by Indo–British troops, capitulates on 15 January.
1761 – Shah Alam II Mughal army defeated by Indo–British on 15 January at Suan in Bengal. Law de Lauriston's small corps with that army offers stubborn resistance before finally capitulating.
1763 – Pondicherry, Chandernagor and a few small lodges in India with Goree (Senegal) returned to France by Treaty of Paris.
1764 – Compagnie des Indes government at Ile de France and Ile de Bourbon replaced by royal governance.
1770 – The Compagnie des Indes closes its books. Its territories in the East gradually revert to the royal government during the next two years.

Introduction

Antecedents

The French East India companies emerged during the first half of the seventeenth century with the goal of opening trade routes to Asia and the Far East where they had been preceded by other maritime European nations. India was the prime objective, but the first settlement in 1642 was Fort Dauphin on the southern coast of Madagascar off East Africa. It was not a successful foray and was finally abandoned as we relate in Chapter 2. It did, however, spawn a successful settlement at the island of Ile de Bourbon (now the French overseas department of La Réunion) eventually followed by the settlement of Ile de France (now Mauritius). The location of these islands in the Indian Ocean gave them a certain strategic and military importance, especially from the early eighteenth century as seen in various chapters. However, the French interest in Africa did not end at Madagascar, but went on in Senegal and the Guinea Coast later in the seventeenth century as shown in Chapter 13.

The overwhelming interest was to reach India and establish trade lodges and commercial relations there. This was achieved from 1668. India, being the seat of one of the greatest ancient and sophisticated civilisations on the globe, was an infinitely more complex country in all aspects of human endeavours.

To understand events in India and other countries bordering the Indian Ocean during the seventeenth and eighteenth centuries, it is necessary to go back to the seventeenth century. The historiography of European and American nations has understandably given great importance to Portuguese navigators arriving in India during 1498. They were followed by other European nations in the next three centuries, but their activities in India were minimal and limited to coastal trading until the mid-eighteenth century when the rivalries between the French and British took on an increasingly imperial importance.

India had an estimated population of 130 million souls in 1500, ten million more in 1600 and about 180 million by 1750. By comparison, France as a unified state had the largest population in Western Europe at about 20 to 24 million people.

When the Portuguese arrived in India at the end of the fifteenth century, they encountered local rulers of coastal kingdoms in this very large country that was the seat of a great, wealthy, sophisticated and ancient civilisation. There were enormous business opportunities that could be exploited by trade and commerce between populous India and Europe. The Portuguese inaugurated trade relations and obtained seaport enclaves of which the largest was Goa on the Malabar coast. It was in the interest of both the Portuguese and the Indians coastal rulers to have relatively decent relations.

India is a vast country beyond its coastline on the India Ocean. Since the eighth century, parts of it had been repeatedly invaded by Arabs and Persians bringing the Islamic faith with them. Initially somewhat repulsed, they kept at it and by the end of the twelfth century, Sahab-ub-din had conquered north-western India establishing his capital at Delhi. As in Europe during the Middle Ages, the various kings and princes across India often fought amongst themselves and this was the situation when the

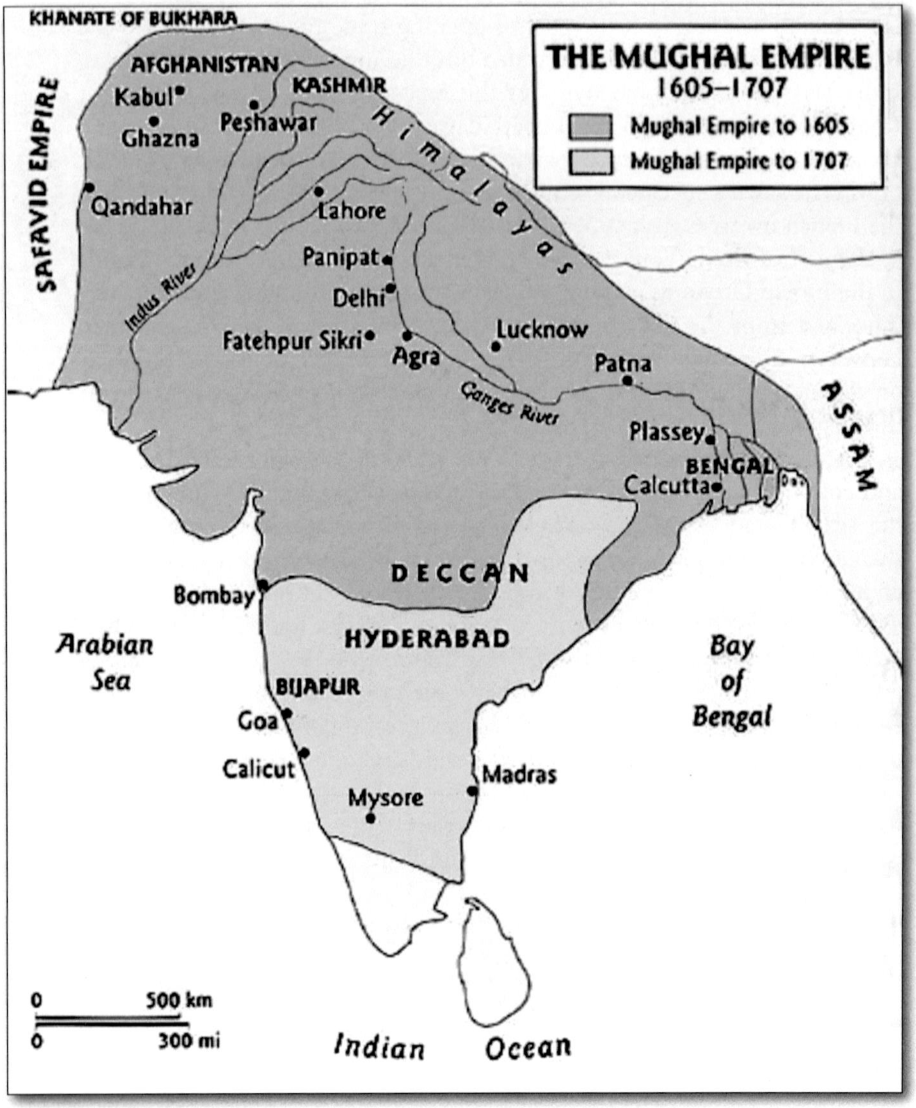

Map of the Mughal Empire, 1605 to 1707. The lighter shaded area indicates the imperial conquests from 1605 to 1707. The first French lodge opened at Calicut in 1668. (Indian Army Official History Department)

Portuguese arrived in 1498. Shortly thereafter, the geopolitics and strategic situation changed radically.[1]

This change was due to the advent of Baber, a Mughal king of Samarkand, whose kingdom had been invaded by Uzbeks from the Central Asia. He found refuge in Persia. Baber had exceptional qualities and was renowned for his quick wit and his ability in making good decisions. His widely varied interests included poetry, art and technology as well as governance. As a military leader, he was versed in military sciences and, seeking to have orderly troops, imposed severe disciplinary actions to marauding soldiers, which was rather unusual anywhere at that time. Baber was also a charismatic and energetic leader that, with the help of Persian Shah Ismail, regained his kingdom and then set his eyes on India after conquering Afghanistan. After a few exploratory incursions on the Indian border, he learned that Ottoman Sultan Selim I had conquered Syria and Egypt in 1517 thanks to technologically superior weapons: light cannon deployed as field artillery.

Large cannon used for sieges were known in India. On the other hand, the Indian armies did not generally take light firearms into account; when Baber attacked the fortress of Bajaur on India's north-western border during 1519, his musketeers were laughed at by the defenders until some were hit by shots. This was obviously not noteworthy at the sultan's palace in Delhi. On 20 April 1526, Baber with his invading Mughal army was at Panipat near Delhi to face a great Indian army led by Sultan Ibrahim Lodi. Against hordes of Indian cavalry and hundreds of elephants, Baber, who was the better tactician, deployed field artillery and elite formations of musketeers, which stopped the main Indian attack while Baber's mounted archers erupted upon the rear of the sultan's army. Panic spread and Sultan Lodi was killed with many of his troops.

Baber then assumed the throne at Delhi as the Great Mughal and achieved imperial status by later conquests or submissions largely thanks to militarily superior force armed with light field artillery. As a ruler, he treated the conquered populations as subjects in a great state rather than as serfs. When Baber passed away in 1530, he ruled over much of northern and central India. The ultimate goal was the unification of India as a Mughal imperial superpower.

Succession to supreme power could be a complicated and bloody affair in the sixteenth and seventeenth centuries. The conflicting claims, murders, beheadings, civil wars and massacres that then went on in western Europe were also common in oriental palaces until a strong and relatively wise leader won and assumed power. Such a pretender was Akbar who had shared his father's exile in Persia and Afghanistan before he assumed throne. When Great Mughal Humayun died in 1556, his illiterate son Akbar was only 13 years old, but also outstandingly brilliant,

1 On early India, see: Hermann Kulke and Dietmar Rothermund, *A History of India* (London & New York: Routledge, 1998), chapters 4 and 5; Abbé Guyon, *Histoire des Indes orientales anciennes* (Paris: Lottin, 1744); David Nicolle, *Mughul India 1504-1761* (London: Osprey MAA 263, 1993) with plates by Angus McBride; Arnold Toynbee, *La grande adventure de l'humanité* (Brussels: Elsevier, 1977).

Baber's Mughal forces armed with field artillery defeats Indian forces at Panipat, 20 April 1526. This battle was one of the most important in the history of India as it led to the creation of the Mughal Empire under Baber as the Great Mughal. Print after Ambrose Dudley. (Private collection; author's photo)

gifted with an amazing memory, always seeking new ideas that could be applied in a pragmatic manner. During his young exile in Afghanistan, he observed and learned from its experienced warriors sparking an interest in military affairs that eventually made him an outstanding general. His aim was, much as Baber, to further expand the Mughal empire that would lead to a unified Indian peninsula.

Secure after thwarting a pretender in 1557, Akbar was wise enough not to impose Islam on Hindus and instead abolished the hated tax on non-Muslims thus largely rallying the majority of India's population. The next years were of conquests and submissions such as Gujarat (1574) and Bengal (1576). The Mughal empire was now very extensive going as far as Samarkand, Baluchistan, Kandahar and parts of Afghanistan. Besides being a good general, he organised government services to supervise the administration of his huge empire. The Mughal imperial armies were very large, well armed and mostly made up of Muslim officers and soldiers whereas the civil servants were usually non-Muslims.

With the seventeenth century came the roots of the rapid disintegration of the Mughal Empire. Shah Jahan who became emperor in 1628 annulled the policy of tolerance towards the non-Muslims living in the empire who made up the majority of its people while declaring war on the independent states in the Deccan. The territorial zenith of the Mughal empire was achieved in the reign of Aurangzeb who was Great Mughal from 1658 to his death in 1707.

Southern India was not immune from the Mughal empire and, besides the spread of Islam, many aspects of Persian culture in the arts and architecture, including fortifications, were increasingly seen in the Deccan (central India) and beyond. Some of Aurangzeb's troops made forays deep into the south and sacked Surat in 1664.

Usually warring amongst themselves, the princes of the southern Deccan, Mysore, the Carnatic, and coastal fiefdoms of the Malabar and Coromandel coasts reacted to the military threat and united under Sivagi's Marathas who defeated a Mughal invading army in 1665. Aurangzeb's troops of course reacted resulting in many decades of warfare. By the eighteenth century, warfare had exhausted the empire in particular and the rest of the country in general. Direct imperial central authority collapsed after Aurangzeb's death succeeded by near independent states whose princes competed against each other. These states may have been more or less independent, but they took seriously what went on in the Great Mughal's court in Delhi. Even after Aurangzeb's death, the Great Mughal still wielded sizeable influence in the political intrigues and power struggles of states, even those that were outside of his power. His approval and blessing to the winner of a power struggle was very much sought to ensure the legitimacy of the new ruler whose succession would be announced by a imperial decree and followed by gifts of luxurious protocolary robes, headdress, arms and jewels.

By that time, European explorers, navigators and businessmen with soldiers had been sailing not only through the Indian Ocean for many decades, but around the world crossing all its oceans in their search to find heretofore unknown lands and their riches. America had yielded such promises by conquest. Asia was much farther away, had enormous populations, great imperial civilisations and numerous land armies that were technologically somewhat comparable to Renaissance European troops. Clearly, India and China could not be conquered by the sword. Unless their empires disintegrated… This is what happened in India from the early eighteenth century.

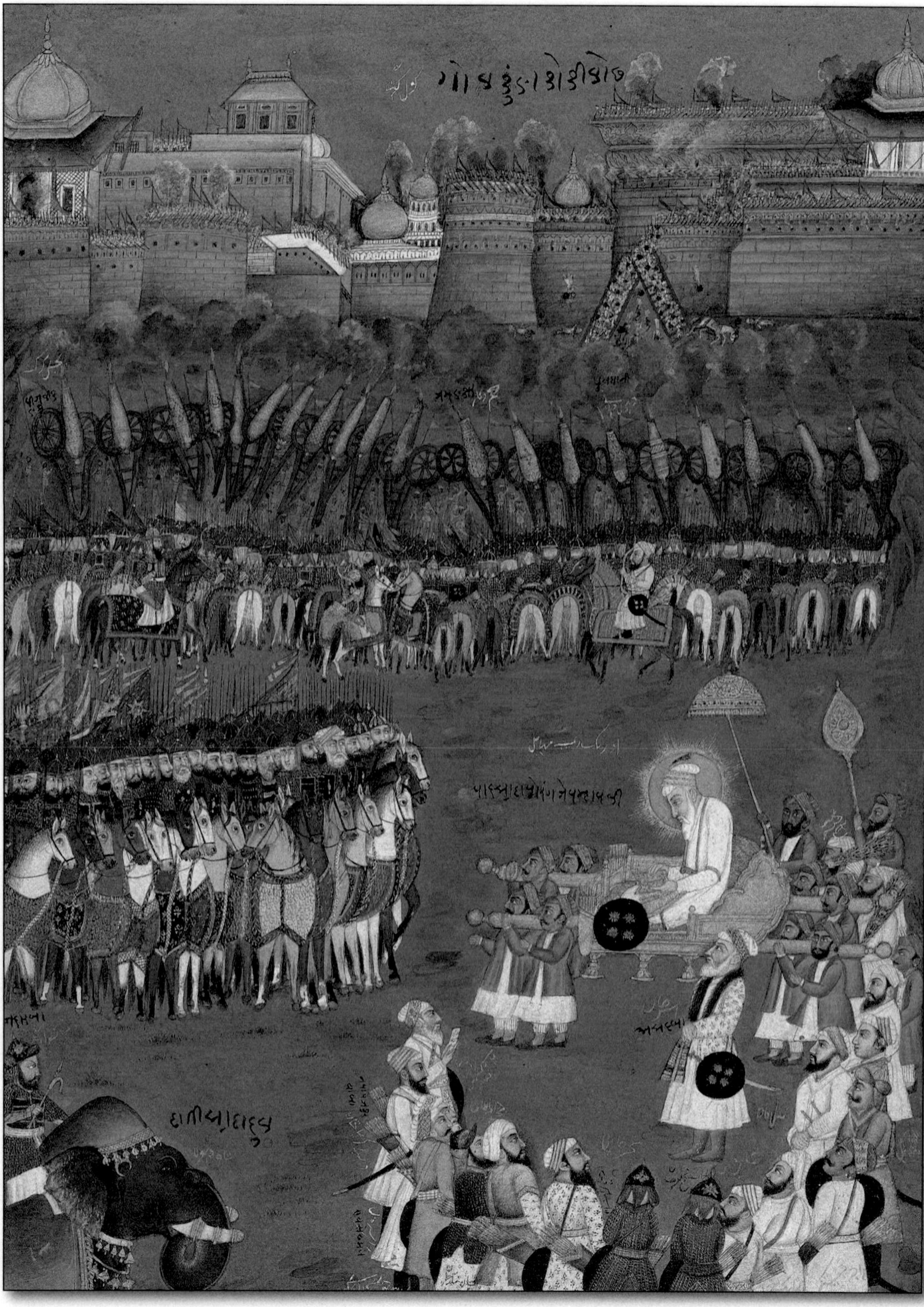

Mughal Emperor Aurangzeb at the siege of Golconda, 1687. This painting shows the emperor on a litter surrounded by senior officers and bodyguards. The many cavalrymen, some of whom are mounted archers, are nearly all seen wearing chainmail coats and metal helmets. The brass guns are served by gunners dressed in light blue clothes and turbans. The fortress of Golconda was taken securing central India to the empire. (Anne S.K. Brown Military Collection)

1

France's Trading Companies 1611-1719

When Portuguese navigators reached India in 1498, this opened enormous trade potentials between Europe and Asia by going east around the aptly named Cape of Good Hope into the Indian Ocean to India, China and as far as the Pacific Ocean. Western European ships were then at the leading edge of world maritime technology and could much more easily reach countries as far as Japan, conduct trade and bring back Asiatic products to Europe by sea.[1]

This was a far more convenient, safer and faster way of transporting sizeable cargoes than by land using the so-called Silk Roads going from China and northern India through Persia (Iran) to reach the Ottoman Empire. This could take years by camel caravans, be expensive due to fees paid to local princes on the way and transported a relatively modest amount of goods compared to cargo loaded in a ship. The next decades saw Portuguese outposts appear along the coasts of Arabia and India and further east in the 'spice islands' of Indonesia. Lisbon became the emporium of Asian good and the coastal ports of India and farther east as far as Indonesia greeted European cargoes creating wealth thanks to new maritime trading routes.

In 1581, the Netherlands declared independence from their Spanish overlords, war ensued and the Dutch, being a maritime and trading people, now revealed themselves to also be excellent soldiers and daring sailors. They were innovative shipbuilders and soon had one of the most powerful navies in Europe. Dutch ships soon appeared in the Indian Ocean, not only to trade, but to attack ships from Portugal that was then somewhat unhappily united to Spain. They were no match for the Dutch who gained most of the Portuguese lodges and territories except for Goa and East Timor. In the process, the Dutch East India Company became one of the most powerful and wealthy trade organisations anywhere.

1 On the impact of Western European technology see: Geoffrey Parker, *The Military Revolution. Military innovation and the rise of the West* (Cambridge: Cambridge University Press, 1988 and 1995).

Europe's two other sizeable maritime nations, Great Britain and France, were basically absent when it came to substantial ventures overseas. By the beginning of the seventeenth century, neither nation had sizeable overseas territories. This started to change from the early 1600s with permanent settlements of Englishmen and Frenchmen in North America and the West Indies. The East Indies were drawing more sustained interest too and, as early as 31 December 1600, British 'Merchant Adventurers' received a charter signed by Queen Elizabeth I creating the Honourable East India Company. It was followed by exploratory visits to princes on the Indian seacoast that, after some opposition from the Dutch, resulted in a first 'factory' established at Masulipatam in 1628 followed by others at Madras and Surat. During 1662, Bombay was ceded by Portugal, which had regained its full independence, as the dowry of the Princess of Braganza upon becoming the Queen of Great Britain. By then, the Honourable East India Company was well established in coastal India.

Meanwhile, although there had been a few French travellers, navigators and even missionaries in India, there were still no permanent establishments hoisting the French standard on the shores of the Indian Ocean apart from the rather tenuous Fort Dauphin at Madagascar since the 1640s and a few marooned individuals on Ile de Bourbon (La Réunion) in spite of several monopoly companies having been formed including three successive Compagnies des Indes orientales (Orient or East India Companies).

Real action came following young King Louis XIV assuming autocratic power from 1661. The Sun King, as he became known, wanted the rays of France's sun to reach all parts of the world and set about to have the means to reach his many goals. To reach them, he insisted on an orderly process with defined rules. He had the good fortune to have the outstanding Jean-Baptiste Colbert as his minister of the economy, the navy and overseas expansion. France had the largest population and economy in western Europe and it was at last well managed. The small French navy was transformed into one of the largest and most modern in Europe while the merchant marine was also expanding, often with royal help.

The next endeavour was to organise overseas expansion. The highly successful Dutch East India Company seemed like a good model to Colbert, Louis XIV agreed, and signed the charter creating the fourth Compagnie des Indes orientales (East India Company) in August 1664.

It was certainly not the first nor the last such endeavour by French financiers in search of more fortunes gained by risk capital as seen below:

- Compagnie des Indes orientales: 1611-1642, 1642-1656, 1656-1664, 1664-1719
- Compagnie de la Chine: 1660-1664, 1700-1712
- Compagnie des Indes occidentales: 1621-1664, 1664-1674
- Compagnie du Sénégal: 1673-1681, 1681-1718
- Compagnie de Guinée: 1685-1702
- Compagnie de l'Assiente: 1702-1713
- Crozat's company in Louisiana: 1713-1717

The Paris headquarters of the Compagnie des Indes. It originally was the palace of Cardinal Mazarin, then became a royal property until 1719 when it was turned over to the company. Print after Jean Marot. (Musée Carnavalet, Paris, author's photo)

Each usually had a convoluted existence. An example was the Louisiana company created by one of France's richest financiers, Antoine Crozat, who, with some royal support, sought to create a large and very prosperous colony. Royal authority happily devolved to Crozat the immense territories that went from the Gulf of Mexico to the Great Lakes of North America. The settlement schemes concentrated on developing plantations, founding towns and creating sizeable maritime trade in the Gulf of Mexico.

After four years of efforts, Crozat saw that it was better to pass the privilege on and it was financier John Law's bank that took it under his wing by creating, with royal approval, his Compagnie d'Occident (Western Company) in September 1717. Its aims were broadly the same as the previous company, but Law was more optimistic that he would succeed and, in the process, created a stock market frenzy with shares booming in

John Law, 'king's councillor, comptroller general of finances, inspector general of the bank and of the Compagnie des Indes', 1719. This Scots adventurer-economist is show at the peak of his achievements that included founding the Compagnie des Indes and the Banque de France. (Bibliothèque Nationale de France, Paris)

France. In May 1718, ships with settlers left for the Mississippi where, stock exchange promoters insisted, magnificent and prosperous establishments would soon rise. Law, through his bank, was also obtaining many monopoly trade privileges from the royal government such as beaver export in Canada. Meanwhile, the other East India, China, and Senegal companies were running deficits and might close their books so, to prevent bankruptcy, Law took over some of their monopoly privileges as well. This maze of monopoly privileges and financial operations needed a total reorganisation to keep everything running.[2]

The Compagnie des Indes 1719-1770

The reorganisation occurred in May 1719 with the formation of the new Compagnie des Indes (Company of the Indies), which was the result of fusing many overseas business entities operating in Asia, Africa and America. These were:[3]

- The 4th Compagnie des Indes orientales 1664-1719
- The 3rd Compagnie de la Chine 1712-1719
- The Compagnie d'Occident 1717-1719

Trade at Senegal in Africa, including the slave and gum trade, had its privilege transferred to the Compagnie des Indes. The same went for the Guinea Coast trade whose privilege ultimately went to the Compagnie des Indes. Louisiana also came to the Compagnie des Indes' portfolio in 1719. So was the 'Beaver Privilege' in Canada which, in 1720, granted the export monopoly of its fur trade.

This plan was initially successful, but eventually collapsed during 1720 due to speculative complications resulting in a massive stock market crash, nicknamed the 'Mississippi Bubble' by the British, and political intrigues. This was not directly attributable to John Law, but popular opinion blamed him and he fled France in December.[4]

The new Compagnie des Indes survived these economic traumas thanks to prudent yet innovative management from the 1720s gradually becoming one of the most important businesses in France with

Coat of arms of the Compagnie des Indes, 1719-1770. Illustration in Chevalier Des Marchais' 1724-1726 in *Journal du Voiage de Guinée et de Cayenne*. (Bibliothèque Nationale de France, Paris, Ms. fr. 24223)

2 Joseph Chaillet-Bert, *Les Compagnies de colonisation sous l'Ancien Régime* (Paris: Colin, 1898), pp.21-28 gives a list of all companies and their activities before 1789.

3 Dufrene de Francheville, *Histoire de la Compagnie des Indes avec les titres de ses concessions et privilèges* (Paris: Bure, 1738), p.3 and folding page with table. Paul Lacroix, *XVIIIe siècle: institutions, usages et costumes* (Paris: Firmin-Didot, 1878), pp.225-229.

4 For a short account of these financial events, see: 'Mississippi Bubble' <https://www.britannica.com/event/Mississippi-Bubble> (accessed 26 September 2023).

a large part of its national trade thanks to its overseas territories and its large fleet of merchant ships.[5]

Associated with the East India trade monopolies were the islands of Ile de Bourbon (La Réunion) and Ile de France (Mauritius). Both islands became more important in trade from the 1730s from increasingly large cash crops of coffee and sugar while the harbour of Port-Louis (Ile de France) became not only a stop for ships going to and from India, but a full-fledged commercial harbour with shipyards as well as a base for warships and privateers. India was seen as the main overseas business of the Compagnies des Indes of 1719. Indeed, revenues from India 1726 to 1749 (inclusive) came to a total yearly average of nearly 24 million livres; from 1750 to 1755 (inclusive) the yearly average was slightly over 21 million livres. These profits funded just about all the company's expenses in India, military and otherwise, along with mostly modest revenues from taxes in Pondicherry and its area and a few other lodges. A major shift in revenues came in 1753 with the addition of the northern sirkars whose taxes could cover the cost of the company's army in the Deccan, the garrisons in the sirkars, and still turn a profit of about 20 percent.

Finally, within France were also many substantial revenue sources. The new Compagnie des Indes had monopoly privileges on consumer good like tea, coffee, tobacco, banking, pension plans, running the state lottery and being exempt of many customs fees and taxes. Another much less visible branch of the company was involved in banking. From 1719, Law's bank became the Bank of France, but this was somewhat too close to the operations of the company and the bank became a truly independent entity in 1725.[6]

A Passage to India

In spite of the sailing conditions, it was more profitable, safer, cheaper and faster to conduct trade with Asian countries by sea than by land. Goods going by ship from, say, from Pondicherry to Lorient, did not pay 'protection' money to various officials going by land along the Silk Route and the hold of a large merchant ship carried far more than a caravan. While it was certainly far more convenient and less dangerous to go by sea from France to India and the far East, it was still a journey that took a substantial amount of time.[7]

- Lorient to Ile de France: about four months without stops on the way.
- Lorient to Pondicherry: about six months with stops.
- Pondicherry to Bengal: about 25 days.

5 Many aspects of the company are masterfully presented in the four volumes of Philipe Haudrère's, *La compagnie française des Indes au XVIIIe siècle 1719-1795* (Paris: Librarie des Indes, 1989).

6 Joseph François Dupleix, *Réponse du sieur Dupleix a la lettre du sieur Godeheu* (Paris: Cellot, 1763), pp.66-67, 285. Dupleix's letter was written on 20 May 1755 while sailing to France on board the *Duc d'Orléans*.

7 Jean Boudriot, *Compagnie des Indes 1720-1770 vaisseaux, hommes, voyages, commerces* (Paris: Self Published, 1983), pp.166, 194.

Outbound ships of the Compagnie des Indes, 1740s. Print after a painting by Peter Rindlisbacher. (Private collection, reproduced by kind permission of the artist)

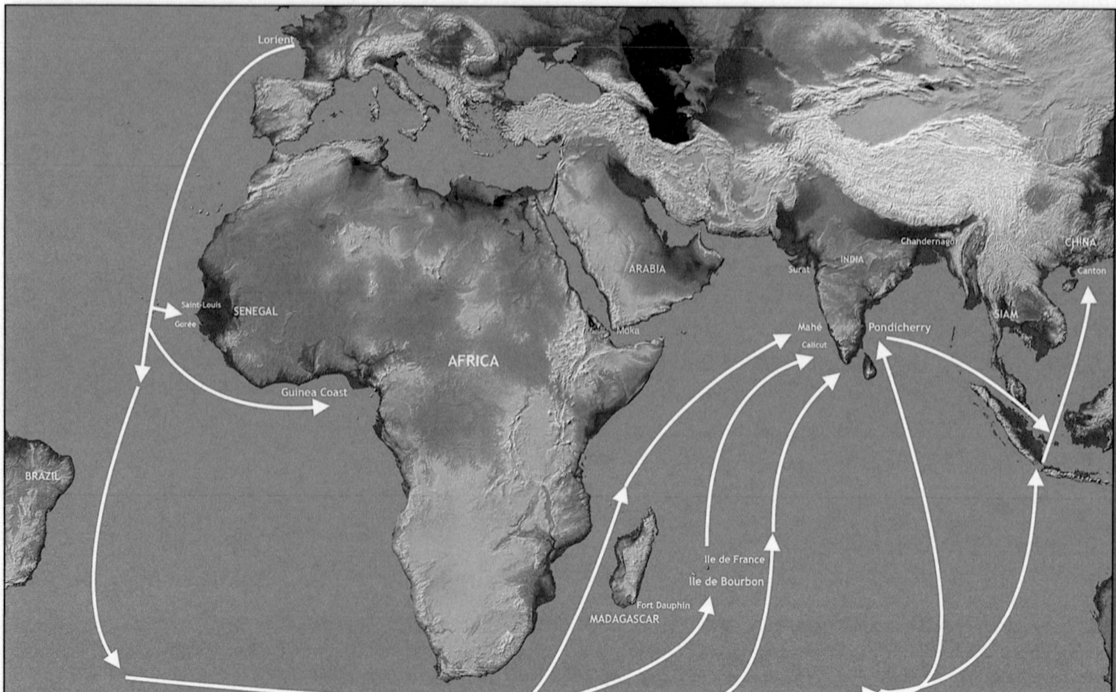

Sea routes of the French East India companies from Lorient to Africa, India and the Far East. (US National Aeronautics and Space Administration (NASA) – digital overlays by the author)

- Lorient to China: about seven-and-a-half months with stops.
- Lorient to China to Lorient: about 19-and-a-half months with stops.

These figures were compiled from the average time for trips for many of the company's ships. Individually, they could vary greatly. The *Cybelle* that left France for India on 28 February 1747 had many stops and came back to France on 23 April 1749 after some 38 months.

Sailing ships were at the mercy of winds that dictated sailing times. In the Indian Ocean, monsoon winds had to be taken seriously into account. There were two main types of monsoons: one blowing from the north-east that brought dry weather and steady wind favourable to sailing in winter; the other being the south-west monsoon during the summer that brought rain, storms making sailing very difficult in June, July and August.

2

Madagascar

The origins and era as to when the island was first settled is obscure and could date from antiquity as well as several different potential ethnic origins. From 1500 when it was sighted by Portuguese navigator Pedralvares Cabral, the great island of Madagascar was often a stop for European ships on the way to India. For instance, the earliest French ships known to have anchored there were from Dieppe in 1527. There was some trade with the coastal inhabitants, but no permanent settlement was made until 1642 when a party of French settlers led by M. de Pronis founded Sainte-Luce at the southeastern end of the island. This was an initiative of one of early and short-lived Compagnie des Indes. Soldiers were also occasionally mentioned in these early settlements. They were recruited, paid, equipped and armed by the company who assumed the expenses so were obviously not very numerous. There were also Malagasy – that is to say, indigenous to Madagascar – warriors that were paid as auxiliary soldiers to the French.[1]

Fort Dauphin

The local inhabitants were not pleased to see the French build a settlement and, after several settlers had been killed by hostile warriors, the settlement was moved in 1643 to a seaside hill further south at Taolankara, which had a good harbour; a fort built there and christened Fort Dauphin. In the following years, Pronis became something of an autocrat, seizing native inhabitants to sell them as slaves, and, in 1647, exiled a dozen settlers opposing him to the uninhabited island of Mascareigne (later Ile de Bourbon and now La Réunion). He was recalled to France.

1 This account of Madagascar is mainly based on: Étienne de Flacourt, *Histoire de la grande isle de Madagascar* (Paris: Cloudier, 1661); Souchu de Renefort, *Relation du premier voyage de la Compagnie des Indes orientales en l'Ile de Madagascar* (Paris: Auburn, 1668), pp.2, 73-75, 157, 165; Hubert Deschamps, *Histoire de Madagascar* (Paris: Berger-Levrault, 1972), chapter III; Villars, *Madagascar 1638-1894 Établissement des Français dans l'Ile* (Paris: Fournier, 1912), chapters 1 to 9; Robert Cornelian, *Histoire de l'Afrique* (Paris: Payot, 1966), Vol.2, pp.352-355

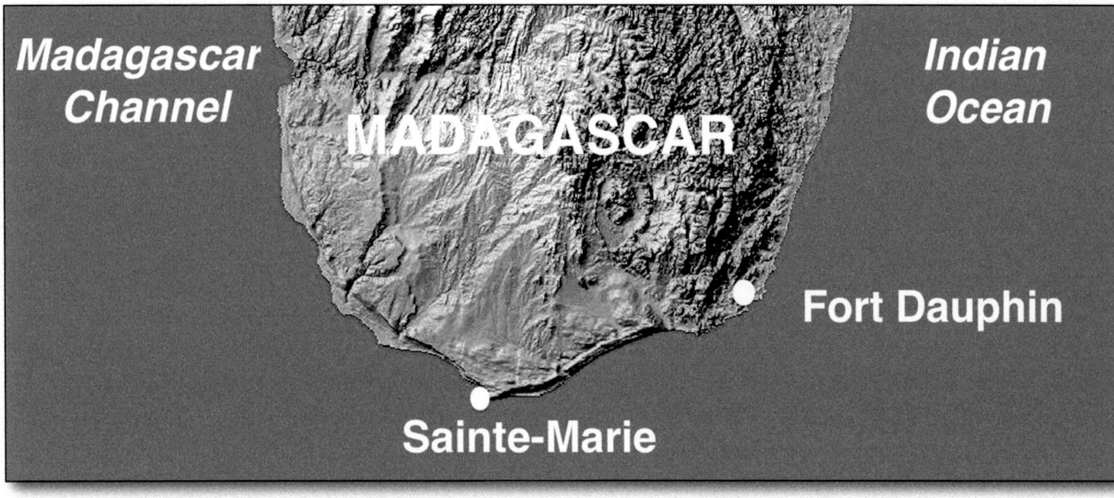

Map of southern Madagascar. (U.S. National Aeronautics and Space Administration (NASA) – digital overlays by the author)

Governor Antoine de Flacourt arrived at Fort Dauphin in December 1648 with a party of settlers and a few soldiers. Thereafter, the Fronde civil wars broke out in France and no ship came to the colony until 1654. Flacourt, who was a well-educated scientist, had some diplomatic successes with the inhabitant nations while holding on with a hundred French settlers at Fort Dauphin and a dozen at outlying Fort Sainte-Marie. Fevers had killed many others before. Antanosi chiefs mustered thousands of warriors that were driven off by the cannons of Fort Dauphin, after which Flacourt and his

Fort Dauphin, Madagascar, 1650s. The flag at the centre of the fort was described as being white with the royal coat of arms. Detail from a map in Flacourt's *Histoire*. (Private collection; author's photo)

Warriors of Madagascar, mid-seventeenth century. Some were hired as auxiliary troops to the French garrison while many others fought against them. All had the same general appearance and weapons. Print after Flacourt's *Histoire*. (Private collection; author's photo)

men successfully counterattacked in July 1651 killing the main chief Dian Ramaka and many warriors and women as well as destroying villages and crops. Other chiefs gradually made their submission. Needless to add that all the Frenchmen had turned into de facto soldiers for their survival; they were surely trained by the few professional soldiers there. In late 1656 however, the company sent four ships to Fort Dauphin having on board 150 sailors and 150 soldiers in the *Duchesse*, 250 sailors and soldiers in the *Maréchalle*, 100 sailors and soldiers in the *Armand* and 75 in a small transport ship. This made about 350 soldiers out of 800 men. Some of the men were prospective settlers who first had to serve three years as soldiers to pay for their transport to Madagascar.

At about that time, a new monopoly company had been formed in France and Flacourt was replaced in 1658 by Pronis who had somewhat amended his previous conduct. The following years were nevertheless disastrous for the small colony. There was warfare against indigenous warriors who attacked and killed isolated Frenchmen. The settlement was beset with deadly fevers, followed by terrible reprisals by the colonists on the inhabitants even as they had dissensions amongst themselves, while fire partly destroyed Fort Dauphin twice. French accounts invariably blame the Malagasy inhabitants for savage cruelty, but a Arabic manuscript reveals that the 'Army of the Whites' had their own terrifying practices on Madagascar's people burning

Sieur de Flacourt accepts homages and gifts at Fort Dauphin from inhabitants of Madagascar in June 1652. This promotion print mentions 'the reduction of the inhabitants of the province of Careanossi…to obedience to the king [of France] by grandees and deputies from the whole country' which, from later events, proved rather optimistic. This print does give a possible idea of the fort's interior and the French soldiers and militiamen being dressed in European fashion and well armed with matchlock and flintlock muskets. The soldiers were enlisted for three years according to Flacourt's *Histoire*. (Private collection; author's photo)

Étienne de Flacourt, governor of Fort Dauphin, Madagascar, c. 1660. Print after Corneille from Flacourt's *Histoire*. (Private collection; author's photo)

towns, killing at random, looting massively and enslaving countless women and children.[2]

In 1664, the new Compagnie des Indes orientales (East India Company) founded by Louis XIV and organised by Jean-Baptiste Colbert included Madagascar in its responsibilities. The following year, four ships with 400 men were sent to reinforce and supply the colony and duly took possession of the colony for the company in a formal ceremony. There was a captain of militia and, at a parade during 1665, some 80 musketeers were present at Fort Dauphin, no doubt a mixture of the settlement's militiamen and soldiers of the company. The troops had a standard bearing a cross that may have been the red flag with a white cross seen on a small boat during a military expedition. The fort was described as having a square plan with two bastions on its landward northern side. Within was a house for the governor, a chapel, a guardhouse and 12 lodgings all of which were made of planks or narrow logs.

On 10 March 1667, a fleet of 10 ships bearing *Lieutenant Général* the Marquis de Montdevergue with settlers, supplies and four infantry companies detached from the royal army regiments of Schulemberg, Duras, Saint-Géniez and La Fère plus 20 men and three officers of Montdevergue's company of guards, in all about 2,000 persons, arrived at Fort Dauphin. The four companies of soldiers were later reduced to two by a royal order signed on 24 December 1668 disbanding the companies of Duras' and Chulemberg's regiments and incorporating their men into the Saint-Géniez and La Fère companies. A financial note of 1666 mentions funds for the men's pay, the expenses of their voyage and 'ammunition clothing [or coats]' indicates they probably had a somewhat uniform dress.[3]

A small party of 19 Frenchmen with up to 4,000 local auxiliary inhabitants penetrated into the interior to trade for supplies but somewhat coercively also pillaged villages, which greatly upset the redoubtable Sihanaka warrior nation. By December 1667, heavy tropical rains and fevers joined with lurking revengeful warriors to force the few French to retreat while many of their now fearful auxiliaries absconded forcing the expedition's withdrawal. This was followed by abandonment of small outposts as the hostile warriors neared, some being even armed with flintlock muskets and ammunition. They were repulsed by a small French party of about 11 men with 600 local auxiliary warriors, recognisable by a white insignia they wore, although many initially fled. There even was an optimistic request to France for 200 more French soldiers so as to conquer the whole island. Colbert did not approve since the Madagascar venture was losing money and priority was instead given to finding markets in India. Meanwhile, auxiliary allied warriors sensed that thing were not going well and they gradually vanished from Fort Dauphin.

2 Flacourt, *Histoire*, pp.423, 456; E.F. Gautier and H. Froidevaux, *Un manuscrit arabo-malgache sur le campagnes de La Case dans l'Imoro de 1659 à 1663* (Paris: Imprimerie nationale, 1897), pp.137-151 for the bone-chilling Arab account translated into French.

3 AC, B, 1, Ordre du Roy, 24 December 1668; AC, C11A, 113, Fonds faits pour les troupes et les officiers pour l'Ile Dauphine [1666]. A somewhat similar arrangement was made for the Carignan-Salières Regiment sent to Canada in 1665. It received brown clothing, the coats lined with grey.

The Marquis de Montdevergue's management was not appreciated by the King and Colbert so he was recalled in 1669 and jailed on arrival in France.[4]

With many of the settlers leaving or dying from diseases at Fort Dauphin, it was decided in 1671 to abandon it in favour of Ile de Bourbon as a site for a colony. Nevertheless, about 200 nearly starved Europeans led by *Major* La Bretèche were still at Fort Dauphin in 1674. By then, they did not dare go out for fear of hostile warriors who surrounded the place. On 17 August, the warriors attacked and about 100 settlers were killed before their attackers withdrew. On 9 September, the fort's guns were spiked, the buildings torched, and 63 survivors sailed from Madagascar in a small boat to Ile de Bourbon.

Pirates and Sainte-Marie

The Compagnie des Indes orientales' interest in Madagascar considerably waned thereafter. Its coast nevertheless offered good anchorage and ships might anchor, trade with the local inhabitants and sail away. By the 1680s, pirates were also finding that great island to be an ideal temporary base. Captain Henry Avery is possibly the best-known pirate in that area because of his capture of a ship that had aboard 'one of the Great Mughals own daughters, with several persons of distinction, who were carrying rich offerings of jewels and other valuable presents to Mecca, where it is usual for all Mohammedans, at least once in their lives, to go a pilgrimage.'[5] Following their expulsion from Nassau in the Bahamas during 1718, more pirates chose Madagascar as a haven to pursue their activities. Within a few years, warships from France, Great Britain, the Netherlands and Portugal sought them in the Indian Ocean so that being a pirate was becoming very hazardous. The governor of Ile de Bourbon offered amnesties that many pirates accepted in 1724. By the time one of the last recalcitrants, a pirate leader named La Buse, was hanged there in 1730, widespread piracy had been largely eliminated.[6]

As the pirates vanished during the 1720s, the Compagnie des Indes sought to establish permanent trade relations with the kingdom of Betsimisaraka in southern Madagascar. As business flourished, the company sought for years to have a permanent base in the area. An agreement was finally signed by Queen Béti of Betsimisaraka and representatives of the company on 30 July 1750 that ceded the island of Sainte-Marie to France and enabled the company to have warehouses and stores on the island. A M. Gosse, the agent of the company, was posted there with several employees, but relations soon became tense with local inhabitants now finding that Gosse and his staff scorned them and had no remorse kidnapping some of them to be sold as slaves. Such actions on the proud and warlike people of Madagascar were

4 A. Martineau (ed.), *Mémoires de François Martin. fondateur de Pondichéry 1665-1696* (Paris: Société de l'Histoire des colonies françaises, 1931), Vol.1, p.119.

5 Daniel Defoe, *History of the lives of all the most notorious pirates and their crews* (London: E. Midwinter, 1725), p.11.

6 Defoe, *History of the lives of all the most notorious* pirates, pp.10-12, also Charles Johnson, *A General History of Pirates* (London: Warner, 1724) and, at Madagascar, Deschamps, *Histoire de Madagascar*, pp.28, 76-78, 87.

bound to have disastrous consequences. One night, when Gosse and his acolytes decided to round up people to fill a visiting slave ship, the inhabitants rose in revolt, killed Gosse with any of his staff they could find and burned down the company's buildings.

After more negotiations with local rulers, a trading post was established at Sainte-Marie in 1753. Two years later, relations had again soured and the ship *Achilles* was sent as reinforcement to 'entirely drive out the people of the country' that wished to dispute the French possession of Sainte-Marie. Nevertheless, relations with local inhabitants had obviously not improved. In 1756, the ships *Gloire* and *Auguste* with 100 of the company's soldiers on board were sent with an engineer. Following a review of business possibilities at the island, it was obvious trade was not likely to flourish. Furthermore, deadly fevers took a heavy toll on the French posted there and so the place was abandoned in 1757.[7]

7 ADR, Co, 435, Conseil supérieur of Ile de France to the Conseil supérieur de l'Ile de Bourbon, 10 June 1755; 465, same to same, 1756; Henry Lachouque, *Les vagabonds de la gloire* (Paris: Copernic, 1980), pp.22-26.

3

On to India

The first French navigators reached India in the early sixteenth century. Some are recorded arriving at Diu during 1526 and, soon thereafter, ships sponsored by Jean Ango, Comte de Dieppe and a famous corsair, went as far as Sumatra, the coasts of India and Persia. The royal interest of King François I was somewhat aroused until 1536 when overwhelmed by European matters. The religious strife and near constant warfare in Europe also marked France for much of the first half of the seventeenth century, the doomed attempts to establish a colony at Madagascar related above being the only major initiative in the east. There had been some royal government interest in eastern ventures during the reign of Louis XIII through his prime minister Cardinal Richelieu, but no substantial investment. A French Compagnie des Indes had been created in 1604 having a trade monopoly in the East Indies, but there soon was strong Dutch East India Company opposition while France was embroiled in various internal struggles as well as the pan-European wars until 1659. The French lack of interest in India changed when 22-year-old King Louis XIV took effective power in 1661. The European wars had ended and he entertained grand visions to confirm his nation as the most important in and beyond Europe. From 1665, royal fleets and army units were sent out to America and the Indian Ocean.[1]

The Marquis de Montdevergue's 1666-1667 expedition to Madagascar aimed at creating a viable colony and naval base on that island. However, it was merely a step to the king's grander objective: establish French trading loges on the coastline of India. Compagnie des Indes orientales directors De Faye and François Caron with a few merchants were also on Montdevergue's ships that arrived at Fort Dauphin in March 1667.

1 This chapter is based on Gabriel Hanotaux and Alfred Martneau (eds), *Histoire des colonies françaises et de l'expansion de la France dans le Monde* (Paris: Plon, 1932), Vol.5, chapters 1 to 3.

François Caron directs the construction of the French lodge at Surat (India) in 1668. Print after Bombléd in the December 1902 *Dépêche coloniale illustrée*. (Bibliothèque Nationale de France, Paris)

Surat 1668

According to royal instructions, Caron was to sail on to Surat in India as soon as possible and establish a trading lodge there. Montdevergue was reticent to let the fleet go at once and it was only on 13 February 1668 that Caron finally set foot in India. There already were a few Frenchmen there: Capucin missionaries led by Father Ambroise de Preuilly. Thanks to skilful diplomacy whose influence extended to the imperial court, de Preuilly, who had previously been informed of the intention to establish a lodge at Surat, had obtained permission for such a French establishment from Mughal emperor Aurangzeb. The new French lodge joined British and Dutch lodges already in Surat, which was then the busiest port in India. Aurangzeb may well have granted permissions simply to encourage more competition amongst European traders. On 12 March of the following year, Compagnie des Indes orientales director De Faye arrived at Surat in full pomp, both he and Caron traveling through the city in two 'large carriages covered with red velvet trimmed with gold, even the wheels being gilded and bearing the coat of arms of the company, which are a fleur-de-lis on [a globe] of the world' with numerous escort to meet the Indian governor and many officials. Other small lodges were also opened at Rajapour and at the Arab ports of Bender Abbas and Bassora in the Persian Gulf.[2]

Visions of prosperity were abruptly interrupted by the ongoing conflict between the Marathas led by Sivaji and the Mughal empire. Surat was not protected by walls although it had a citadel. A large Maratha force had sacked the city from 6 to 10 January 1664. The British and Dutch establishments were sparred at the time, but trade was very perturbed for a while. On 3 October 1670, the Marathas attacked Surat again. The Dutch were spared because they were situated away from the centre. The British were attacked and managed to repulse the looting warriors. At the French lodge, Caron made rich presents to the Marathas who must have also noticed that he had

2 Souchu de Rennefort, *Histoire des Indes orientales* (Leiden: Haring, 1688), pp.395-398.

fortified the lodge. He also wondered if there might not be a safer place to have the company's main lodge in India. He further wanted to tap into the spice trade and opened a lodge in 1671 at Bantam on the island of Java.

The Persia Squadron

Shivaji, leader of the Marathas, circa 1670. Led by this outstanding general, the Marathas became one of the most militarily powerful state in India. Print after a miniature in Langlès' *Monuments ancien et moderne de l'Hindoustan*. (Bibliothèque Nationale de France, Paris)

In France, meanwhile, the expected fantastic profits from the East Indies were not as grand as expected and a worried Compagnie des Indes orientales alerted the royal court. The result was the arrival at Surat on 18 October 1671 of the substantial *escadre de Perse* (Persia Squadron) led by Jacob Blanquet de La Haye as governor and lieutenant general for the king with the powers of viceroy 'in all the Indies'. The squadron consisted of 'six good warships' of the royal fleet and three smaller vessels of the Compagnie des Indes orientales armed with a total of 238 cannon having 1,470 men on board including '400 men of good troops' aboard. The king expected the squadron to 'take a few posts in India and make a few solid establishments for the Compagnie des Indes orientales. It is absolutely necessary embark at least 400 effective soldiers' which was done by detaching part of the Régiment Royal-Marine. There also was La Haye's company of guards, a company of cadets and some officers detached from the King's Musketeers. Furthermore, the king wished that some 600 sailors could also join the troops so as to have a landing force of 1,000 men.[3]

The fleet had left La Rochelle on 30 March 1670 arriving in India some 18 months later. La Haye's instructions were, after a stop at Madagascar, to sail along the Indian coast to show the Sun King's naval power before proceeding to take possession of the eastern part of Ceylon (Sri-Lanka) and also the island of Banca (Indonesia). The fleet experienced considerable difficulties

3 AC, B, 1, Louis XIV to La Haye, 5 May and 3 December 1669; BNF, fonds français, 8027, Mémoire du Roy to Colbert, 25 December 1669; Louis Pauliat, *Louis XIV et la Compagnie des Indes orientales de 1664* (Paris: Calman Levy, 1886), p.307; Paul Kaepellin, *Histoire de la Compagnie des Indes orientales* (Paris: Challamel, 1908), p.30.

sailing to India and had more delays at Madagascar. Once at Surat, cannon salvos in the harbour, gifts for the emperor and grand receptions receiving local Indian princes and officials were given by La Haye while his ships were restored after the long trip with three more joining the squadron. When Caron arrived at Surat from Bantam on 11 November 1671, he found himself very much under the authority of Viceroy La Haye who had his own superior agenda. On 6 January 1672, he sailed from Surat sailing and stopping along the Malabar coast. The fleet was greeted cordially at the Indian ports, but was not allowed to enter Goa by the Portuguese and, on 21 February, a Dutch fleet of 12 ship was perceived. La Haye wanted to attack it, but was persuaded by Caron who was with him to adhere to his instructions and sail for Ceylon.[4]

On 22 March 1672, the Persia Squadron reached be large bay of Trincomalee. Much to La Haye's dismay, a small fort flying the Dutch standard was seen near the shore and another Dutch fort was at Batacolor further south. The Dutch had gotten there first. Nevertheless, La Haye decided to build a fort there as well in spite of a Dutch summons to sail away. He eventually obtained on 8 May a treaty signed by the king of Kandy ceding the bay to France. However, the Frenchmen building the fort were increasingly sick and unfit while food and water were becoming scarce. Finally, on 9 July, the fleet sailed away leaving three ships in the bay because there were not enough sailors to man them due to substantial sickness and death amongst the crews. A small garrison was left in the fort consisting of 90 soldiers, 20 sailors, 30 topasses with about 200 Sri-Lankan auxiliaries.[5] On 11 July, the Dutch fleet led by Admiral and Governor-General of the Dutch East Indies Rijklof van Goers arrived and, after some artillery exchanges with the French fort, landed up to 1,200 men nearby on 16 July who soon cut off the French fort's water source. There was some skirmishing in the following days, but it seemed that the garrison preferred to capitulate if good terms were obtained rather than put up a ferocious fight. On 19 July the French garrison surrendered with the honours of war.[6]

French infantrymen, circa1665-1675. In France, they were clothed with a coat, a pair of breeches, stockings, shoes, shirt, a hat and a cravat. Soldiers sent overseas by the East India Company also had such clothing. Once in the tropical climate of the Indian Ocean, they obviously favoured a lighter dress. Their weapons consisted of a matchlock or flintlock musket with a plug bayonet and a sword. Print after Marbot who based these figures according to works by Van der Mullen. (Canadian War Museum, Ottawa, author's photo)

4 AC, B, 4, Louis XIV to La Haye, 19 October 1672; AC, B, 5, Louis XIV to La Haye, 27 February, 31 August and 3 October 1673

5 Described as 'Portuguese Metis', topasses were 'Christians of the country that dress as Europeans and are descendants of the first Portuguese that came to India, of which they have retained the language.' BNF, NAF, 9381, Father Faucher, Canton (China), 20 December 1724.

6 Martineau (ed.), *Mémoires de François Martin*, Vol.1, pp.329-331, 341-349; A.J.A. Gerlach, *Fastes militaires des Indes orientales néerlandaises* (Zalt-Bommel and Paris: Nonan and

1672-1674 Sieges of Sao Tomé

On 22 July 1672, the French fleet was before Sao Tomé (or Saint-Tomé, St Tome). This Indian port city had been Meliapour until 1504 when taken over by the Portuguese who kept it until 1602 when occupied by the king of Golconde on behalf of the Great Mughal. La Haye's request to anchor and land some of his men was flatly denied by Sao Tomé's governor who did not want any Christians to set foot in his port nor obtain any supplies. Soon thereafter a French sailor landed led by an Indian guide, both were caught and beaten, as was La Haye's interpreter who would be beheaded if he came back to negotiate. Facing such insults, La Haye and the fleet's officers resolved to occupy the city, whose defences were not formidable. On 25 July, French landing parties scaled the walls, scattered the defenders and took the city by storm. Once in control of it, his priorities were to restore the fortifications and organise local markets. The king of Golconde reacted to the capture of the city by making diplomatic contacts with other local kings and the Dutch for assistance while part of his troops went to the outskirts of Sao Tomé and blockaded it. By early August, food shortages were experienced in the city. On 10 August, the French made a sortie to scatter the Indian troops who indeed withdrew while fighting in an orderly way. La Haye, who was leading the French sortie, was nearly killed in a skirmish and went back into Sao Tomé. He transferred the guns from two of his ships to mount them on the city's curtain walls.

The Dutch, who could only profit from the situation, had a further boost in early September when news arrived in India that France and Great Britain were at war with the Netherlands. The British in India were not very enthusiastic about this alliance with the Sun King and largely stayed neutral locally. However, there were about a dozen British ships at Madras: La Haye sent word that their assistance was needed to fight the Dutch common enemy, but the answers were vague. By October 1672, some Dutch officers and soldiers, especially gunners and engineers, had joined the Indian troops around the city. Although numerous, the king of Golconde's Indian soldiers were repulsed several times when some of their trenches approached the city and by the end of the month, the siege ended as they withdrew.[7]

Director Caron then left for France to be succeeded by François Baron while La Haye sailed along the Indian coast from early April 1673 returning to Sao Tomé on 5 June. He was hoping for some support from local Indian princes, but they were lukewarm on the idea of sending help and thereby upsetting the Dutch whom they rightly felt were the most militarily powerful Europeans in the East Indies at that time.

The Dutch and the king of Golconde had meanwhile been preparing to retake Sao Tomé. In late August and early September, the large fleet of Rycklof van Goens was cruising off the Coromandel coast in spite of renewed reminders from La Haye that Great Britain was allied with France against the

---

Borrani, 1859), p.94. This Dutch version mentions that 600 men, French and Indians, were captured with 112 guns at Trincomalee.

7 BNF, Ms Français 6090, Premier voyage de M. Carré en Orient (1669-1672), p.4.

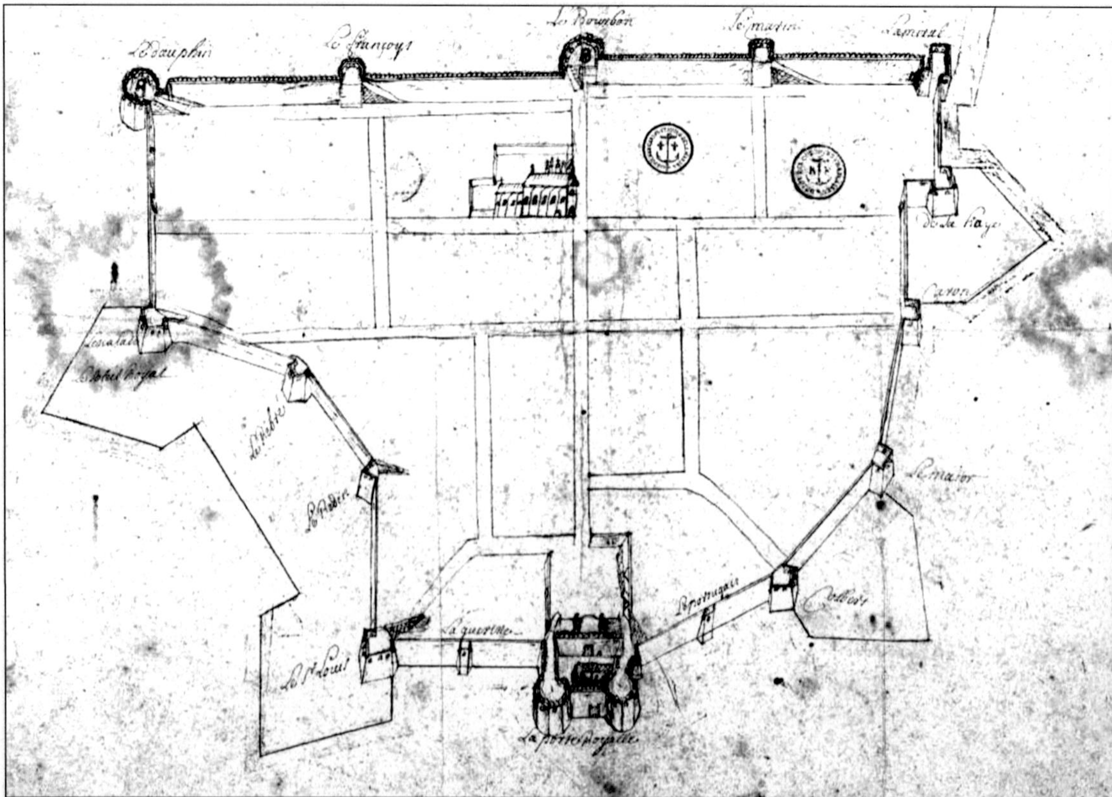

Plan of Sao-Tomé, India, 1672. It was taken by the French on 25 July 1672. The outlines show bastions that the French may have wanted to add to Its Medieval style walls with turrets. Indian and Dutch troops recaptured it on 6 September 1674. (Archives Nationales Outre-Mer, 25DFC 327B)

Netherlands. The Dutch did not trust the British and 22 ships under Cornelis van Quaalberg attacked the 10 British ships of William Base off Masulipatam on 1 September 1673. The engagement was a hard fight according to Martin who encountered seven British Honourable East India Company ships on 11 September. They had lost two ships dismasted and captured by the Dutch while a third was 'sunk to the bottom' or 'ran ashore rather than strike her colours' according to Low. The Dutch had about 500 casualties. Even if the British had wanted to assist the French, they were now neutralised by the Dutch. Ironically the Treaty of Westminster taking Great Britain out of the alliance with France war had been signed, but this was unknown in India.[8]

In mid-September, the Dutch fleet anchored off Sao Tomé, landed some 500 Dutch soldiers and 500 Indian troops that made their junction with the king of Golconde's Indian army. On 18 September 1673, they invested Sao Tomé for a second siege. In the following weeks, the Dutch built a fort as

8 N.A.M. Rodger, *The Command of the Sea* (London: Penguin/National Maritime Museum, 2004), p.86; Martineau (ed.), *Mémoires de François Martin*, Vol.1, p.516, Kaepellin, *Histoire de la Compagnie des Indes orientales*, p.113 and p.62 and Charles Rathborne Low, *History of the Indian Navy* (London: Bentley, 1877), Vol.1, p.62 and Gerlach, *Fastes militaires des Indes orientales néerlandaises*, p.94 mention this battle, but seemingly not Jean Sutton, *Lords of the East The East India Company and its Ships* (London: Conway, 1981) although on p.149 the list of vessels lost or only having a single year of service indicate four ships for 1673: *Advice*, *European*, *John & Alexander*, and *Jonah*. We have not encountered a precise name for this naval battle.

a command and supply base at Trivileany (situated between Sao Tomé and Madras) that also could protect the besieging army from an unlikely, but still possible, relief force attacking the rear of the Dutch lines. Furthermore, the king of Golconde's cavalry was clearing out and burning nearby villages.

For all that, the garrison of Sao Tomé was in a fighting mood as the Dutch found when, on 25 September, the French made a vigorous sortie and cleared out the Dutch who had advanced trenches in the range of two musket shots from the city's walls. Almost incredibly, the second siege lasted over a year, the French garrison making many sorties and repulsing every assault under La Haye's courageous leadership. But there could be no relief and a capitulation was signed on 6 September 1674. The garrison was granted the honours of war and La Haye with 530 men sailed to France.[9]

'Nan va Halva' (Breads and Sweets), circa 1690. This image of an Indian man shown accepting bread and sweets from a European 'infidel' was a warning that growing western influence had negative and corrupting aspects. As such, it is a remarkably early statement of the foreboding some Indians had. This plate by Muhammad Baha' al-Din al-Amili illustrated a book of morals made at Aurangabad in the Deccan. (Metropolitan Museum of Art, New York. Purchase, Friends of Islamic Art Gifts, 1999. DP235872)

Pondicherry Acquired, 1673

Further north meanwhile, Compagnie des Indes orientales official Bellanger de Lespinay had obtained permission on 4 February 1673 from Prince Chirkam Lodi, who ruled southern India for the rajah of Bijapour, to open a lodge at the coastal village of Pondicherry. Its anchorage was not well protected, but it was well sited being at the central hub of the Coromandel coast. Belanger foresaw that it could become a major trade centre and so did the prince who further made it known to the Dutch who protested. The prince replied he saw nothing wrong in the French being their neighbours because they were also neighbours in Europe.

Capture of the Fortress of Valdaour, 1676

The lodge at Pondicherry had barely been established that its area was engulfed into a princely succession war during 1676. Prince Chirkhan Lodi favoured trade with France, while his rival Nazirmohammed, king of Gingee, wanted to expel the French. François Martin, director of the Pondicherry lodge, had about 50 French soldiers of the Compagnie des Indes orientales so he immediately needed more soldiers; he obtained 300 Indian sepoy soldiers from Prince

9 AC, B, 5, Louis XIV to La Haye, 3 October 1673 announced departure of the *Rubis* with 100 soldiers to reinforce Sao Tomé. It reached Surat at an unknown date, probably left the soldiers there, and arrived back at Port-Louis (France) on 21 June 1676 as per Kaeppelin, *La Compagnie des Indes orientales*, pp.654-655; Gerlach, *Fastes militaires des Indes orientales néerlandaises*, pp.94-95.

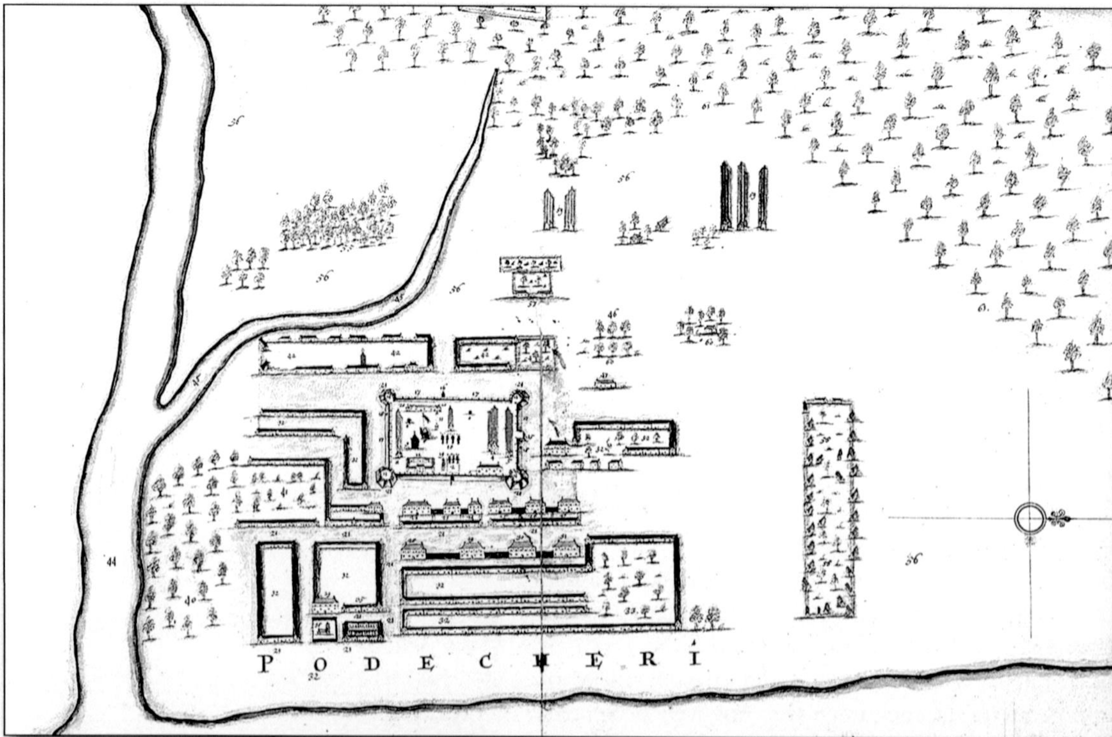

Plan of Pondicherry during the later 1680s. The compound of the Compagnie des Indes in the centre of the town was, by permission of Indian Prince Ram Raja, fortified from 1687 with walls on a rectangular plan with four round turrets at its corners. (Dutch National Archives)

Chirkhan along with permission to fortify the Pondicherry lodge with a wall. Martin's 300 Indian soldiers were armed with French muskets and trained by French cadres in manoeuvres and discipline as practiced in the Sun King's army. They could be said to have been the first Indian sepoys in French service.

Meanwhile, Martin had obtained intelligence, through one of his older servants disguised as a merchant, that Nazirmohammed's favourite residence was the fortress of Valdaour situated only 10 kilometres northwest of Pondicherry. It had a garrison of about 300 well-armed sepoys and also housed the soldier's families, servants and Nazirmohammed's harem. His refusal to pay tribute to Chirkhan Lodi and the rajah degraded into open warfare. Martin confidently assured Chirkhan Lodi that he would take Valdaour, a task that seemed impossible to most. Every morning and late afternoon, the sepoys in Valdaour were paraded and drilled, sometimes by Nazirmohammed himself, but everyone took a nap during the hot early afternoon. This time was chosen by Martin at the best to stage a surprise attack. Accordingly, on 24 September, the old merchant was before the gates of Valdaour that were opened to let him in. Hidden behind bushes nearby, Martin with two French officers and some 40 French soldiers with about 60 Indian sepoys now rushed in, overpowered the guards, secured the weapons and cannons of the sleeping garrison that wakened as prisoners, took the harem where Nazirmohammed was and apprehended him. This astounding capture of Valdaour basically gave the advantage to Chrikhan and a truce favourable to him eventually ended the hostilities.

This vigorous surprise capture became known all over India and erased whatever tarnish the French might have since the departure of La Haye's squadron followed by the fall of Sao Tomé in 1674. Martin and his few French soldiers with trained Indian soldiers had achieved an incredible military action. The tangible benefit eventually came from the raja who, through the influence of Chirkhan Lodi, made the concession of Pondicherry to France permanent and confirmed the permission to build a wall to protect it.[10]

The following years were relatively quiet. Attempts by the French and British to have lodges at Bantam (Indonesia) to trade for spices did not please the Dutch who, as rulers of that area, convinced these competitors in April 1682 that they should go back to India. In 1686 however, the French company successfully established a lodge at Chandernagor destined to become the main post in Bengal.

10 Martineau (ed.), *Mémoires de François Martin*, Vol.2, pp.39, 62, Kaeppelin, *Compagnie des Indes orientales*, pp.159-160; Tambi Pourouchotman, 'Nos Cipahis de l'Inde', *Armée, Marine, Colonies* (1927), p.580.

4

Fiasco in Siam, 1680s

During the 1680s, the Compagnie des Indes orientales became involved with a mooted expansion into Siam (Thailand). This was due to interest manifested by both King Louis XIV of France and King Phra Narai of Siam in having closer diplomatic, commercial and military relations. The Sun King wanted to expand trade relations beyond India while King Phra Narai sought ways to circumvent the preponderant influence of the Dutch East India Company by having more trade relations with France. Siamese Prime Minister Constantine Phaulkon, said to be a Greek adventurer, also favoured closer links with France in particular and other European nations in general.

Both the Dutch and the British trading companies had modest lodges in Bangkok while the French had Roman Catholic missionaries there who had received land to build a mission. They had influence at the court of King Phra Narai and convinced him to send ambassadors to Versailles to open relations with France. In 1680, the Compagnie des Indes orientales had sent instructions to Pondicherry to open a lodge at Bangkok. On 3 September, the Sieur Deslandes-Boureau landed in Bangkok and, by 1682, he had secured a trade agreement. Two years latter, King Phra Narai sent two mandarins to France as ambassadors where they were received by Louis XIV at Versailles' Hall of Mirrors with considerable interest and cordiality. The ambassadors told Louis XIV that King Phra Narai wished he would send a French embassy to Siam.

At that point, Louis XIV and his ministers thought, through what information they had from the French missionaries, that the king of Siam and most of his subjects were favourable to converting to Roman Catholicism and that the situation seemed ripe to spawn trade and military activities in this kingdom. It should be noted that embassies from Muslim countries also had similar ambitions. These manoeuvres naturally raised alarm and tensions from the Buddhist monks, whose faith was that of the overwhelming majority of Siamese during a period of a certain religious tolerance in their country. In France meanwhile, the Sun King was about to revoke the edict of Nantes thus abolishing Protestant French Huguenots' right to practice their faith in the kingdom. The Siamese surely had no idea of the European religious wars, but they were wise enough to realise that religious intolerance could

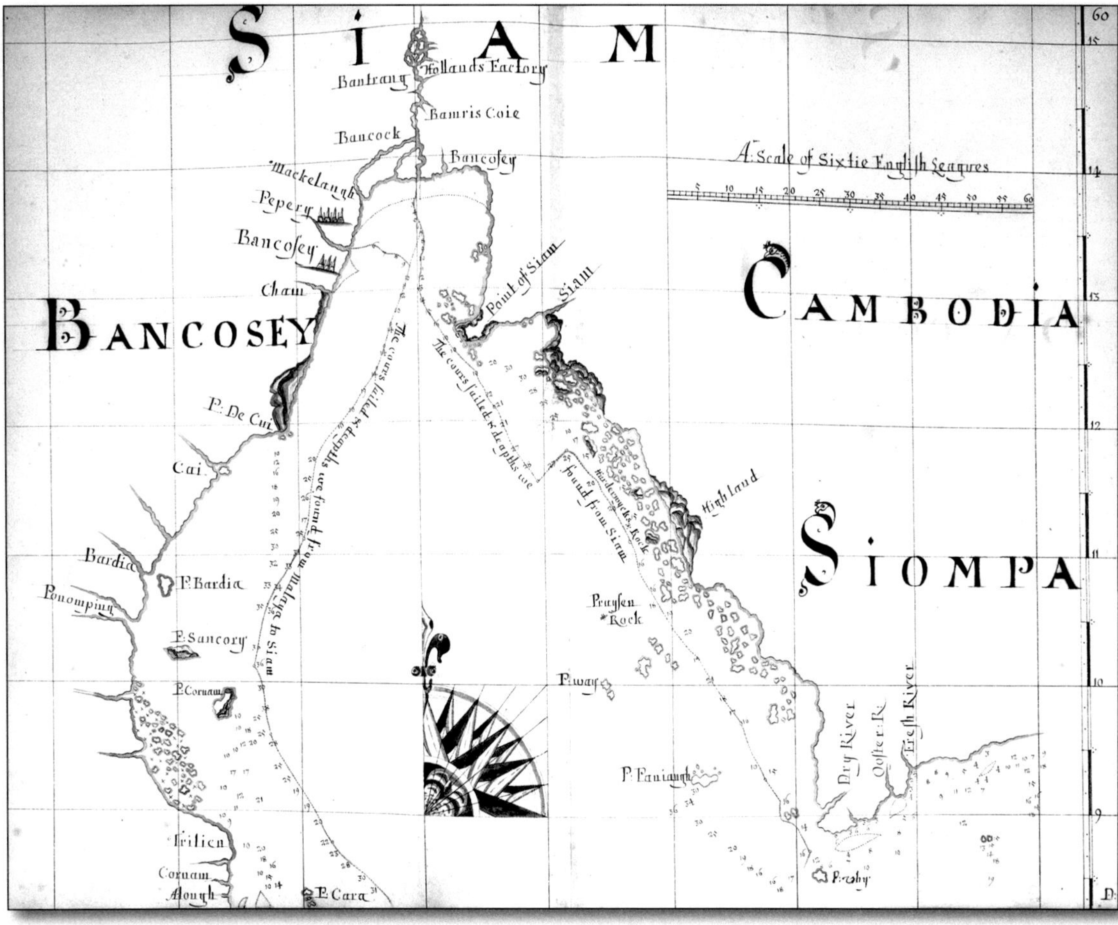

Map of Siam and adjacent territories, late seventeenth century. From the manuscript nicknamed the 'Buccaneer Atlas' by William Hacke. (Library of Congress, Washington)

have disastrous effects and were, on the whole, satisfied with their Buddhist faith. On 21 January 1685, King Louis XIV wrote a letter to King Phra Narai presenting the Chevalier de Chaumond as his ambassador to Siam notably thanking him for the protection granted to French missionaries, promising great commercial and diplomatic advantages while inviting him to convert to the Roman Catholic church.[1]

The Chevalier de Chaumond and the Abbé de Choisy arrived safely in Bangkok with their suites and presented this letter with presents to King Phra Narai on 18 October 1685. Siamese protocol was altered so that the elaborate procession of the Sun King's ambassador, which included French mounted trumpeters, could see King Phra Narai without crawling on the ground as even Siamese mandarins had to; the French officers led by Chaumond, who wore a richly brocaded 'colour of fire' coat embroidered with gold, were

1 On these aspects, see notably: Alan Strathern, *Thailand's First Revolution? The Ayutthaya Rebellion of 1688 and Global Patterns of Ruler Conversions to Monotheism* (Singapore: Asia Research Institute Working Paper No. 258, National University of Singapore, May 2017); Anon., *Voyage de Siam des pères jésuites* (Paris: Seneuze, 1685), pp.190-208; Abbé de Choisy, *Journal du Voyage de Siam* (Paris, 1741), pp.212-260.

Bangkok, capital of Siam, circa 1662-1663. This would have been the general aspect of the city (also called Juda) at the time when the French expeditions reached it. With its many golden pointed roofs, it was unlike anything Frenchmen of the 1680s had ever seen before. The royal quarter was at upper left. Painting attributed to Johannes Vinckboons. (Rijkmuseum, Amsterdam. SK-A-4477)

allowed to sit. A treaty was then signed that included a type of free trade agreement with no taxes levied on the Compagnie des Indes orientales and the cession of a seaside territory as a base the French could fortify.[2]

The French embassy returned to France with three Siamese ambassadors who were received at Versailles on 1 September 1686. All seemed superb at Louis XIVs court. A major expedition to Siam was to be prepared in France, with six warships under Commandant l'Aulnay de Vaudricourt. A number of officials, officers, missionaries and scientists as well as a vast number of gifts for King Phra Narai and Constantine Phaulkon were on board.

Furthermore, Prime Minister Constantine Phaulkon had asked that a strong contingent of French troops be posted in Siam. Therefore 12 companies of infantry led by *Maréchal de Camp* (major general) Des Farges and *Lieutenant-colonel* de Bruant were organised and boarded the fleet with a detachment of 10 Bombardier de la Marine with a bombardier officer and a king's engineer to plan the fortifications. They were to garrison the French lodge and harbour ceded in Siam. Each infantry company had 50 soldiers led by three officers for a total establishment of 600 men and 36 officers. The companies were formed during 1687, partly from the navy's existing marine companies, later known as Compagnies Franches de la Marine, and partly from recruits. These 'soldiers were not to be told they are going to Siam otherwise they will desert' which gives an idea of recruiting practices of the time. A special Siam military establishment was created in the budget for these companies under the responsibility of the ministry the king's navy.

2 *Mercure Galant*, February 1685, p.290 also mentions the hope that one day Siam would 'become Catholic'; Preede Phisphumvidhi, 'La Révolution de 1688 au Siam d'après des sources militaires françaises', mémoire de maîtrise, Université Silpakorn, Bangkok, 2002, pp.33-34 quoting Louis XIV to King of Siam, 21 January 1685 in Archives des affaires étrangères, Vol.862, p.153; Maurice Besson, *Vieux papiers du temps des isles* (Paris: Société d'éditions géographiques, maritimes et coloniales, 1925), pp.135-137. The Siamese report of the visit to France is reproduced in L.-B. Rochedragon (trans.), 'Phonga-Vadan (Les annales officielles Siamoises)', *Bulletin de la Société de géographie de Rochefort*, Vol.12 (1890), pp.186-195.

These were royal troops, not soldiers of the Compagnie des Indes orientales. This was the largest contingent of French troops ever sent to the Orient.[3]

Shock in Bangkok

The fleet arrived in Siam and the French ambassadors with retainers, officers and some 500 soldiers landed at Bangkok on 18 September 1687. The appearance of so many Frenchmen accompanied by an infantry battalion came as a shock in the country in all classes of society from mandarins to humble folks. They arrived at a time of political instability as the regime of King Phra Narai was increasingly questioned while his Prime Minister Constantine Phaulkon was detested by many Siamese who were unhappy that foreigners such as the French had gained so much influence at the royal court. In 1686, Siamese Prince Macassar Dai had led a sizeable revolt at Laburi which had been defeated loyal militia levies.[4]

The only truly regular troops of the Kingdom of Siam were the royal guards. They were recruited amongst foreigners, mostly 'maures' (of Islamic faith) and Japanese men-at-arms (possibly samurai). During the fall of 1687, the king also raised a French-style guard cavalry company of 'cadets' amongst Siamese nobility led by the son of Des Farges. A fourth group that never arrived was a company of lifeguards made up of Frenchmen that King Phra Narai asked Louis XIV to send him and to which the king of France agreed. From the colours of their uniforms, he was recreating the red and the blue household troops of Louis XIVs guards. For most Siamese, the prospect of having French foreigners as guardsmen and commanding its new Siamese unit could only be seen as yet another cession to the Europeans by the king and especially his loathed prime minister.[5]

In Siam, armies were raised by somewhat forced levies during hostilities. Vagabonds were the first to be enlisted forcibly or kidnapped followed by poor

3 Martineau (ed.), *Mémoires de François Martin*, Vol.2, pp.518-519; Phisphumvidhi, 'La Révolution de 1688 au Siam d'après des sources militaires françaises', p.41; Kaepellin, *La Compagnie des Indes orientales*, pp.219-220; AM, B3, 53, de Montmor to Minister, Le Havre, 12 December 1687; AC, F1A, 4, Estat de la dépense...du detachment des Vaisseaux que Sa Majesté a envoyée à Siam...1688. Each infantry company had 41 soldiers, one drummer, six *caporaux*, two *sergents* led by a *capitaine*, a *lieutenant* and an *enseigne*. The artillery detachment consisted of seven bombardiers, two *capitaines d'armes* (junior sergeants), one *sergent* and one *enseigne*. There were also two surgeons with two assistants. The Siam establishment of Compagnies Franches de la Marine existed in the budget until 1692.

4 Phisphumvidhi, 'La Révolution de 1688 au Siam d'après des sources militaires françaises', pp.17-18

5 Approval of the French company of guards for the king of Siam was made by Louis XIV in early March 1689 led by Sieur d'Éragny. It was to consist of 80 troopers including three officers. Weapons, clothing, equipment, kettle drums and trumpets were made in France at the expense of the king of Siam as were horses once in Bangkok. Their uniform was 'red with a wide gold lace' as per *Mercure Galant*, March 1689, pp.145-146; AC, C1, 27, Instructions pour le Sieur Desfarges, Versailles, 10 March 1689 and Traité pour la compagnie des gardes du Roy de Siam, Paris, 15 March 1689. Some '...blue material to make coats' for the company of cadets from de Beauchamp's 'Relation originale de la revolution de Siam' as per Phisphumvidhi, 'La Révolution de 1688 au Siam d'après des sources militaires françaises', p.235.

men who could not pay mandarins to be exempted from military service. There were few elephants and cavalry, and not much artillery; most men were on foot, had no firearms and carried mostly edged weapons. They were commanded by mandarins interested in military matters. Siam had won a war against Burma some years before, so its troops were not to be underestimated, especially when the national pride of the population was aroused.[6]

Most French soldiers were posted in Bangkok with others at Lopburi and at the seaport of Mergui on the Bay of Bengal. One of the officers, the Chevalier de Forbin, was to recruit some Siamese and train them as soldiers 'drilled exactly as in France' while King's Engineer de La Marc was drafting fortification plans. The opposition to the government of Prime Minister Constantine Phaulkon mainly consisted of mandarins, religious bonzes and the country's vast population of peasants led by Phra Petracha, then the most influential and powerful mandarin at the royal court. Phaulkon's brutal persecutions to protect his personal monopoly of all foreign trade had caused an economic depression as well as much aversion to foreigners amongst the population. During the next months and into 1688, supplies to the French troops were diminishing as was their pay and many soldiers were perishing from sickness. Furthermore, King Phra Narai was said to be increasingly ill.[7]

Siamese Revolution May 1688

What became known as Siamese Revolution broke out in May 1688 at Lopburi led by Mandarin Phra Petracha with about 15,000 men. Constantine Phaulkon was in that city and, in February, reacting to rumours of a revolt, received a reinforcement of two French-trained companies of Siamese soldiers and *Maréchal de Camp* Des Farges with 80 French soldiers in April. About 8,000 rebels appeared to also be approaching Bangkok and Des Farges was recalled to the capital to prepare its defence. In Lopburi, Constantine Phaulkon was unable to gather enough troops to defend himself. On 18 May, Phaulkon with a few French soldiers was arrested by Mandarin Phra Petracha's troops who occupied Lopburi and executed him shortly thereafter. On 20 May, the death of King Phra Narai became known. Phra Petracha proclaimed himself the ruler of Siam. Through all this, the royal guard had simply vanished…[8]

In a matter of days, the situation of the French in Siam had totally changed. Some soldiers and missionaries were held as prisoners by the

---

6 Rochedragon (trans.), 'Phonga-Vadan (Les annales officielles Siamoises)', Vol.11, pp.282-283.

7 Martineau (ed.), *Mémoires de François Martin*, Vol.2, pp.556-557; Phisphumvidhi, 'La Révolution de 1688 au Siam d'après des sources militaires françaises', pp.19-20, 235.

8 Royal and political succession in Siam was usually a bloody affair as seen in Rochedragon (trans.), 'Phonga-Vadan (Les annales officielles Siamoises)', Vol.11, pp.90-92; Michael Smithies (trans. and ed.), 'Four unpublished letters from Desfarges, Beauchamp, and Vollant, survivors of the siege of Bangkok in 1688', *Journal of the Siam Society*, Vol.92 (2004), pp.64-104. Jean Vollant des Verquains, *Histoire de la Revolution de Siam arrived en 1688* (Lille: J.-C. Malte, 1691) is an account of the often tragic fate of the royal family, the prime minister and their families as well as giving some aspects of the siege..

Siamese who rallied to Phra Petracha's banner to drive the French out of Siam. This also extended to the British. In the previous months the French troops had occupied the citadel, whose defences they had improved, and also the western fort of Bangkok. Their only salvation seemed to be able to hold out as long as possible. Circumstances now made Des Farges the *de facto* leader of the French and, on 7 June, he ordered the evacuation of the western fort after spiking its 19 cannon, in order to regroup all his meagre forces and supplies in the citadel.

The siege proved to be an outstanding and somewhat desperate defence that lasted five months and four days. During that time, Phra Petracha also ordered the British out of their factory at Bangkok and they found refuge in the citadel held by Des Farges and about 200 to 300 officers and men. The Dutch were in better terms with the Siamese and some of their gunners with mortars bombarded the citadel, but to no avail. The Siamese besiegers built eight redoubts around it, which did not stop French sorties. The Siamese also forced their French prisoners to work as slave labourers on the siege field works such as trenches so that the defenders would have to shoot at them; they did and the walls were not breached. It must be pointed out that the numerous Siamese were civilian men levied to serve temporarily while the French garrison consisted of regular soldiers defending an obviously strong fortress. At length supplies were running out and a capitulation was

Plan of the fortifications at the siege of Bangkok, 1688. The French citadel was bastioned and its officer's quarters had four bastions acting as an ultimate defence keep. At lower left is the western fort, which had a cavalier for its guns overlooking the river. It was evacuated by the French at the outset of the siege to concentrate their troops in the citadel. It was surrounded by trenches and artillery batteries. Plan from *Histoire de la révolution de Siam*. (Author's photo)

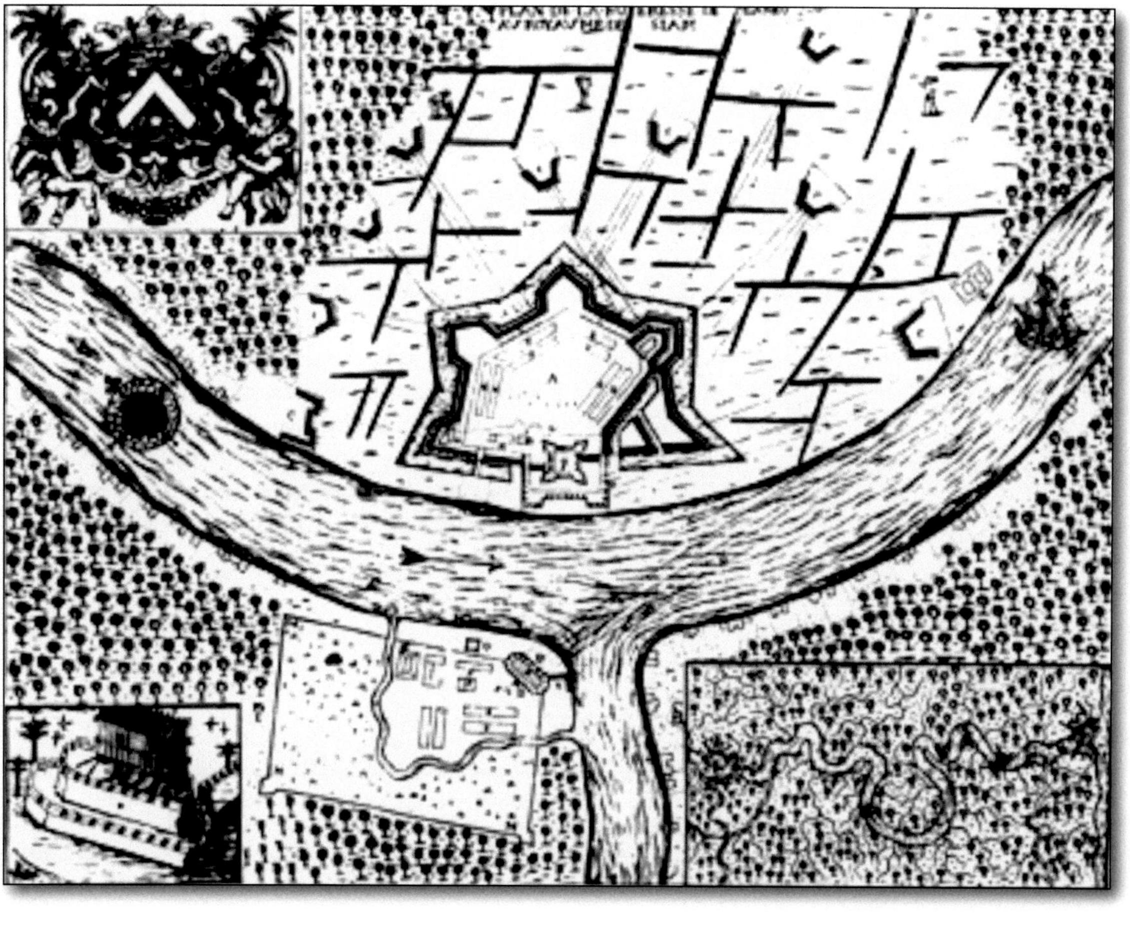

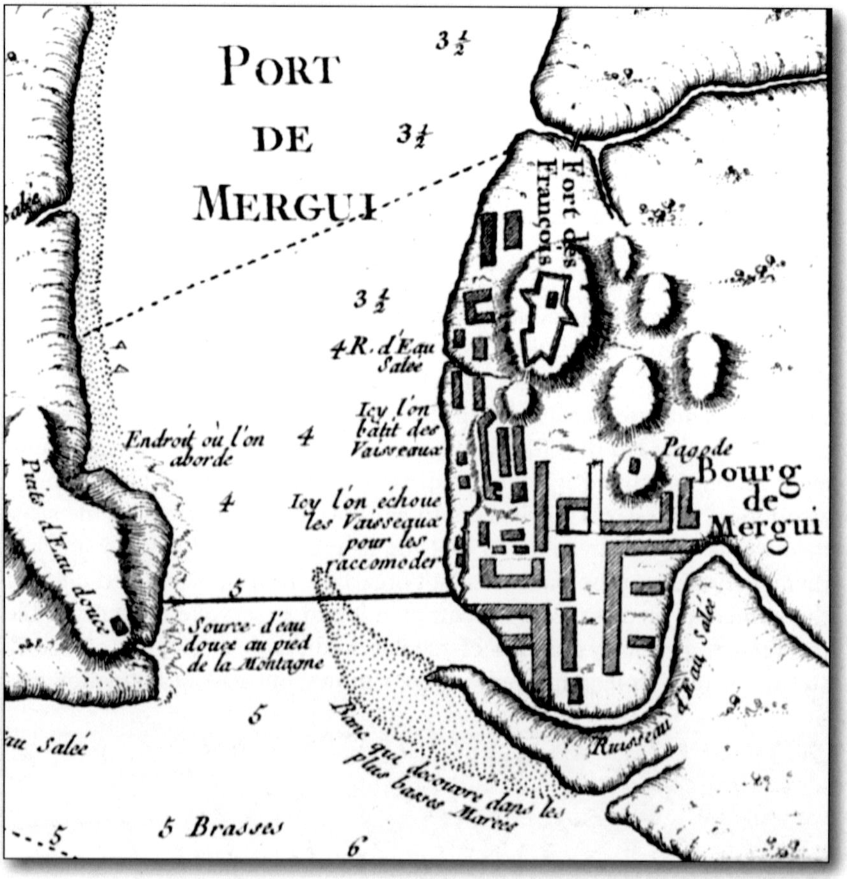

Plan of Mergui and its harbour. The 'Fort des Français' (French fort) is shown on the town's main height. A French detachment of four companies was posted there in 1688 until it sailed for Pondicherry. From Bellin's *Petit atlas maritime*. (Ministère des Armées)

finally agreed to, which granted the evacuation of the remaining French and British who left Bangkok for Pondicherry on 2 November 1688. A French detachment of four companies led by *Lieutenant-colonel* Bruant at Mergui also managed to reach Pondicherry. Another three companies sent to Siam during 1689 were redirected to Pondicherry. Minister of the Navy Seignelay ordered the remnants of these troops to be sent back to France.[9]

The Dutch, who supported the revolutionaries, managed to remain in the good graces of the Siamese as helpful traders and, eventually, so did the British who were also allowed to remain in Siam. News from Europe arrived stating that war had broken out and that they were now allies against the French. As for Siam, it was soon mostly forgotten by the competing European powers.

9 Much more details on Siam's revolution and Bangkok's siege are given in Phisphumvidhi, 'La Révolution de 1688 au Siam d'après des sources militaires françaises' which includes five journals of French officers, also, the *Mercure Galant* of December 1689, pp.28-47, January 1691, pp.75-93 and December 1694, pp.99-108; Kaeppelin, *La Compagnie des Indes orientales*, p.219; AC, C1, 24, Siege de Bancoq, 1688.

5

India and the Indian Ocean, 1690s-1744

Louis XIVs overtures and bad luck in Siam had not produced much profit of any kind for anyone, but at least the Compagnie des Indes orientales had not been forced into bankruptcy. It still had its main lodge at Pondicherry on the Coromandel coast with a new one since 1686 at Chandernagor in Bengal and the older and less active one at Surat on the Malabar coast.

In 1690, the Sun King and the company outfitted a fleet of six ships for India, half of them warships and the others merchantmen under the command of *Capitaine de Vaisseau* Duquesne-Guitton, which sailed from France on 2 March. War had been declared in Europe and, on 3 July off the East African coast, the squadron encountered the British Honourable East India Company ship *Philip Herbert* that had sailed from England with 150 soldiers to reinforce the garrison at Bombay of which about 130 remained alive, the others already dead from disease. It was captured and burned after a short fight. On 28 July off Ceylon, the 38-gun *Écueuil* captured the Dutch East India Company's ship *Monfort* and its rich cargo, which was great news in terms of prize money for the 350-man crew of the French warship.

Once in India, the squadron sailed to Madras on 25 July finding nine Dutch and five British merchant ships in the harbour protected by a fortress armed with 80 guns. After a robust cannonade, Duquesne-Guitton withdrew, went to the Bay of Bengal, loaded up goods at Belassor and sailed for France on 30 December. On the whole, not much had been accomplished by this small, too small really, squadron.[1]

The company sent four ships that sailed for India at the end of April 1692 under Commandant Dandennes arriving at Surat on 26 October. At that time, in spite of hostilities in Europe, the British and French had convened a local truce of sorts spawning decent relations especially as there were very

1 Robert Challes, *Journal d'un voyage fait aux Indes orientales* (Rouen: Michael, 1722), Vol.2, pp.86-96, 123-140, 220-233, 330-344. Readers wishing a wonderfully humorous account of Challes' cruise on board *L'Écoeuil* must read W.H. Lewis, *The Splendid Century: Life in the France of Louis XIV* (London: Sloane, 1953), chapter XI on sea travel.

An assault during a siege in India, late seventeenth century. This detail from a large Indian wall hanging shows Indian infantry assisted by European gunners attacking a fortification defended by Indian and European soldiers. (Metropolitan Museum of Art, New York. Harris Brisbane Dick Fund and Louis V. Bell Fund. 2014.88)

Attack on a large fortification in India, late seventeenth century. Only European troops wearing coats, cravats, breeches, stockings, brimmed hats and, for an attacking group (lower right) what appears to be some type of black caps are seen battling each other in this detail from a large Indian wall hanging. Surprisingly, no Indian warriors, unless some might be topas, are represented. (Metropolitan Museum of Art, New York. Harris Brisbane Dick Fund and Louis V. Bell Fund. 2014.88)

few British ships in the area although Dandennes captured a few small ones on the way to India. The Dutch were a different matter. They had extensive establishments in present-day Indonesia and Ceylon rounded out by many factories along the Indian coast. Their naval force was the most powerful in the area and was based at Batavia (now Jakarta) whose squadrons cruised the eastern seas. Since 1690, they had reinforced their naval and military forces so that by early 1693, only a large fleet with many warships could oppose them. A squadron of 10 Dutch ships was already at Ceylon. Learning of this, Dandennes detached one ship to Bengal and sailed from Surat heading back to France in February 1693.[2]

The Dutch Capture Pondicherry, 1693

The French lodges were thus left with very minimal protection. The Dutch East India Company now saw its opportunity to attack Pondicherry and mustered a large force led by Admiral Laurens Pit consisting of 1,500 European troops from Java and Ceylon, 600 'Macassar' soldiers from Java and hundreds of Cingalese in Dutch pay, siege artillery consisting of 15 to 20 brass cannon, 24 field guns and six mortars. All boarded a fleet of 19 warships manned by 2,000 Dutch sailors with a multitude of transport and smaller vessels. The fleet appeared off Pondicherry on 23 August 1693 and some 2,000 men landed two days later led by Commandant van der Ploen that soon encircled the city. They built four batteries and dug trenches. There were skirmishes outside Pondicherry on 30 and 31 August as Dutch troops neared the walls.[3]

The fortifications at Pondicherry consisted of a medieval-style somewhat rectangular wall with round turrets upon which were mounted a few guns, a shore battery of four 18 pounder guns and a small redoubt. The garrison led by Governor François Martin consisted of about 50 French soldiers and up to 500 Indian auxiliary soldiers, notably some 200 Rajputs. Dutch batteries opened fire on 31 August and were answered by accurate shooting of the French guns on the fortifications. However, the walls proved vulnerable to the Dutch cannonballs. The following days saw more cannonades and skirmishes, but it became increasingly clear that the town could not resist for very long and some 300 of the Indian soldiers in the garrison deserted.

By 4 September, there remained only two or three serviceable French cannons and Martin considered retreating to the solidly built Jesuit's church to make a last stand. However, the next day, 200 Dutch and 300 Macassars divided in three corps supported by two cannon attacked the church simultaneously and its defenders barely had time to withdraw. It was, as Martin recalled, an 'irremediable disaster' followed by the desertion of the remaining 200 Rajputs. Part of the fort and the shoreline were still held by the French soldiers, but, fearing their cannons facing the sea would be captured, they blew them up. The next day, after some shooting, a cease fire

2 Kaeppelin, *La Compagnie des Indes orientales*, pp.299-304.
3 Gerlach, *Fastes militaires des Indes orientales néerlandaises*, p.116.

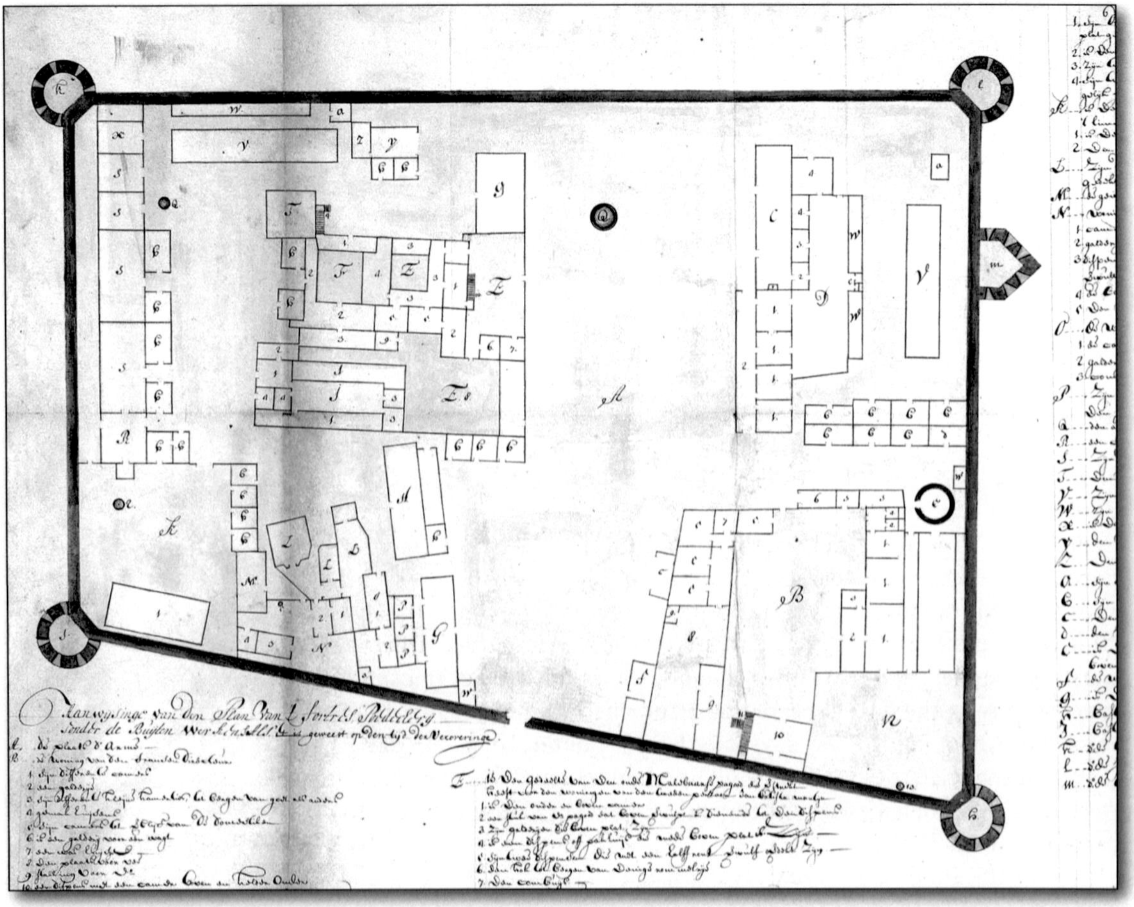

Dutch plan of the Compagnie des Indes' fortified compound at Pondichéry in 1694. (Dutch National Archives. AMH-5399-NA)

was agreed to, and negotiations led to signing an honourable capitulation on 7 September. The following day, the remaining and somewhat heroic French soldiers marched out with lit matches for their muskets, drums beating, colours unfurled and their two remaining cannons.[4]

The other French lodges at Surat and in Bengal could be vulnerable to Dutch attacks also. At this time however, the Mughal Empire under Emperor Aurangzeb was still powerful and Indian princes could intervene with considerable forces to stabilise a situation between squabbling Europeans. They were interested in trade and the competition between European lodges was best if relatively balanced. The Dutch knew this and although they had superior naval and military resources, they also had to contend with nearly constant challenges from local princes and kings in Indonesia and Ceylon.

There was as well the possibility that a squadron from France might arrive. Indeed a small squadron of six ships (including three royal warships) led by Serquigny d'Aché arrived at Surat on 14 January 1696. Cruising up the coast in late February, he sighted a Dutch fleet of eight ships, some having 50 and

4 Martineau (ed.), *Mémoires de François Martin*, Vol.3, pp.366-384; Kaeppelin, *La Compagnie des Indes orientales*, pp.310-313; G.B. Malleson, *History of the French in India* (London: Longmans, 1868), pp.26-27.

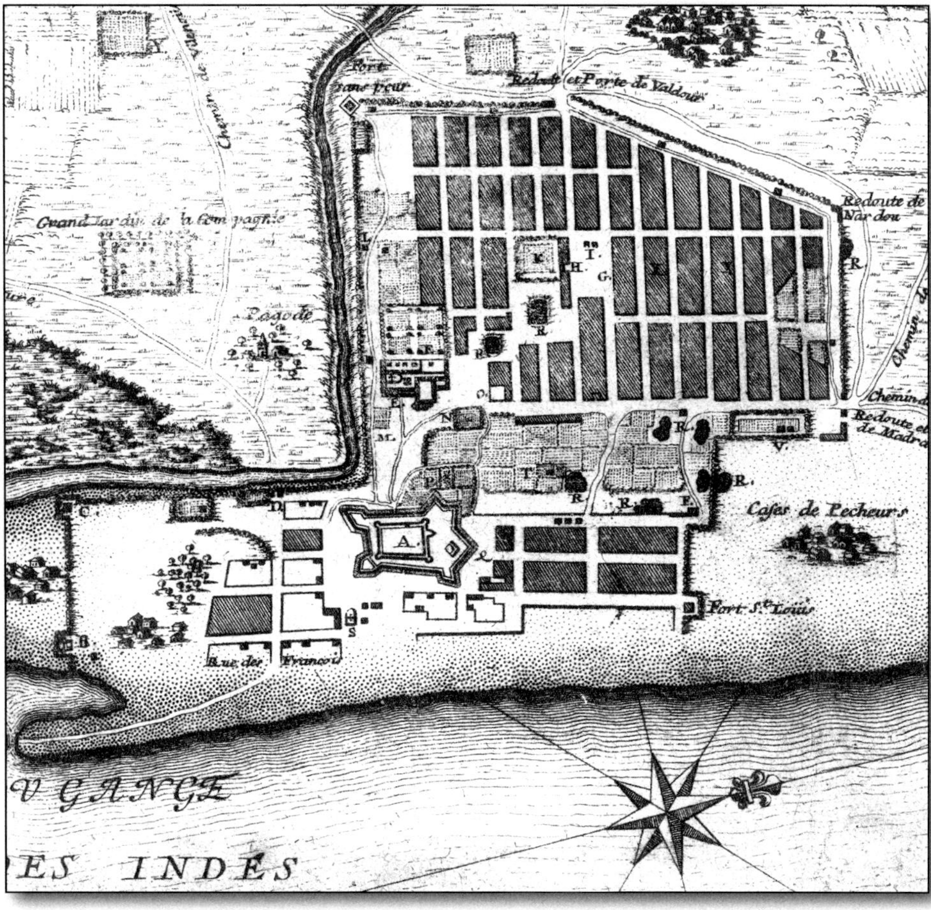

Plan of Pondicherry, circa 1699-1700. The letter A is at the centre of the old French fort with turrets around which the Dutch built new bastioned walls between 1693 and 1699 and possibly also the palisades around the city. Detail from a plan by N. de Fer. (Private collection, author's photo)

60 guns. After some manoeuvring, he attacked the Dutch north of Goa on 7 March; the battle was basically a long cannonade at the term of which the Dutch withdrew and the French followed them. A council of war was held deciding not to engage again for fear of heavy damages that could be inflicted by the superior Dutch fleet and Serquigny d'Aché went back to Surat. More Dutch ships were reinforcing their fleet and the French squadron sailed for France on 26 April. Some trading went on nevertheless in Surat and Bengal with single merchant ships hazarding long voyages from and to France.[5]

In Europe, the War of the League of Augsburg was ended by the Treaty of Ryswick signed on 21 September 1697. One of its many clauses provided for the return of Pondicherry to France. The Dutch evacuated the town on 3 September 1699 and François Martin was back as its governor.[6]

5 Kaeppelin, *La Compagnie des Indes orientales*, pp.327-329

6 Gerlach, *Fastes militaires des Indes orientales* néerlandaises, p.117. The French paid the Dutch 1,600 gold 'pagodas' (96,000 livres) in compensation for the fortifications that the Dutch had built at Pondicherry.

Consolidation in India and the Far East 1700s-1740s

In September 1699, two detachments of 30 men each belonging to the Compagnies Franches de la Marine were landed under the command of navy *Lieutenant de Vaisseau* de Livernan and assigned to garrison Pondicherry. A *sergent* with 20 recruits of the Compagnie des Indes orientales troops arrived later and were incorporated into the two companies. This was clearly insufficient and the marines were paid less than soldiers of the company who, in turn, were paid less than the departing 200 Dutch soldiers. Martin resorted to enrolling 180 topasses to strengthen the garrison while more soldiers of the company from France arrived the following year. In 1701, the garrison stood at three companies of 50 French soldiers each and more company recruits allowed the marines gradually to return to France. By 1706, there were five companies maintained by the Compagnie des Indes orientales but reduced to four in 1709 and to three in 1713. Europe was at war again from 1702. This time, there was a truce of sorts in the East Indies and, in Pondicherry that now had 60,000 inhabitants, the emphasis was to reinforce its fortifications notably by building its citadel under the direction of Engineer de Nyon. This was inaugurated on 25 August 1706. There were no major military events during the war, which ended in Europe and this was known in Pondicherry by October 1713. By then, François Martin had passed away seven years earlier and the next seven years saw substantial administrative mismanagement in all fields. By 1720, the garrison was said to be indolent and the upkeep of the fortifications neglected.

Nevertheless, business in India was improving after the European wars, but the Compagnie des Indes orientales was practically bankrupt due to huge debts accumulated in the war years. As seen above, it was saved from the brink by its incorporation into the multinational Compagnie des Indes from 1719. A period of consolidation followed, which was fostered by a positive outlook at opportunities to be found in India. In 1721, trade at the lodge of Surat was disappointing and it was closed as a main post. More trade was also sought with major coastal towns of the Persian Gulf and the Red Sea as well consolidating sea voyages from Pondicherry to Canton in China and creating naval bases and establishments at Ile de France (the former Mauritius abandoned by the Dutch) and agriculture of cash crops at Ile de Bourbon (La Réunion) thus creating a web of routes in the Indian Ocean. The benefits were apparent. The revenues from India and China that did not reach two million livres before 1719 rose to 15 to 18 million by the late 1730s leaving a net benefit of some 10 million yearly to the company.[7]

7 Hanotaux and Martneau (eds), *Histoire des colonies françaises et de l'expansion de la France dans le Monde*, Vol.5. pp.94-103,132; Martineau, *Dupleix*, Vol.1, ch.1; Bluzet, 'Les Indes pendant la guerre de Succession d'Autriche 1740-1748', École de guerre navale, 1933, p.4. A director with a few employees was kept at Surat for minor transactions.

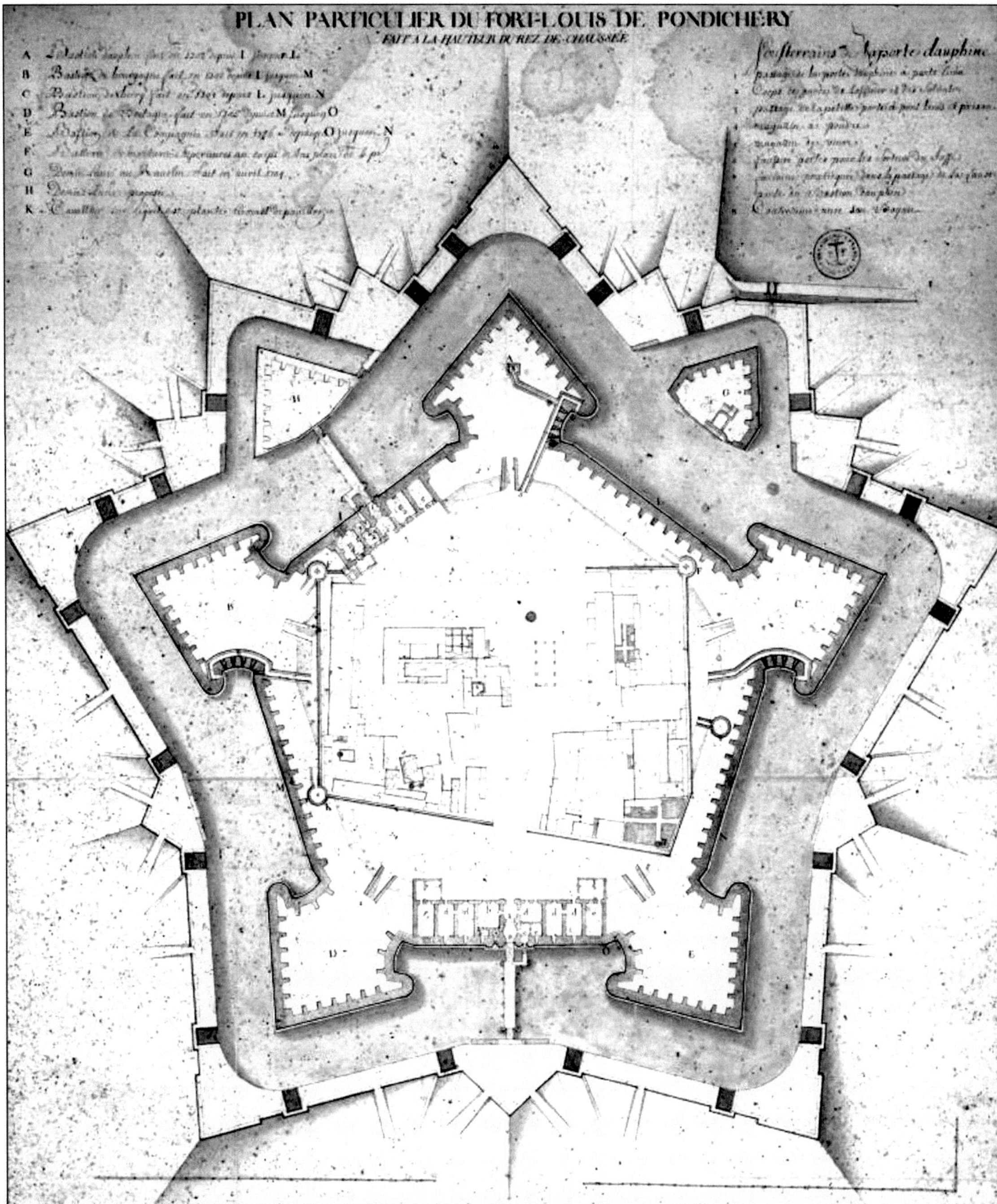

Plan of the Saint-Louis citadel at Pondicherry, 1709. This plan made two and a half years after its inauguration shows vestiges of the previous fortified compound consisting medieval-style of round turrets linked by walls now within the much larger citadel. (Archives Nationales Outre-Mer, 26DFC10A)

Ile de Bourbon and Ile de France

Two large uninhabited islands west of Madagascar had been sighted by Arab navigators during the ninth century and by the Portuguese in 1507. They remained unsettled until 1638 when a Dutch settlement was attempted at Mauritius while French convicts from Madagascar were marooned on Ile de Bourbon in 1642 followed by settlers during the 1660s and 1670s. The Dutch abandoned Mauritius in 1710 and the French took possession of it in 1715. Both islands were administratively under a governor general. Until 1721, the islands did not have a garrison of regular troops when the Compagnie des Indes sent soldiers to Ile de France. Ile de Bourbon had a garrison from 1723.

Fertile Ile de Bourbon developed into a plantation economy, notably of coffee, sugar and also spices as well as food crops. Slaves largely from Madagascar provided some labours although they were not in great numbers before the latter half of the eighteenth century. Many of the European settlers were small farmers and hunters whose ability for accurate shooting on land or at sea made them famous and feared.

Ile de France saw real development from the 1730s when energetic and far-seeing Bertrand-François Mahé de La Bourdonnais became governor general. Unlike its sister island, Ile de France had two good harbours and La Bourdonnais turned its capital, Port Louis, into a naval base and shipyard ideally situated on the route to India. Sugar plantations also brought wealth to the islands and, in wartime, privateers. Roads and fortifications were built. La Bourdonnais thus turned the island into a prosperous French colony and a port of call on the sea journey from Europe to India and the Far-East.[8]

Mahé de Malabar 1725

In India itself, the company still wanted a large lodge on the Malabar coast and, some years earlier, permission had been granted by the local prince of Coringote to establish a post at the mouth of the Mahé River. A French embassy duly signed with King Bayanor the cession of land to build a lodge there on 2 April 1721 in return for trade advantages. Mr Adams, the chief factor of the British Honourable East India Company at the factory of Tellicherry, was not pleased and soon suggested to the king that he should have second thoughts about the French. Things dragged on and by the time the company's ship *Argonaute* landed a modest party to occupy the place in October 1723, Adams had convinced the king to change his mind and he therefore ordered the French out of Mahé, which they duly evacuated in April and May 1724.

The Compagnie des Indes was not amused. On 29 October 1724, six company ships armed for war appeared off Mahé with 250 European soldiers and 100 topasses on board led by Commandant Pardaillan-Gondrin. At

8 Hanotaux and Martneau (eds), *Histoire des colonies françaises et de l'expansion de la France dans le Monde*, Vol.6.

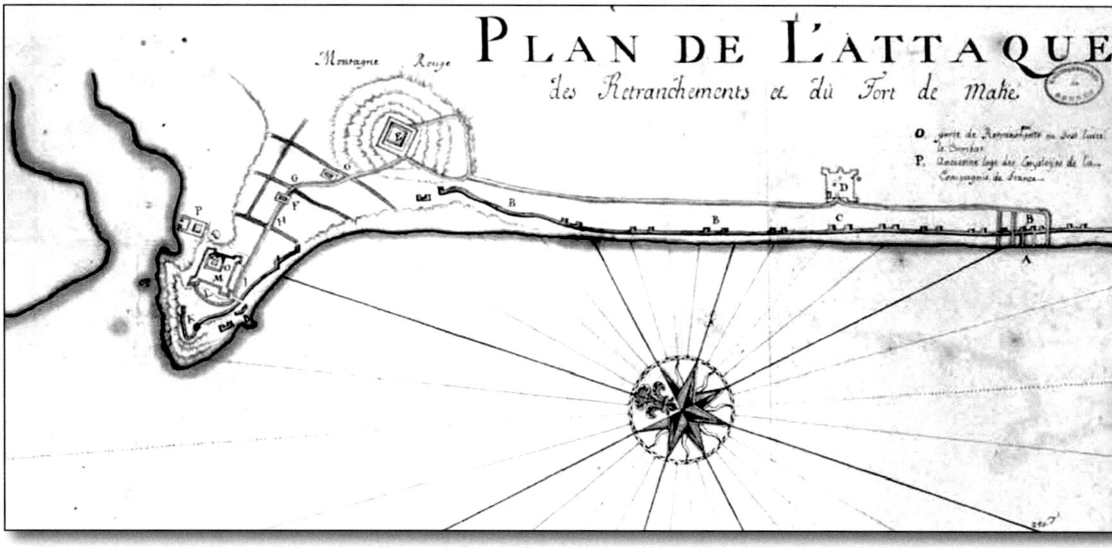

Plan of the French attack on the entrenchments and fort at Mahé on the Malabar Coast, 1726. The line from the landing to the fort is the road of the French force. At right, 'A' and 'B' show where the French force landed and built trenches, 'C' is the French camp, 'D' is the redoubt on the 'Montagne Rouge' (red mountain), 'O' and 'G' are minor defence works on the road, 'M' is the fort whose stone walls were half built. (Bibliothèque de Rennes. Ms0297)

dawn on 2 December, the troops landed at about two kilometres south of the river. The king had about 3,000 men along the shore and those at the landing spot were driven off by artillery and pursued by the French troops to the gates of a nearby fort, which the French then stormed and captured after some robust swordplay and bayonet fighting. The Indian opponents were said to have suffered 200 to 300 casualties, the French 13 killed (including two officers) and 33 wounded. Besides Pardaillan-Gondrin, Major Simon de La Farelle, Engineer Didier and a young officer of the company's navy named La Bourdonnais were noted for distinguished conduct. Mahé was thus secured and the lodge built although there was resistance at times by armed groups in the surrounding countryside encouraged by Adams who supplied arms and ammunition. However, Pardaillan-Gondrin was also a good diplomat with several local princes and the king signed a peace treaty on 8 November 1725. The British Honourable East India Company finally agreed to it on 10 March 1728.[9]

Moka 1737

The town of Moka (now Mukha), at the southern end of the Red Sea, was the main port of Yemen and renowned for its trade of fine coffee. In 1709, the governor of Moka and a representative of the Compagnie des Indes orientales signed a trade treaty regarding coffee and a lodge was opened there. Later on, the governor and treasurer of Moka caused losses to the Compagnie des Indes by not applying some clauses of the treaty so as to

9 E. Lennel de La Farelle (ed.), *Mémoires du chevalier de La Farelle sur la prise de Mahé 1725* (Paris: Chalamel, 1887), pp.8-53; 1725; Hanotaux and Martneau (eds), *Histoire des colonies françaises et de l'expansion de la France dans le Monde*, Vol.5, pp.104-107. Adams was later relieved and censored by Honourable East India Company for having unduly spent its funds in what seems to have been his private war when France and Great Britain were at peace.

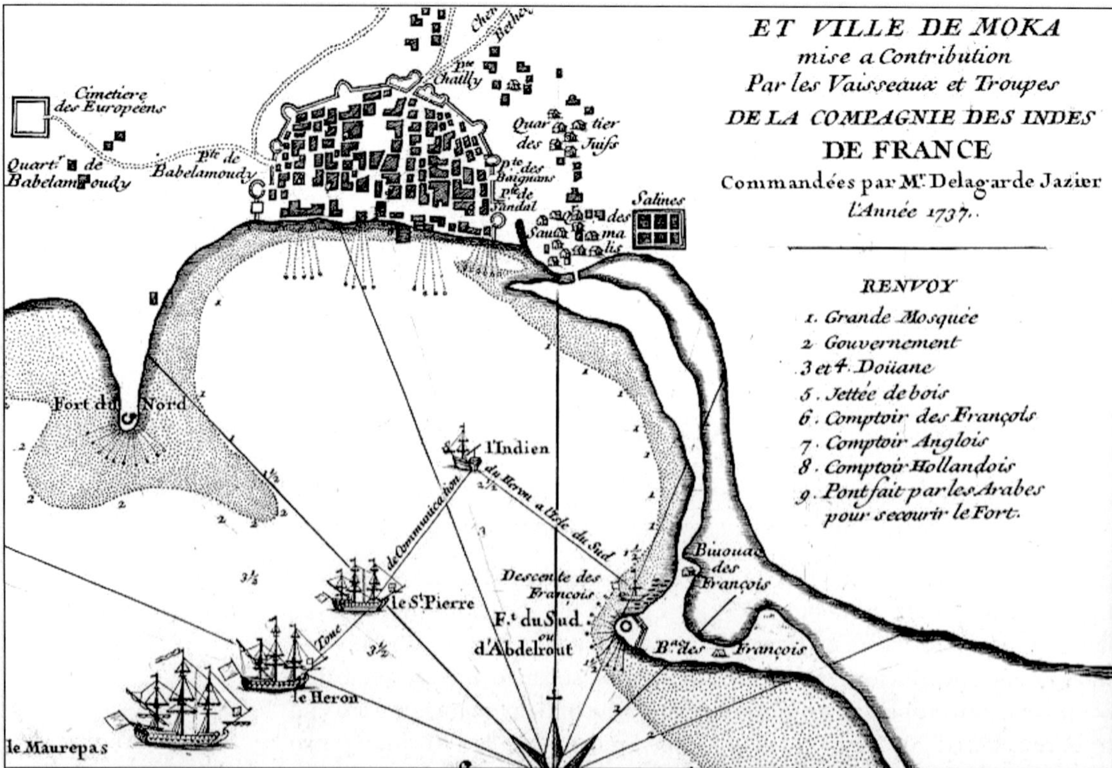

Plan of the attack on Moka by ships and troops of the Compagnies des Indes, February 1737. (Bibliothèque Nationale de France, Paris)

divert some revenues to themselves. Negotiations failed during the mid-1730s and the company obtained royal agreement from France to organise a military expedition to Moka. The fleet led by *Capitaine* de la Garde-Jazier assembled at Mahé consisted of four ships from India and a fifth from Ile de France. The Compagnie des Indes soldiers detached from garrisons from India and the islands were organised into a temporary landing corps of three companies of 94 soldiers each with 40 sailors, making 322 men plus officers. They were trained in various exercises including throwing grenades and landing operations so that when they appeared before Moka on 25 January 1737, they were deemed ready for action.

The rather alarmed governor of Moka sent boats with presents while mustering the town's garrison. During the next days, bad weather prevented further operations while letters were exchanged between Garde-Jazier and Moka's treasurer that did not produce any diplomatic progress. The weather improved and, on 1 February, the fleet bombarded the town while all of Moka's batteries opened fire, but caused little damage. The town was also lightly hit although its population was said to be very affected by these events and some blamed the governor and his officers for provoking a 'war' with the French.

The bad weather persisted so that any military operations were next to impossible until the night of 14 to 15 February when French longboats full of soldiers approached the shore near the 'Fort du Sud' (southern fort), being detected only as they landed. The French troops scattered the defenders at the beach, went to the fort's walls, threw in grenades, fixed bayonets and stormed it suffering only a few casualties while its surviving garrison ran off. Many more defenders came out of Moka to wipe out the French, but they were stopped by volley fire and artillery salvos manned by French gunners in the fort. The defeated defenders retreated into town. French casualties amounted to four soldiers killed and 12 wounded while the defenders admitted to 80 including 42 found dead in and near the fort. There followed a long truce and negotiations that now involved representatives of the king of Yemen resulting in mutual agreement in a new treaty that essentially put in force the 1709 agreement. The king of Yemen and the Compagnie des Indes were anxious to restore the lucrative coffee trade to its full capacity, especially as France was becoming a nation of coffee drinkers. The fleet sailed back to India on 21 July.[10]

Governor General Dumas welcomes the widow and family of Nabob Dost Ali Khan as refugees in Pondicherry, 26 May 1740. The nabob had been slain in battle by the Marathas who later had to withdraw. Governor Dumas' humane gesture had favourable diplomatic consequences for the Compagnie des Indes. Print after Bombléd in the December 1902 *Dépêche coloniale illustrée*. (Bibliothèque Nationale de France, Paris)

Blockade of Pondicherry by the Marathas 1740

The next challenge to the Compagnie des Indes in India was far more serious, and threatened all its establishments in the Carnatic including Pondicherry. It was due to the eroding authority of the Mughal Empire causing bloody dynastic struggles and the increasing power of the Marathas. In 1739, the king of Tanjore wanted to get rid of the nabob of Arcot so he called on the Marathas to carry this out. They accordingly marched into the Carnatic with over 200,000 men led by Ragogy Bosla who defeated the smaller army of the nabob of Arcot, who was killed in battle, on 20 May 1740. This battle, which had been very bloody, occurred four leagues west of Pondicherry and, the next day, the survivors of the nabob's army arrived at the city's outworks seeking safety.

The nabob had been an ally of the French and his family, including his widow and son, asked Governor-General Pierre-Benoît Dumas to grant them asylum in Pondicherry. It was a very delicate situation, but Dumas and the Pondicherry council accepted on the spot. Dumas greeted the widowed princess personally with guards of

10 *Relation de l'expedition de Moka en l'Année M.DCC.XXXVIII sous les orders de M. de la Garde-Jazier* (Paris: Chaubert, 1739); Louis Moreri, *Le Grand Dictionnaire historique* (Paris: Libraires associés, 1739), Vol.7, p.599. Following the 1737 campaign, the Moka coffee trade transactions could be made directly in its harbour by ship's officers, eliminating the need to have a lodge there. It was closed in 1741.

honour and artillery salutes as she and her large suite, which included 80 elephants, entered the city. The situation was not as desperate as it seemed for the French. The city's fortifications were in decent condition with numerous guns and the garrison of about 1,200 French and topas soldiers had been augmented by about 4,000 sepoy soldiers gradually recruited since 1737 by Dumas. Furthermore, Dumas had urgently called on Governor-General Bernard-François de La Bourdonnais at Ile de France to sail to Pondicherry as soon as possible with all the forces he could muster.

Months passed as the Marathas terrorised and looted much of southern India including many smaller European lodges. Finally, in January 1741, Ragogy was outside Pondicherry and summoned Dumas to deliver the dead nabob's widow and son as well as pay a huge tribute. Dumas answered on 21 January asking why would he attack the French who had always sought good relations with the Marathas. He further mentioned that he and his officers would be 'severely punished by the king of France, our master, whose justice and power are known all over the world, if we did the smallest action against his intentions and his glory', adding that his soldiers would fight anyone who would 'unjustly attack'. Further letters exchanged did not change the situation although Ragogy now could see from occasional skirmishes and French cannon fire that taking Pondicherry would require a very difficult siege operation that might not succeed. Part of his troops were already further south besieging Trichinopoly when it was learned that Indian princes further north were mustering an army to invade Maratha territories. He eventually made a truce with Dumas and marched north with his troops.[11]

La Bourdonnais and Mahé 1741

Dumas' call for help at Pondicherry was only seen by La Bourdonnais on 14 August 1741 when he arrived at Ile de France from Europe leading a naval squadron. He lost no time mobilising the island's militias while organising an expeditionary corps that left on 22 August arriving at Pondicherry on 30 September. By then, the Marathas had long departed, but Governor-General Dumas asked La Bourdonnais if he could lead his squadron and troops to Mahé, which had been blockaded for 18 months by the somewhat piratical forces of local princes. La Bourdonnais sailed on 22 October arriving at Mahé on 23 November, having trained his troops on assault tactics during the voyage. His force consisted of eight companies of French soldiers amounting to about 400 men and 500 sepoys.

On the nights of 3 and 4 December, the Franco-Indian troops constructed undetected a four-gun artillery battery at about 200 metres from the enemy forward positions. At dawn on 5 December, enemy warriors saw the battery which they attacked immediately and were repulsed. La Bourdonnais had planned a general assault that day and divided his troops into two columns

11 Anon., *Lettres édifiantes et curieuses écrites des missions étrangères, mémoires des Indes* (Lyon: J. Vernarel, 1819), Vol.8, pp.179-193; Hanotaux and Martneau (eds), *Histoire des colonies françaises et de l'expansion de la France dans le* Monde, Vol.5, pp.121-124.

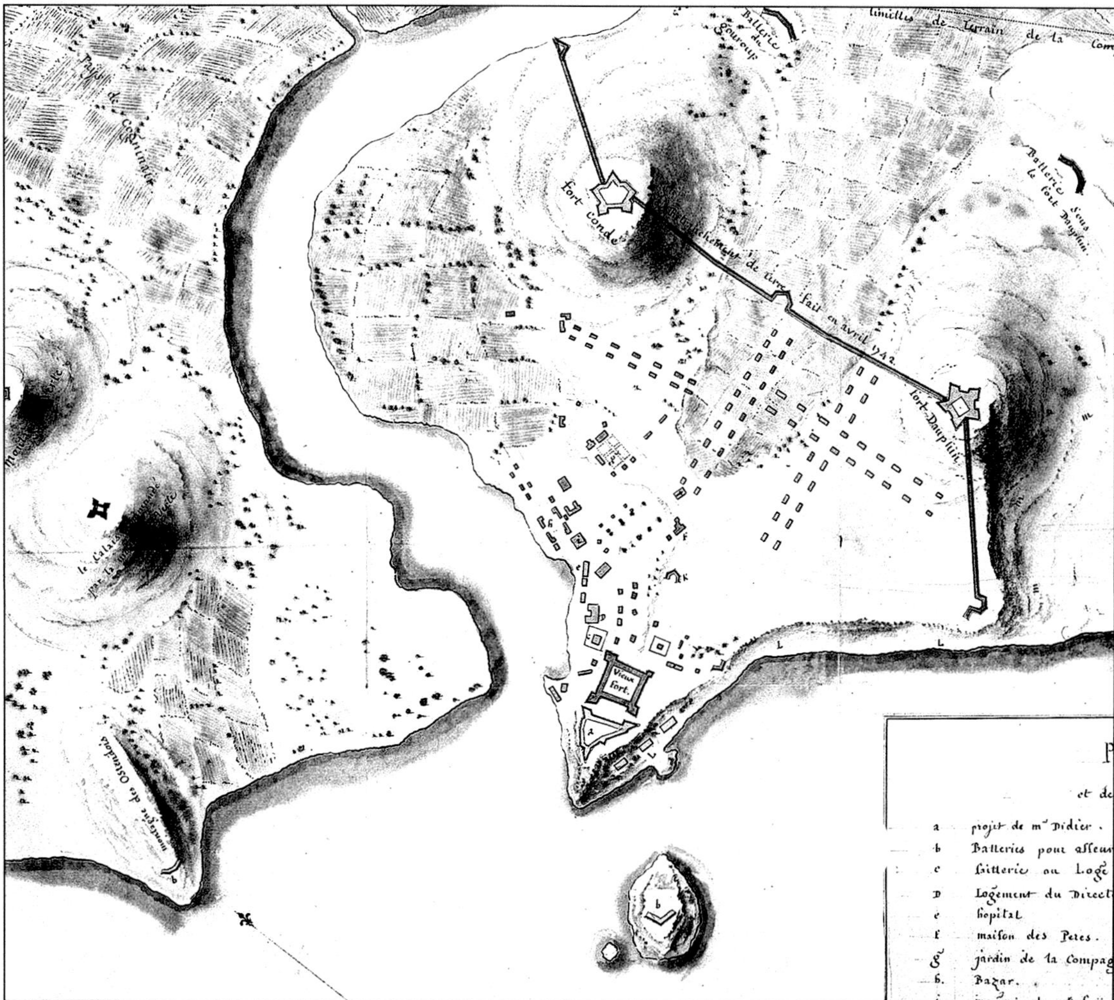

Fortifications at Mahé on the Malabar Coast, 1742. A year after La Bourdonnais' relief of this lodge and its 'Vieux Fort' (old fort – at bottom centre), a number of defensive works had been added, notably an earthen entrenchment completed in April 1742 connecting two redoubts (Fort Condé and Fort Dauphin). (Archives Nationales Outre-Mer, 29DFC19B)

which he now ordered to attack after his eager soldiers had begged him to do so. The enemy force was estimated to be about 8,000 strong whose strongest positions were two earthen forts. Neither enemy gunfire nor field obstacle prevented the soldiers and sepoys with La Bourdonnais charging ahead from reaching the forts, scaling the walls and bursting into a more numerous rabble that soon broke and fled being unable to resist to a disciplined assault. Some defenders were very brave 'Naire' caste warriors that fought to death and never surrendered, but the French volleys and bayonets nevertheless prevailed and all enemy positions were taken. The French lost 56 men killed and 120 wounded while the estimated enemy loss was about 500 men killed. Negotiations followed and a peace agreement that definitively secured Mahé was made on 22 January 1742.[12]

12 Pierre de Gennes, *Mémoire pour le sieur de La Bourdonnais, avec pièces justificatives* (Paris: Delaguette, 1750), pp.28-31; Pierre Crepin, *Mahé de La Bourdonnais* (Paris: Leroux, 1922), pp.165-171.

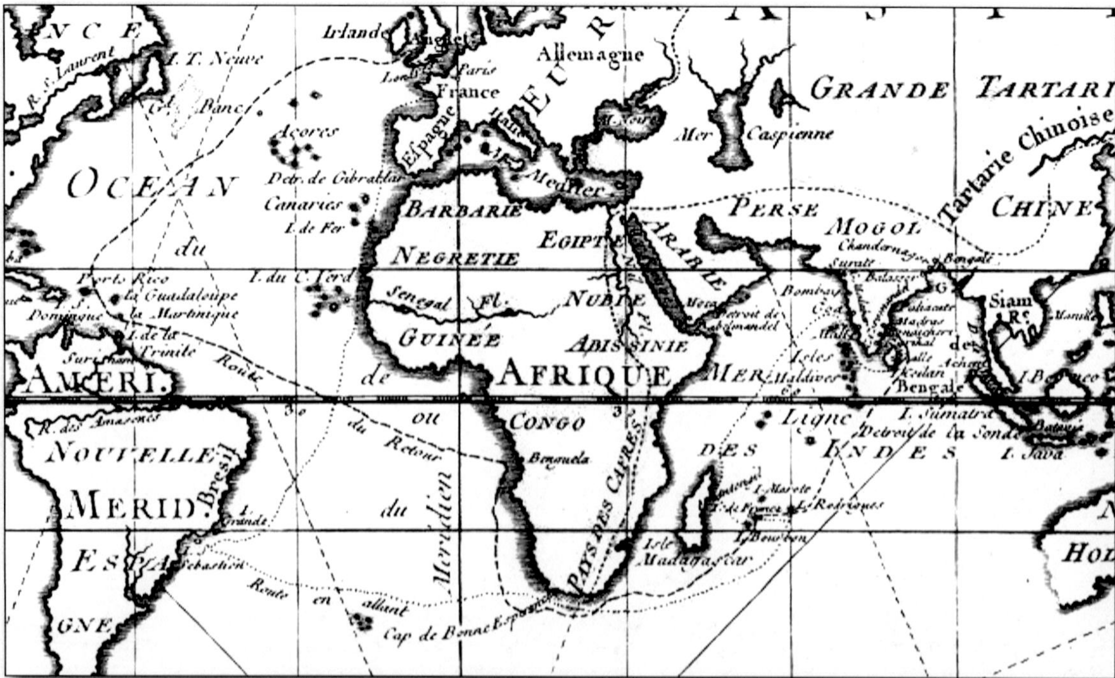

La Bourdonnais' routes to India and back, 1740s. This map with La Bourdonnais' memoir of the East Indies shows some of the main routes. The line with small dots starts at Lorient, France, goes south to Brazil, turns east going past the Cape of Good Hope and north-east to Ile de France, west to the coast of Madagascar and north-east to the area of Goa in India, East round Sri Lanka and North to Pondicherry. The way back is shown in small bars from Pondicherry sailing south-west to Ile de France, round the Cape of Good Hope and north up the African coast, turning west across the Atlantic to the West Indies and north-east France. Such a voyage and back could to take about a year and a half. Centre detail of a map after Chambon. (Private collection, author's photo)

The determined stance by Dumas at Pondicherry and the relief of Mahé by La Bourdonnais were noticed in princely courts throughout India and, in general, their firmness was admired; the compassionate treatment given to the fallen nabob's widow and his family was also much approved. This raised the diplomatic reputation of the French in the great sub-continent. As it were, Dumas now retired to France and was succeeded in January 1742 as Governor-General by Jean-François Dupleix, a near genius of geopolitics and strategy destined to raise French influence in India to its apex.

6

The War of the Austrian Succession 1744-1748

Jean-François Dupleix was born at Landrecies on New Year's day of 1699 into a prosperous family that had interests in the East India companies and, in 1715, young Jean-François was sent on a grand tour to see India. He liked it in and, in 1720, became a member of the Pondicherry council. Having a good business sense, he made his own fortune during the following decade. Recognised as a bright and able administrator, he was appointed director of the lodge at Chandernagor in 1730. Under his energetic and shrewd administration, Chandernagor prospered becoming the second most important French lodge in India. On 14 January 1742, he was promoted to the post of governor general.

Bust of Jean-François Dupleix, Governor General of French India, 1742-1754. Print after Bombléd in the December 1902 *Dépêche coloniale illustrée.* (Bibliothèque Nationale de France, Paris)

In July 1746, a French naval squadron led by La Bourdonnais anchored at Pondicherry. He was destined to be lauded by future French historians for his accomplishments at Ile de France and Ile de Bourbon as well as in India during his short passages there. He went to sea at 10 years old, was an *enseigne* in the Compagnie des Indes orientales' navy by 1713, sailing in southern seas as far as the Philippines in the following years. He had an avid curiosity and, during the long crossings, learned from some passengers on board who were delighted to teach to this obviously brilliant young mind subjects such as advanced mathematic (from a Jesuit missionary) and engineering and tactics (from King's Engineer M. Didier). His military capacities

Bertrand François Mahé de La Bourdonnais, 1740s. Born in Saint-Malo in 1699, officer of the king's navy, governor general of Ile de France and Ile de Bourbon (1733-1748). Print after portrait. (Private collection, author's photo)

became quite useful against pirates on the Indian coast finally coming back to his native Saint-Malo in 1733 to marry his sweetheart. His reputation as an energetic, bright and action-minded officer reached Versailles and, in 1735, he was appointed Governor-General of Ile de France and Ile de Bourbon. His administrative talents transformed these Indian Ocean islands into strategically important commercial and military bases. Their outstanding strategic importance was soon proven when Pondicherry and Mahé were blockaded by hostile Indian princes during 1740-1741 (see chapter 5).[1]

This success was repeated. In mid-April 1746, La Bourdonnais sailed from Ile de France to India. All his ships were short of sailors and most of them did not have 'the necessary training to serve on warships', so he divided them into companies to be trained in weapon's drills. Officers were also offered lectures on military manoeuvres. To have more sailors, Africans *Caffres* were incorporated into the companies.[2] On 1 June 1746, his nine ships had 3,342 men on board including 720 African sailors and 300 to 400 men that were sick. The squadron was off the coast of India at month's end on the way to Pondicherry to deliver much needed species and supplies; this was the primary objective La Bourdonnais had in his instructions from Versailles.[3]

Naval Battle of Negapatam 1746

On the morning of 6 July 1746 when off Negapatam on the Coromandel coast, La Bourdonnais' squadron came into view of six British Royal Navy warships led by Commodore Peyton. They immediately sailed to meet the French ships who formed a line and prepared to fight them. La Bourdonnais noted that, from noon, the approaching ships took in some of their sails to slow down. The French squadron's only true warship of the king's navy was the *Achille* of 60 guns, of which the heaviest were of 18-pounder calibre.

1 L.C. Mahé de La Bourdonnais (ed.), *Mémoires historiques de B.F. Mahé de La Bourdonnais*, (Paris: Policier et Chatet, 1827), pp.2-24.

2 The French *Caffre* shares its linguistic origins with the English-language Kaffir but does not appear to have acquired the same offensive conotations, beyond those implicit in all European attempts to impose racial classifications on the peoples of their empires. It should nevertheless be understood that the term is used in this work as reflecting the usage of the seventeenth and eighteenth centuries and that no offence is intended thereby.

3 Mahé de La Bourdonnais (ed.), *Mémoires historiques de B.F. Mahé de La Bourdonnais*, pp.74-76, 85.

Naval battle of Negapatam, 6 July 1746. La Bourdonnais' *Achilles* (centre) was the only true French warship in his squadron, has other ships being armed merchantmen. Although Commodore Peyton had six Royal Navy warships, he was compelled to withdraw. Print after Guérin's 1846 *Histoire maritime de France*. (Author's photo)

The others were ships of the Compagnie des Indes. There was one with 36 guns, three with 34 guns, one with 30 guns, two with 28 and one of 26 guns. All their guns were 12 and 8-pounders. The total came to 310 guns. La Bourdonnais further reported Peyton's British squadron's six ships as having one of 74 guns, two with 56 guns, one with 50 guns, one with 40 guns and a frigate with 20 guns for a total of 296 guns, of which the heaviest were of 24 pounder calibre. There were 1,320 men on board. The French squadron had a slight advantage in the number of guns, but the much more numerous heavy calibre guns of the British warships gave them a true ballistic advantage.[4]

La Bourdonnais' account of the battle, which started at 4:30 p.m., was very short:

> First of all, three of our ships were put out of combat and the British, who had put out all their sails, would have crushed the *Neptune*, which remained alone in front, had I not caught up with them. At that time, the combat became more serious than ever. My ship received for a quarter of an hour all the enemy's shots. Finally, rebutted by our resistance, they withdrew at 7:30 p.m.[5]

---

4 Numerous British and French sources give different numbers of guns to ships of both fleets. We have opted for La Bourdonnais' count as it was important for him to have fairly accurate information as to guns and their calibres. The Compagnie des Indes ships were: *Bourbon*, *Phénix*, *Neptune*, *Saint-Louis*, *Lys*, *Duc d'Orléans*, *Renommée* and l'*Insulaire*. There was also a small tender most likely unarmed. The British ships were: *Medway*, *Medway Prize*, *Harwich*, *Preston*, *Lively* and *Winchester*.

5 La Bourdonnais (ed.), *Mémoires historiques de B.F. Mahé de La Bourdonnais*, pp.85-87; Louis Joseph Philippe, Comte de Rostaing, 'Expedition de La Bourdonnais dans la mer des Indes en 1746', *Revue maritime et coloniale*, 1880, pp.72-5, 427-429; Robert Orme, *A History of*

Some of the battle's highlights were that the *Achilles* fired a third of the French squadron's 3,000 shots. This ship's fast firing rate was favoured by a flintlock firing mechanism invented by the Chevalier de Rostaing. Nevertheless, some French ships were battered and *Insulaire* had lost its masts, thus frustrating La Bourdonnais' wish to pursue and board the British ships. Both squadrons spent the night far from each other. In the morning, the British squadron approached the French to within artillery range and then turned away heading for Trincomalee (Sri Lanka) leaving control of the Coromandel coast to the French squadron.[6]

La Bourdonnais also had to obey the wishes of Versailles and so the squadron anchored at Pondicherry on the evening of 9 July. Having made repairs to his ships, La Bourdonnais sailed out of Pondicherry on 4 August looking for Peyton's squadron. It was spotted off Negapatam on 17 August and La Bourdonnais immediately gave the chase hoping to engage with the faster *Achilles* alone long enough for the rest of his slower-sailing squadron to catch up. The pursuit went on all night and into the morning when, forming a line, Peyton considered engaging the French, but as he came closer, changed his mind and with the agreement of his officers, sailed off towards Sri Lanka, the pretext being that the French ships had more guns than at the previous engagement![7]

This engagement has sometime been described as 'inconclusive' which seems odd when one of the two contestants left not merely the waters off Negapatam, but India's coast altogether for the safety of Trincomalee. The French now had naval predominance. A remarkable factor considering the forces involved. Except for one warship, the military navy of Louis XV was nowhere to be seen in India and it was the Compagnie des Indes' merchant ships 'armed for war' that had prevailed over a fleet of warships belonging to Britain's Royal Navy.

La Bourdonnais takes Madras, 1746

La Bourdonnais had wanted to attack Madras as early as July, but Dupleix had been reluctant seeing this enterprise as too risky. He still had doubts in early September because there was also the possibility that Peyton could appear again, especially if four more British warships, rumoured to be sailing towards India, joined him. To La Bourdonnais, it was all the more urgent to attack swiftly and Dupleix with the Pondicherry council finally agreed.

---

the Military Transactions of the British Nation in Indostan from MDCCXLV [1745] (London: Nourse, 1775), Vol.1, pp.61-64; Bluzet, *Les Indes pendant la guerre de Succession d'Autriche 1740-1748* (Brest: École navale de guerre, 1933; typescript at BNF), pp.20-24; Herbert W. Richmond, *The Navy in the War of 1739-48* (Cambridge: Cambridge University Press, 1920), Vol.3, pp.193-198; Charles Rathbone Low, *Her Majetsy's Navy* (London: Virtue, c. 1890), Vol.1, pp.189-191.

6 Rostaing, 'Expedition de La Bourbonnais dans la mer des Indes en 1746', p.73.

7 Some historians, perhaps in embarrassment, have since qualified this battle as 'indecisive' which has been usually retained in anglophone publications and websites.

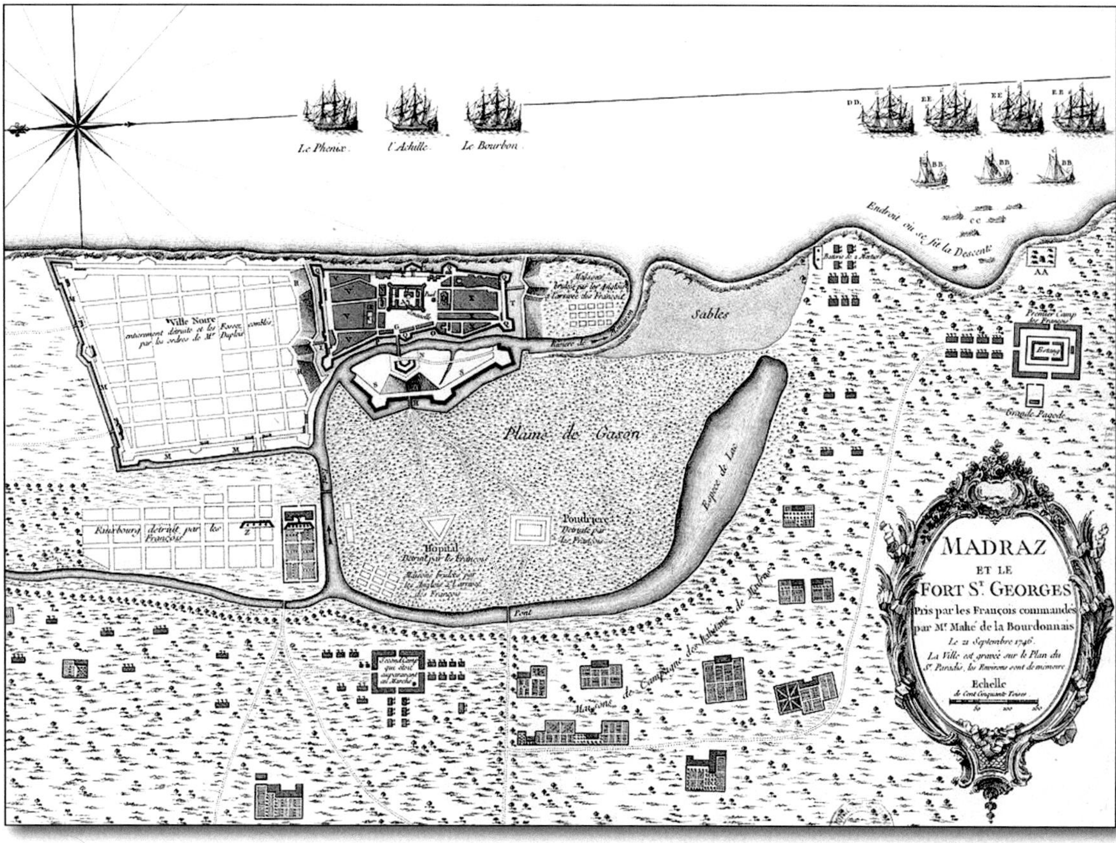

Plan of the siege of Madras and Fort St George, September 1746. At top centre are the ships *Pheonix*, *Achille* and *Bourbon* facing the city and fort. At upper right is the landing site and first camp of the French forces. At lower bottom is their second camp with, just above, two batteries containing ten mortars. Plan by the engineer, Sieur Paradis. (Bibliothèque Nationale de France, Paris)

By 15 September, 1,100 European soldiers, 400 sepoys and 400 *Caffres* from Ile de France and Ile de Bourbon had landed near Madras and were investing the city. About 1,880 sailors were on board the French fleet. The city's British garrison was estimated at about 500 when there were actually only about 200 soldiers and 100 British civilians; the citadel of Fort St George basically defended the European quarter. On 17 September, construction of field fortifications and siege batteries started and the next day, some Indian troops allied to the British attempted to skirmish towards the French camp, but they were swiftly beaten back and sought safety farther out in the countryside. The much larger Indian part of the city was largely abandoned by the British while, on 18 June, the European part was bombarded by the two French land batteries and the three largest ships of La Bourdonnais' squadron.

Governor Morse knew he could not hold out for long, and, on 20 September, negotiations took place. La Bourdonnais warned the British that if there was an assault, it would be impossible to restrain the sepoys who looted and the 'ferocious *Caffres* who think anything is allowed during a city's assault'. The capitulation was signed on 21 September. Governor Morse presented his sword to La Bourdonnais who immediately gave it back and entered Madras with 1,500 men largely to restore order mainly because some of the British soldiers had mutinied, some even saying they did not mind being executed if they could kill the French general indicating that their discipline had collapsed. The French troops therefore imposed strict police authority, British soldiers and sailors were transferred to the French ships and Madras was secured.[8]

The surrender of Madras led to a bitter dispute between La Bourdonnais and Dupleix regarding their jurisdictions and powers. Both had the post of governor-general, La Bourdonnais of the Ile de France and Ile de Bourbon that basically concerned naval power and influence in the Indian Ocean, whereas Dupleix ruled French establishments on mainland India with all the territorial ramifications. They were strong-willed men of talent with imperial visions. Both clashed almost as soon as they met, and each encamped himself solidly in his respective prerogatives claiming executive power in areas that were far from being clearly defined. It is not our purpose in this book to present in detail these disputes, which affected the conditions that the British garrison had agreed to; they are related in British histories. There also were numerous lesser-known contestations of authority affecting the French troops and ships at Madras that left local commanders in a confusing situation. On 29 October, La Bourdonnais sailed from Pondicherry never to return. [9]

La Bourdonnais accepts the British capitulation of Madras, 21 September 1746. Print after Bombléd in the December 1902 *Dépêche coloniale illustrée*. (Bibliothèque Nationale de France, Paris)

After a stop in the West Indies, he reached France on 22 February 1748 and was in Versailles seeing ministers and officials a few days later. However, he had been preceded by many memoirs and letters signed by Dupleix, the Pondicherry council and other officials, all damning his conduct while in India and accusing him of many sins including treason. On 2 March, he was arrested by royal order and detained in the Bastille for the next three years until declared innocent and released. He passed away in 1753. Voltaire considered La Bourdonnais to have been 'an audacious genius' like France's greatest sailors and the only one that had maintained 'the honour of the standard of France in Asia.' The judgement of History has since agreed with the great philosopher.[10]

8 The main source on the siege of Madras has been Mahé de La Bourdonnais (ed.), *Mémoires historiques de B.F. Mahé de La Bourdonnais*, pp.95-123; J.W. Fortescue, *A History of the British Army* (London: Macmillan, 1899), Vol.2, pp.180-181.

9 H. de Closets d'Errey (ed.), *Résumé des lettres du conseil provincial de Madras avec Mahé de La Bourdonnais, Dupleix, le conseil supérieur et divers* (Pondichéry and Paris: Bibliothèque publique, 1936) is a remarkable source regarding this dispute, much of which regarded military details.

10 Voltaire, *Fragments sur l'Inde, sur le général Lalli et sur le comte de Morangiés* (Unknown Publisher, 1773), pp.14-18.

Fort St George at Madras, mid-eighteenth century. Print after I. Van Ryne published in 1754. (Rijkmuseum, Amsterdam. RP-P-1932-439)

Adyar/Sao Tomé 1746

Carnatic Nabob Anwarudeen had been very concerned during the French attack on British Madras, to the point of threatening to send an Indian army to remind everyone that territories were granted to European nations only for trade. They were ultimately still part of the domain of Indian princes. Dupleix had shrewdly replied that, in fact, the French were taking possession of Madras on their nabob's behalf and had even hoisted his standard there after the place capitulated. The nabob's understanding of the agreement with Dupleix was that once the French had taken the place, they would simply leave and let him add it to his domains. Weeks passed and the French showed no sign of leaving. By late October, Anwarudeen had enough and, in the traditional fashion of Mughal India, sent his son Maphuze Khan at the head of an army of 10,000 men to convince the French of the wisdom of turning over Madras or else his army would invest and storm the city.

Council director d'Eprémesnil, in charge at Madras, had received instructions from Dupleix: under no circumstances was Madras to be delivered to Maphuze Khan. The city's situation was not hopeless because its fortifications were adequate and it had a French garrison of some 3,000 Europeans including some 900 sailors plus sepoys. By the end of October, Maphuze Khan and his troops were outside Madras and started the siege works to invest the city. They had a rude surprise on 2 November when *Capitaine* Dubernat de la Tour led 300 men with two field guns in a sortie that scattered masses of charging cavalry with his rapid firing artillery shooting five to six shots a minute assisted by infantry firing disciplined musket volleys. The French raiders then charged into the terrified enemy's abandoned camp before retiring back into Madras. They had no casualties while their opponents had about 70 killed. Maphuze Khan then cautiously moved his army to the shores of the small and shallow Adyar (also called

Sao Tomé) River just south of Sao Tomé to intercept a Franco-Indian force marching north from Pondicherry.

Sure enough, on the morning of 4 November, *Capitaine* Louis Paradis, an engineer, was nearing the Adyar River leading 230 French and 700 sepoys soldiers to reinforce Madras; they now faced Maphuze Khan and his army. No doubt, Maphuze Khan and his officers were sure of an easy triumph and elimination of Paradis' small force. Indeed it would serve as a warning to the French as well as to other Europeans that they were tolerated in India by the grace of their princes who could, if they wished, deploy huge armies to back up their will.

Accordingly, Maphuze Khan's army now gathered in battle formation. Besides cavalry and war elephants, his foot troops consisting of fusiliers, swordsmen, pikemen and gunners were deployed in four corps. Facing this multitude advancing towards his French soldiers and sepoys, Paradis could only hope against such heavy odds that charging the enemy might save some of his command and all his men thought the same. Retreat meant slaughter by waves of cavalrymen and perhaps worse if taken alive. It was certain death except for the thin survival chance granted by the unpredictable gods of war. Paradis ordered the advance, took the lead and all crossed the fordable Adyar River heading towards the nearest enemy corps.[11]

According to Ananda Ranga Pallai's journal, Maphuze Khan's fusiliers were formed in three ranks with four guns that opened fire on the advancing Franco-Indians also formed in line, but their shots either fell short or proved totally inaccurate. Within fairly close range, Paradis' troops stopped and fired a devastating volley 'making many men fall dead' on the spot. Seeing this, Maphuze Khan's surviving fusiliers panicked, threw away their muskets, broke ranks and ran spreading fear to the whole army. Paradis' soldiers now attacked with their bayonets into terrified masses fleeing into Sao Tomé. To seal the victory, a French reinforcement column out of Madras arrived in the field and attacked the enemy's rear. Maphuze Khan was on foot and, seeing his army evaporate, his fear overcame bravery and he ran to climb into his elephant and run off. The charging French soldiers and sepoys overran the enemy camp making prisoners and seized some 30 camels, 60 or 70 cattle, 40 or 50 horses, supplies, cloth and money. Ananda further reported the French casualties as two sepoys wounded while 'no other man received so much as a pin's jab'. Maphuze Khan's army had at least 200 to 300 killed.[12]

Ananda had a far-seeing conclusion when he wrote that Indian rulers 'would not be able to do whatever they wish' in the future. Indeed, a single battalion had defeated a whole army. News of Maphuze Khan's army's total collapse near the banks of the Adyar River spread through India like wildfire. As small as the battle may have been, its astounding result crossed a threshold: it was the first time a European-trained force, always small-sized in India, had utterly defeated a far larger Indian prince's army. Awe and fear-

11 Orme, *A History of the Military Transactions of the British Nation in Indostan*, Vol.1, pp.75-77; P. de Vaissière, *Dupleix* (Paris: Plon, 1931), pp.87-89.

12 Julien Vinson (trans. and ed.), *Les Français dans l'inde : Le journal d'Anandarangappoullé 1736-1748* (Paris: Leroux, 1894), pp.141-142.

inspiring huge armies were now proven to be totally vulnerable to European battlefield tactics, discipline and weapons technology. As Fortescue aptly wrote: 'With this action it may be said that the dominance of a European nation in India was assured. Hitherto the native armies had been treated with respect. Their numbers had given the impression of overwhelming strength… Now the spell was broken…' What was more, we must add, this was done by the brave and efficient soldiers, be they sepoys or French, in the service of the Compagnie des Indes. Fortescue further concluded: 'The memory of Paradis should be honoured in England since he taught us the secret of the conquest of India.'[13]

Ile de France Attacked, 1748

In the summer of 1748, the British forces gained naval superiority in the Indian Ocean thanks to Rear-Admiral Edward Boscawen's squadron of 25 ships including six warships, notably HMS *Namur* of 74 guns, arriving from Great Britain. His primary objective was to attack Ile de France. The obvious reason for this expedition was that while there were no good harbours at Ile de Bourbon, there were two fine harbours at Ile de France, one of which, Port-Louis, also called Port Nord-Ouest, was the island's capital. During the governorship of La Bourdonnais in the later 1730s, it had seen considerable development as a naval base and shipyard where Compagnie des Indes ships could refit safely from winds and storms, find ample fresh water, supplies and be repaired. Vessels of modest tonnage were now also built there. Furthermore, French warships and corsairs found it an excellent base to control the centre of the Indian Ocean and therefore the trade routes to India. Should French naval power become prevalent, when sufficient warships led by talented commanders were present, it could cut off the way to and from India. In wartime, the island could thus turn into a strategic nightmare for Britain's eastern trade in general and the Honourable East India Company in particular. Thus, Boscawen's instructions stressed the 'taking of the island of Mauritius [Ile de France] is of the greatest consequence, which the Admiral' would give 'his utmost endeavours to succeed in it' before going on to the coast of Coromandel.[14]

The fleet was accordingly in sight of the island on 4 July and approached Port-Louis. Aboard were nearly 1,400 European regular royal army troops plus about 800 marines. Boscawen and his officers could now see that Ile de France had a rugged and traitorous coastline with reefs and cliffs that made landings hazardous. The British estimated the whole French force to be 500 soldiers and 200 militiamen. This was rather optimistic for the regular soldiers because the garrison had three companies that would total 300 men if at establishment strength, which was very rarely the case, while the number of militiamen, when including Africans, would have been about

13 Fortescue, *A History of the British Army*, Vol.2, pp.183-184.

14 Richmond, *The Navy in the War of 1739-48*, Vol.3, pp. 218-219. Bowcawen's instructions include a detailed plan of operations from which we have quoted.

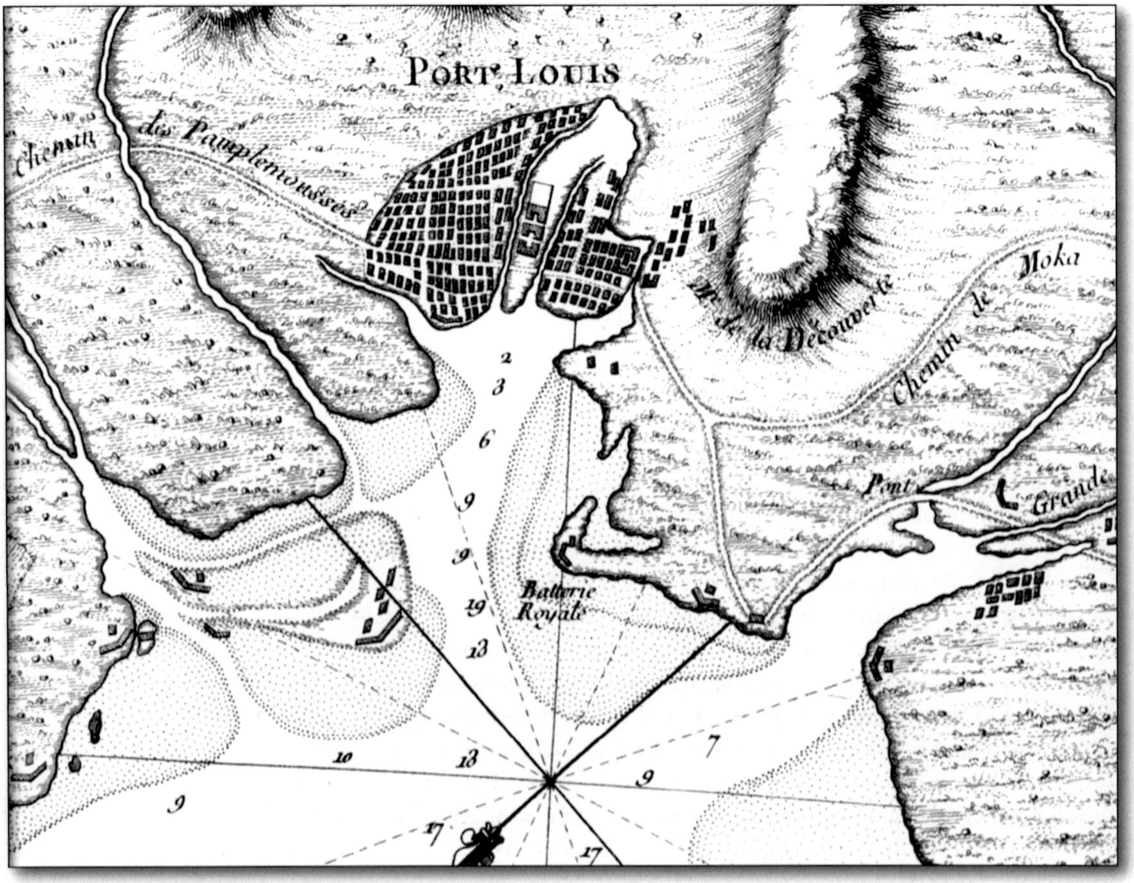

Port Louis, Ile de France, mid-eighteenth century. As can be seen, entering the harbour could be hazardous due to sandbanks and reefs. The single mortar that drove British warships away was most likely on Mont de la Découverte. Several batteries are shown, but they were probably fewer in 1748 when Boscawen unsuccessfully sought to land troops and bombard the unfortified town. Detail from a map in Bellin's 1764 *Petit atlas maritime*. (Author's photo)

300. Its harbour had many merchant ships, but only one French warship, *Alcide*, 64 guns, described by Orme as a 'large ship of two tiers lay at anchor, with her broadsides across it' whose *Capitaine de Vaisseau* Kersaint had posted at the harbour's entrance.[15] Boscawen may have cautiously wondered if there were more French warships in the harbour and anchored his ships outside within artillery range. Observing this manoeuvre was *Capitaine* Louis Joseph Philippe, Comte de Rostaing who commanded the artillery at Ile de France—later destined to become one of the best-known gunners of his era for his innovations regarding ordnance. As Boscawen was about to find out, Rostaing had prepared the island's defence with batteries and had further provided militiamen with light field guns to help them repel enemy landing parties.[16]

The British estimated they were being fired upon by eight different batteries planted upon the shore, as well as from forts at the entrance of the

15 Orme, *A History of the Military Transactions*, Vol.1, p.97.

16 Colonel Aldercron's 39th Regiment of Foot is generally said to be the first royal army infantry unit in India in 1754. However, the 12 new Independent Companies in Boscawen's expedition totalled 1,381 officers and men at a cost of £23,716 pay for 366 days were also royal troops as per: Royal Archives, Windsor (UK), GEO/ADD/35/8, 1742-1757 Army estimates and accounts, Estimate…1748.

harbour, which was rather exaggerated. On a hill called Petite Montagne overlooking the harbour's entrance, a singe mortar did open fire. Its second shell came close to a warship, which was possibly the 60-gun *Pembroke*. As Private James Miller of the Independent Companies put it, 'They fired sharply upon us from their Forts, and our ships return'd them as merely…' After that near miss, the fleet cautiously moved further back and stayed offshore for several days. Meanwhile the island's troops and militiamen were gathering on the hills bordering the seashore.[17]

Eventually, a British warship came closer and bombarded steadily a specific area on the shoreline to destroy a French hidden battery, which, unbeknown to the British gunners, were just some cut down tree logs. Comforted by the fact that the French had not fired back at all from what they though was now a destroyed battery, a landing to secure a beachhead was now mooted. That evening a British frigate and a few smaller warships approached the bay at Petite Rivière intending to land troops at that isolated and unsettled area. As they neared the shore, the British were suddenly greeted by unseen Ile de France militiamen firing muskets and field artillery. Furthermore, many drums could be heard beating the alarm in the distance announcing French reinforcements so the British withdrew. The British 'uselessly attempted to make landings' and were foiled, later reported Governor-General Pierre David who led the defenders, because the militiamen on the coast 'were so well prepared to receive' attacks that 'nothing serious was attempted' by the British who kept their distance and 'would only fire a few cannon shots every once in a while. However, before their departure, [the British] honoured the colony by a general salvo of two hours by all the ships that did not cause the least harm.' The squadron then sailed on to the Coromandel coast on 9 July.[18]

Curiously, some British accounts mention that Boscawen's force did not attack due to bad winds, heavy surf and bad weather. This does not match the French accounts which do not mention climate as a great protective factor, but do relate foiled landings and cannonades. Lack of precise intelligence on the strength of the French also seems a weak reason to leave; there were some

---

17 J.H. Leslie, (ed.), 'The Diary of James Miller', *JSAHR*, III (1924), p.212 and extracts from Boscawen's report on p.213. Miller, a Scots soldier of the Jacobite army captured at Carlisle in December 1745, later sentenced to death but given the option to enlist in the corps of 12 Independent Companies bound for the East Indies, which he did with many others. On 17 October 1749, the Independent Companies numbered for the 1st Battalion: 624 (including 33 officers), 2nd Battalion: 627 (including 34 officers), total 1,251. The companies were then disbanded, some of their men joined the troops of the Honourable East India Company while others, including Miller, went back to Great Britain.

18 Pierre David, 'Le Sénégal et les îles orientales de l'Afrique', in Pierre Margry (ed.), *Relations et mémoires inédits*, (Paris: Challamel, 1867), pp.371-372; Albert Pitot, *L'Ile de France Esquisses historiques 1715-1810* (Port-Louis, Ile Maurice: Pezzani, 1899), pp.57-58; Vaissière, *Dupleix*, p.97; Orme, *A History of the Military Transactions of the British Nation in* Indostan, Vol.1, pp.95-98; Ferdinand Macon de saint-Elier, *Tableaux historiques, politiques & pittoresques de l'Ile de France aujourd'hui Maurice* (Port-Louis: 1839), pp.102-103; Louis Joseph Philippe, Comte de Rostaing, 'Expedition de La Bourbonnais dans la mer des Indes en 1746', *Revue maritime et coloniale*, March 1880, pp.427-429; Charles Rathbone Low, *Her Majetsy's Navy* (London: Virtue, c. 1890), Vol.1, p.194; Fortescue, *A History of the British Army*, Vol.2, p.188; Richmond, *The Navy in the War of 1739-48*, Vol.3; Rodger, *The Command of the Sea*, p.254.

2,100 British regular troops aboard, more than enough to overcome at most 600 French soldiers and militiamen.

Siege of Pondicherry, 1748

The three French warships of *Captaine de Vaisseau* Jean-Baptiste Bouvet de Lozier had defied Commodore Thomas Griffin's British squadron and, during June 1748, managed to bring supplies and 300 soldiers to reinforce French forces in Madras. Obviously, Bouvet de Lozier could not compete against Boscawen's fleet and wisely withdrew. It was, related Orme who was in India at the time:

> [The largest] marine force belonging to any one European nation that had ever been seen together in the East Indies; for it consisted of more than 30 ships, none of which were less than 500 tons burden, and 13 of them men of war of the line. Every person attached to the English cause, who beheld this formidable force, was elated with joy, from expectation of its success, and no one doubted that the loss of Madras would be revenged by the capture of Pondicherry.[19]

Boscawen, who had been named commander of both sea and land forces in India, was of course resolved to take Pondicherry. He arrived with British regular royal army troops consisting of 12 independent companies of 100 men each, 800 marines and 80 Royal Artillery gunners. Furthermore, up to 1,800 of the sailors were organised into landing brigades. Once ashore, this force was joined by Honourable East India Company European troops with, in addition, 120 Dutch and 300 topas soldiers totalling some 3,720 Europeans. There further were about 2,000 Honourable East India Company sepoys. In mid-August, three British ships appeared at the head of Pondicherry's harbour and, in a defiant gesture, anchored there a buoy surmounted by a British flag. Dupleix, the senior French commander of the French garrison, quickly found two sepoy volunteers that swam to the buoy at night, took the flag and triumphantly brought it back to the city boosting its morale. It needed it. There would be a siege and Pondicherry's garrison consisted of some 1,000 French Compagnie des Indes soldiers and about 3,000 men who were mostly Indian sepoys, topasses, peons and a few hundred African *Caffres* in the company's service. Apart from about a hundred marines detached from warships, there were no French royal troops. In all, Dupleix had about 4,100 soldiers. He further had issued weapons to the few hundred civilian resident Frenchmen able to bear arms. The ordnance in the city consisted of about 100 guns.[20]

---

19 Orme, *A History of the Military Transactions*, Vol.1, p.98; Fortescue, *A History of the British Army*, Vol.2, p.189-191; C.T. Atkinson, 'In the Days of John Company: The Deployment of the King's Troops in India', *JSAHR*, XXXII (1954), p.111; Vaissière, *Dupleix*, p.94.

20 The main sources used for the siege of Pondicherry are: BNF, Manuscrits Français 8971, 'Relation du siège de Pondichéry levé par les Anglois le 18 8bre [October] 1748', folio 85 to 100 and 'Relation du siège de Pondichéry par les Anglois en 1748', folio 127 to 145; 'Relation du Siege de Pondichéry', *Gazette* (1749), pp.229-250; Royal Library, Windsor (UK), RCIN

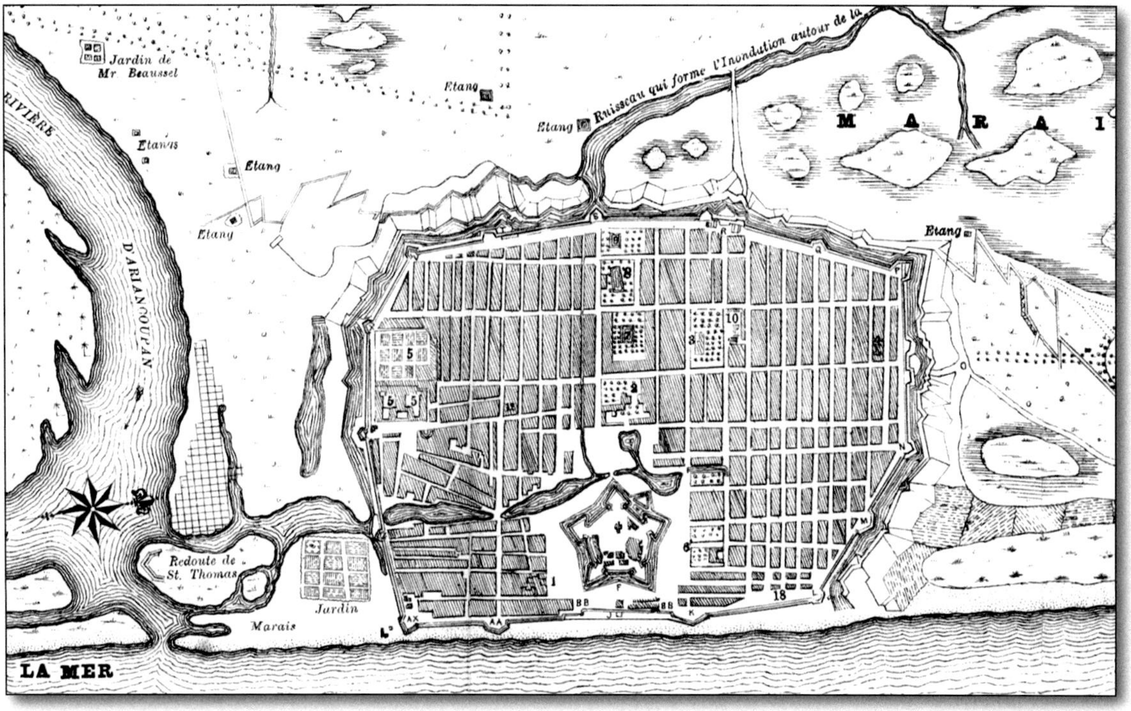

Plan of Pondicherry, 1748. The city was difficult to approach because it was surrounded by marshes (*'marais'*), ponds (*'étangs'*) and wetlands as well as a wet moat outside of the curtain walls. The northern side (right) was somewhat more accessible and a large British battery built there is the only one shown. None of the French batteries are shown; they were mostly in the bastions. British bombardments appear to have mainly come from the fleet anchored off the shore and a bomb ketch on the Ariancopang River, south of the city (left). Print after a map dedicated to Dupleix. (British Library, London)

An amusing anectode of the 1748 siege of Pondicherry occurred in August when Boscawen defiantly had a buoy surmounted by a British flag anchored in the French harbour. Dupleix retorted with two sepoys who swam to the buoy at night, took the flag (as shown) and triumphantly brought it back to the city's cheering defenders. Sketch in the 30 January 1943 *Siroco*. (Bibliothèque Nationale de France, Paris)

On 23 August, Dupleix received information that there was great activity to the south of Pondicherry with British troops at Cuddalore (Gondelour) were marching north while 14 warships including the *Namur* anchored east of Ariancopang (Ariancoupon) whose fort was held by about 400 French troops. Lieutenant Doyle of Fraser's Marine Regiment described it as a 'square Entrenchment, fortified with demi bastions'. The British thought it was held by perhaps a hundred French sepoys. Some 700 men, including four companies of British 'marine grenadiers', tried to storm it that day without even having ladders to the walls; they were repulsed with substantial losses. Boscawen landed sailors with artillery to bombard the fort, but Chief Engineer Louis Paradis, in command at Fort Ariancopang, had 60 of d'Auteil's dragoons and sepoy cavalrymen who charged them: the British sailors and soldiers panicked while the dragoons charged with such fury that British commander, Major Stringer Lawrence, was taken by surprise as his startled troops ran from the trenches.

The British came back in force and methodically put in place proper siege procedures, and the place was bombarded. Rather than just endure the shells, Paradis made a sortie against the British trenches, but this time the Indo-British soldiers were ready and it was repulsed. On 30 August, British efforts finally had some luck on their side during a sortie by 400 sepoys, 500 *Caffres*, D'Auteuil's Dragoons and Bussy's Volunteers who were effectively countered by British troops and the French sepoys ran off; however the dragoons and volunteers then charged the British capturing the town major of Cuddalore and a captain of marines before withdrawing. Soon thereafter, a British shot hit a French powder cart causing a disastrous explosion killing 46 men and grievously wounding as many. This spread disorder amongst the French troops, rendering Ariancopang that became untenable, and they withdrew on Paradis' orders. The next day, an elated Boscawen gave a ball to which the English ladies of Cuddalore were invited to celebrate this victory, and promised to soon give another ball in the governor's palace at Pondicherry.[21]

The British troops moved up to the outskirts of Pondicherry on 6 September, but the British engineers had the first parallel trenches dug much too far from the northwest corner of the city at about 1,500 metres when it

---

731043.1.b, 'A short journall, of the siege of Pondicherry, from / the time of our march, till our return to Fort St Davids [c.1748]' by Lt. John Doyle of Fraser's Marine Regiment; Vaissière, *Dupleix*, p.99-112; Leslie, (ed.), 'The Diary of James Miller', pp.213-220, which also large extracts of Boscawen's account of the siege; Fortescue, *A History of the British Army*, Vol.2, p.189-191. According to Paul Harris Nicolas, *Historical Record of the Royal Marine forces* (London: Boone, 1845), Vol.1, p.34, the total of marines with Boscawen was 850 to 880 men while Doyle's journal states 700. One of the marines in Fraser's Regiment was the later famous Hannah Snell, a woman who passed for a man and who was wounded at Pondicherry by 'a ball in the groin, which she herself extracted two days afterwards. Eleven other wounds in both legs rendered her removal to the hospital at Cuddalore absolutely necessary, and having returned home…her sex was not discovered until her discharge.'

21 The British 'grenadiers' reported in French accounts were actually marines, Lieutenant Doyle of Fraser's (45th of the line or 2nd Marine Regiment) was present at the siege and specifically mentions 'marine grenadiers' in his journal. This would seem to indicate that grenadier companies were formed with the elite marine soldiers. At that time, British marines wore high-fronted cloth caps with a rounded top. British grenadiers who also wore high cloth caps, but with a pointed top, that were worn by all marines from 1755 until 1768.

should have been at about that distance. While the engineers may have been 'utterly ignorant of their business' to quote Fortescue,[22] it was not an easy place to approach because of large swamps and morass being around outside much of the city's curtain walls and bastions. Its coast was full of rocks and shoals that prevented ships sailing closer, while the entrance to the Ariancopang River, south of the city, was very narrow and well protected. Inside, Dupleix revealed himself to be an energetic and tireless military leader of the besieged city. The initial worries of the garrison and inhabitants were quickly changed into optimism as Dupleix and his officers seemed to be everywhere inspecting daily the progress of defence works, mustering and arming every European able to bear arms, and inspiring his troops. A church transformed as a refuge by Madame Dupleix during bombardments was fortified, like many other places, with coconut tree trunks and cotton bales soaked with water. When the British bombarded, the population stayed calm, the troops determined; a story went around that when a bomb exploded near Dupleix, he was unhurt and kicked the bomb's fragments joking it was worthless junk.

In the late afternoon of 11 September, a sortie to destroy a British trench being built on the north-west side of the city was made. A party of some 1,200 men went out, led by Paradis, consisting of Bussy's Volunteers, La Tour's and Goupil's grenadiers companies, d'Auteil's dragoons, sepoy cavalrymen and infantrymen, *Caffres* and topasses handling two 6-pounder field guns. They were seen by sailors in the masts of British ships offshore and this was signalled to the troops on shore. As the French neared the trench they expected to be lightly guarded, about a thousand British troops waiting for them opened a withering fire in three successive volleys. Many attacking soldiers and officers were hit including Paradis who was mortally wounded

Dupleix leading the defence of Pondicherry, 6 September to 15 October 1748. Wet cotton bales and coconut tree trunks were used to protect batteries and buildings. Sketch in the 30 January 1943 *Siroco*. (Bibliothèque Nationale de France, Paris)

22 Fortescue, *A History of the British Army*, Vol.2, p.189.

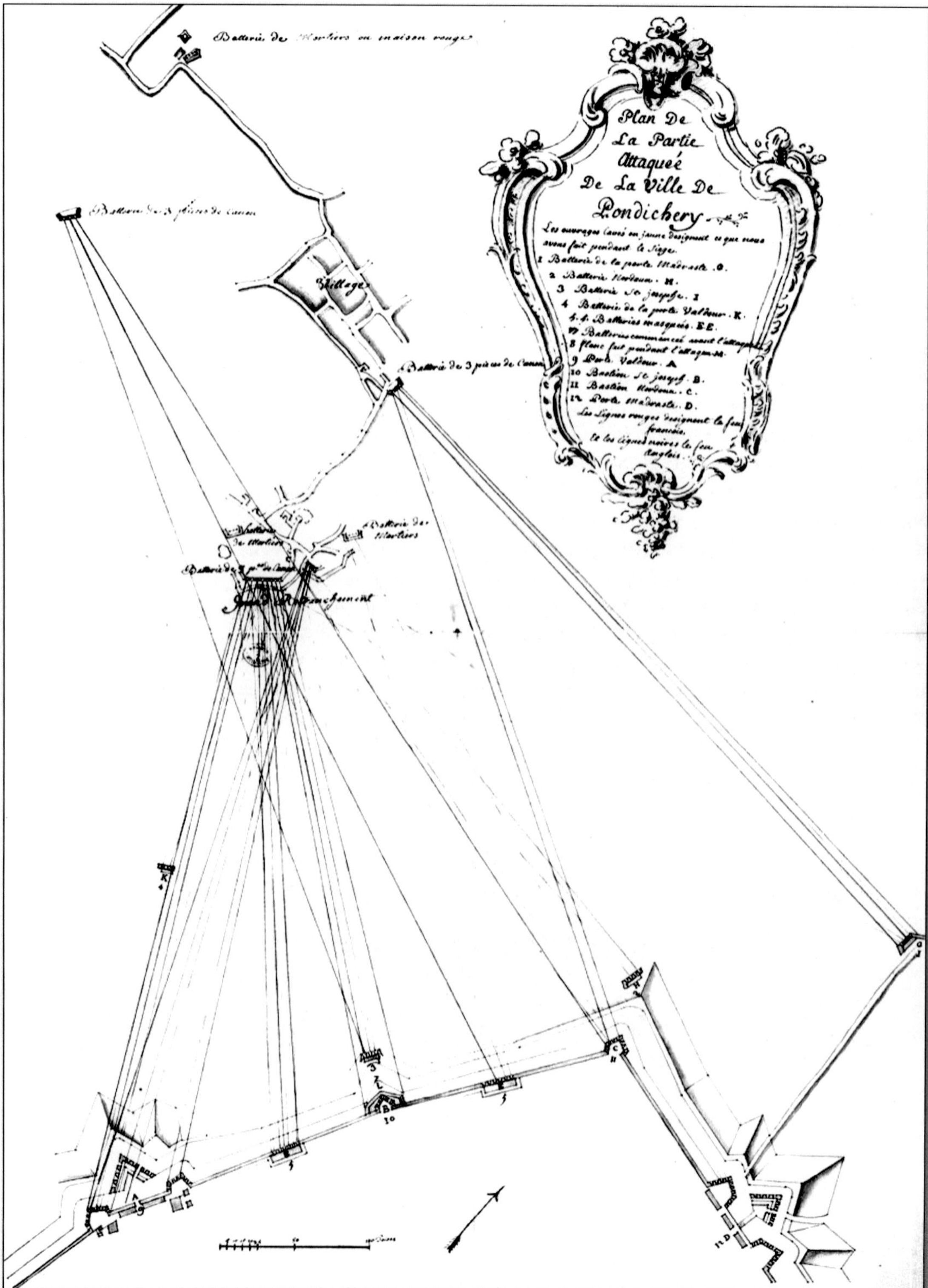

Opposing British and French batteries at Pondicherry, October 1748. The lines between the outside British batteries (centre and top) and the French along the curtain walls and bastions (bottom) are shown. The West is at top and the North at right on this manuscript plan in Vol. NAF 9146. (Bibliothèque Nationale de France, Paris)

and deplored as the greatest loss by the French. The grenadiers, dragoons and volunteers managed to cover the retreat by the pursuing British who were led by Captain Robert Clive.

Nevertheless, the city's defences were not breached and its garrison remained resolute. Boscawen opted for intensive bombardment to terrify its population and, hopefully, pierce some of the walls. The British land batteries and ships increased their rate of fire. Between 10 September and 10 October, an estimated 40,000 cannonballs were shot at the city; indeed so many that the French fired back some of them since they did not have as many in store; a bomb ketch on the South side fired 1,000 shells on the citadel of Fort Saint-Louis and its area without causing serious harm while 3,800 shells were fired from mortar batteries on land. Dupleix on his side was having batteries built to face those of the opponents; his cannons seemed to appear everywhere.

On 25 September, a Mughal standard was hoisted on a hill some distance to the north of the British camp. Some 200 Indian cavalrymen with camels and two elephants had been sent by the local Nabob Anwarudeen to observe the siege. Nabob Anwarudeen was finally answering in his own way Boscawen's appeal to join his British force with 2,000 cavalrymen. The troopers that now appeared were said to be an advance party to more Mughal troops. If Pondicherry should fall to the British, they would come to ransom or loot the city and its inhabitants. However, which side Indian princes might support depended very much on whichever local Europeans won or lost militarily and, by extension, diplomatically. In this instance, Nabob Anwarudeen's 2,000 cavalrymen and those on observation departed after three weeks when it became clear that the city would not fall.

The second half of September and the early part of October were spent mainly in artillery duels and trench raids. Of the latter, French sepoys sneaking out of Pondicherry were particularly active; on 25 September, they caused a dozen British casualties escorting an ambushed supply convoy and on 3 October captured two field guns with their limbers during a raid. Not to be outdone, the *Caffre* soldier/warriors in French service were especially adept at approaching, nearly naked, the British trenches during the dark of night, shooting at a redcoat or an Indian worker, and vanishing, a tactic that spread fear and slowed down the progress of the trenches. Although not a professional soldier, the charismatic Dupleix displayed outstanding energy, mustering everything in the city that could be useful in its defence such as building counter batteries as soon as the British had built their own batteries and proclaiming he would be satisfied only when he could point four French guns to one British. Morale was high amongst the defenders.

The same could not be said of the British attackers. The competence of the engineers could be called into question although the marshy ground did not favour whatever they did; on 26 September, the batteries were finally completed, but proved inferior to the French ones on the city's walls. Health of the troops was now an increasing problem, with some 700 British soldiers sick, and the monsoon rains were arriving. A council of war called by Boscawen on 30 September had to conclude to the inevitable: the city could not be taken and the siege had to be raised. Nevertheless, from 7 to 12 October, the British, perhaps out of spite and frustration, fired some 20,000

The British set fire to their camp outside Pondicherry on 15 October 1748 as they retreated from Pondicherry. Sketch in the 30 January 1943 *Siroco*. (Bibliothèque Nationale de France, Paris.)

rounds into Pondicherry; there were casualties and fires destroying homes suffered largely by civilians, but everyone sensed the British had lost their gamble.

The British spent the next days destroying their batteries and hastily removing stores, embarking the sick and wounded as well as fit sailors and soldiers while the rest of the troops marched to Fort St David. On 16 October, Boscawen's fleet sailed away while everyone in Pondicherry celebrated shouting '*Vive le Roi*!' and '*Vive Dupleix*!', along with fireworks, canon salvoes and banquets. French casualties amounted to 104 soldiers killed including three officers and 94 wounded including six officers one of which was Indian *Colonel* Chekassem of the sepoy cavalry. The British loss amounted to 757 soldiers, 43 artillerymen and 265 sailors for a total of 1,065 Europeans.[23]

23 The casualty figures are from the *Gazette* (1749), p.250 and Nicolas, *Historical Record of the Royal Marine Forces*, Vol.1, p.36.

7

Princely Alliances

During 1748, Nizam-ul-Mulk, viceroy of the Deccan died aged at about 100 years old. His grandson Muzaffar Jang (also Murzapher or Muzaffer Jung) was his designated successor to the viceregal throne, but his uncles Nasir (or Nazer), Salabat and Ghazi-ud-din all laid claim the throne. In the following months, civil war gradually erupted in much of central and southern India.

Up until then, both the French and the British had usually refrained from meddling heavily into the plots and politics of Indian princes unless it concerned their immediate safety and trade advantages. During the late War of the Austrian Succession, there had been various contacts between Indian princes and the French and British companies. Hardly had Boscawen's fleet sailed away that eyebrows were raised in Pondicherry when it was learned that the British were now supporting previous Rajah Sauhojee of the kingdom of Tanjore against the new rajah so as to obtain Devicotah near the French lodge at Carical in Tanjore. The old rajah would regain his throne. Indeed, 800 British troops with 1,500 sepoys led by Major Lawrence attacked the fort at Devicotah on 23 June 1749. The first assault met with strong resistance and a party led by Robert Clive, then a young officer, was nearly overcome by Tanjoran cavalry with Clive barely escaping; Lawrence renewed the attack with all his European troops and finally overcame resistance and took the place. The British then decided to keep Tanjore and told Sauhojee it would give him a pension if he retired quietly from public affairs. Naturally, this dishonourable act of the Honourable East India Company became widely known and harmed British influence at Indian courts for a while. This was seen by the French as a direct British intervention in Indian politics with the obvious intention to become the champions of dethroned princely rulers.[1]

Dupleix too could play these games; he had a great interest and ability in the strategies of diplomacy, including its covert and double-dealing arrangements. From 1742 when he became governor general, he had indulged in Indian-style politics and got better at it as years passed, Now,

1 Fortescue, *History of the British Army*, Vol.2, pp.192-193; Martineau, *Dupleix*, Vol.3, pp.89-90.

like a tiger let out of his cage, he came up with much grander secretive plans. In eighteenth century India as elsewhere, a ruler might have all the trappings and pageantry of supreme power, but real authority was often shared more or less openly. There were allies and challengers. Dupleix was aware of this and, having heard of British secret negotiations in the spring of 1749 that led to their occupation of Devicotah, he came up with his own secret overtures.

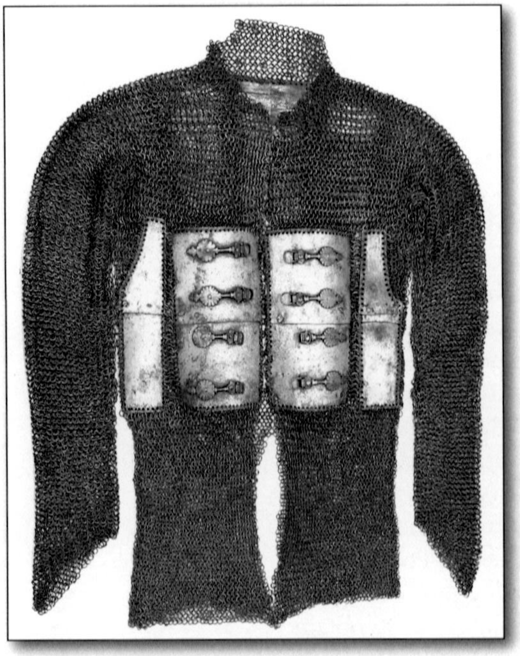

Indian warrior's chain mail shirt with steel plates, mid-17th century. This type of protective garment was popular well into the eighteenth century. (Metropolitan Museum of Art, New York. Purchase, Arthur Ochs Sulzberger Gift, 2000-sfsb2000.595_001)

Armoured Indian cavalryman, eighteenth century. He wears a helmet, a chain mail shirt with steel plates with brass or gilt fasteners and edging, dark red sash with a brass-hilted Katar, chain mail trousers with dark red trousers underneath, buff shoes, brass-hilted Talwar sabre and round shield. Reconstruction by F.P. Todd based on armour seen at the Tower of London. (Anne S.K. Brown Military Collection, author's photo)

Amoor 1749

Muzaffar Jang, grandson and designated successor of the decease *soubab* or viceroy, had been chased out of the Deccan by his uncle Nasir Jang who assumed this position with approval from the chaotic imperial court in Delhi. He and another prince in the same situation, Chanda Sahib, appealed to Dupleix to help them regain their thrones. Dupleix agreed as long as they would cede the city and territory of Vellenour to the Compagnie des Indes if successful. They agreed and Dupleix dispatched some 420 French soldiers, 100 topasses and 2,000 sepoys led by Commandant d'Auteuil seconded by *Capitaine* Busy, who joined the princes' troops on 23 July at Vellore near Gingee. This army may have gathered up to 28,000 men, half of them cavalry according to Ananda's diary.

To counter them, Carnatic Nabob Anwarudeen was coming with an army of 20,000 men including 12,000 cavalry, with 220 elephants and 26 guns. Anwarudeen was the subject and partisan of Nasir Jang, usurper to the viceregal throne, as well as leaning towards the British. Dupleix remembered Anwarudeen with scorn for his unfriendly attitude at the time of the sieges of Madras and of Pondicherry.

Anwarudeen arrived in the Eastern Ghauts confident of a victory to settle the succession of viceroy of the Deccan and thereafter, maybe go east towards Pondicherry and take it. On 3 August 1749, the two armies clashed at Amoor (also Ambour, Anur) west of Arcot. Muzaffar Jang was in nominal supreme command with Chanda Sahib as second in command of the Indo-French army, but tactical operations were under the French officers who ordered attacks. The first attack on Anwarudeen's troops, who were obviously good and steady soldiers, was repulsed. The second attack was personally led by d'Auteuil and involved more of the French soldiers and sepoys, but they wavered along with their Indian allies when he was wounded.

Bussy now took over actual command of the army and led a third attack. His feeling that Anwarudeen's troops were becoming unsteady proved correct; they had lost many men to the disciplined volleys of the French soldiers, topasses and sepoys. This time, Bussy ordered an advance by his French troops who opened fired at very close range; their rapid and steady volleys at last broke the enemy's resistance and Bussy ordered a general charge. Panic broke out and when Anwarudeen tried vainly to rally his army, he was killed by two musket shots and fell off his elephant. The French corps, which bore the brunt of the fighting, had 12 killed and 63 wounded Europeans, plus about 300 sepoys killed and wounded. Muzaffar Jang's and Chanda Sahib's allied army's casualties may have been about the same. Anwarudeen's army's casualties is also unknown, but were surely much higher; thousands had been captured, and it was destroyed as a military force.[2]

The victory was complete and part of the defeated troops switched sides and joined Muzaffar Jang. Most importantly, it was a confirmation that the

2 Martineau, *Dupleix*, Vol.3, pp.92-95; J.F. Price and K. Rangachari (trans.), *The Private Diary of Ananda Ranga Pillai, Dubas to Joseph François Dupleix* (Madras: Government Press, 1904-1928),Vol.6, pp.124, 162.

1746 Battle of Adyar/Sao Tomé was not a coincidence. The superiority of the European way of war was confirmed.

Pomp and Circumstance by Indian Armies

Muzaffar Jang and Chanda Sahib knew they had been saved by Dupleix's shrewd political manoeuvres and the French soldiers and sepoys of the company. They further wished to appear in triumph at Pondicherry with their much-expanded army following the Battle of Amoor. By the time it reached the area of Pondicherry, it numbered about 23,000 infantry, 14,000 cavalry, 216 elephants and another 6,000 men armed with crossbows and matchlock muskets followed by an 'infinite multitude' of people with baggage. Chanda Sahib arrived first with part of the army. The following account of the elite of their troops parading into the city as well as the honours bestowed upon Dupleix, as related by a Jesuit missionary, is a remarkable display of Indian prince's lavish protocols. It was actually was done in two parts. The first part consisted of Chanda Sahib's contingent:

> They made their entry in the city saluted by all its artillery. The governor [Dupleix], who greeted them at the [city] limits, walking along with all the marks of distinction associated with his dignity. At the head [of Muzaffar Jang's and Chand Sahib's forces] was an elephant having a white flag upon which were five suns. Two other elephants followed with *nabates*, a type of kettle drums that only nabobs can have. After that was another elephant having a white flag with a gold embroidered sun. At his sides were two camels with kettle drums. They were followed by a mounted officer holding a white standard embroidered with red and green and a golden hand holding a sword. 500 horsemen holding their swords then marched passed followed by 60 French dragoons who escorted M. Dupleix's palanquin. To his right were held 12 small white standards [each] with a gold sun. At his left was the palanquin of Chanda Sahib having at his sides eight green standards bearing [each] a gold sun. His suite consisted of an elephant marching in front bearing his green flag; of 3,000 cavalrymen; of 200 of his life guards with drawn swords and of 400 lancers [meaning here pikemen or lance bearers on foot] and crossbowmen. His palanquin was surrounded by 12 *chopdars* or bearers of orders, armed with long canes and of six other holding silver maces. This parade marched to the fortress where Chanda Sahib gave to M. Dupleix his gifts consisting of a magnificent headdress ornamented with a bouquet in the shape of gold aigrets ornamented with diamonds, of a *cabaye* being a robe made of gold and silk material and a gold embroidered sash. Chanda Sahib himself put the cap on M. Dupleix's head and this ceremony was accompanied by the sound of the artillery in the fortress.[3]

Two days later, the *souba* Muzaffar Jang arrived at Pondicherry, was greeted by Dupleix and entered the city with 5,000 cavalrymen sword in hand.

3 Anon., *Lettres édifiantes…*, Vol. 8, pp.229-230.

Pageantry was again at the heart of this second parade:

A prince reviewing his troops, eighteenth century. Print after a miniature in Langlès' *Monuments anciens et moderne de l'Hindoustan*. (Bibliothèque Nationale de France, Paris)

> His flag was white having at its centre a half sun on one side and a golden crescent on the other. It was carried by an elephant. There followed 1,000 lancers marching accompanied by two elephants, each bearing two small two-pounder cannons. They were followed by 800 camels loaded with armed rockets, which the Moors use in battles instead of grenades. There followed an infinite number of flags and standards who were the badges of the dignity of all the superior officers making up the *souba*'s [Muzaffar Jang's] suite. After that came an elephant bearing a black standard ornamented on one side with a hand holding a silver sword and a on the other side a crescent and a half-sun. This elephant was surrounded by 24 others with their little towers on their backs where were seated the senior generals that accompanied Muzaffar Jang. After which marched 500 cavalrymen armed with arrows. Muzaffar Jang himself arrived with his eight-years old son and the son of Chanda Sahib at his feet on his prodigiously tall elephant. At his right, an elephant carried the standard called *Maimnavatte* and all the small standards, which were the marks of dignity of his grandfather Nisam-Moulouk. His guard consisted of 10,000 cavalrymen superbly dressed bearing drawn swords. He was escorted by 24 *soubdars* with silver maces and 100 *chopdars* armed with long canes. A white standard ornamented with a a sun and a crescent was before him. The parade was closed by 12 elephants bearing the mother, the wife and the rest of the family of the *souba* in their little *ckeiroses* or little covered towers. They were guarded by 5,000 men armed with matchlock muskets, 1,000 lancers and crossbowmen, and 1,000 cavalrymen. The rest of the army camped in the areas of Villenour with all the prisoners.[4]

The immediate benefit of the victory at Amoor was substantial. The Compagnie des Indes was gaining revenues from territorial taxes as agreed and this was essential to pay its military expenses. Not only did Dupleix settle his accounts, but he was finally rid of Anwarudeen. His protégé, Muzaffar Jang, was now ruler of the Deccan with Chanda Sahib by force of arms thanks to his assistance. Most of all, French influence might now extend west into central India.

4 Anon., *Lettres édifiantes…*, Vol.8, pp.230-231. Extract from an account of the events in 1749 by a Jesuit missionary that may also have been a chaplain with the French troops.

Dynastic Struggles in the Early 1750s

Early in 1750, Nasir Jang, *soubab* of central India, interpreted the elevation of Muzaffar Jang as an act of rebellion against the authority of the crumbling Mughal empire and proceeded to muster a very large army. Amongst his motives were for him to be the effective ruler of central and southern India with imperial blessing. This turn of events was obviously the contrary to everything Dupleix and his Deccan allies were hoping for. The surprising situation of the near-defunct Mughal empire was that it still existed; the Great Mughal was still reigning in Delhi and, although now nearly powerless militarily, all the ambitious and near-independent princes in the land vied to manipulate the imperial court for largely protocolary approvals and traditional honours. It was indeed the only influence it had left and it was considered important for powerful princes to promote traditional Mughal protocol, hoist imperial standards, receive imperial robes and gifts.

It certainly must have helped Nasir Jang to raise his army during 1750, which some rumours overestimated as having some 300,000 men. Over half of them were various types of camp followers, merchants and families of soldiers. There were also about 1,300 Indo-British troops including 450 Europeans led by Major Stringer Lawrence. In March 1750, Nasir Jang led his impressive army into the Carnatic. Seeing this, the forces and allies of Muzaffar Jang and Chanda Sahib largely evaporated and they both arrived at Pondicherry on 15 March seeking support and protection. True to his promise, Dupleix found some Indian troops and money for them and sent Commandant d'Auteuil with an Indo-French force of 1,100 Europeans and sepoys and what was left of Muzaffar Jang's troops (about 10,000 men of which 6,000 were cavalry) to approach Nasir Jang's army. When the French saw the countless hordes afar on 4 April, many officers refused to go further as it meant certain defeat for their men and themselves; indeed, 13 French officers deserted on the spot, but 10 others remained and distinguished themselves by their conduct. A council of war decided to withdraw and, in the early morning, some thousands of Nasir Jang's cavalry attacked forward positions. Disaster was averted by the steadfastness of officers and men; the hurried retreat was well covered by steady volleys into the masses; the French lost about 60 casualties (including 19 Europeans) but it was estimated that up to 4,000 attacking cavalrymen had been hit by musket and light artillery fire. Meanwhile, either Muzaffar Jang was captured or, some said, rallied with his cavalrymen to his uncle who henceforth treated him more as a prisoner than an ally. Either way, he was one of Dupleix's trump cards in the great game and Dupleix was not about to let him down.[5]

Things seemed desperate for the French, but Dupleix was in a fighting mood. He opened some negotiations with Nasir Jang that even included

5 BNF, Ms Français 12087, Abrégé de la guerre des François dans l'inde…, 1746-1751; Martineau, *Dupleix*, pp.112-121. The 13 officers were later arrested in Pondicherry and given a chance to redeem their conduct. By October, two of them, des Essards and Sainte-Colombe, had even gone beyond that and were mentioned in dispatches for outstanding services.

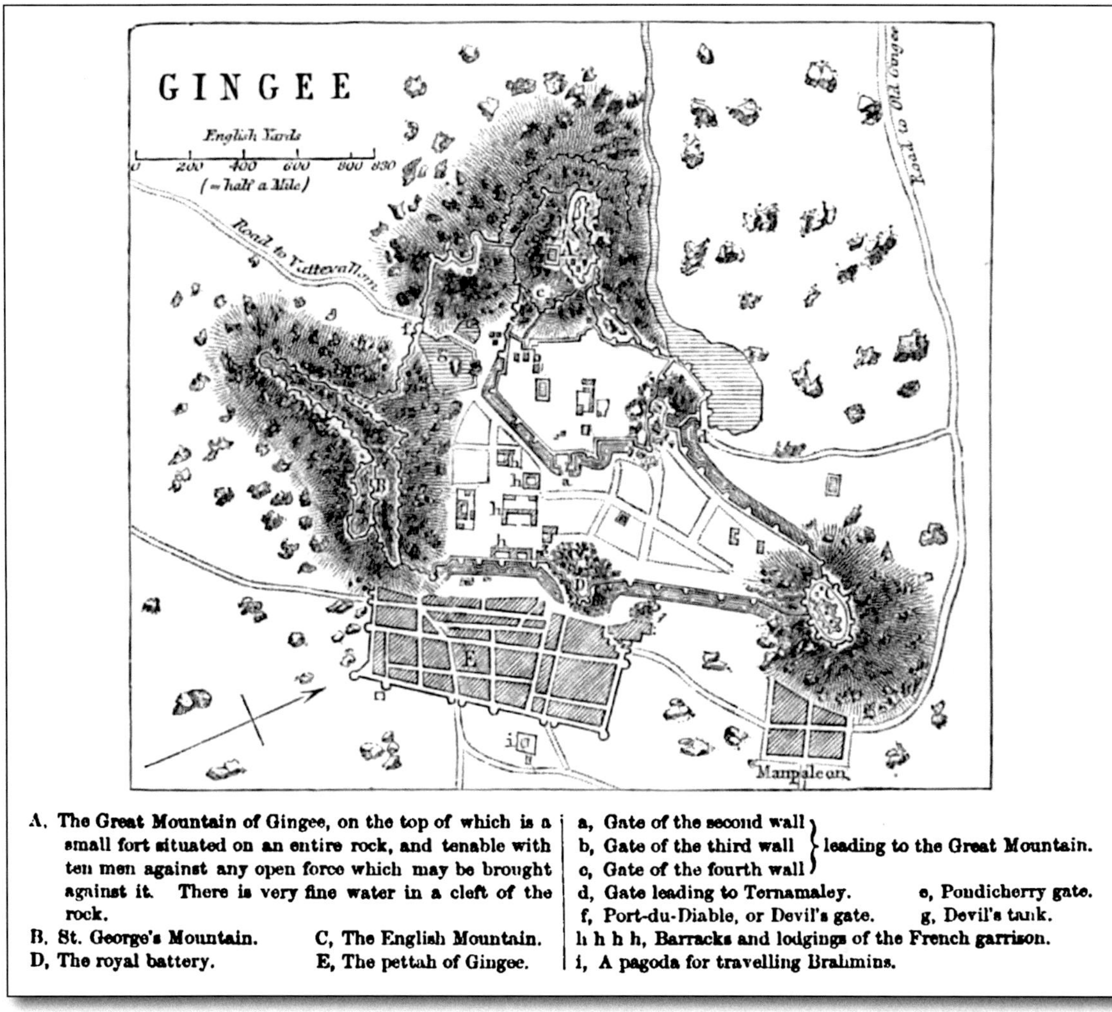

Plan of the Fortress of Gingee, circa 1750. This was one of the most important and esteemed impregnable fortresses in India. Its capture by a daring attack of French soldiers and sepoys amazed all of India. From Beveridge's 1862 *A Comprehensive History of India*. (Author's photo)

demands for the liberation of his nephew Muzaffar Jang. The negotiations of course failed by 24 April, but Nasir Jang obviously had some hesitations and did not go further east than the area of Gingee. On the night of 27 April, Commandant Latouche led an Indo-French raiding party of 3,000 men on Nasir Jang's sleeping camp that caused surprise and total confusion amongst his army. Up to a thousand men in the camp may have been lost. On 30 April, the huge army broke camp and marched west while Lawrence and his Indo-British detachment went back to Fort St David. In the following months, small Indo-French parties shadowed Nasir Jang's army resulting in various minor skirmishes.

A period of relative calm also followed between British and French officers including commanders Lawrence and Latouche having cordial enough relations, sometimes even exchanging gifts such as bottles of French and Rhine wines while being careful not to advance into each other's territory. For his part, Nasir Jang was assuming more in a warlike spirit. The forces of Mohamed Ali, the son of Anwarudeen killed at Amoor, who had fled to Trichinopoly now formed part of his army. They became an advance guard of about 15,000 men that moved east. Dupleix had sent reinforcements in that area too and, on 31 July, Commandants d'Auteuil, Bussy and Latouche had some 2,500 sepoys, 1,000 Indian cavalry and 1,200 Europeans. The advance parties then clashed at Karamangalom near Trivady followed by more robust fighting on 1 August that resulted in Mohamed Ali's retreat. As Ananda later noted, Mohamed Ali's defeat was really also a defeat for Nasir Jang. It also meant that Mohamed Ali's great fortress of Gingee was more vulnerable.[6]

Gingee September 1750

Gingee (Gingi or Gingy) was the capital of the small kingdom bearing the same name. In 1750, it was part of Mohamed Ali's domain. An anonymous French author who obviously knew the country considered it was:

> [T]he strongest of all the cities in India, its situation making its approach extremely difficult. [The citadel of] Gingee is fortified by three equally steep and high mountains on the side of the plain and of the city; these mountains are linked by a thick and very high wall, whose masonry is immune to cannonballs by the solidity of the cement that secures the stones. On each of these mountains, that are accessed by very difficult paths, towers carved in the rock can be seen and a very deep cistern, whose purpose is to preserve ammunition and food.[7]

As formidable as it was, there was some neglect in maintaining the walls of the city at the foot of the citadel's hills. In early September 1750, Commandant Bussy thought its capture should be attempted to which commandants d'Auteuil and Latouche agreed. Late on 11 September, Bussy's Indo-French detachment profited from the decrepit city fortifications and quickly dispersed its defenders. Night was falling as the citadel's guns opened fire on the city, which did not harm the attacking force. The morale of the garrison did not seem very high and the French commanders waited until it was pitch black to assault the hills. Shooting in the dark caused a few casualties to the French and sepoys led by Gallaud, a gunner, as they approached the highest hill, called the great mountain, that had a gate while its defenders threw grenades ineffectively; another party led by Saint-Georges, Véry and Lenormand sneaked up another hill nearby and, at four in the morning, stormed and took it at the cry of '*Vive le Roi*!'. This was a signal to Gallaud; he now blew up the highest hill's gate and his men rushed in easily dispersing its defenders; the defenders posted higher were also overcome and at dawn, the citadel was secured.

The Indo-French troops had 10 men killed and 11 wounded. The defenders' casualties are unknown, but would have been much higher. Dupleix had not initially given much importance to Gingee, but he now realised that his forces henceforth controlled this nearly impregnable citadel with its geo-strategic importance. Indeed, the news of its capture spread

6 Martineau, *Dupleix*, Vol.3, pp.132-134.

7 Anon., *Tableau historique de l'Inde* (Bouillon: Société Typographique, 1771), pp.66-67.

'terror' in Nasir Jang's army and resounded throughout India. The least that can be said was that Nasir Jang was deeply disappointed, enraged and redoubled efforts to strengthen his forces so as to become the most powerful prince in the sub-continent. His prime target was the increasingly powerful French that opposed him.[8]

Nasir Jang's Defeat near Chettipet 16 December 1750

During the fall, Nasir Jang mustered, by promises or by threats to other Indian princes, tens of thousands of men yet again. By December, his army was truly huge, even by Indian standards. It consisted of 45,000 infantrymen, 40,000 to 45,000 cavalrymen, 700 elephants and 360 cannon all of which amounted to at least 100,000 men (but no British auxiliaries) plus a probably equal number of servants and camp followers all of whom were slowly marching southeast from Arcot towards Gingee. Once that great fortress was captured, he reasoned the remaining Indo-French troops would collapse and Pondicherry could easily be taken.

The Indo-French contingent sent out to oppose this multitude was led by Commandant de Latouche and numbered 800 European soldiers, 3,500 sepoys, 1,500 auxiliary Indian cavalrymen and 20 cannon (including 10 'minute' guns) for a total of about 6,000 men. The elite of the French European troops were partly the same men that had defended Pondicherry in 1748, namely de Puymorin's grenadiers, Bussy's volunteers led by St Georges, Kirjean's volunteers, Le Normand's dragoons plus a company of *Étrangers* (foreigners) led by one 'Kane' who were likely British deserters.[9]

By any European logic, Nasir Jang's advantage of 20-to-one would quickly result into the total annihilation of Larouche's force. However, this was India in the mid-eighteenth century during the era of the collapsing Mughal Empire. Its imperial, royal and princely politics were dominated by double-dealing, treason and assassinations. Added to this were the British and the French as new players into these great, treacherous and often deadly Indian power games. Thus an army leader such as Nasir Jang could have doubts about the loyalty of some of his troops. Dupleix was indeed secretly involved in a plot with three nabobs who led part of Nasir Jang's huge army. They wished to oust him, free Muzaffar Jang and divide the spoils amongst themselves instead of trying to capture Pondicherry, a task made much more difficult since the capture of Gingee by the French.

The engagement started early in the morning of 16 December 1750 at some distance north of Chettipet. The little Indo-French army was divided

8 BNF, Ms Français 8971, Précis historique…, 1749-1753 and 12087, Abrégé de la guerre des français dans l'inde…, 1746-1751; Alfred Martineau, *Bussy et l'Inde française 1720-1785* (Paris: Société de l'histoire des colonies française, 1935), pp.16-20. Dupleix mentioned enemy casualties at about 2,000 which seems much exaggerated.

9 BNF, Ms Français 8971, Victoire sur Nezerzingue par l'armée française commandée par M. de La Touche le 16 décembre 1750; BNF, Ms Français 12087, Relation de la victoire remportée sue Nazerzingue par l'armée française commandée par M. de Latouche le 16 décembre 1750. Unsigned but by an unknown soldier in the battle.

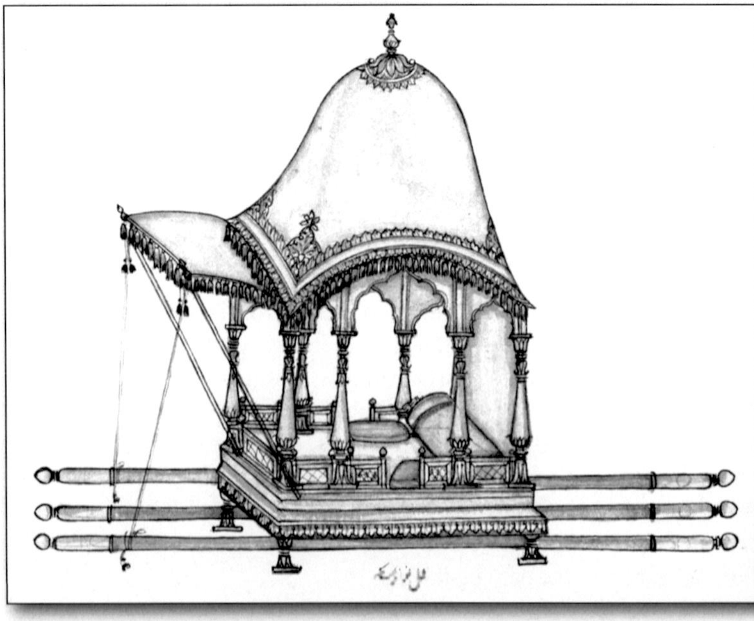

Senior officer or prince's 'nalki' palanquin, mid-eighteenth century. The 'nalki' type was the luxury version that was seen in processions borne by carriers holding the brass-tipped rods on their shoulders or fastened on the back of an elephant, which was also done on military campaigns. Its elaborate decoration included a polished brass or even gilded dome. Watercolour by Navaz Singh. From the album 'Eléphans, Palanquins et autres usages indiens'. (Bibliothèque Nationale de France, Paris, Col. Gentil bequest, RH n° 280)

Any Indo-European army in India during the eighteenth and nineteenth centuries was followed by a large horde of dromedaries, bullocks, mules, ponies and some elephants hauling supplies of all sorts attended by a multitude of camp followers 'who far exceed the number of fighting men' be they French, British or sepoys. This early-nineteenth-century view would have been identical a century or more earlier. Detail from a print from Captain Ludlow's circa 1825 album of *Bengal Troops on the Line of March. A Panoramic Sketch.* (Private collection, author's photo)

into three divisions: Bussy leading the right of the line, Kerjean the left wing, de Villeroy the centre, the sepoys on foot and mounted on the flanks of the wings and acting effectively in European fashion 'as men used to fight alongside the French' recalled a French soldier. Nasir Jang first disposed his army behind his artillery. At about the early dawn, his forward parties were advancing when, to their surprise, they were checked by de Puymorin's grenadiers while at the same time, the Indo-French army rapidly advanced in battle formation towards the Nasir Jang's huge, but largely undefended camp supported by the French artillery. 'The enemy had previously never shown such resistance. When we charged on one side, it attacked on the other side. But our small force fired on all sides' wrote a French soldier. The presence of Nasir Jang, seen on his elephant in the battlefield, encouraged his own men to scoff at death. Many indeed were killed or wounded from the terrible holes made in their closely massed charging troops by the French gunners firing several rounds a minute serving their light 'minute' cannons, and the steady volleys of the European and sepoy infantry. If victory was to be achieved, it could well depend on Nasir Jang being captured, wounded or killed. As its losses rose, the enemy attacks weakened and some of them retreated. At this point, Nasir Jang started to withdraw too.[10]

A French soldier in the midst of the fighting related that the Indo-French troops were cautiously advancing

> ...in good order when we perceived in the middle of the enemy army, the colour our companies being hoisted as high as possible on top of an elephant; this circumstance startled us and it was followed by a considerable number of white standards [of France] being displayed on all sides. M. de Latouche, who knew what this was all about, ordered us to reduce our shooting and to shout *Vive Le Roy*. We did not know what this manoeuvre meant and we still advanced in good order when a man came on behalf of Muzaffar Jang and M. de Latouche that Nasir Jang had been killed by our shooting. This good news redoubled our shouts of *Vive Le Roy* and we entirely stopped shooting. [11]

What had happened had been secretly prepared for three months. At a critical point of the battle, the nabob of Carnoul, who led a considerable number of his Pathan troops, would hoist a blue colour with a white cross provided secretly by Dupleix as a signal to the other two nabobs to change sides. That nabob further sought personal revenge; his father had been murdered by Nasir Jang. Indeed, Nasir Jang had also ordered the murder of Muzaffar Jang before the battle, but the would-be assassin wisely delayed such an action. Instead, he was freed when the white standards were hoisted and soon joined Commandant Latouche while the remnants of the formerly huge army fled from the field of battle.[12]

As for Nasir Jang's death, accounts do not quite agree as to how it happened. It might have been from the Indo-French troop's shooting, it might have been from a double barrel musket given by Dupleix to the nabob of Carnoul when he caught up with Nasir Jang on his elephant, or it may have been at the hands of the nabob of Cuddapah. Either way, one of the nabobs cut off Nasir Jang's head and later presented it to Muzaffar Jang.[13]

On 26 December, Dupleix received the protocolary imperial insignias from Muzaffar Jang. He was now amongst the most senior and powerful princes in India.

---

10 BNF, Ms Français 12087, Relation de la victoire remportée sue Nazerzingue…, by an unknown soldier.

11 BNF, Ms Français 12087, Relation de la victoire remportée sue Nazerzingue…, by an unknown soldier; Anon., *Lettres édifiantes*…, Vol.8, pp.295-299.

12 BNF, Ms Français 8971, Relation des principaux événements arrivés aux Indes dans la province du Carnate et le long de la Côte Coromandel entre les François et les Anglois…, July 1749 to 17 October 1752.

13 Martineau, *Dupleix*, Vol.3, p.144 gives options as to how Nasir Jang was killed.

Nasir Jang killed and beheaded by the Nabob of Canoul at the battle of Chettipet on 16 December 1750. Print after Bombléd in the December 1902 *Dépêche coloniale illustrée.* (Bibliothèque Nationale de France, Paris)

Dupleix receives the imperial insignias from Muzaffar Jang, soubab of the Deccan, on 26 December 1750. Print after Bombléd in the December 1902 *Dépêche coloniale illustrée.* (Bibliothèque Nationale de France, Paris)

8

Into the Deccan 1751-1758

Commandant Bussy and his Army in Central India

On 15 January 1751, Dupleix sent a small French corps from Pondicherry led by Commandant Bussy deep into the Deccan to help allied Nabob Muzaffar Jang consolidate his power at his capital of Aurangabad. Bussy initially had only 2,100 soldiers of which only 300 were French, yet they achieved great importance as the backbone of the forces led by allied Indian princes in central India. Thanks to Bussy and some of his officers who turned out to be gifted in the perilous paths of Indian princely diplomacy as well as leading troops in battlefields, that army of a few hundred European soldiers supported by a few thousand sepoys became the key force in the Deccan.[1]

Other princes in central India opposed Muzaffar Jang and, some three weeks after leaving Pondicherry, part of his army was secretly plotting to depose him. On 14 February, Muzaffar Jang's loyal troops attacked the plotters who were soon dispersed, but a reckless Muzaffar Jang exposed himself too much in the pursuit and was killed. It was small, short and bloody battle. The chief of the opponents, the nabob of Carpe was also killed with 2,000 of his officers and men with at least 1,000 of Muzaffar Jang's army. Bussy's corps was not heavily engaged except for two wounded out of a dozen French dragoons that were part of Muzaffar Jang's bodyguards.

Bussy was suddenly in the middle of an Indian political and command crisis. The death of Muzaffar Jang threatened to cancel the agreements he had made with Dupleix and thus seriously harm French influence in central India. All loyal Indian and French senior officers urged that a new ruler had to be named as soon as possible; Bussy, whose diplomatic talents now emerged, was

1 The main sources for the Deccan are: Albert Depréaux, 'Les uniformes de la Compagnie des Indes d'après un journal inédit de la campagne du Décan 1751-1755', *Revue de l'histoire des colonies françaises*, No. 54, Vol.XIV (1926), pp.144-180. This includes remarkable extracts from a French gunner's journal. The original is in BNF, Nouvelles aquisitions françaises 9338 that, regrettably, has not yet been digitised; Martineau, *Bussy*, pp.24-233; BNF, Ms Français 8971, Précis historique de l'origine de la guerre enterprise par M. Dupleix…just'en 1753; BNF, Nouvelles aquisitions françaises 9146, Correspondance de Dupleix avec la Compagnie des Indes.

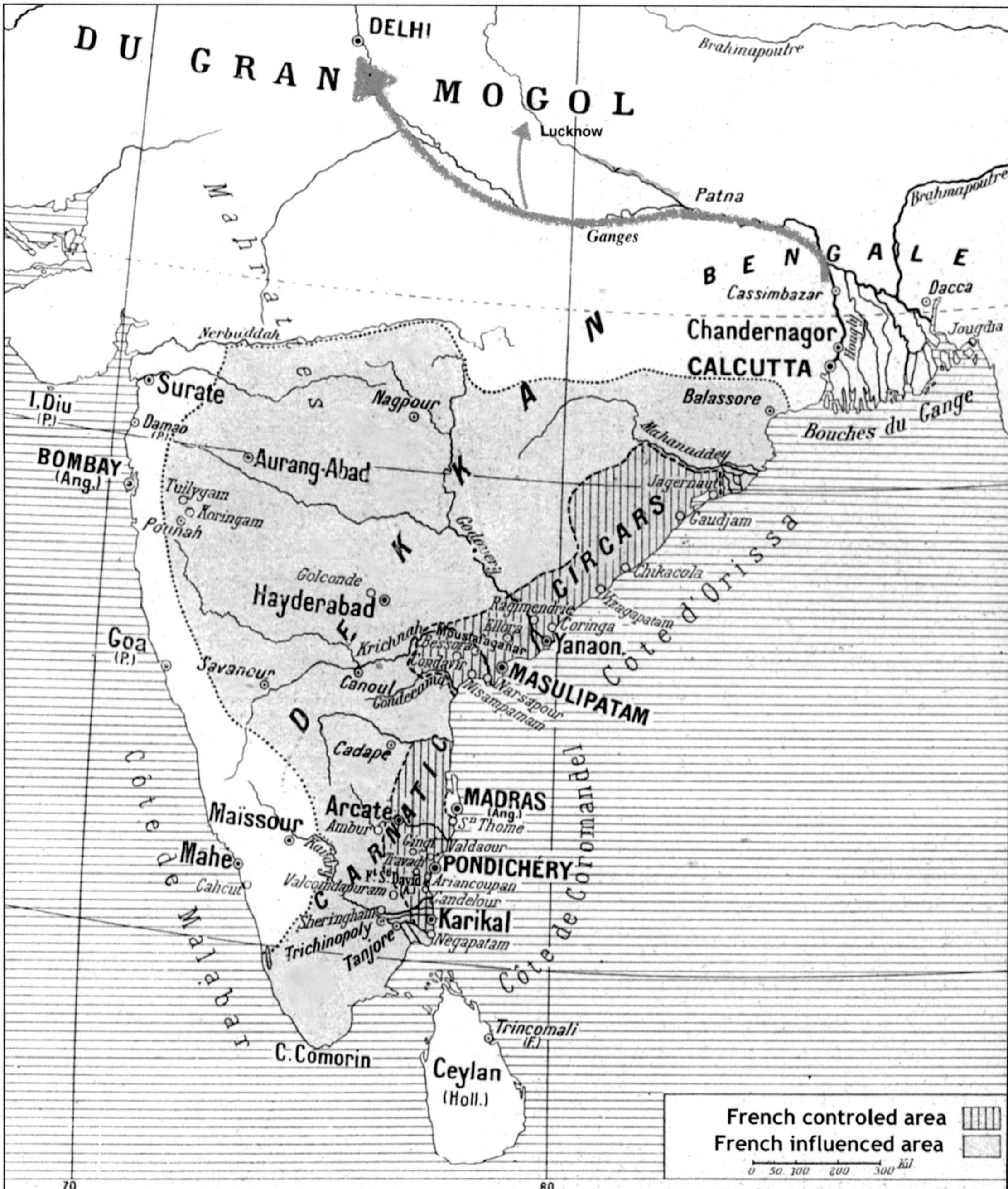

Map of India, mid-eighteenth century. The vertical lines indicate areas under French control, the shaded areas being those under French influence. The arrows to Delhi and Lucknow show the 1757-1758 penetration of Law de Lauriston's column as far as Delhi. (Author's photo)

Charles-Joseph Patissier, Marquis de Bussy-Castelneau. He was born in 1720 in a military family, entered the royal army in 1733 as *lieutenant*; *capitaine* in 1735, to Ile de France in the troops of the Compagnie des Indes in 1736 and Pondicherry in 1742 where he learned India's language, showed distinguished conduct at Madras, Pondicherry, Ambour, Gingee, the Deccan, Dautalabad and Wandewash where he was captured by the British. An outstanding diplomat, he was arguably the finest tactician of French India and came back to India leading the French expeditionary force of 1782-1783. He remained in Pondicherry after the end of the hostilities and passed away there in 1785. Print after portrait. (Author's photo)

invited to preside a meeting that rapidly reached an agreement and Bussy designated Salabat Jing, uncle of the deceased, to be nabob.

The army continued its march west. Bussy then learned that a Maratha army of some 20,000 men under General Balagirao wanted to intercept him. For Bussy and Salabat Jing, it was most important to reach Aurangabad and consolidate the nabob's government. For his part, Balagirao may have thought that he did not have enough troops while likely wondering if the Indo-French contingent, although small, might be very difficult to overcome. So he accepted Bussy's offer of two lakhs of rupees to withdraw. On 12 April, Salabat Jing made a triumphant entry at Hyderabad in Mysore and, after crossing central India, arrived at the capital, Aurengabad, on 18 June 1751. A few days later, about 100 French marines of the king's navy provided a small reinforcement for Bussy's corps.

North-east View of Hyderabad. Bussy's troops entered the city on 21 April 1751 greeted with 'exclamations of joy, Muslim blessings, according to the customs of these people' related a French soldier. Print after Francis Jukes. (British Library, London)

The summer and early autumn were mostly quiet in the Deccan, but it was only a facade. Salabat Jing's elder brother Guaziuddin Khan announced he was the legitimate nabob and was rallying support amongst some nobles. The threats became very serious when the Marathas sent an army of 60,000 led by Balagirao to support Guaziuddin Khan's claim. Facing this threat and a somewhat discouraged Salabat Jing, Bussy reasoned that the best defence was to attack and marched towards Poona, the Maratha's capital. War was declared on 23 November. He had some 420 French soldiers, 5,800 French-trained sepoys and about 60,000 Indian warriors rather loosely loyal to Salabat Jing. The two opposing Indian armies approached each other, but there was some hesitation and, for weeks, only skirmishes between small out parties.

Marathas Defeated

By 3 December 1751, Bussy was in reach of Balagirao's Maratha camp and decided to raid it. There was an eclipse of the moon that night and, profiting from the ancient Indian legend of the evil celestial dragon devouring the moon that night – in response to which as much noise as possible was made by all to chase him away – Bussy with his French soldiers and sepoys attacked the camp in the early hours of 4 December. The noise-making and praying Maratha warriors were totally surprised, confused and panicked, with even a stark naked Balagirao fleeing to nearby hills. Had Salabat Jing's cavalry charged, the Maratha army would have been wiped out. One assumes they were also making noise to scare the dragon. As it was, Balagirao managed to rally many of his men and, on 10 December, attacked a 11,000 men detachment of Salabat Jing's army that included Bussy's troops. The Marathas were repulsed with sizeable losses by the Indo-French corps' disciplined volleys and quick-firing artillery. Their losses may have been up to 6,000 men including 2,000 killed and 34 senior officers against trifling Indo-French casualties. Moreover, their capital was now threatened. Bowing to the inevitable, they signed a truce on 17 January 1752.

Intrigues and treacheries took up much of the year in the various princely courts of the Deccan resulting in the assassination of Salabat Jing's prime minister, some of his opponents raying around Guaziuddin Khan's claim to rule the Deccan. There was no sizeable military action during 1752 in that area, but Bussy was on his guard because if his small army and diplomacy failed, the Deccan would be lost and, ultimately, this would threaten the French in the Carnatic and Bengal. A relief of sorts was Guaziuddin Khan's death by poison in October.

Bussy later became quite ill (from natural causes) and, in February 1753 went to rest on the coast at Masulipatam. His command passed to Commandant Goupil who did not prove equal to the task. He soon lost the esteem of his troops whose discipline loosened while his princely ally wondered about him.

Upon recommendation of Bussy, Prince Lasker Khan had become Salabat Jing's prime minister. The prince convinced Goupil to post elements

The great mosque at Aurengabad. On 20 June 1751, Salabat Jing accompanied by Bussy's Indo-French troops made a triumphant entry into the city. Its imposing mosque was built from 1645 by order of the Mughal emperor. Print after a miniature in Langlès' *Monuments ancien et moderne de l'Hindoustan*. (Author's photo)

of the Indo-French corps at both Hyderabad and Aurengabad, thus fatally weakening it. He was secretly plotting with Prince Gazi Oudin to expulse the French, but the latter was mysteriously poisoned, most likely by one of his Indian princely enemies. Lasker Khan, whose plot was undiscovered, wisely kept quiet.

On 15 June 1753, Bussy was back at Hyderabad and found the political situation as confused as ever; he rallied nearly all his troops there and by 1 September, obtained again substantial funds to pay and equip them and marched to Aurengabad without opposition arriving in November. He was greeted in triumph by Indians who saw him as the only chance for stability. To maintain his troops and officials, he obtained the tax revenues of four Sirkars (provinces) and several other areas. As Dupleix wrote on 18 December 1753, 'the French are the protectors, friend, referees and mediators' of the Indian populace while 'procuring to the Compagnie des Indes wealthy establishments and ensured to Salabat Jing the heritage of his ancestors.' As for Lasker Khan, he was replaced as prime minister by the more trustworthy Chanavas Khan. On 28 April 1754, near-viceregal powers were devolved to Bussy by Dupleix to negotiate with Indian rulers.[2]

2 Dupleix quoted in Hanotaux and Martneau (eds), *Histoire des colonies françaises et de l'expansion de la France dans le Monde*, Vol.5, p.207

Consequences of Dupleix's departure in the Deccan

On 1 August 1754, Godeheu arrived at Pondicherry to replace Dupleix as governor general. This badly-timed decision of the Compagnie des Indes directors in Paris did not have immediately disastrous effects on Bussy's troops at their base of Hyderabad. In time however, the rumour mill did its work with the help of British propaganda that suggested to Indian rulers that the French were unreliable. However, when the province of Maisour did not pay taxes in 1755, Bussy mobilised his troops and the money soon came. There was nevertheless an uneasy feeling in Indian courts that Godeheu had nowhere the understanding of Indian diplomacy and the subtle firm hand it required. Bussy was thus left without answers for instructions while some Indian rulers in central India interpreted Dupleix's recall as a sign that King Louis XV, ruler of France, had lost interest in India and thus in their alliances. On the contrary, the British seemed even more interested than ever to link with Indian rulers. More British royal warships and soldiers were seen arriving.

Bussy's corps, abandoned as it was by authorities in Pondicherry and by political changes in the Decan, was increasingly affected negatively. Support in soldiers, supplies and money from Pondicherry dried up. On 18 July 1755, the company of elite volunteers was disbanded and its men incorporated into the artillery. Four days later, the Portuguese company was disbanded, half of the topasses released from service and everyone's pay reduced. Many others deserted.

To obtain resources to pay, feed and equip his troops, Bussy simply could wait no longer for instructions from Pondicherry and agreed to join his corps with Nabob Salabat Jing's troops in return for substantial amounts of money. A joint expedition of Salabat Jing's and Bussy's troops towards Mysore regarding unpaid taxes by its princes resulted in an amicable agreement. Bussy's reputation as a military leader and skilled diplomat was such that Great Mughal Alamgir II in Delhi offered to take him with 1,200 French soldiers into his service. It was a tempting offer although it meant that up to a third of the company's army in India would be partly controlled by the Mughal's imperial court. Governor-General Duval de Leyrit (who had replaced Godeheu in February 1755) responded that such a decision could only be made with the knowledge and consent of the Compagnie des Indes directors in Paris so that this matter was laid aside.

Local princely feuds went on in the Deccan and, from 5 to 25 May 1756, an army under Salabat Jing with a French corps led by Bussy besieged the city of Savanour defended by Balagirao's Marathas troops. There was no capitulation, but rather a peace agreement between Salabat Jing and Balagirao whose political philosophy now wondered if they might not unite their forces to rule central India without French or British allies. Money and privileges were no longer arriving from Pondicherry since Dupleix had been replaced and local rulers now wondered why the French troops were still in their midst. Bussy wondered too and assembled his troops to withdraw from the Decan. There were no incidents until the corps entered Hyderabad on 14 June. Soon thereafter, the city was blockaded by a large Maratha army.

French infantrymen of Bussy's Indo-French army in the Deccan repulse an attack by the cavalry of an enemy Indian prince, early 1750s. The Indian opponents were very brave but, as seen in many battles, could not overcome the European battlefield linear tactics. Print after Bombléd in the December 1902 *Dépêche coloniale illustrée*. (Bibliothèque Nationale de France, Paris)

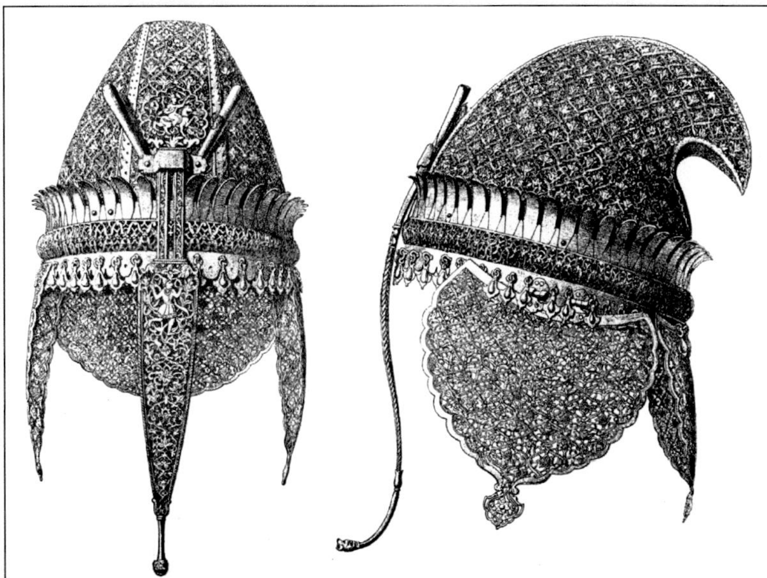

An eighteenth-century Maratha officer's helmet. This exquisite helmet was made of pierced ironwork with gilt enhancements. From Egerton's 1880 *An illustrated handbook of Indian arms*. (Author's photo)

Bussy used the palace of Charmal as his citadel and called for help from Pondicherry. The next weeks were replete with skirmishes, notably a sharp one on 30 June between Bussy's German hussars and Maratha cavalry.

On 10 August, the besieged learned that a relief army with 500 French troops was arriving led by Commandant Jacques-François Law who, the next day, met and defeated a Maratha force at Mognapara, but it took three more days to scatter the enemy and finally enter Hyderabad on 14 August. Maratha casualties were estimated at 3,000 men while the French lost three officers and about 30 men. The area was secured and Bussy stayed at Hyderabad with his corps until 16 November 1756, leaving there only 200 men under a subaltern officer.

Meanwhile, news that France and Great Britain were at war reached Bombay on 6 October 1756.

Bussy was marching eastward when he learned of the British occupation of French lodges in Bengal and he responded by having his troops occupy all the largely indefensible British factories of Vizagapatam, Madapolam, Ingeram and Banderoulanka on the Sirkars and Orrisa coast. The British could not react immediately with their troops being occupied in Bengal, but these events by Bussy's Indo-French corps had sobering repercussions amongst Indian courts in the Deccan insofar as French influence was concerned. Nevertheless, their plotting went on during the following year that threatened Salabat Jing in favour of the more popular Nizam Ali. Learning of this, Bussy mustered his troops and arrived at Hyderabad in January 1758, marched on and occupied by a ruse the fortress of Daulatabad held by Nizam Ali's troops. Bussy used it as his base of operations to secure Salabat Jing's authority the spring. On 11 May at Aurengabad, Nizam Ali had Prince Hyder Jing, Chanavas Khan and his son assassinated. Bussy and Salabat Jing mustered their forces to restore some order during the next weeks. By then, Nizam Ali had fled with a few horsemen. Bussy marched his troops to Hyderabad.

He had hardly arrived there when he received a letter from *Maréchal de Camp* the Comte de Lally on 14 July 1758 ordering him to withdraw all his troops from the Deccan and elsewhere except for a detachment to guard the Sirkars and Masulipatam under the Marquis de Conflans. Lally wished to have all the French troops available to attack the British on the Coromandel Coast. Three days later, Bussy and his army left Hyderabad and marched towards Pondicherry. Thus ended the extraordinary adventures of the Franco-Indian army in the Deccan.

Mahé and the Malabar Coast, 1750-1761

This area was relatively quiet during the whole decade. There were no outstanding military operations between the opposing French and British forces. There were, however, the inevitable plots and conflicts in local Indian princely courts in which commanders and troops at Mahé might be involved. In 1751, Commandant Louet had, after approval from Dupleix, granted the protection of France to the king of Nelissoram who felt threatened the king of

Badnour. Commandant Collé took command in 1756 and sought to reduce expenses resulting in the small French outpost of Matlaye being overrun and nearly all of its small garrison killed. This was more of a banditti attack than a princely or British plot. The policy of the French commander at Mahé was primarily of strict neutrality on the Malabar coast insofar as Indian princes were concerned. Matlaye was reoccupied and its fortifications improved.

Another outpost requiring a small Franco-Indian detachment from Mahé was at the Maldive Islands under Commandant Le Termeiller where they provided the actual security and authority for the population.[3]

Carnatic Campaigns, 1751-1756

The fortress city of Trichinopoly on the southern shore of the Cauvery River was situated in a strategically important place. In 1750 or early 1751, both Dupleix and British Captain Robert Clive had mooted the same basic strategic vision regarding this fortress: its occupation would be a definite advantage to achieve the domination of the southern part of the Carnatic. It could further be a diversion and create a front of attrition that would gradually weaken the army that would besiege Trichinopoly.[4]

Dupleix did not have the approval of his council regarding its occupation while Clive obtained immediate support from the new British Governor Thomas Saunders who had arrived in India during October 1750. Once in office, he learned of the defeats suffered by Indian princes favourable to the British at Gingee later compounded by the defeat and death of Nasir Jang in

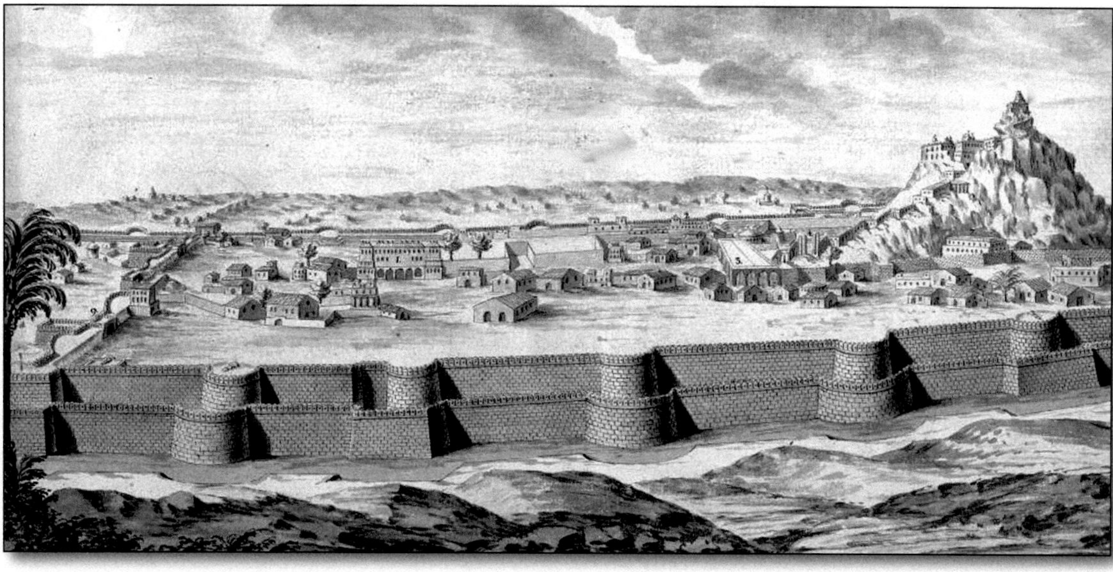

View of Trichinopoly, 1742. Situated on the southern shore of the Cauvery River, this Maratha stronghold was taken by the Nabab Sabber-Aly-Kan in 1738 after a two-year siege and retaken by the Marathas on 26 March 1742 following three months of siege. Only the more substantial buildings are shown; there were many more smaller ones. It was occupied by the British in 1752 and repeated French attempts to capture it were repulsed in the following years. (Archives Nationales Outre-Mer, 25DFC00234C.)

3 This intervention was a result of a feud by two kings of the Maldive islands with Ali Raja of Canmore who had seized and imprisoned them for years.

4 Unless otherwise noted, much of this narrative on Trichinopoly is taken from Martineau, *Dupleix*, Vols.3 and 4; Orme, *A History of Military Transactions*, Vol.2, books 2 and 3; de Vaissière, *Dupleix*, chapters 4 and 5.

December. Saunders immediately saw great threats to British interests due largely to Dupleix's actions and, in February 1751, wrote of the directors of the Honourable East India Company that the French were gaining influence and even raising their flag near the British territories. He further warned that these French gains made in peacetime could be much greater if war was officially declared in Europe. Saunders did not wait for an answer from Great Britain. He rallied relatively easily Indian princes such as Mohamed Ali and, in March, sent 600 Indo-British troops to reinforce his garrison at Trichinopoly.

The French council in Pondicherry now realised that they should have taken Dupleix's advice and taken Trichinopoly. Dupleix now sent Chanda Sahib and his 8,000 men to which 400 French soldiers was added under Commandant d'Auteuil. Some 500 British, 100 Africans and 1,000 sepoys with 1,200 of Mohamed Ali's warriors under Captain Gingen and Lieutenant Clive with more troops joining them marched out to intercept the Indo-French corps. This occurred in July 1751 near Valconda on the road between Trichinopoly and Arcot. Soon after the French opened artillery fire, the British troops panicked and ran back to the fortress so that most British troops in the Carnatic were blockaded in Trichinopoly.

Trichinopoly was a well fortified city featuring a double wall easily defended with a small almost inaccessible citadel on a steep rocky height. It could really only be taken only by assault or starved into surrender. For this, Commandant Jacques-François Law, who had replaced d'Auteuil in September 1751, would have needed at least 20,000 disciplined men or a very tight blockade. He certain did not have enough troops so the siege could only be a blockade that was not tight enough to intercept supply convoys in spite of observation posts to detect them.

British reinforcements arriving from Great Britain managed to get into the fortress while Clive went to Madras and convinced Saunders to create a diversion by attacking Arcot, Chanda Sahib's capital. It was an open city with decrepit fortifications that was easily taken. Learning this, Chanda Sahib detached 11,000 men with 150 French soldiers led by his son, Raju Sahib, to retake Arcot, which was occupied on 4 September 1751. However, its fort acting as a citadel had been rendered defensible by Clive's 120 European soldiers and 200 sepoys who successfully resisted early attacks. On 25 September, now reduced to 80 Europeans and 120 sepoys, they repulsed a major assault on the fort that included elephants with steel plates on their head trying to break down the gates. Raju Sahib's Indian army suffered over 400 casualties to British fire while the defenders only had six. Discouraged, Raju Sahib raised the siege of Arcot and withdrew.

Covrepauk, 1752

In late February 1752, an Indo-British force of some 380 British soldiers and 1,300 sepoys (later reinforced to 1,800) with six field guns under Clive marched out of Madras hoping to find and divert some of the French forces tasked with the capture of Trichinopoly. There was indeed a Indo-French force led by *Capitaine* Véry de Saint-Roman of about 400 French troops and 2,000 sepoys, many of which were cavalry, with nine pieces of field artillery lurking about to the south of Madras, looking to intercept any Indo-British relief column. Clive learned that the French were at Covrepauk (or Caveripacom; about 20 kilometres from Arcot/Arcate) and marched to meet them. It was a trap. The French knew the Indo-British force was coming and placed their guns in a field battery behind a dense grove of mango trees protected by a ditch and a bank with the troops sheltered in a dried-up stream.

Apparently without much information regarding the French positions, Clive boldly attacked Véry's troops at Covrepauk at about four in the afternoon of 14 March 1752. The two forces had vigorous musket and cannon duels, the French guns gaining the advantage during the next four hours. The cavalry that formed the main part of the French force (Clive had no cavalry) was not engaged in any manner. The sun set but some light was henceforth given by the moon in a clear sky. By then Clive had more information on the French positions and it was clear that the French cannon were knocking out his artillery and would win the battle. In a daring move, Clive joined his men resisting at the at the dried-up stream while detaching part of his troops under Lieutenant Keene to outflank and attack the rear of the mangrove battery that was reported as unguarded.

Plan of the Battle of Covrepauk, 14 March 1752. Fortescue's *History of the British Army*, Vol.2. (Author's photo)

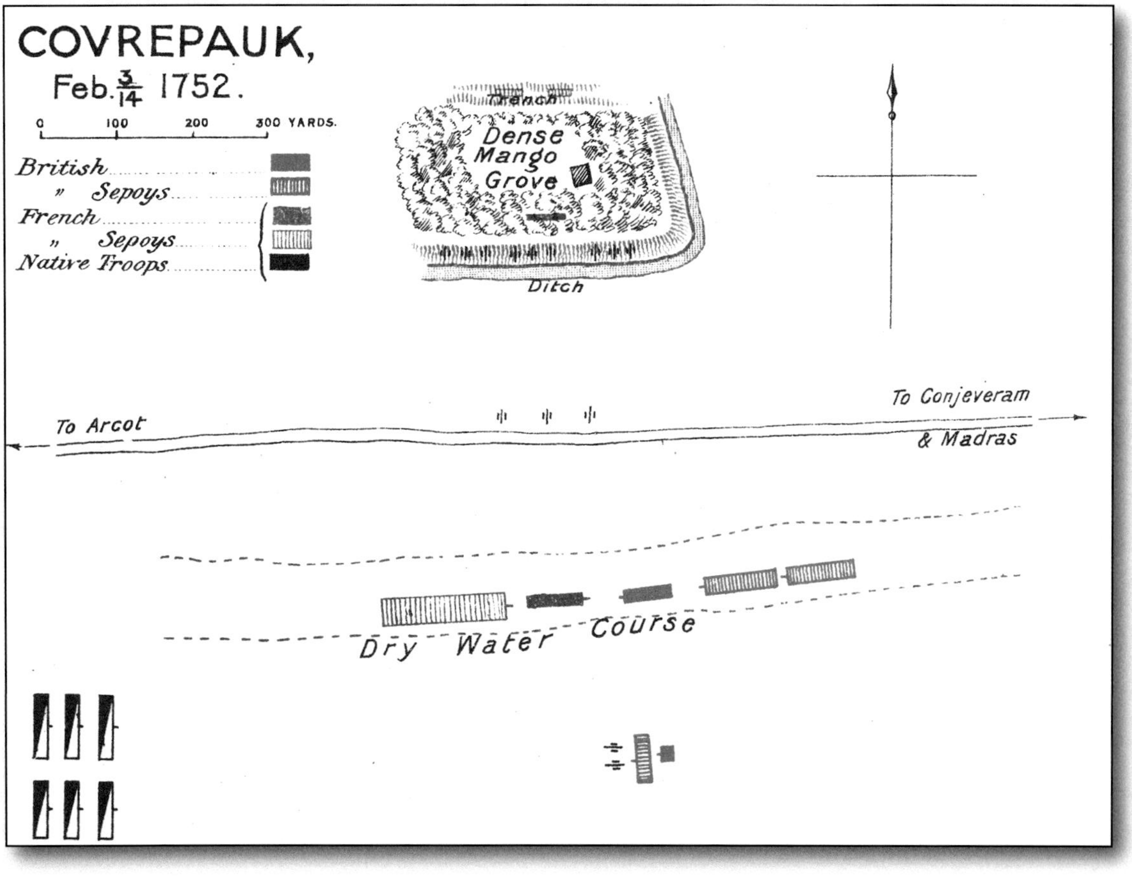

Anglo-Indian troops overcome the French field guns at Covrepauk, 14 March 1752. The British force under Robert Clive was slightly weaker than the Franco-Indian force, but it was better led. Clive had part of his troops outflank at attack the French rearguard as darkness fell in the evening. The surprised French force panicked, the British soldiers and sepoys swept all before them, as shown, overwhelmed three field guns and three mortars. Print after Stewart Orr. (Private collection, author's photo)

Keene and his men managed to move undetected until it arrived near the rear of the French battery. Keene sent Ensign Symmonds ahead to reconnoitre, but he was soon challenged by French sepoys; he deceived them answering in French and passing for a French officer, went back to lead his own British detachment to the battery's rear. At 30 metres from it, it fired a general volley on the startled Indo-French troops: they panicked and this quickly spread to their whole force. This totally changed the course of the battle, the British soldiers and sepoys now sweeping all before them and taking nine field guns and three cohoorn mortars. Clive lost about 40 Europeans and 30 sepoys while Véry's losses amounted to some 50 French and 300 sepoys killed with 60 more French made prisoners. The rest of the Indo-French force retreated into the fort at Covrepauk.[5]

Ongoing Actions at Trichinopoly

This engagement upset Dupleix's plan to tighten the blockade around Trichinopoly and it also secured Arcot for the British. The tables had turned and Lawrence marched out of Fort St David leading 400 British soldiers, 1,100 sepoys and eight guns towards Trichinopoly. Learning of this, Dupleix instructed Jacques-François Law to leave a small Indo-French force around Trichinopoly, march out and intercept Lawrence. Law's rather timid attempts failed and Lawrence's troops relieved Trichinopoly on 29 March 1752 while the Indo-French forces withdrew.[6]

More actions around Trichinopoly followed, notably on 26 April when Clive had a close call with his camp attacked by d'Auteuil's men who were eventually repulsed; on 7 May Lawrence captured the outlying fort of Coilady and d'Auteuil was outmanoeuvred and captured by Clive on 9 May while retreating to Valconda with his force of 100 Europeans and 800 sepoys. The British now dominated the area of Trichinopoly from which the Indian

5 Fortescue, *A History of the British Army*, Vol.2, pp.204-208; Orme, *A History of the Military Transactions*, Vol.1, p.212; C.B. Malleson, *The Decisive Battles of India* (London: Allen, 1883), pp.18-31, 98; Martineau, *Dupleix*, Vol.3, pp.274-275. Apart from Ensign Symmonds speaking French, the confusion may have also been due to the fact that some French troops had red uniforms whose details might not be perceived to be British on a moonlit night.

6 Malleson included Covrepauk in his *Decisive Battles of India* as an engagement that showed to the Indians that the Brritish could also be as redoubtable as the French. While a notable engagement, Orme and other British historians since have not given it such a status. French sources too do not give it an overwhelming strategic importance and Dupleix's translator did not mention it in his diary.

Indian soldiers on the march, 1755. This illustration from a cartouche on a map by William Jenings provides a rare glimpse at Indian soldiers as seen by a European. All are armed with edged weapons so were likely in the service of an Indian prince allied with the British Honourable East India Company; soldiers of princes allied to the French Compagnie des Indes would have been generally similar. From 'A Plan of the Army's March from Trichinopoly to Madura' that appears to have been made after the truce made on 29 September 1754 and formalised in January 1755. (British Library, London)

army of Chunda Sahib had wisely departed. Law's Indo-French force of 800 French troops and 2,000 sepoys was now trapped without hope of relief and instead of trying to break out, an utterly discouraged Law surrendered on 13 June 1752.

The French front in the Carnatic seemed to have largely collapsed at the time, but it soon regained some vigour thanks to the boundless energy of Dupleix to muster all the resources he could as well as deploying his mastery in the political intricacies of India's princely politics. During the summer, he received the confirmation from the Great Mughal's court in Delhi of his elevation to the status of nabob of the territories south of the Kistnah (or Krichna) River. He wisely selected Raju (or Raza) Sahib, son of the assassinated Chunda Sahib, to be the ruler of the area under his guidance.

There were many more engagements during the summer in various areas, but Dupleix managed to assemble a sizeable force to attack Trichinopoly again. He had 450 European soldiers and 2,500 sepoys under Commandant Astruc, 8,000 Mysore warriors, 3,000 Maratha cavalrymen and 'a rabble' of 15,000 Indian infantrymen for a total 28,500 men. By early July 1752 they had occupied most of the outlying fortifications including the Five Rocks. Lawrence had detached 200 British sepoys to a rocky hill called the Golden Rock who repulsed a first assault. Lawrence went out on 7 July and outmanoeuvred the somewhat disorderly Indo-French troops around

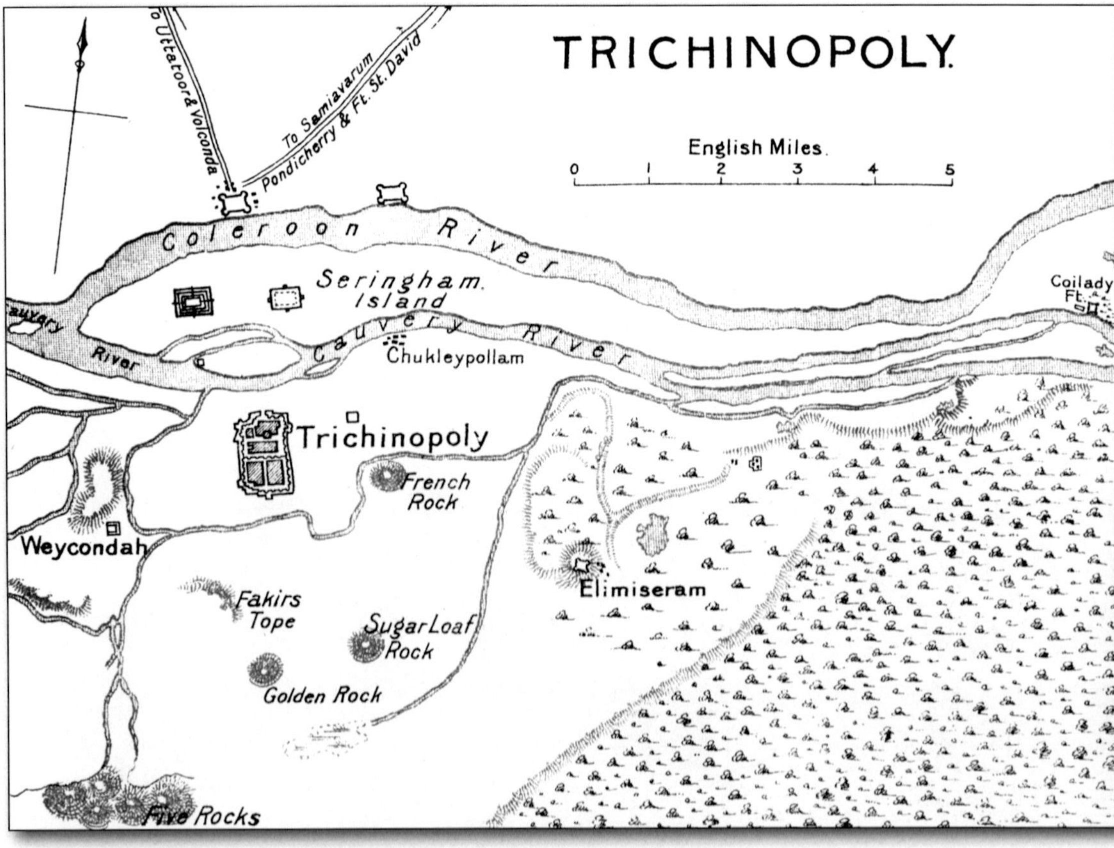

Map of the vicinity of Trichinopoly, mid-eighteenth century. Fortescue's *History of the British Army*. (Author's photo)

Golden Rock that eventually broke and fled when attacked. Astruc resigned and was replaced by Commandant Brennier. He courageously tried to invest Trichinopoly again from July 1752 resulting in various engagements, notably for the Golden and Sugar-Loaf rocks, but Lawrence proved to be the better tactician. There were many more remarkable actions of courage displayed by all for another two years in the four failed attempts to capture Trichinopoly that could fill volumes. We recommend Fortescue's history as the clearest short account. The Indo-French troops withdrew from Trichinopoly during the autumn of 1754.

Certainly, it was possibly Dupleix's pride that led him to such an obstinate pursuit of such a goal without adequate resources. It enormously drained the morale, the finances and the number officers and men of the company's troops fit for service. As such, it was surely his greatest military error as Governor-General of French India.[7]

7 Fortescue, *A History of the British Army*, Vol.2, pp.198-236

Fusilier, Garrisons of Lorient, Louisiana and Senegal, 1720s – early 1730s.
Artwork by Patrice Courcelle © Helion and Company. For details, see Colour Plate Commentaries.

Fusilier, Compagnie des Indes troops, India, Ile de France and Ile de Bourbon, mid-1720s to mid-1730s.
Artwork by Patrice Courcelle © Helion and Company. For details, see Colour Plate Commentaries.

Company of Gentlemen Cadets, New Orleans Militia, Louisiana, December 1729.
Artwork by Patrice Courcelle © Helion and Company. For details, see Colour Plate Commentaries.

Sepoy Fusilier, Compagnie des Indes troops, Coastal India, late 1740s.
Artwork by Patrice Courcelle © Helion and Company. For details, see Colour Plate Commentaries.

Fusilier, European Companies, Compagnie des Indes troops, Coastal India, circa 1750-1761.
Artwork by Patrice Courcelle © Helion and Company. For details, see Colour Plate Commentaries.

Sepoy Fusilier, Compagnie des Indes troops. Nellore District, India, circa 1750-1755.
Artwork by Patrice Courcelle © Helion and Company. For details, see Colour Plate Commentaries.

***Enseigne* with colour, European Companies, Compagnie des Indes troops, India, circa 1750.**
Artwork by Patrice Courcelle © Helion and Company. For details, see Colour Plate Commentaries.

***Enseigne* with colour, Sepoy Companies, Compagnie des Indes troops, India, circa1750.**
Artwork by Patrice Courcelle © Helion and Company. For details, see Colour Plate Commentaries.

Artilleryman, Bussy's Deccan Army, Compagnie des Indes troops, India, April 1751.
Artwork by Patrice Courcelle © Helion and Company. For details, see Colour Plate Commentaries.

Caffre fusilier, Bussy's Deccan Army, Compagnie des Indes troops, India, July 1751.
Artwork by Patrice Courcelle © Helion and Company. For details, see Colour Plate Commentaries.

Grenadier, Company of Grenadiers à cheval, Bussy's Deccan Army, Compagnie des Indes troops, India, November 1754.
Artwork by Patrice Courcelle © Helion and Company. For details, see Colour Plate Commentaries.

Fusilier, Law de Lauriston's Compagnie des Indes corps in north-central India, circa 1759-1761.
Artwork by Patrice Courcelle © Helion and Company. For details, see Colour Plate Commentaries.

Demise of Dupleix

The imperial visions of Dupleix were not shared by directors and stockholders of the Compagnie des Indes in France. Peace had been signed in Europe in 1748 and they expected that business and profits to substantially increase. Instead, war continued in India whose pertinence was not easy to understand in Paris. Nevertheless, between 1750 and 1754 inclusive, the company made a notable effort to increase substantially its garrison in India. Overall, some 4,349 men including 72 officers were sent during those years.[8]

The company's officials and the government in Versailles were apprehensive regarding Dupleix's near independent administration; there were rumours of vast fortunes and of the governor general's luxurious lifestyle in the Orient; of glowing victories and yet few ships arriving in France loaded with riches. As early as 1753, it was suggested that a commissioner with executive powers be sent to India. The Minister of the Navy Machault agreed and convinced senior company administrator Charles Robert Godeheu de Zaimont (1710-1794) to go to India to replace Dupleix. He landed at Pondicherry on 2 August 1754. Dupleix had instruction to return to France at once.[9]

Godeheu was more of an administrator than a career diplomat or soldier. He may have been a fine business manager, but lacked the statesmanship necessary in India. His outlook appears to have entirely lacked the diplomatic finesse and geo-strategic vision of his predecessors Dumas and Dupleix. The views of the company's conservative shareholders in France now prevailed and the new administrator of India was more like an inward-looking auditor.

Nevertheless, much of his duties concerned the army maintained by the company in India and this required a strategic outlook from its commander. Regarding military leadership, he had no military command experience yet could be a martinet. He sought to 'reestablish order and discipline everywhere, which was what mainly lacking in the army' in India according to his own account. His solutions were predictably managerial. Amongst the measures taken was the creation of 'Commissaires des Guerres' (war office commissioners) like in the royal army to look after logistics, financial management and auditing. Another creation was a 'bureau des troupes' (administrative office) to look after various bureaucratic details. A large 'camp of discipline' was set up near Pondicherry. This last measure could be useful to train more fully the many recruits sent in the last four years. However such training had been given to French and sepoy soldiers for many years previously, as proven by their remarkable battlefield performances. They

8 Anon., *Mémoire pour la Compagnie des Indes contre le Sieur Dupleix* (Paris: M. Lambert, 1763), pp.62, 101. The troops sent included a contingent recruited by Jacob Fischer, a then famous mercenary corps leader, consisting of 'nearly all Germans, Lorrain, etc' numbering 41 officers, 939 soldiers, 34 women and 4 children 'of which a company of hussars' embarked for India on 1 May 1754 as per AC, D2C, 41, Volontaires embarqués par Fischer pour la Compagnie des Indes, 1 May 1754.

9 BNF, Fonds Français 385, Compagnie des Indes. Journal du voyage de M. Godeheu, fait en 1754. It in fact ends on 16 February 1755 and is followed by a valuable annotated subjects table.

were already quite familiar with European drill, delivered effective volley fire in action and made disciplined bayonet charges. What they now needed was a talented commander.[10]

A Controversial Peace Agreement

In spite of all the previous fighting in India since 1749, Godeheu felt he was in a peace mission and, during the fall of 1754 negotiated a truce that was signed with British Governor Saunders on 26 December 1754. It affirmed that both companies would be politically neutral and have strictly commercial activities. This came after the British government had decided to assist the Honourable East India Company by sending six Royal Navy warships with Aldercron's 39th Regiment of Foot and 72 Royal Artillery gunners from the regular army that arrived at Madras in October 1754. It could be argued that Godeheu's timing could not have been worse, especially when reinforcements from France were diminishing.[11]

News of this treaty caused dismay amongst allied Indian princes who interpreted its clauses as a withdrawal of French military and diplomatic assistance. Did this mean that the Compagnie des Indes would thereafter only maintain its activities to its lodges? In that perspective it could even be taken in Indian princely palaces as treason. The French forces in India were certainly still redoubtable; the question now raised was would the government in Pondicherry deploy them to secure its allied or favourable Indian princes as in previous decades? The answer was now far more ambivalent forcing any prince to consider other options such as warming their relations with the British.[12]

Furthermore, while Godeheu's withdrawal of the troops blockading Trichinopoly in October 1754 was really the only logical decision he could make, it also sent a signal that the company's forces might be weakening.[13]

10 Anon., *Mémoire pour la Compagnie des Indes contre le Sieur Dupleix*, p.94.

11 TNA, WO 379/1, Distribution of His Majesty's Land Forces (by year); TNA, WO 380/16, Notes on regiments: 39th Foot, 12 companies (936 NCOs & privates) to India 1754; Richard Cannon, *Historical Record of the Thirty-Ninth or the Dorsetshire Regiment of Foot* (London: Parker, Furnivall, and Parker, 1853), p.14; M.E.S. Laws, *Battery Records of the Royal Artillery 1716-1859* (Woolwich: Royal Artillery Institute, 1952), p.14. More gunners followed by the creation of four Royal Artillery companies for India.

12 Martineau, *Dupleix*, Vol.4, pp.441-443 reproduces the 11 articles of the treaty.

13 BNF, Fonds Français 385, Journal du voyage de M. Godeheu, 12 October 1754.

9

Bengal

Chandernagor

The French established lodges in Bengal from the later seventeenth century. Chandernagor on the Hooghly River was the oldest, being founded in 1675 with the town and adjoining area granted to France by Mughal Emperor Aurangzeb in 1688. It was the only lodge in Bengal with a bastioned fortification, Fort d'Orléans, built from 1691, whose upkeep was somewhat neglected at times. Its chief was also the local superior officer. Chandernagor was the largest French lodge in Bengal and served as the central depot for the merchandise to and from other smaller lodges as well as being the main harbour for ships. Each of the smaller lodges had a trade or service specialty. Patna, further west, bought saltpetre and sold French cloth; Cossimbazar mostly acquired silk; Balassor had modest trading and it was there really to assist ships entering the Ganges, especially those without pilots; Dacca, further east (in present day Bangladesh) brought mainly linen and embroidery; Jougda, at the entrance of the Brahmapoutre River brought a variety of local products. Except for Chandernagor, the garrisons were modest and were included under Chandernagor's only in the general returns when in fact all lodges had a detachment.[1]

The European lodges in Bengal were not a great concern to the Indian rulers of the mid-eighteenth century. They were far more worried about the invasions of the Marathas and Afghans who had made some inroads from 1747. Aliverdi Khan, who ruled Bengal with imperial approval since 1740, died of natural causes at 80 years of age on 9 April 1756. He was succeeded by Surajah Dowlah who is remembered in history as one of the more inhumane, cruel and sadistic rulers to ever have sat on a throne. In his memoirs, Law de Lauriston, who was well aware of the questionable practices of some princes in Indian courts, described him in a paragraph that sends shivers down one's spine:

1 In the mid-eighteenth century, the population of Chandernagor consisted of about 500 Europeans, 400 Armenians, muslims and topasses, 20 to 22,000 Indians in 52 different castes including some 1,500 Christians. S.C. Hill, *Three Frenchmen in Bengal* (London: Longman, 1903), pp.14-15.

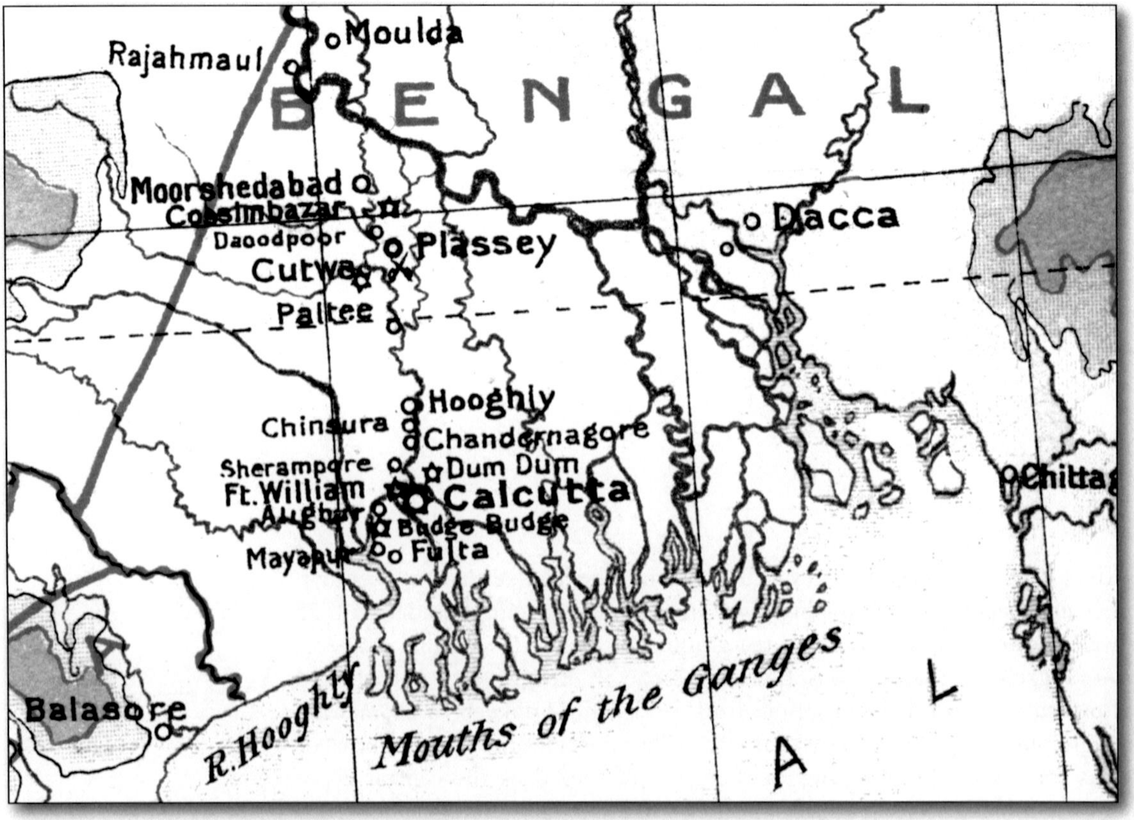

Map of Bengal. Fortescue's *History of the British Army*, Vol.2. (Author's photo)

Interior of the French lodge at Chandernagor, 1722. (Archives Nationales Outre-Mer, 27DFC2A)

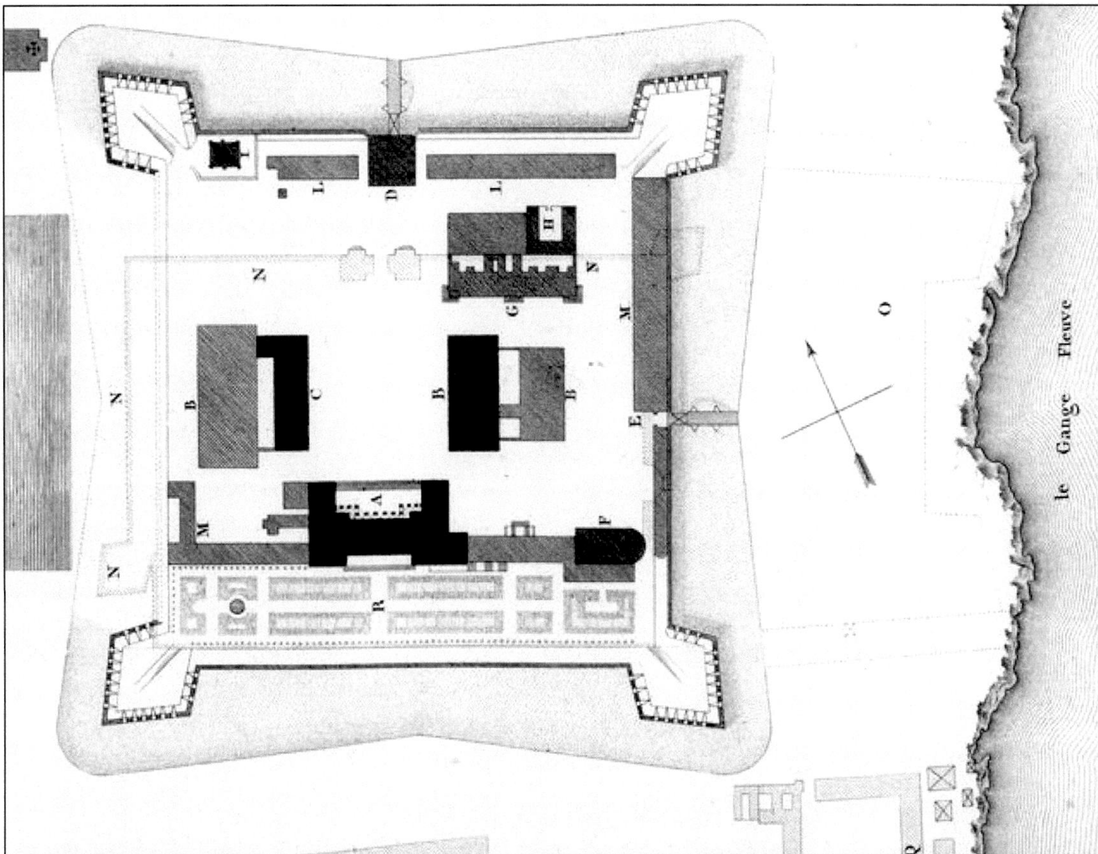

Plan of Fort Orléans at Chandernagor, 1749. This plan by M. Mouchet of the Compagnie des Indes shows the expanded fort in 1749 and also, faintly, the outline of the former curtain walls and bastions as well as the older buildings in black. By 1756, it was described as nearly decrepit having no glacis, no moat facing the Ganges River and the other sides facing land having moats without water and barely four feet deep, walls of brick and earth only one and a half feet wide, its 16 guns spread in the four bastions all needing new carriages. Print in Langlès' *Monuments anciens et moderne de l'Hindoustan*. (Bibliothèque Nationale de France, Paris)

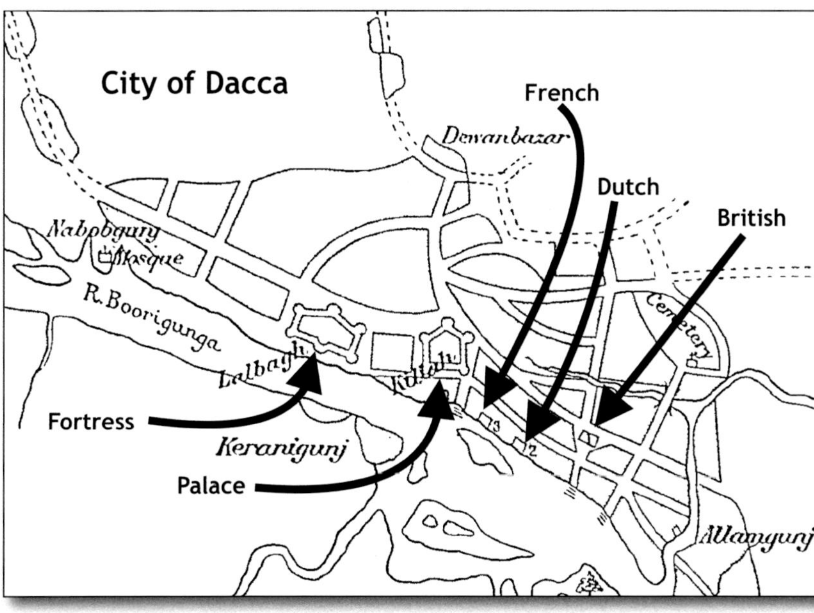

The European lodges at Dacca in eastern Bengal. The French lodge was situated next to the palace. Map in the 1903 *Three Frenchmen in Bengal*. (Author's photo and digital additions)

> Surajah Dowlah, a young man of twenty-four or twenty-five, [had a] very common appearance. Before the death of Aliverdi Khan the character of Surajah Dowlah was reported to be one of the worst ever known. In fact, he had distinguished himself not only by all sorts of debaucheries, but also by a revolting cruelty. The Hindu women are accustomed to bathe on the banks of the Ganges. Surajah Dowlah, who was informed by his spies which of them were beautiful, sent his satellites in disguise in little boats to carry them off… When it became necessary to get rid of some great lord or minister, Surajah Dowlah alone appeared in the business, Aliverdi Khan retiring to one of his houses or gardens outside the town, so that he might not hear the cries of the persons whom he was causing to be killed.[2]

It was supposed that Surajah Dowlah had his uncle poisoned shortly before Aliverdi Khan's death to ensure his own elevation as nabob. Once in power, he soon expressed his scorn for the British and somewhat good feelings for the French. Law de Lauriston and other French chiefs appear to have been more diplomatic than the British with the new nabob, but had no illusions as to the unpredictable and cruel aspects of his character and rule as related above. There was certainly no way to offer the slightest military or moral resistance. The British appeared to be in a stronger position due to their large establishment at Calcutta. But the new nabob thought it was no match for the forces that he mustered to get rid of the British.

Surajah Dowlah takes Calcutta 1756

Accordingly, Surajah Dowlah leading an Indian army of some 70,000 men occupied the British lodge at Cossimbazar on 4 June 1756 and marched to the outskirts of Calcutta. The town was surrounded and siege operations began on 15 June by an attack on a redoubt that was repulsed causing heavy casualties amongst the assault troops. More attacks followed and the garrison retreated into Fort William, the town's citadel. One of the defenders related that:

> The whole number left in the Fort being 250 effective men, we held out till the 20th in the evening when the ammunition being near spent, a flag of truce was hung out. During the parley from the walls, the back gate was betrayed…and we were obliged to surrender at discretion. The same night 170 of us were crammed into a hole not large enough for 50 of us to breathe in; the effect of it was, that only 16 were alive next morning. Four of us were sent to the Nabob's camp, and put into irons; but what became of the other 12 that escaped hell in miniature, I have not been able to learn. [3]

2 Quoted in Hill, *Three Frenchmen in Bengal*, p.66.

3 S.C. Hill, (ed.), *Bengal in 1756-1757. A Selection off Public and Private Papers Dealing with the Affairs of the British in Bengal during the Reign of Siraj-Uddaula* (London: Government of India and John Murray, 1905), pp.102-103; Anon., *Lettres édifiantes…*, Vol.7, pp.281. The beaten 'uttered lamentable cries that spread terror', leaving other prisoners fearing when their turn would come to suffer the same tortures. These accounts were from missionaries that had been jailed in chains by unhappy Indian officials or princes. The description given by

The infamous 'Black Hole of Calcutta' was an utterly awful place where these events occurred to that are just as revolting today.

At length, the survivors were sent to 'Maxadavad' (the nabob's capital Mooreshedabad) from where Mr Howell, one of the survivors, sent a letter on 7 July to Jean Law de Lauriston, chief of the nearby French lodge at Cossimbazar, describing their distress. Law de Lauriston, 'with great politeness and humanity, sent them not only clothes, linen, provisions and liquors, in great plenty, but [also] money.' Their story becoming known, they 'received every possible relief, not only from the kindness of the French and Dutch chiefs, but from the Arabian merchants.' On 25 July, Surajah Dowlah ordered their release.[4]

Water! Water! the poor British prisoners gasped in the Black Hole of Calcutta, June 1756. The city was taken by Surajah Dowlah's army. Of 170 British prisoners shut in a small room on the night of 20 June, only 16 were alive by the next morning. Print after Stewart Orr. (Private collection, author's photo)

The capture of Calcutta by Nabob Surajah Dowlah was of course intolerable to the British and could be reversed because the French military presence in Bengal was negligible. At length, a British force of 900 European soldiers (including 250 of Aldercron's 39th Regiment of Foot) and 1,500 sepoys under Robert Clive on board a naval squadron led by Vice Admiral Charles Watson that included four Royal Navy warships arrived before Calcutta on 30 December 1756 and started to bombard the city. The nabob's garrison panicked and the town and Fort William were occupied the same day. Predictably, Surajah Dowlah and his army of 40,000 men appeared before Calcutta in early February 1757 and encamped outside its eastern walls. On the night of 4-5 February, Clive made a daring raid through the nabob's army camp that spread terror and confusion amongst his troops. This convinced him to make a truce with Clive.

---

two priests shut in prison at Tanjore was so horrific that it was not printed. Unfortunately, for common Indian people, being in a 'public' prison at that time guaranteed a traumatic experience. Prisoners were packed in a room so that they only had space to sleep; at dawn guards would come to beat and torment some of them every day. Some would die from beatings, suffocation and other ailments. As bad as some prisons may have been in Europe, they could not match those in India and thus cause the outrage provoked amongst all Europeans when the horror of the Black Hole became known.

4 J.Z. Howell, 'A Genuine narrative of the sufferings…Black Hole…in June 1756', *Annual Register*, 1758, pp.278-286. Howell eventually reached the Dutch lodge at Corcemandel from where he embarked for England.

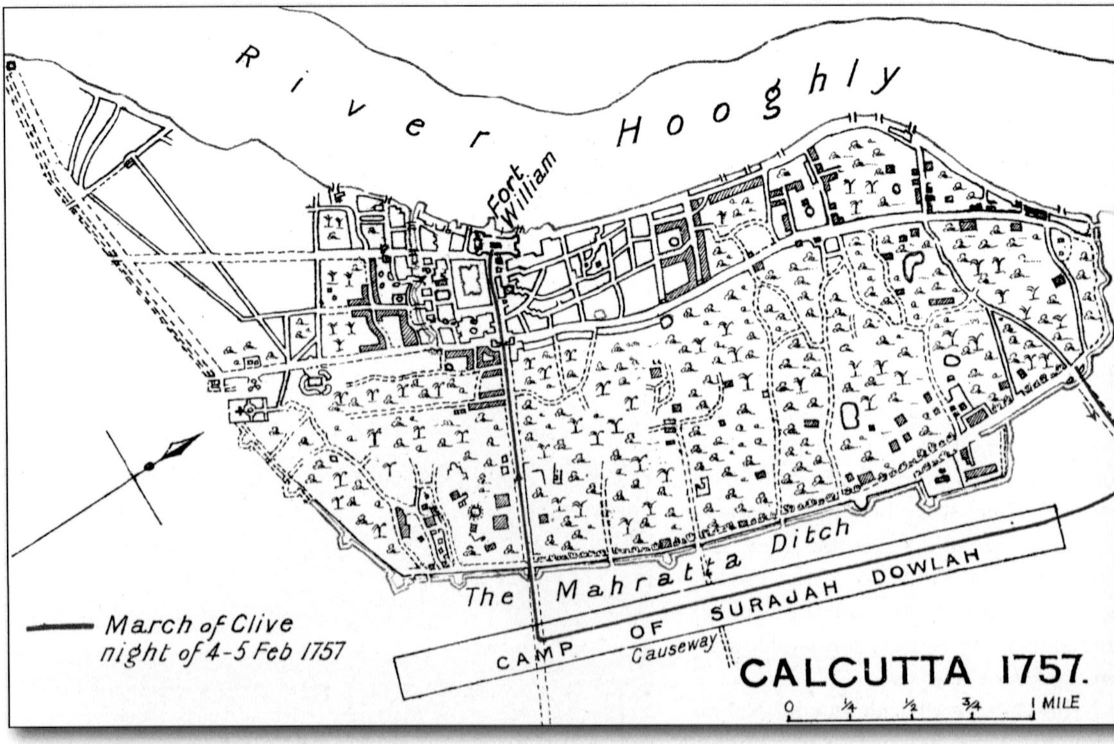

Plan of the Indo-British forces' capture of Calcutta, night of 4-5 February 1757. Fortescue's *History of the British Army*, Vol.2. (Author's photo)

French troops had not been part of Surajah Dowlah's army; they hardly had enough men to garrison Fort Orleans at Chandernagor and their other smaller lodges. Furthermore, British warships dominated naval access to Bengal on the Hooghly and Ganges rivers. Meanwhile, Clive had received reinforcements and attacked Chandernagor on 14 March 1757. Commandant Renault only had 146 defenders who resisted bravely during bombardments by Watson's ships until the capitulation was signed on 23 March.

Plassey 1757

Surajah Dowlah's position as nabob was becoming delicate. There were practically no French soldiers of the Compagnie des Indes left in Bengal except for about 50 gunners with the nabob's army. Many subaltern princes increasingly wished to get rid of him and conspired to replace him with Meer Jaffier, his military commander. Clive was also secretly a party to the plot. By 4 June, he had made a secret agreement to support the conspirators. Meanwhile Surajah Dowlah made amends and convinced Meer Jaffier to remain loyal, or so it seemed, as he assembled his army at Plassey to fight the British. He had 35,000 men on foot, 18,000 cavalrymen and about 50 cannons for a total of about 53,000 men. On 23 June, Clive reached Plassey with 850 European soldiers, 50 sailors, 100 topasses and 2,100 sepoys with

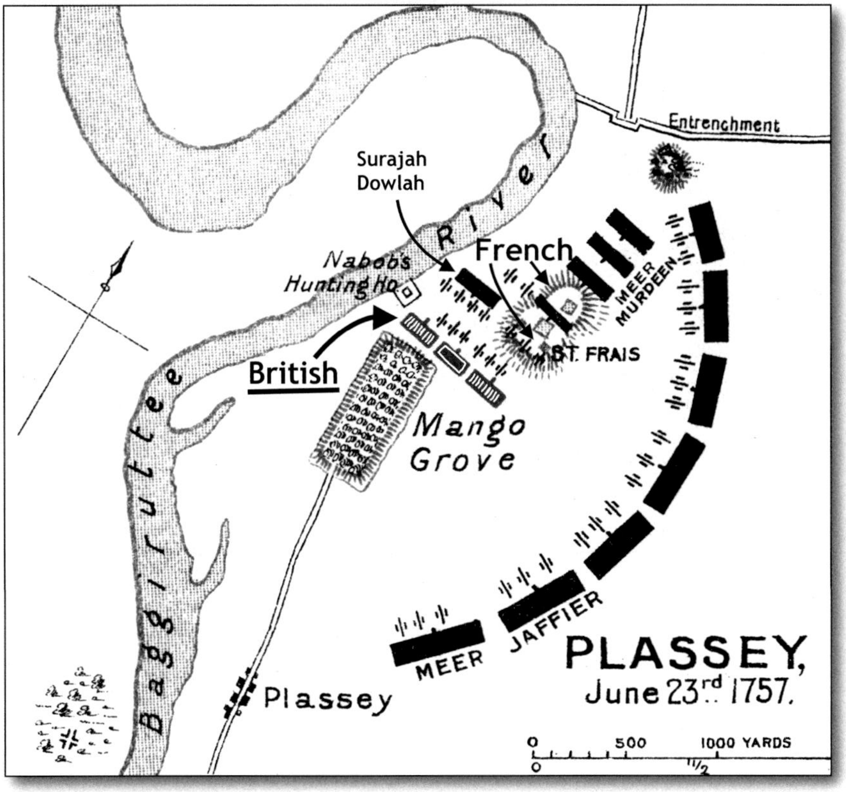

Plan of the Battle of Plassey, 23 June 1757. Fortescue's *History of the British Army*, Vol.2. (Author's photo)

eight 6-pounders and two howitzers formed into two divisions for a total of some 3,000 men.[5]

It looked like a most uneven match, but the deployment of Surajah Dowlah's huge force was anything but orderly with some of it approaching and others not, notably Meer Jaffier's corps on the left flank of the nabob's army. Its heavy cannons were slowly advancing on platforms pulled by bullocks while its numerous cavalry was really a large and disorderly groups of horsemen. The only somewhat organised troops seemed to have been the French gunners under Commandant Saint-Frais serving four light field guns set up at a water tank on a low hill; at eight in the morning, they fired the first salvos of the battle. It was answered by the British Royal Artillery detachment. The early part of the battle was mainly an artillery contest lasting until 11 in the morning that did not cause heavy losses. By then, Clive decided not to advance further and wait until dark so as to attack the nabob's camp.

Shortly thereafter, a heavy downpour of rain drenched both armies. However, the British managed to keep their powder dry; this was not the case for much of the nabob's army. Nevertheless, his most faithful general, Meer Murden, thought the British were in the same predicament and advanced.

5 Our account of the battle of Plassey is mainly based on British sources, notably Fortescue, *A History of the British Army*, Vol.2, pp.418-423; Orme, *A History of the Military Transactions*, Vol.2, pp.173-179; Malleson, *The Decisive Battles of India*, pp.35-70. We have not encountered primary source accounts from French soldiers who fought there, only less trustworthy reports from hearsay.

The Nabob of Bengal's artillery on its movable platform, drawn up against Clive's Indo-British troops at the battle of Plassey, 23 June 1757 Print after Richard Caton-Woodville from *The Illustrated London News*, 23 September 1893. (Private collection, author's photo)

Nabob Surajah Dowlah arriving on the battlefield of Plassey, 23 June 1757. Print after Richard Caton-Woodville from *The Illustrated London News*, 23 September 1893. (Private collection, author's photo)

British salvos and volleys were far more effective and casualties added up rapidly in the nabob's army; its cavalry bolted, the nabob's artillery was still largely un-deployed and Meer Murden himself was mortally wounded. Surajah Dowlah then pressed Meer Jaffier to take command and beat Clive and his troops. He of course agreed. Once with his troops, he sent a message to Clive and did not move. Surajah Dowlah then mounted a camel and left the battlefield with an escort of 2,000 cavalrymen heading for his palace at Moorshedabad. His army at Plassey now had no effective leadership.

Clive correctly saw 'that his only chance was to press the attack home before the resistance to him could assume any organised form' to quote Fortescue. Some of the nabob's army fought stubbornly in their 'own irregular fashion' while Saint-Frais' field guns were still 'well and regularly served' by their gunners. Clive then realised that Meer Jaffier's corps was not engaging meaning that he was in fact changing sides. This meant the British right flank and rear would not be attacked. He thus made a two-pronged attack on the disorganised masses and on the small hill, which was taken. It was untenable for the French gunners who left their guns and retreated. The Battle of Plassey was essentially over at five in the afternoon with the British soldiers and sepoys occupying the nabob's army's camp and field fortifications. The losses of his army are unknown, but must have been substantial. The Indo-British casualties came to 16 sepoys killed and 36 wounded, seven British killed and 13 wounded. As a result, the territories of Bengal, Orissa and Behar were gained by the British.[6]

The Loss of Bengal

Following the battle of Plassey, Meer Jaffier detached forces

> [T]o follow and arrest Surajah Dowlah. He was captured in the neighbourhood of the mountains of Rajmehal and conducted to Moorshedabad where he was put in prison. Two days later he asked to bathe himself which was permitted; he was in the bath when the son of Meer Jaffier and several other conspirators entered the chamber and stabbed him in the most shocking manner. His head was cut off and placed on the point of a pike, his body was thrown on the back of an elephant and paraded through all the streets of Moorshedabad. Thus miserably perished this proud nabob, who shortly before had spread terror through the country and made all the European nations tremble, a thing which none of his predecessors had dared to attempt...he was naturally brave, but he was born cruel and gave himself up to the most violent excesses... His gross injustice towards everybody caused his death to be little regretted by anybody.[7]

6 Fortescue, *A History of the British Army*, Vol.2, pp.423-424; P.R.C., 'The British Casualties at Plassey', *JSAHR*, XXVI (1948), pp.80-81.

7 Hill, (ed.), *Bengal in 1756-1757*, p.241. This extract is from a manuscript titled 'Revolution in Bengal'; Law de Lauriston's *Mémoire*, pp.169-171 is somewhat in the same tone.

Armour for an elephant, June 1757. This impressive artifact is said to have been amongst the trophies taken at the Battle of Plassey and brought back to England by Clive. From an old image in the Todd Albums. (Anne S.K. Brown Military Collection, author's photo)

General Meer Jaffier, 1750s. He was the senior commander of the army of the Nabob of Bengal, Surajah Dowlah, until he defected to Clive's army during the Battle of Plassey on 23 June 1757. To reward him, the British made him Nabob of Bengal. He has an orange-and-gold turban adorned with a feather plume, a 'jigha' (ornament similar to an aigrette), and a 'sarpati' (horizontal tripartite ornament). Around his neck are strands of pearl with an emerald pendant. He wears an emerald and ruby armlet with matching bracelets, and an archer's thumb ring. Gold brocaded waist sash that matches the gold brocaded border and trimming of his long coat. Yellow shoes with floral scrolls. Tucked into his sash on his far side is a sword and the handle of a katar dagger. (Courtesy Los Angeles County Museum of Art. Gift of Mr and Mrs Frank Neustatter (M.72.42))

By then, whatever French troops there might have been in Bengal had evacuated however they could, some towards the Carnatic, but others actually went west into the heart of India as far as Delhi (see next chapter). As for Bengal, it was now British. Plassey was a military and diplomatic turning point that would be very hard to reverse, even with substantial reinforcements from France. On 29 June, Clive installed Meer Jaffier as nabob with powers, in 'plain language, that the [British Honourable East India] Company should be the true sovereign and Meer Jaffier its puppet.'[8].

8 Fortescue, *A History of the British Army*, Vol.2, p.425.

10

North Central India 1757-1761

An Expedition to Delhi

A much lesser know yet quite fascinating episode was the foray of the modest-sized detachment led by Jean Law de Lauriston that went from Bengal to as far as Delhi, the imperial capital. He had been sent to Bengal in 1744 and became chief of the French lodge at Cossimbazar three years later. He served there another 10 years proving to be an efficient diplomat.[1]

Nevertheless, by early 1757, the British were gaining the upper hand in Bengal; Chandernagor, the main French lodge there was besieged in March and it was clear that it would fall to the much superior British forces. Before it surrendered, a few officers, a few volunteers and about 80 European soldiers, most of whom were British deserters that had enlisted in French service, managed to escape with about 30 sepoys to make their way to Cossimbazar. Law de Lauriston knew the British were hoping to capture the deserters at his lodge, much to their fear. Nabob Surajah Dowlah favoured a peaceful surrender and had even arranged for a Mr Watts and Law de Lauriston to meet at his palace. However, the rather undiplomatic Watts practically ordered Law de Lauriston to surrender to which he answered that if he ever did, it would be to the nabob and not to the British. It was of course hopeless to resist when the British did arrive and the best option was to abandon the lodge. The Comte de Carryon had also evacuated the French lodge at Dacca and his group joined the troops assembling at Cossimbazar.

In all, Law de Lauriston's force consisted of 14 officers, six volunteers, a chaplain, two surgeons, a translator and about 175 European soldiers with 100 sepoys. The artillery consisted of two 3-pounders, two 2-pounders and six 1-pounders. On 16 April 1757, they went out of Cossimbazar marching

1 This chapter is nearly all based on: Law de Lauriston, *Mémoire sur quelques affaires de l'Empire mogol, 1756-1761*, which is the very best source. It can be downloaded from the Internet Archive at <http://archive.org/details/mmoiresurquelqueOOIawj>. Jean Law de Lauriston (1719-1797) was the brother of Jacques-François Law and both had landed in India during 1742. Jacques-François Law had distinguished himself at the 1748 siege of Pondicherry, but had been less fortunate four years later at Trichinopoly.

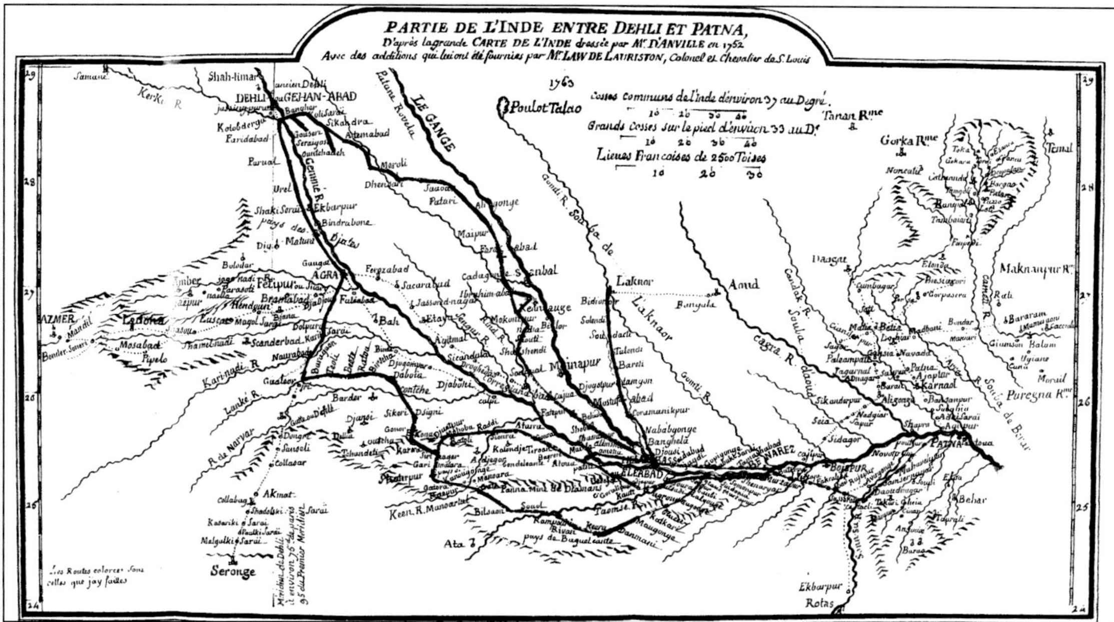

Map of India between Delhi and Patna, c. 1758-1761. Based on Danville's 1752 map of India, Commandant Law de Lauriston drew up this map, which shows the travels of his small force from Patna all the way to Delhi, a side foray to Lucknow and back as well as various detours. He mentions indicating the travels in coloured lines on the original and so far vanished map, but this greyscale print with doted and solid lines is still impressive. (Print from Law de Lauriston's memoir published in 1913, author's photo)

An archer of a prince's Indian army, mid-eighteenth century. Archer were still common in the Indian armies at that time. Unsigned drawing. (National Gallery of Canada, Ottawa)

The entrance to the Mughal imperial palace at Delhi. Commandant Law de Lauriston and his small force arrived there in early April 1758 and met the 'Chazada› Ali Gohar who was the imperial crown prince. Print after W. Purser. (Private collection, author's photo)

westward across much of Bengal eventually reaching Patna. From there, they followed the Ganges River westward arriving at Benares on 2 August 1757. Law de Lauriston considered it to be one of the finest looking cities in India. It was then a city of bankers described as 'the treasure of India' and was an 'open city' without fortifications because it was in no one's interest to attack and loot it. The raja of Benares nevertheless felt that this unusual armed column would be better at Allahabad, which was reached on 14 August. They could stay there for months if they liked. The curiosity of the nabob residing at Laknaor (Lucknow) resulted in an invitation to Law de Lauriston to visit him. So, with three officers and a few sepoys as escorts, he went up to Lucknow and saw the nabob with his officials to which the sepoys gave a demonstration of French military drill. After courteous diplomacy the French party came back to the column at Allahabad on 18 October.

Law de Lauriston's objective was to reach Delhi, the capital of the Mughal Empire to 'show the flag' and exert French influence in an area hitherto unvisited by any substantial group of Europeans. His column was a small one, but it was now in an area of India where most inhabitants had never actually seen Europeans. The appearance of these French soldiers and Indian sepoys in March 1758 naturally caused amazement.

Attack Repulsed

For Prince Dourdjousingue of the 'Djates' (or Jats), here was an opportunity to harvest some laurels and he accordingly mandated a force of about 10,000 cavalrymen to attack and capture the French column at its camp near the Calini River; Law de Lauriston had been warned and, on 24 March at three in the morning, raised his camp and marched slowly so as not too loose his baggage. In the morning, Dourdjousingue appeared with his cavalry intending to break into the French column that now assumed a battle formation with its light artillery pieces in support. The charging cavalrymen were immediately repulsed suffering heavy losses in every attack due to disciplined musketry volleys and quick-firing guns shooting grapeshot; Dourdjousingue's Indian fusiliers were then deployed without success against accurate volleys fire and grapeshot. Law de Lauriston then had his men ford the river covered by some of his sepoys who excelled as light infantry skirmishers. More Jat cavalrymen caught up with the column across the river, some of them being utterly brave charged again in vain, many being killed by bayonets. Defeated, Dourdjousingue's men retreated.

French casualties were very light at 14 wounded (including six sepoys) while Dourdjousingue's force had at least 150 men killed and many more wounded it was later learned. In this part of India, this relatively minor and unknown engagement was the first time that a large traditional Indian force faced a European-trained corps. The news of this victory was said to have produced the same amazement in northern India as had been seen after similar engagements in the Carnatic since 1746. Law de Lauriston marched on to Delhi.

Delhi and the Taj Mahal

Delhi was reached in early April and Law de Lauriston was introduced to the 'Chazada' (also Shahzada) Ali Gohar who was the crown prince designated to succeed the old emperor. At that time, the political situation of the near-defunct empire was very unstable with the Marathas basically dominating the area and, to a certain extent, the imperial court which was itself the scene of bitter and sometimes bloody events and plots. The Chazada's 'vizir' (or prime minister) for instance was 'the slave of the Marathas', noted Law de Lauriston who quickly had to learn Indian imperial diplomacy in order to survive. Fortunately, he was a learned man who had a certain command of Indian and Persian languages as did the Chazada who gave him a ceremonial imperial dress and liked to dine with him. There was considerable confusion about Europeans in the imperial court; some courtiers thought Law de Lauriston was an envoy of Robert Clive in Bengal while other wondered from what country originated Bussy! As for the Chazada, he wanted to lead an army into Bengal to get rid of Surajah Dowlah who ruled like a tyrant and invited Law de Lauriston and his men to join him. He replied that he would, but had no money so that was arranged. Law de Lauriston's detachment left the area of Delhi on 30 April 1758 to go south to Agra.

The detachment arrived at Agra on 8 May and saw its impressive fortress. In that area, the French soldiers marvelled at the magnificent mausoleum of the Emperor Akbar 'which must have cost immense sums and would honour the most accomplished architect in Europe.' Slightly further on, they came

The fortress at Agra with its impressive gate, from a nineteenth-century photograph. Law de Lauriston and his men arrived at Agra on 8 May 1758. Law de Lauriston observed that it had two curtain walls, 'very high and much better built' than the fortress at Delhi. (Library of Congress, Washington)

The Taj Mahal much as seen by French officers and soldiers in May 1758. Their commander Law de Lauriston described it as a building 'crowned by five domes, all made with marble, outside as well as inside, ornamented with mosaics' and 'more perfect' than any other. Today, everyone in the world agrees with him. In May 1758, very, very few usually lone European travellers/explorers had ever seen it and it was all but unknown outside of India. Law de Lauriston with his French officers and soldiers of the Compagnie des Inde's army were most probably the first large group of Europeans to see this sublime example of the world's architectural art. Unsigned Indian painting, late-eighteenth or early-nineteenth century. (Bibliothèque Nationale de France, Paris. OD-83(A))

upon the Taj Mahal, mausoleum of the wife of Emperor Shah Jahan made of marble and noted by a clearly very impressed Law de Lauriston's as being 'even more perfect' than Akbar's. Law de Lauriston, his French officers and soldiers of the Compagnie des Indes' army were most probably the first large group of Europeans to see this sublime example of architectural art.

With the Mughal Army

The Indian Mughal army that Law de Lauriston's small Franco-Indian corps joined was under the nominal command of the Chazada Ali Gohar, but actually led by Maratha Prince Hytelrao with whom everything had to be cleared. Prince Hytelrao was not particularly fond of Law de Lauriston and his small Franco-Indian force so that, by treacherous manoeuvres, he exposed it to an opposing Indian force's surprise fire outside Fort Gouzerte on the road eastward. The French reaction was immediate and the fort was taken quickly by assault while Hytelrao and his men stayed out of range. Having lost four men, Law de Lauriston was outraged and so was the Chazada, which led to Hytelrao and his corps leaving the Mughal army. The expedition was cancelled, but there were more forays in which the small Franco-Indian corps participated in the following months. It was not, however, an integral part of the Chazada's army as yet.

Being on Bengal's western border, the city of Patna had previously been garrisoned by a modest Indo-British detachment since 1758. The Chazada felt this was an infringement of his rights. Viceroy of Bengal Meer Jaffier and Clive disagreed and sent about 15,000 men to reinforce Patna under Major Caillaud and Prince Meerun. However, by early February 1760, the Chazada and his sizeable army were within sight of Patna. By then however, the Governor of Patna, Raja Ramnarain, had assembled a larger army of about 40,000 men, nearly all Indian levies; there were otherwise only 170 British soldiers and five companies of sepoys. On 9 February, Raja Ramnarain advanced on the Chazada's army and was compelled to retreat back into the city. On 22 February, Caillaud and Prince Meerun's relief force were nearing Patna and the Chazada's army was defeated, but not decisively, when he tried to stop the Indo-British force. More manoeuvres followed and

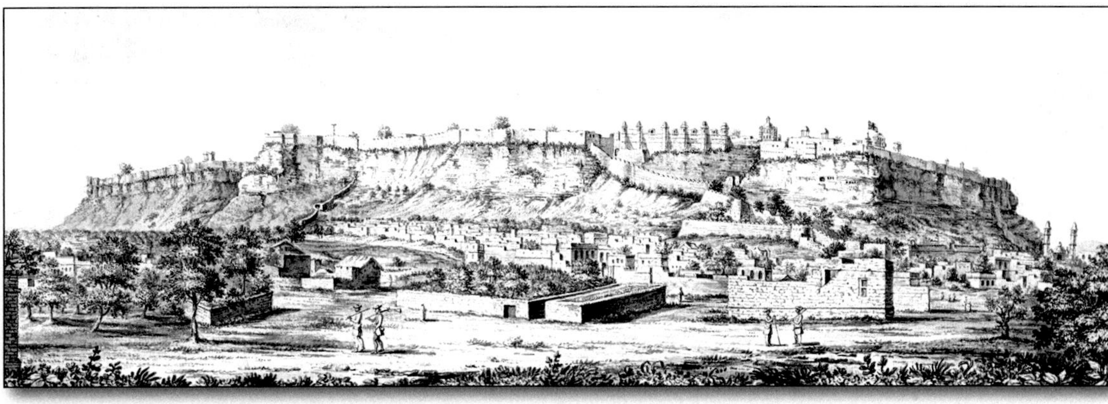

The great fortress at Gwailor. Law de Lauriston and his column saw it when they arrived there on 14 May 1758. He described it had having one curtain wall situated on a very steep hill estimating that 'this fortress must be impregnable by the people of this country' concluding that it could only fall by starving its garrison. Print after William Popham. (British Library, London)

The great fortress at Gwailor. Print after William Popham. (British Library, London)

Law de Lauriston's small Indo-French corps joined the Chazada's army in early April, but did not have the opportunity to participate in an attack on the city that was repulsed on 28 April. The siege was finally raised in May 1760.

Following the Chazada's failed siege of Patna, the French corps was sent south in late May 1760 with about 4,000 Marathas to attack the fortress of Soupy, a dependency of Patna. It was a work built on an octagon plan, with a moat, double curtain walls and a succession of four gates had to be passed to go in. Its garrison had about 2,000 men; there were no British troops. Law de Lauriston did not have heavy artillery and knew that the Marathas fought well in the field, but less so in sieges while his French soldiers and sepoys were very suited for siege assaults. Since he had few troops, he felt the only recourse lay in a surprise night attack by his men simultaneously on the four gates, which he saw as the weak point. He first made a false attack shooting muskets and light

Chazada (Crown Prince) Ali Gohar, mid-eighteenth century. Commandant Law de Lauriston met Chazada (or Shahzada) Ali Gohar in Delhi in April 1758 and later accepted his invitation to join his Mughal army. He became Mughal Emperor Shah Alam II in 1760 and reigned largely powerless until his death in 1806. Beveridge's 1862 *A Comprehensive History of India*. (Author's photo)

artillery at about nine in the evening and eventually retired an hour later to make the garrison think it would be quiet the rest of the night. But at three in the morning, his men quietly approached the first gate unseen, set fire to it and tore it down, axed down the second gate and blew up the third and fourth gates within a few minutes while the French guns poured ricochet shots on the turrets and curtain walls. The waking garrison made a desperate stand, but fled if they could when their commandant was killed along with about a hundred of his men and at least as many being wounded. The allied Marathas finally arrived to participate in looting the place that had been solely taken by the French soldiers and sepoys. Seven sepoys were killed and a dozen others wounded including a few Europeans.

Meanwhile, in late 1759 or early 1760, the Mughal Emperor Alamgir II was assassinated in Delhi. The details of his murder were only known publicly in May 1760 following the abandonment of the siege of Patna. The Chazada Ali Gohar had known about it for months, but had reasons to keep it secret. After rallying sufficient support although he was the designated successor to the throne, he became Emperor Shah Alam II. At this time, a Mughal emperor of India was largely a protocolary title because true power over most of the country had passed to various area princes without forgetting the increasing influence French and British East India companies. There nevertheless was a great durbar celebration where he received homages from Indian officials and officers and named princes to high posts. Even Law de Lauriston was on the honours list being named 'Mirateche' (Master of Fire or Grand Master of the Artillery).

Later that year, Law de Lauriston's corps participated in the capture of the fortress of Mannepour south of Patna. Shah Alam's army stopped at a distance from the fortress while the French corps approached, took cover from musketry fire by its garrison of about 900 men, quickly made fascines and installed four of the heavier calibre cannons and fired with little effect on the gates so aimed higher. One cannonball went through the apartment where the commander of the fortress was. This terrified him and he asked to capitulate as long as it would be to Europeans. This was granted and the garrison came out with the honours of war, their weapons and baggage between the French soldiers and sepoys. Once in the fortress, it was found to have no artillery or ammunition, which better explained the hasty capitulation. The French casualties amounted to four wounded.

Suan 15 February 1761

In early January, Law de Lauriston's small French force was still with Shah Alam's Indian army, which was slowly marching east towards Bengal. It had up to 40,000 cavalry, about half being of bad quality, unpaid and lacking weapons. The French contingent numbered only 125 Europeans and 200 sepoys who were said to be the only troops armed with muskets; the French also served their 10 light calibre cannons from 3- to 1-pounders. An Indo-British army was marching west to stop Shah Alam and end the blockade of Patna. It consisted of some 30,000 cavalry and 15,000 fusiliers led by

Cassimalikhan with a British contingent of 650 Europeans and about 5,000 sepoys led by Major Carnac; its train of artillery coasted of about 15 guns, ranging from 4-pounders to 12-pounders.

On 15 January 1761, the opposing armies met near the village of Suan (called Elsa by Law de Lauriston) at six or seven in the morning when the British were seen advancing in good order towards Shah Alam's army. No effective field fortifications had been built by Cassimalikhan to stop the advancing Indo-British and it was a most disorderly mass of men, some mounted on elephants, that mustered half-heartedly. The French corps was ordered to occupy a very exposed position in front of the army, which Law de Lauriston interpreted as a way by Cassimalikhan to get rid of his corps; it was already formed in a line with its artillery at about 200 steps in front of the imperial Indian army so he refused to obey this order. Once in range, the Indo-British troops stopped, quickly set up their guns and open fire on the Indian confused mass, killing many men, horses and elephants within 15 minutes. Cassimalikhan, totally frightened, ran off followed by thousands of panicked men. The French corps could only retreat, but to another position while leaving behind only one gun and reaching the village of Suan, until it was totally surrounded and capitulated 'with three or four officers and 30 or 40 soldiers that were with the pieces [of artillery] with me.' It was at 'about four in the afternoon.'

Law de Lauriston was quite humble in his relation of the conduct of his men and himself as the battle ended. Arthur Broome, the historian of the Indo-British Bengal army later revealed the gallantry of the small French corps. The British, he wrote:

> ...continued to pursue them [the Emperor's Indian army], but speedily came in contact with Monsieur Law [de Lauriston], who, with his [French] party, had taken up a position to cover the retreat. This gallant and able officer...made up his mind to make one final and desperate stand on this occasion, and either to succeed or perish in the attempt. The English immediately advanced against this detachment, which was drawn up in line, with their Artillery, consisting of 6 pieces, in front...as the columns approached, the French guns opened upon them, but fortunately at such an elevation that almost all the shot flew over the heads of the English, who closed upon them rapidly but steadily with shouldered arms, without attempting to return a shot, and leaving a party to secure and guard the captured guns as they passed, rushed on to encounter the line of French Infantry; but the latter, astonished at this coolness and determination, broke at once and fled in disorder, leaving Monsieur Law with 13 or 14 of his officers, and some 50 men who stood by their commander and their colours.
>
> This gallant little band of gentlemen and soldiers appeared determined to sell their lives dearly, and prepared for a desperate resistance; but Major Carnac with Captain Knox and the other English officers, respecting this spirited conduct, halted their own men and advanced alone to the little party, raised their hats and saluted them with the courtesy they merited; the Major then requested Monsieur Law to surrender, pointing out the utter hopelessness of resistance and the inutility of attempting it, when all had been done that skill or bravery could effect. Monsieur Law replied that if permitted to surrender as they were, he would agree

> that they should be considered prisoners of war, but that he would only give up his sword with his life. Anxious to save the lives of such brave men, the Major readily consented, and Monsieur Law and his officers gave themselves up, but were permitted to retain their swords.[2]

It was at about four in the afternoon on 15 January 1761 that this extraordinary and largely unknown saga that had started in April 1757 ended. Law de Lauriston kept his sword, but lost that day all his baggage, the most valuable to him being all the papers given to him 'by the prince' that included a treaty of mutual assistance signed by Shah Allem due, no doubt, to rather rapacious Indo-British soldiers. He nevertheless went on to praise the treatment received by Major Carnac and later by 'McGwire' at Patna where the French prisoners of war were taken. Most of them later dispersed and went to the Deccan.[3]

As for Shah Alam II and those who remained with him, he was pursued by the Indo-British forces until, realising his hopeless military situation, he surrendered at Patna in the hope that his imperial status would be recognised. The British wisely saw the great political advantages he could bring and proclaimed him as the Mughal emperor at Patna and in Bengal thus bringing him some revenues while coins were henceforth minted with his name. In effect, the British Honourable East India Company now assumed the tax collection of the Mughal Empire.[4]

Barely half of a century earlier, a Mughal emperor still had considerable power and unrivalled influence over India. Even a decade earlier, a *firman* signed by the emperor with his imperial gift of the luxurious honour robe and cap was considered the greatest of honours one could hope for. With the defeat of Shah Alam II and the remaining imperial forces at Suan, imperial prestige was given a very hard blow that, in time, announced the eventual end of an imperial structure that became diplomatically and militarily irrelevant.

2 Arthur Broome, *History of the Rise and Progress of the Bengal Army* (Calcutta: Thacker, 1850), p.325.

3 The papers also included a manuscript Persian-French dictionary that Law de Lauriston had compiled in the previous five years, which was his most regretted loss. Law de Lauriston, *Mémoire*, pp.461-470 has been our main source on this battle. Editor Martineau also included in it the British reports of it, notably that of Major Carnac.

4 Toynbee, *La grande adventure de l'humanité*, p.525.

11

Metropolitan Reinforcements

The Comte de Lally and His Troops

Once war had been declared between France and Great Britain, thought was given to sending reinforcements to India as well as to America. These reinforcements were drawn from the king's metropolitan army. By mid-November 1756, the rumour mills amongst courtiers in Versailles were fed by the 'preparations at the port of Lorient [that] continue in their mysterious ways' as well as troop movements in western France. According to the Duc de Luynes, it seemed 'certain that M. de Lally [also Lally-Tollendal, Lally de Tollendal], *maréchal de camp*, will be in command' of infantry five battalions 'including three Irish'; by late December, the total infantry had been reduced to three battalions that were the Irish Régiment de Lally, the 2nd battalion of the Régiment de Lorraine and the 3rd Battalion of the Régiment de Berry. In the event, this last was instead sent to Canada and replaced by the 1st battalion of Lorraine for India. There was also to be a battalion from the regular metropolitan army's Corps Royal de l'Artillerie, a numerous staff including '3 brigadiers who are Messrs. d'Estaing, de Landivisiau and a M. de Lally' who was 'a relative' of the commanding general. The total was supposed to 'come to about 4,000 men.'[1]

The contingent of regular metropolitan army troops going to India had royal regulations that specified their peculiar organisation. On 10 November 1756, Lally's Irish and the two battalions of Lorraine were ordered to have nine companies of 60 men each (one of grenadiers and eight of fusiliers) per battalion. Furthermore, 150 artillerymen of the Corps Royal de l'Artillerie were detached to India where they would form upon arrival three companies

1 On Lally's campaigns in India, see L. Dussieux and E. Soulié (eds), *Mémoires du Duc de Luynes sur la cour de Louis XV* (Paris: Didot, 1864), Vol.15; Marc Chassaigne, *Le Comte de Lally* (Paris: Société de l'histoire des colonies françaises, 1938), chapters 2 to 7; John Cornelius O'Callaghan, *History of the Irish Brigades in the service of France* (Glasgow: Cameron and Ferguson, 1883), pp.345-351; Fréville, 'Lally et Bussy aux Indes (avril 1758-mars 1761), *Revue des questions historiques*, January 1907, pp.138-184 (article partly based on papers of Bussy and the Marquis de Nazelle in private archives).

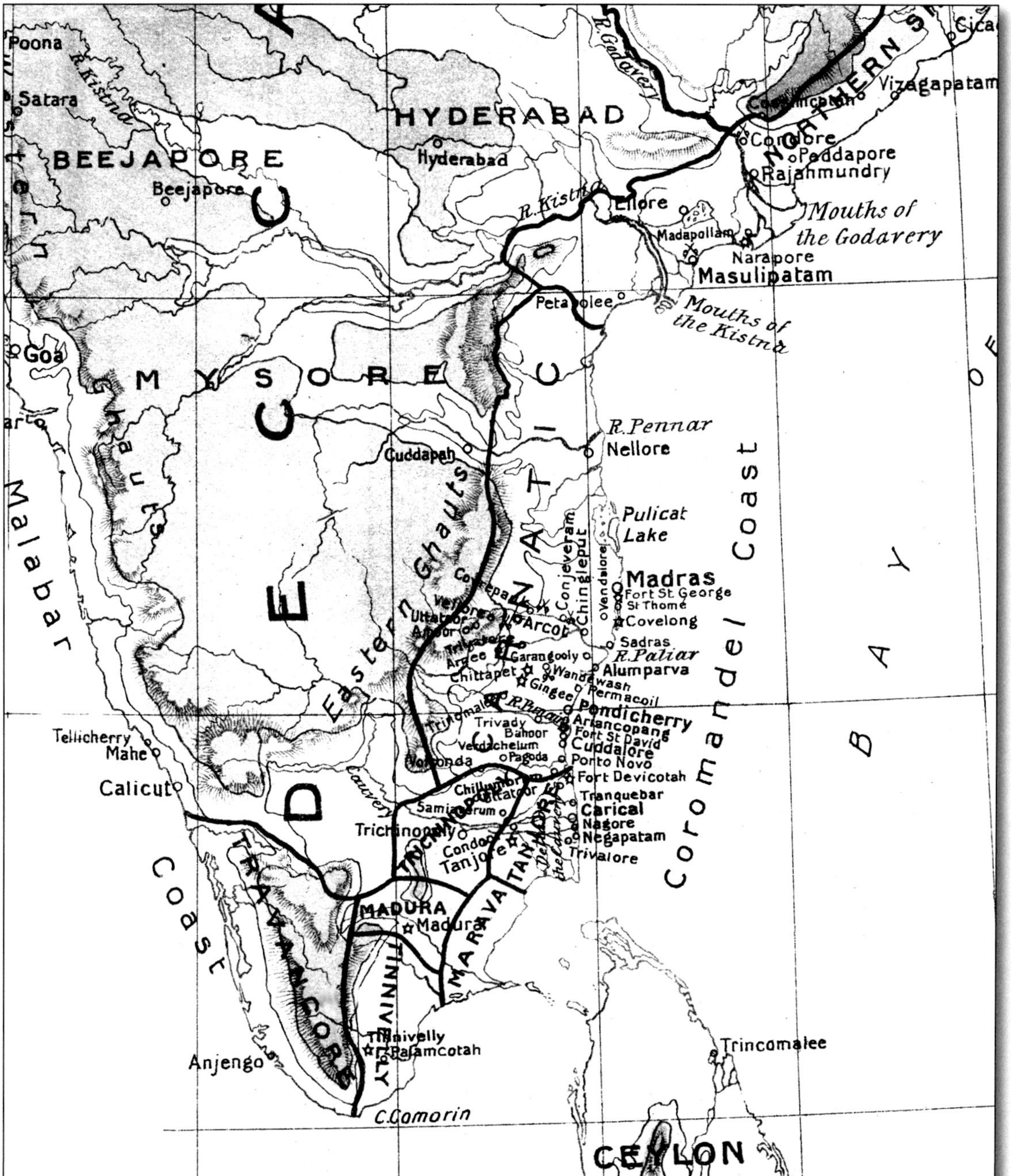

Map of Southern India. Fortescue's *History of the British Army*, Vol.2. (Author's photo)

of 103 men each including four officers, presumably by incorporating 150 Compagnie des Indes gunners.[2]

Another royal order of 1 December 1756 must have been received with resignation by the Compagnies des Indes troops. It ordered them to give precedence 'on all occasions' to the royal army and 'troops of the navy when ashore' and further stipulated that the general of the forces sent to India was the supreme commander of all forces. A further order of 6 December 1756 concerned the establishment of the Compagnie des Indes European troops in India specifying that 10 companies would form a battalion. One battalion 'de l'Inde' was eventually formed in India and campaigned with Lally's army. The company's troops were not well considered by Lally and, by 1759, their officers and men could hardly stand him.[3]

The fleet was led by *Chef d'Escadre* (Rear Admiral) the Comte d'Aché. It was divided into two divisions. The first division had 19 ships including eight warships under the Chevalier de Soupire. It sailed from Lorient on 6 March 1757 and arrived at Pondicherry on 8 September. The Régiment de Lorraine and 50 gunners were immediately landed. The squadron then went back to Ile de France to wait for the second division

D'Aché himself sailed from Lorient on 3 May 1757. His second division consisted of the king's warship *Zodiaque*, 74 guns, and the Compagnie des Indes ships *Vengeur*, 54 guns, *Bien Aimé*, 58 guns, *Centaure*, 58 guns, *Dauphin*, 42 guns, *Condé*, 44 guns, and *Moras*, 44 guns, the frigate *Diligente*, 26 guns, the corvette *Pénélope* with the transport ships *Thérèse*, *Pacifique*, *Saint-Luc* and *Emeraude*.[4]

Except for the *Zodiaque*, all others vessels were Compagnie des Indes merchant vessels that were armed with additional guns. This may have made them redoubtable, but they were not conceived to be warships. A smallpox epidemic amongst sailors made d'Aché call at Rio de Janeiro where the fleet remained for two months. It arrived at Ile de France on 16 December 1757, seven-and-a-half months after departing from France. D'Aché then spent another two months refitting his ships at Ile de France and finally arrived at Pondicherry on 28 April 1758, nearly a year after leaving Europe. The new Governor-General and commander in chief of all French forces in India, the

---

2 AC, F3, 238, Ordonnance du Roi Concernant le Corps de Troupes que Sa Majesté destine à faire passer aux Indes Orientales, 10 November 1756. The order gave the strength of the artillery companies to be formed in India as: one *capitaine*, one *capitaine-en-second*, one *lieutenant*, one *lieutenant-en-second*, three *sergents*, four *caporaux*, four *anspessades*, 88 gunners, artificers or bombardiers. These establishment changes were not recorded in the annual *État militaire de France* since these royal troops were on duty for the Compagnie des Indes as per 'Detail des Reductions et Incorporations…1762', Royal Archives, UK, Ms GEO ADD 35 12, p.60. For abstract histories of the Régiments de Lorraine and Lally see Louis Susane, *Histoire de l'infanterie française* (Paris: Dumaine, 1876), Vol.5, pp.306, 366.

3 AC, F3, 238, Ordonnance du Roi Pour le service des Troupes de Terre & de Marine que Sa Majesté envoie dans l'Inde, & de celles attachées au service de la Compagnie des Indes, 1 December 1756 and Ordonnance du Roi Pour les troupes attachées au service de la Compagnie des Indes, 6 December 1756; Voltaire, *Fragments sur l'Inde*, pp.106-107.

4 On D'Aché's campaign in India see C. Saint-Yves, 'L'expédition de l'Inde. Les Instructions du gouvernement de Louis XV au comte d'Aché', *Bulletin de géographie historique et descriptive*, 1907, pp.293-316; Jonathan R. Dull, *The French Navy in the Seven Years War* (Lincoln: University of Nebraska, 2005), pp.116-117, 141, 153, 172-173.

Three grenadiers of the Régiment de Lorraine, 1758-1761. According to the 1758 *État Militaire*, its regimental uniform consisted of a white coat with white collar and cuffs, red waistcoat, white breeches, brass buttons (three to each cuff and pocket), gold laced hat. (1759 Taccoli manuscript, Royal Library, Madrid)

Thomas Arthur, Comte de Lally, Baron de Tollendal. He was born in France on 13 January 1702, the son of Sir Gerard Lally, an Irish Jacobite officer, entered the French army in 1721, served with distinction in the wars of Polish and Austrian Succession, promoted *brigadier* in 1746, *maréchal de camp* two years later, governor general of India in 1756 where he arrived in 1758. Print after E. Fitz in O'Callaghan's 1883 *History of the Irish Brigades*. (Author's photo)

Comte de Lally with his own regiment of infantry, had finally arrived. About 400 men had been lost through sickness during the voyages.

Cuddalore and Fort St David

French intelligence had correctly learned that a British squadron was in the vicinity of Madras under Vice Admiral George Pocock leading the *Tiger*, 60 guns, *Cumberland*, 66 guns, *Salisbury*, 50 guns, with the frigates *Bridgewater* and *Triton* both of 24 guns. Had d'Aché not spent so much time in Brazil and Ile de France, he would have likely vanquished Pocock, but that opportunity was now lost. On 28 March 1758, reinforcements led by Commodore Stevens had previously arrived in India from Great Britain. The *Elizabeth* and *Yarmouth*, both of 64 guns, *Weymouth*, 60 guns, *Newcastle*, 50 guns, and the frigate HMS *Queensborough* were now part of Pocock's squadron doubling its strength.

On 29 April 1758, the French fleet of nine ships was near Cuddalore landing the troops so as to attack the place when Pocock's squadron of seven ships appeared. D'Aché's fleet had 476 guns to Pocock's 428 guns, but this advantage in firepower could be misleading. As in 1746 (see chapter 6), the French had only one ship-of-the-line of the king's navy, the *Zodiaque*, the others being Compagnie des Indes ships converted into occasional warships whereas all the British fleet consisted of true warships of the Royal Navy manned by trained officers and battle-experienced sailors. It was a definite advantage for the British. Nevertheless, the Compagnie des Indes's navy could give a stiff fight. The engagement was a bloody four hour cannonade that ended in a draw from which d'Aché, who was wounded twice but not gravely, disengaged although he was not beaten.

Meanwhile on land, Lally sent the Comte d'Estaing with 700 men to take the town of Cuddalore, which surrendered on 4 May. The French now pressed against Fort St David near Cuddalore, which Lally's instructions from Versailles specified that it should be his prime target. French siege batteries were built in mid-May. By then, Lally had about 5,000 men, half of them sepoys, while the British garrison numbered about 1,600 men of which 600 were Europeans. The fort capitulated on 2 June 1758 after a siege of 18 days and was demolished by the French. Devicotah also surrendered. It was an auspicious beginning for Lally who announced that his policy was: '*Plus d'Anglais dans la peninsule*' (No English in the [Indian] peninsula).[5]

D'Aché's Naval Support

Lally's next objective was Madras. He asked d'Aché to provide naval support for its siege; the admiral did not agree mentioning the bad state of his crews and the damaged ships that could not be repaired adequately at Pondicherry, but he finally agreed after Lally threatened to arrest him. On 2 June d'Aché's fleet went off towards Carical; an angered Lally ordered him to sail to Pondicherry which d'Aché reached on 17 June. The feud between the two French commanders was now very bitter and both stood on their points of honour. On 27 July, Pocock with his repaired ships was now off Pondicherry. D'Aché sailed out the next day and after some manoeuvres, the rival fleets engaged again off Carical on 3 August with the same indecisive results, but with the rigging of the British ships more badly damaged.

Lally now asked d'Aché to start the siege of Madras by bombardments and a blockade; the admiral again flatly refused pointing to his damaged ships and heavy casualties. After a council with his officers securing their agreement, d'Aché stated that his ships needed repair and their crews provisions; after calling at Pondicherry, the French fleet sailed on 2 September 1758 to Ile de France, the admiral adding that that island might be attacked by a British fleet. With this extraordinary move, the French and their allies in India were left without any substantial naval support. Pocock was so surprised that he thought it was a trick and had the French fleet followed. Its destination was indeed Ile de France and there it stayed for over a year.

5 Voltaire, *Fragments sur l'Inde*, pp.92-97.

On 29 September 1758, British Major Brereton of Draper's 79th Regiment leading 4,000 Indo-British troops (including 2,500 sepoys) attacked the fortress town of Wandewash and was repulsed by about 1,100 European Compagnie des Indes troops under Commandant Diogane. This modest French victory was overshadowed by the enormous long standing problem of lack of money to pay Lally's Indo-French forces. On 17 October, both battalions of the Régiment de Lorraine mutinied because they were owed eight months' pay. They threatened to raise the money themselves by seizing it from the inhabitants if they were not paid within four days. The Pondicherry council swiftly levied a tax on all Europeans and paid a substantial advance to the mutineers which calmed them down. They later obtained the full amount with an amnesty and were back on full duty by 21 November. This of course could have repercussions in the Compagnie des Indes troops and sepoys who also had arrears due. Lally mustered all the money he could and even sold the wine rations to raise money to fund his army.[6]

Madras December 1758-January 1759

For Lally, the consequences of d'Aché's departure and the empty treasury coffers were very serious. Nevertheless, to find new resources his army, which had 2,700 European infantrymen and 300 cavalry, he advanced into Madras on 13 December 1758. It was defended by 1,750 British and 2,200 sepoys under Stringer Lawrence. Early in the siege, the Comte d'Estaing, one of the senior French officers, was captured by the British. The defenders withdrew gradually from what was called the Black Town, which had many wealthy residences. When the French soldiers penetrated it, many soon broke ranks and indulged in widespread looting. One of the French senior officers described the scene as an 'immense looting of the troops in the Black Town' that included 'large stores of strong liquors that favoured drunkenness… It was a situation that had to be seen' to be believed. The siege works and the security of the trenches 'were carried out by drunken men.' The Régiment de Lorraine was the only one that was exempt from this drunken contagion. Other units revelled in it and the Régiment de Lally 'surpassed' everyone. From that resulted 'the most shameful and destructive scenes' due to insubordination and the breakdown of discipline. 'We saw officers join the soldiers and a thousand other infamous acts' the detail of which, although very true, would seem to be a 'monstrous exaggeration.'[7]

The British garrison was grouped in Fort St George, the seaside citadel of Madras. The next day, it staged a remarkable sortie from the fort made by two columns, one under Colonel Draper of 500 men with two field guns to attack the French right in the Black Town and the other under Major

6 Alfred Martineau (ed.), *Correspondance du Conseil superieur de Pondichéry et de la Compagnie des Indes…* (Pondicherry: Société de l'histoire de l'Inde française, 1920-1930), Vol.5, p.5; Voltaire, *Fragments sur l'Inde*, pp.100-101.

7 Voltaire, *Précis du siècle de Louis XV* in *Oeuvres de Voltaire* (Paris, 1831), Vol.21, pp.320-321 citing the journal of an unnamed general officer.

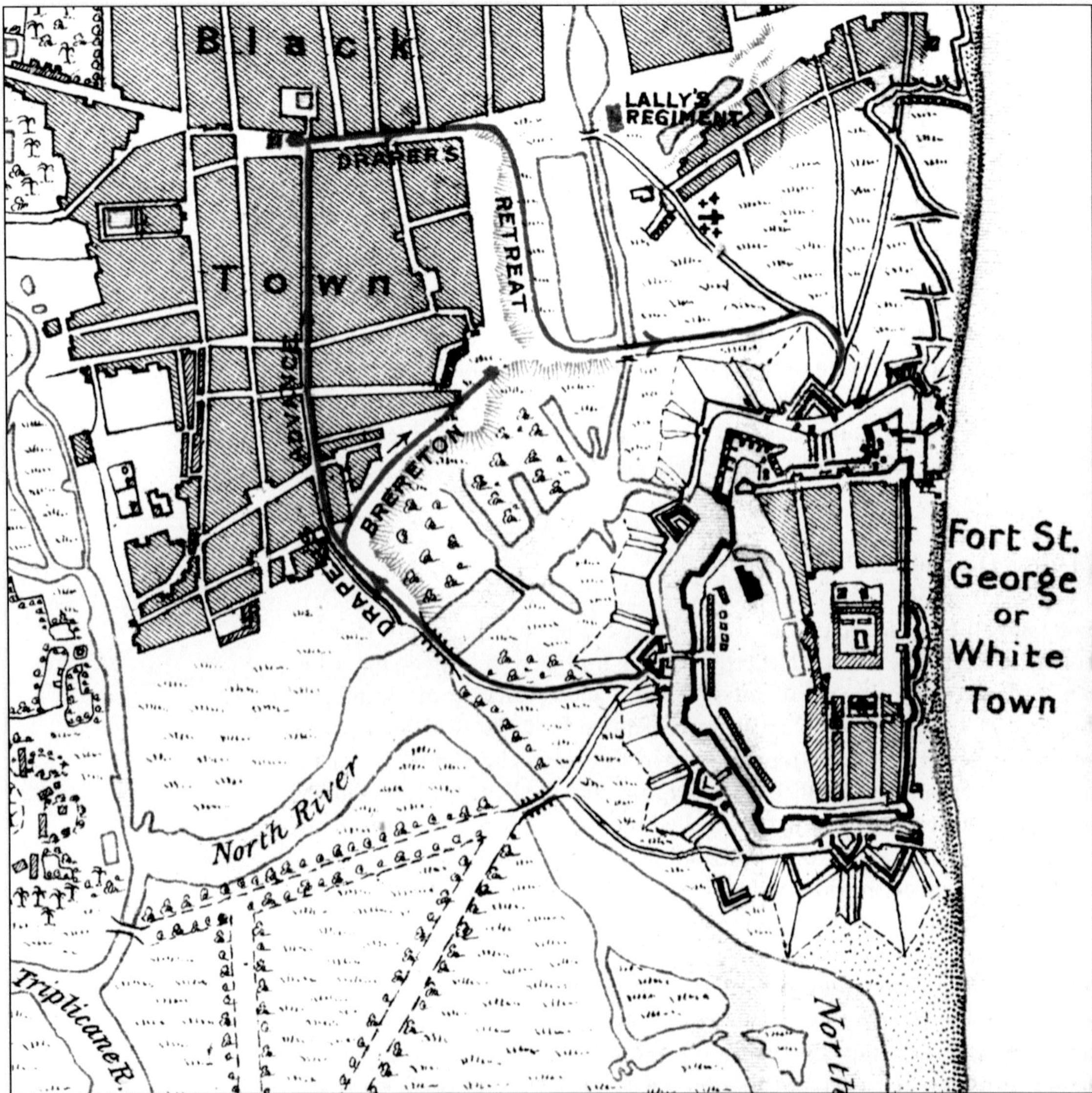

Plan of the 14 December 1758 sortie from Fort St George in Madras. Fortescue's *History of the British Army*, Vol.2. (Author's photo)

Brereton of 100 men to cover the retreat, which cost some 200 casualties in Lally's force. Nevertheless the French rallied and chased the British, who also had about the same number of killed and wounded, back to Fort St George. Thereafter, French siege batteries pounded the fort for weeks. In spite of repulsing a French assault on 9 February 1759, the garrison's position was becoming untenable. Fortunately for the British, Pocock's Royal Navy ships appeared with troops on board on the 16th and the siege ended. Lally hurriedly withdrew leaving some 52 guns behind.

Further north, an Indo-British force 500 Europeans and 2,000 sepoys under Lieutenant Colonel Forde was sent down from Calcutta to support Raja Anunderraj of the Northern Sirkars who had revolted against the French and occupied Vizagapatam, which Forde's troops reached on 20 October 1758. Commandant Conflans there had about the same number

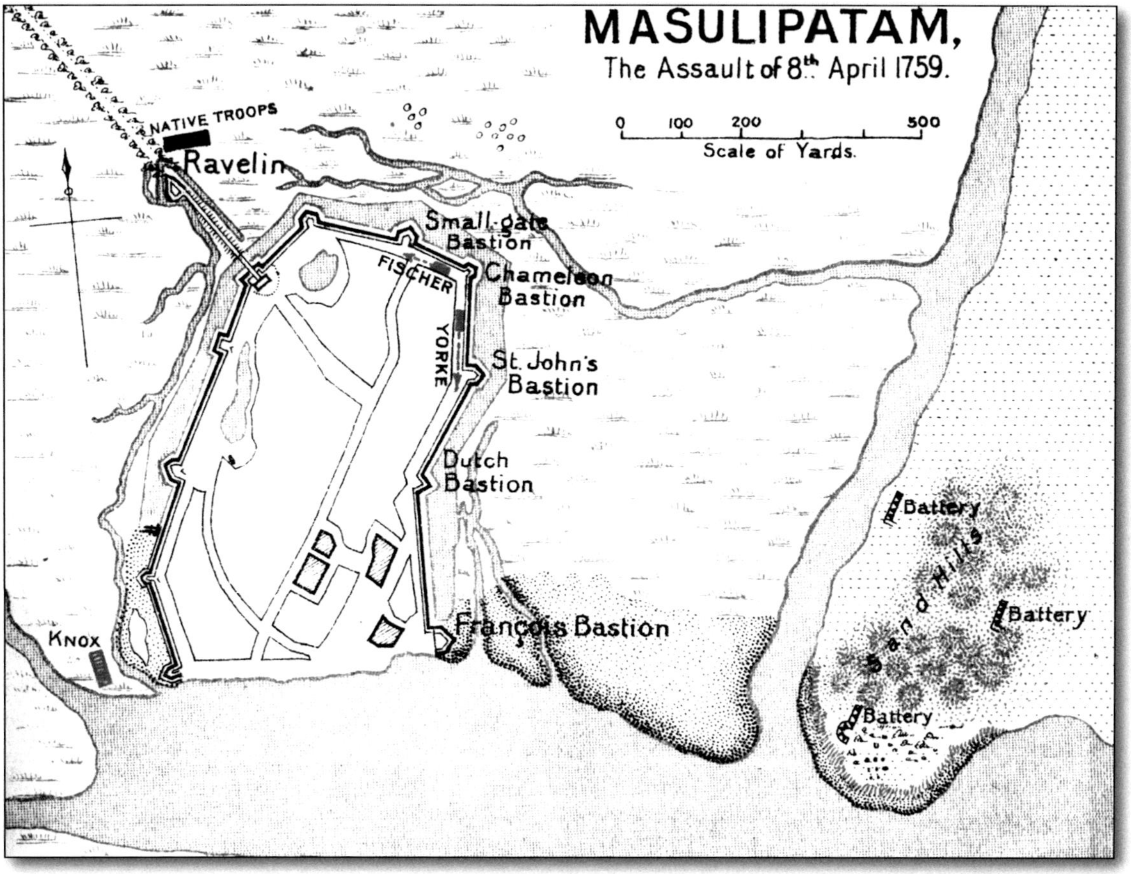

Plan of the British assault of 8 April 1759 on Masulipatam. Fortescue's *History of the British Army*, Vol.2. (Author's photo)

of French and sepoys, less Indian allied soldiers. Conflans proved to be the lesser tactician and Forde's troops eventually arrived in front of Masulipatam on 6 March 1759. The was one of the most important French fortified lodges on the Coromandel coast. Its siege started the next day and the place was taken by assault on 8 April. The Compagnie des Indes' troops and prestige in the Deccan, Bengal and now the Sirkars, so high in the days of Dupleix, had largely vanished. Viceroy Salabat Jing was compelled to recognise British authority a month later.

In the Carnatic, there were many manoeuvres and engagements during the rest of the year that slowly drove back Lally's forces towards Pondicherry and its adjacent territories. Morale in the army had sunk since Lally's 'bad success at Madras' because many did not forgive him 'for having been unfortunate; and on his side he did not forgive those who hated him.' The pressure was not only military; the treasury coffers were still empty creating considerable problem for the cohesion of the army. Lally's violent criticism of the company's management did nothing to raise spirits. In October, part of the Pondicherry garrison mutinied for lack of pay. Oddly enough the ringleader was suspected to be a Jesuit chaplain. A desperate arrangement by the Pondicherry council was the issue of 5,000,000 livres in credit notes to pay soldiers and supplies. Doubts as to the likelihood of ever being paid in actual money depressed the value of the notes by some 80 percent so that everyone

Fusilier, Compagnies franches de la Marine, 1750s. Detachments of marines from warships of the king's navy served in India, notably at the sieges of Madras in 1746, Pondicherry in 1748, with Bussy's troops in the Deccan during 1751 and Lally's troops in 1758-1761. The uniform was a grey-white coat with blue collar, cuffs, turn backs, waistcoat and breeches, yellow metal buttons and hat lace, white gaiters. Watercolour by Michel Pétard. (National Historic Sites, Parks Canada)

lost money. Groups of mutinous soldiers were increasingly flaunting military discipline that could hardly be enforced by soldiers who were unpaid. Of some 500 French company soldiers taken at Trichinopoly that were exchanged for an equal number of British prisoners, 200 mutinied and 60 of those deserted to the British![8]

A glimmer of hope appeared over the horizon on 10 September 1759 with the return of d'Aché's fleet, but he was met by Pocock's Royal Navy ships at Cuddalore and withdrew to Pondicherry after a two hour battle with Pocock unable to follow him. He brought 380,000 livres in money and 400,000 livres in diamonds into Pondicherry on 16 September. Lally and the council begged him to stay, but to no avail. D'Aché sailed away on 27 September abandoning French India to its fate.

Another slight glimmer was the news from France that Bussy was promoted to *brigadier* and second in command of the troops in India. Lally, who disliked Bussy, tasked him to use his diplomatic skills to convince the relatively neutral Bassalet Jing to support the French; the Indian prince was no fool and flatly refused. Lally did obtain 2,000 cavalrymen from the Marathas.

Wandewash 1760

The fortress town of Wandewash held by the French was said to be the most important in the province of Arcot and thus the key to its conquest. In September 1759, a first British attempt to take it had been repulsed. But, as Voltaire put it, only 'delayed its future ruin'. Sure enough, the Indo-British army led by Colonel Eyre Coote was south of the Palear River and invested the town of Wandewash on 27 November 1759, which was breached on the 30th and capitulated. Nearby Carangooly was invested on 3 December and surrendered on the 10th. Lally absolutely had to retake Wandewash to protect Pondicherry and, by 10 January 1760, advanced his army towards that town. Coote marched out to engage him.[9]

On the early morning 22 January 1760, Coote's advance guard reached the vicinity of Wandewash. Some 3,000 troopers of Lally's Mahratta cavalry charged the Indo-British, but were driven off when two British guns opened fire at close range causing heavy casualties. The main Indo-British force now arrived formed in two battle lines. Coote very skilfully manoeuvred his troops

8 Voltaire, *Fragments sur l'Inde*, pp.106, 112; Hanotaux and Martneau (eds), *Histoire des colonies françaises et de l'expansion de la France dans le Monde*, Vol.5, p.241.

9 Voltaire, *Fragments sur l'Inde*, p.111.

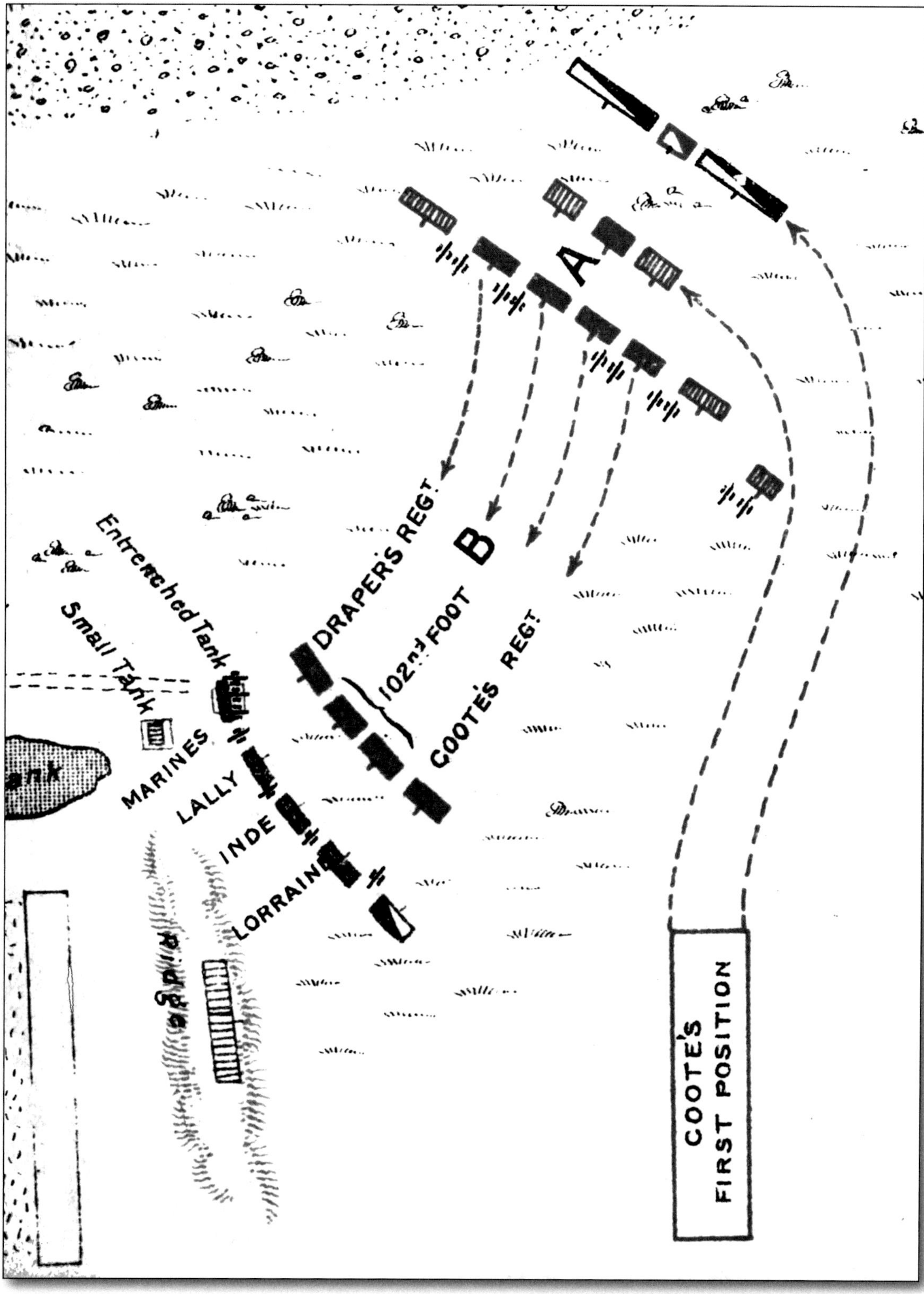

Plan of the battle of Wandewash, 22 January 1760. Note that the '102nd Foot' was the 1861-1881 denomination of the Madras European Regiment, which formed the centre of the line at Wandewash. Fortescue's *History of the British Army*, Vol.2. (Author's photo)

so as to permit communications with the besieged garrison of Wandewash while menacing the French army's flank and rear. Lally hurriedly came out with the whole Indo-French army, so Coote predisposed his troops in an oblique line forcing Lally to place his troops in a single line parallel to Coote's line. It was about noon. From his right were European cavalry troopers, the Régiment de Lorraine Regiment, the Bataillon de l'Inde and Régiment de Lally on the left with marines serving four guns in an entrenchment for a total of 2,250 Europeans supported by 1,300 sepoys. Coote's army was now placed in three lines made up of Draper's 79th Regiment, the Madras European Regiment and Coote's 84th Regiment, with Royal Artillerymen serving 16 guns for a total of about 2,000 Europeans, 2,100 sepoys and 1,250 Indian cavalry troopers, the sepoys and cavalry forming most of the second and third lines.

Coote's line advanced. When still out of range, Lally's European cavalry and notably the German hussars charged and scattered Coote's Indian cavalry making up most of his third line until it came up to British sepoys, European cavalrymen, and two guns that fired at point blank range. This broke up the charge and the hussars retreated. The Indo-British troops then halted while French guns fired largely out of range. An excited Lally ordered his line to advance while Coote's lines, in typical British fashion, waited for the opponents to come into close range to fire. At about one in the afternoon, the range closed and volleys were fired. Lally then formed the Régiment de Lorraine into a column of 12 men wide ordering a bayonet charge, a typical French battlefield practice. The British soldiers of Coote's 79th opened fire at close range causing heavy casualties, but still the brave Lorraine soldiers penetrated the line, only to be overwhelmed on their flanks, the survivors running away and spreading fear amongst Indo-French sepoys.

As the Indo-French troops were being rallied, a British shot hit a French tumbril full of ammunition causing a huge explosion that swept about 80 men including their commander the Chevalier de Poet at the marine's entrenchment battery, the survivors fleeing in panic followed by sepoys nearby. Bussy, who commanded the left flank, brought the Régiment de Lally to cover the breach, but Draper's 79th Regiment was already on the spot and, after various manoeuvres, surrounded Bussy and part of the Régiment de Lally who were made prisoners. The battle was now essentially lost and the Bataillon de l'Inde that held the centre of the French line retreated in good order with the sepoys who had refused to obey Lally's questionable order to charge the British. The Indo-French army suffered about 600 Europeans casualties of which some 200 perished and 160 were made prisoners. The Indo-British had 63 killed and 124 wounded. The sepoys on both sides had few casualties as this battle involved mainly European soldiers.

The morale of the French troops sank even lower. The night after the battle, Busy, who was now prisoner on parole in Coote's camp, spoke to a few French deserters who claimed to speak for some 700 of their absconded comrades who wished to rejoin their units if Lally would grant them a pardon.[10]

10 *London Gazette*, 23 September 1760; Fortescue, *A History of the British Army*, Vol.2, pp.463-469; Martineau, *Bussy*, pp.281-285; Chassaigne, *Lally*, pp.120-134.

Fall of Pondicherry 1760-1761

Following his decisive victory at Wandewash Coote did not immediately march on Pondicherry, wisely putting the priority on attacking the outlying forts and towns that flew the French standard. Lally first withdrew to the next to impregnable fortress of Gingee possibly hoping to lure the British into a lengthy and costly siege. Coote left him there and took Chittapet on 29 January 1760, Timmery on 2 February, Arcot on 9 February, Trinomalee on 29 February, Permacoil and Alumparva in early March. He sent a strong force under Major Monson with Royal Navy assistance to take the important port of Carical that surrendered on 5 April. These garrisons would have been troops of the company whose losses were substantial. Just for Chittapet, Timmery and Arcot, the total rose to at least 417 Europeans and 600 sepoys made prisoner apart from the unknown number of casualties and deserters. Not only were Europeans absconding, but there were *Caffres* deserting and 'crowds' of sepoys who were greeted by the British who paid them regularly.[11]

View of Pondicherry in 1760. There are many plans, but few views of the city. This view shows the citadel and the curtain walls at the city's centre as seen from the harbour. The white standard of France is prominent. (Print of a photo taken of a document in 1935 at the Tanjore palace library and reproduced in Chassaigne's *Le Comte de Lally*)

Since 18 March 1760, 14 Royal Navy warships had been blockading sea access to Pondicherry. Lally, who came back to the city, at last realised that part of his remaining troops in outlying garrisons would be lost and ordered most of them to regroup in the city. The French collapse worried Hyder Ali, ruler of Mysore, who was an admirer of the armament, fast volley fire, discipline, manoeuvres, uniform clothing, orderly and administrative practices of European troops compared to those of the ineffective Mughal armies. Once in power, he transformed his army by modernising its

11 Chettiput: 142 French (including the Chevalier de Tilly and 4 officers), 300 sepoys, nine guns; Timmery: one *sergent* and 30 men, six guns; Arcot: eight officers, 236 men, about 300 sepoys, 22 guns and four mortars. As per *London Gazette*, 23 September 1760; *New York Gazette*, 8 December 1760; Voltaire, *Fragments sur l'Inde*, pp.114-116. The troops were owed 10 months' pay.

'Hyder Ally, Commandant et Chef des Mahrattes', late 1750s-early 1760s. This print published in Paris seemingly during 1762 appears to be from a likeness made by a European artist in India, being attributed to one 'J. Year, del.' According to Typoo Zaeb's memoirs, he and his generals wore a uniform he had conceived consisting of a white silk jacket with golden flowers and yellow lining and cords, a white silk waist sash and a red and orange turban. (Anne S.K. Brown Military Collection)

armament with flintlock muskets, sought French artillery, trained his troops according to European manoeuvres and procured red uniforms for them like the sepoys in European service. His army was thus becoming potentially more effective to face European troops. Diplomatically, he leaned more toward the French who were the only ones able to restrain the increasing power and influence of the British so as to keep a balance and thus provide more independence for princely states such as Mysore.

Hyder Ali and the Pondicherry superior council entered into something like a mutual assistance agreement on 30 April 1760. He would detach 6,000 men from his army, half of them cavalry, in return for 10 cannon, the towns of Dourgour and Elevanassour, and half of the conquests and booty taken from the British. In the next few months, the French troops were trickling back into Pondicherry. The Mysore corps totally defeated on 17 July an Indo-British detachment sent to check its advance and did indeed approach the Pondicherry area led by Hyder Ali's trusted brother-in-law Hussein and Noclon Sahib. They were cautious as their intelligence reported the gradual withdrawal of Lally and his diminishing troops. It was obviously too late to help the French so they gradually withdrew back to Mysore.[12]

Relieved of Hyder Ali, Coote did not yet have a strong enough army to successfully invest and besiege Pondicherry in August. Reinforcements arrived on 2 September consisting of more Honourable East India Company troops and half of Morris's 89th Highland Regiment with more Royal Navy warships. Two days later, Lally made a raid aiming to surprise the British camp, but this unluckily miscarried for the gallant French troops who were repulsed. By mid-September, the city was effectively blockaded. By then, the money had run out since August to pay the 1,100 sepoys and they deserted in massive numbers.[13]

One of the unfortunate incidents of the siege affecting negatively its defence was due to undiplomatic Lally, who by late September, had disgusted nearly all the European civilian men able to bear arms in the city by his imperious ways. To make the British believe that the regular garrison was very numerous, he ordered all European civilians to parade on the beach outside the city's walls armed and 'wearing uniforms'. Only members of the council and religious orders were exempted. What happened instead was a large crowd of the company's employees and merchants, many of them armed, filled the courtyard of Lally's residence

12 E. Guénin, 'Documents inédits sur l'histoire et la géographie de l'Inde française', *Bulletin de la Société Académique Indo-Chinoise*, Volume 1 (1881), p.83.

13 The most extensive account of the siege of Pondicherry seems to be in Chassaigne, *Lally*, chapters 11 to 13.

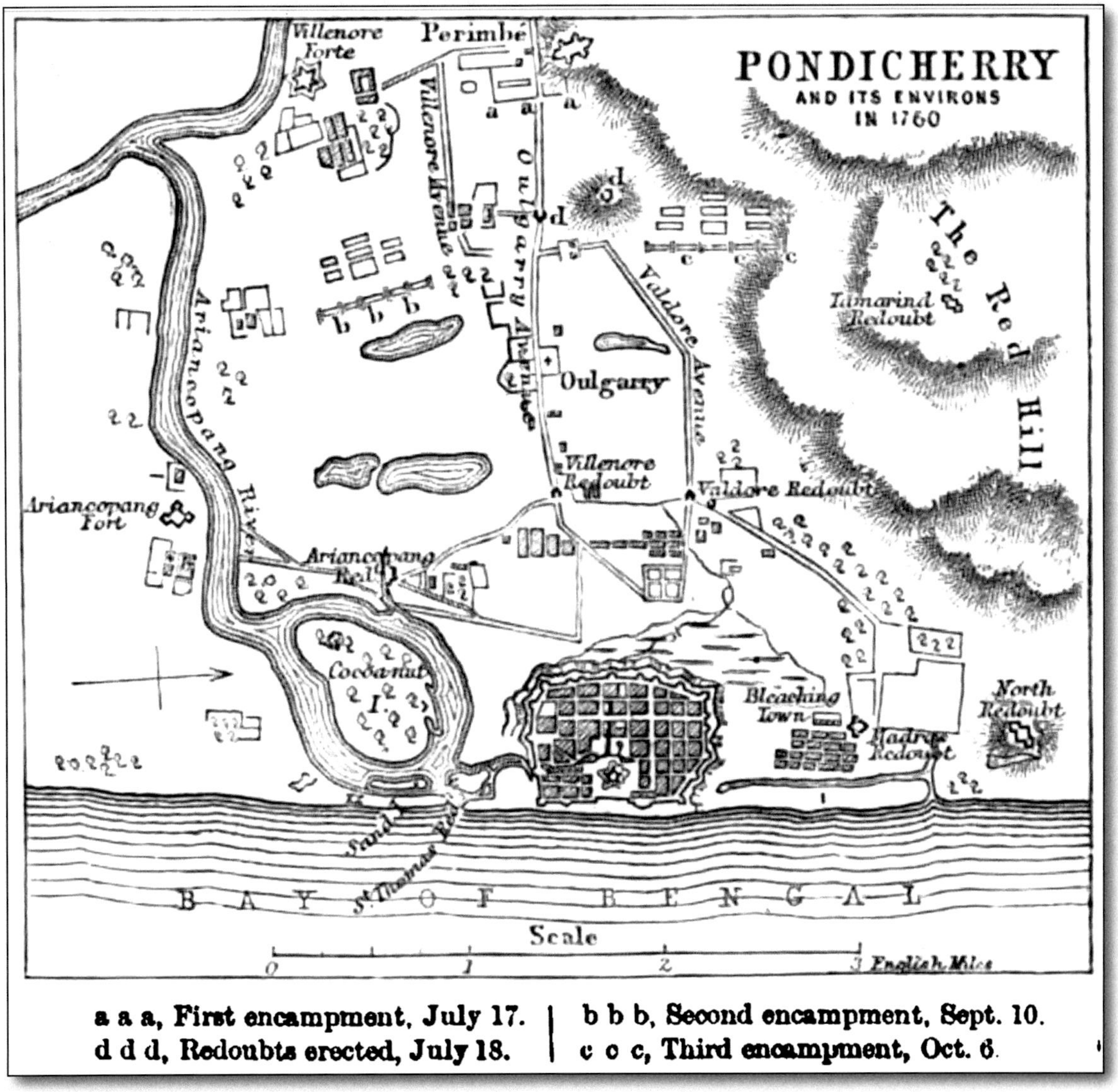

Plan of the siege of Pondicherry, 1760. Beveridge's 1862 *A Comprehensive History of India*. (Author's photo)

shouting that they would not muster outside the walls nor wear uniforms since they were civilians and not soldiers and would only obey Governor de Leyrit. Lally, who had stayed indoors rather than face his critics, made the ultimate 'public relations disaster' by having the protesters disarmed by a couple of grenadiers companies with fixed bayonets and arresting a few council members. From then on, Lally had lost all moral authority and was utterly despised by just about every European civilian in the city. Placards damning him appeared posted in the streets; a plot to free the council members was rumoured; many inhabitants now felt he had betrayed the king and the nation and he even found a note with a death threat. As weeks passed and conditions degraded in the city, its population as well as a presumably substantial part of the garrison had no confidence left in their commander. In October 1760, the number of European men that could contribute to Pondicherry's defence was estimated at 2,741 not including

The Comte de Lally in the last days of the siege of Pondicherry, January 1761. His mood is suitably shown as sombre. Print after Philippoteaux in Guizot's 1876 *Histoire de France*. (Author's photo)

a few dismounted cavalrymen, about 40 of Lally's guardsmen, sailors and hospitalised men.[14]

At midnight on 9 December, the guns in four new British batteries started to bombardment the city, which did not seem to have been intense. By the later part of December, nearly all food supplies had been expended including animals; even cats and rats were on the menu (see chapter 16 for details on rations during the siege). From 31 December 1760 to 2 January 1761, a very violent hurricane descended upon Pondicherry and its harbour. Three Royal Navy ships sank with all hands, three more were driven ashore, three lost all their masts and a fourth most of them; only two were less affected including the flagship blown away offshore. The winds also devastated the British field fortifications just outside the city and it was even hoped that the siege might end. Such optimism soon fell to near despair as the ships blown away came back while field fortifications were repaired within a week. By 12 January, there remained only two days of already much reduced rations left in Pondicherry.

On 15 January, the city's capitulation was agreed to. The next day, Orme related:

> In the afternoon, the garrison drew up under arms on the parade before the citadel, the English troops facing them. Colonel Coote then reviewed the line, which, exclusive of commissioned officers, invalids, and others who had hid themselves, amounted to 1,100, all wearing the face of famine, fatigue, or disease. The grenadiers of Lally and Lorraine, once the ablest-bodied men in the army, appeared the most impaired, having constantly put themselves forward to every service; and it was recollected that from their first landing, throughout all the services of the field, and all the distresses of the blockade, not a man of them had ever deserted to the English army. The victor soldier gave his sigh (which none but banditti could refuse) to this solemn contemplation of the fate of war, which might have been his own.[15]

14 Antoine Fantin-Desodoards (trans.), *Révolutions de l'Inde pendant le dix-huitième siècle ou mémoires de Typoo-Zaeb*, (Paris: Bridal, 1796), Vol.2, pp.338-339; Voltaire, *Fragments sur l'Inde*, pp.122-124; Hamont, *La fin d'un empire français aux Indes*, pp.255-259; Chassaigne, *Lally*, p.202.

15 Orme, *Military transactions*, Vol.2, No. 2, pp.722-723.

The state of the French troops at the surrender of Pondicherry, 15 January 1761, stood as follows:

King's Troops:

- Artillery: one *lieutenant-colonel*, one *major*, one *capitaine*, one *lieutenant-en-premier*, one surgeon-major, two secretaries, three artificers, six miners, one volunteer, one *sergent-major*, 11 *sergents*, eight *caporaux*, four *anspesades* and 42 gunners. Total: 83.
- Régiment de Lorraine: one *lieutenant-colonel*, 16 *capitaines*, 13 *lieutenants-en-premier*, three *lieutenants-en-second*, one chaplain, one adjutant, one surgeon-major, two secretaries, one *sergent-major*, 28 *sergent*, one drum-major, seven drummers, 43 *caporaux*, 31 *anspesades* and 178 privates. Total: 327.
- Régiment de Lally: one *lieutenant-colonel*, 13 *capitaines*, 14 *lieutenants-en-premier*, one quartermaster, one surgeon-major; one *sergent-major*, 20 *sergents*, one drum-major, 10 drummers, 139 privates and 29 invalids. Total: 230.
- Compagnies franches de la Marine: seven *capitaines*, six *lieutenants-en-premier*, two *lieutenants-en-second*, one adjutant, one secretary, 278 non-commissioned officers and men. Total: 295.

Total King's troops: 935.

Company's Troops,

- Artillery: two *capitaines*, five *lieutenants-en-premier*, two *lieutenants-en-second*, four *enseignes*, one adjutant, one commissary, two assistants, nine volunteers, one *sergent-major*, 10 *sergents*, one drum-major, three drummers, six *caporaux* and 45 gunners. Total: 94.
- Cavalry: one *capitaine*, two *lieutenants-en-premier* and 12 privates. Total: 15.
- Bataillon de l'Inde: one *major*, 12 *capitaines*, 11 *lieutenants-en-premier*, 10 *lieutenants-en-second*, 10 *enseignes*; one chaplain, one adjutant, one surgeon-major, two secretaries, one *sergent-major*, 17 *sergent*, one drum-major, 10 drummers, 15 *caporaux* and 99 privates. Total: 192.
- Invalids: one *major*, one adjutant, one captain of the gates, three secretaries, one *sergent-major*, 22 *sergents*, one drummer, 15 *caporaux* and 79 privates. Total: 124.
- Volunteers of Bourbon: one *capitaine*, one *lieutenant-en-second*, three *enseignes*, one adjutant, one *sergent-major*, two *sergents*, one drummer, four *caporaux*, two *anspesades* and 24 privates. Total: 40.

Total: Company's troops: 465.

Grand total: 1,400.[16]

16 *The Daily Advertiser* (London), 22 July 1761. Voltaire, *Fragments sur l'Inde*, p.124 mentions the garrison as 700 French and 300 sepoys, which was obviously a too low estimate.

The Comte d'Estaing's Naval Raids 1759-1760

Apart from the fighting on mainland India, there were also some actions in other areas due to the daring Charles-Henri, Comte d'Estaing, a scion of ancient French nobility. In the spring of 1759, he had been captured by the British during the failed attack on Madras and was released on parole on the condition that he would not fight in India. He accordingly left India and arrived at Ile de France on 14 June 1759. He became interested in serving at sea and learned all he could about sailing. His objective was to be able to conduct naval raids on British establishments outside of India. Governor-General Magon at Ile de France supported his ambitions and allowed him to use two ships of the Compagnie des Indes with their crews as well as detaching 100 soldiers of the island's garrison, 60 volunteers and 200 Africans *Caffre* soldiers to serve as marines and assault troops. D'Estaing used his own money to finance the expedition.[17]

The *Condé*, 50 guns, and *Expédition* sailed on 1 September 1759 and, on 3 October captured the *Mamoudy*, a large 600-ton merchant ship, along with a few small craft. Two days later, d'Estaing attacked Muscat (Sultanate of Oman) situated near the entrance of the Gulf of Oman, whose Iman was friendly to the British, captured the 26-gun British ship *Merry*, bombarded Muscat's harbour fortifications and sailed away.[18]

On 13 October, the French squadron appeared before Bandar Abbas on the northern shore of the Strait of Hormuz. The governor of this Persian (now Iranian) port had ceded land to the British Honourable East India Company to build a factory and a fort to coordinate and protect its trade route going into Arabia as far as Bagdad. Until that day, it was a very quiet area. The British fort's garrison was very small and it capitulated the next day after a British frigate, the *Speedwell*, ran aground trying to get away. The fort was blown up and d'Estaing sailed east from the Gulf of Oman. While he crossed the Indian Ocean, he captured several ships so that he had a small squadron by the time he reached Sumatra.

On 7 February 1760, he was off Fort Natal, one of the British Honourable East India Company's establishments on the island of Sumatra, whose defenders seeing 'two large French ships' surrendered the same day. On 3 April, d'Estaing landed his troops near Fort Marlborough at Bencoolen, the main British factory on Sumatra, which capitulated immediately followed by all its minor outstations on the island. The French force at Bencoolen eventually departed after destroying the fort and the outstations. Some

17 Robert Calmon-Maison, *L'amiral d'Estaing 1729-1794* (Pari: Calman-Levy, 1910), pp.45-78; Léon Guérin, *Les marins illustres de la France* (Paris: Belin-Leprieur, 1846), pp.596-597. At the Battle of Bouvines on 27 July 1214, the Comte d'Estaing had saved King Philippe-Auguste at a critical moment. The grateful king had honoured the family by granting it the use of the royal arms and livery, a unique privilege.

18 On the Sultanate of Oman's fortifications and arms, see Ruth Rhynas Brown and Robert Douglas Smith, 'The Forts and Castles of Oman', *ICOMAM Magazine – Sutanate of Oman Special Issue* (Summer 2011), pp.10-17, 24-31, 86-88.

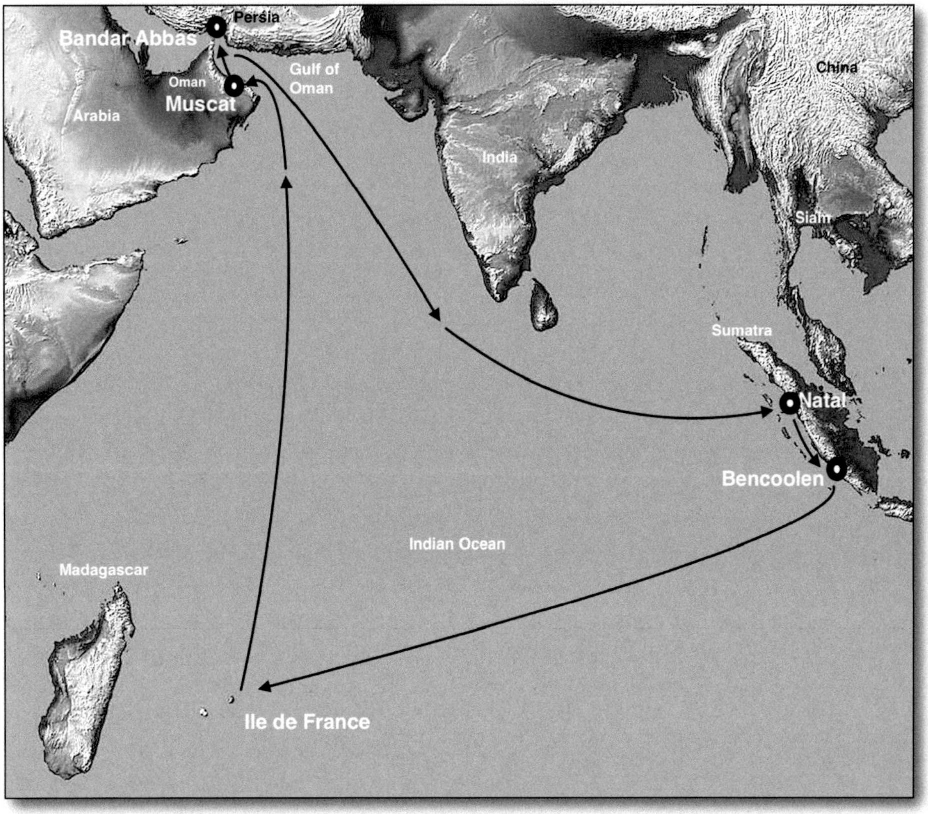

Map of the Indian Ocean showing the wide ranging 1759-1760 raids of Count d'Estaing. (NASA – digital overlays by the author)

View of d'Estaing's raid on the harbour of Muscat, 5 October 1759. The French squadron burst into the harbour of Muscat, the main port of pro-British sultan of Oman, captured two ships and destroyed the merchant ships. Print after Duplessis. (Bibliothèque Nationale de France, Paris)

British soldiers and sepoys left at Bencoolen did what they could to guard the place until relief finally arrived during 1761.[19]

As for d'Estaing and his men, they eventually arrived in France when its repeatedly-defeated navy was near to being the nation's shame. Their victorious raids were thus lauded as saving the nation's honour at sea.

19 Alan Harfield, *Bencoolen A History of the Honourable East India Company's Garrison on the West Coast of Sumatra 1685-1825* (Barton-on-Sea: A and J Partnership, 1995), pp.171-183; Dull, *The French Navy in the Seven Year's War*, p.173.

12

Aftermath

The Fate of Lally

The Comte de Lally certainly had many shortcomings, but he was nevertheless a brave general who impressed his opponent. Colonel Coote later wrote that no one could have a higher opinion of Lally than himself. Lally had prevailed over obstacles that Coote thought to be insurmountable and that there was not other man in India that could have kept his army together without pay nor any other resources. What Coote probably did not know in detail was Lally's violently abrasive and intemperate character spiced with all manners of tantrums, insults and threats. This in an age when genteel manners and politeness were prized amongst the aristocratic French. The predictable reaction of most French officials, officers and enlisted men quickly resulted in a total lack of respect for, and confidence in, their hated commander-in-chief. It was even said that an onlooking Indian prince wondered for what reason had King Louis XV sent a crazy general as the Governor-General of French India.

These opinions and gossips arrived in France in the form of about 200 officers sent back with Lally after the fall of Pondicherry. Royal government and Compagnie des Indes officials were horrified. Back in Paris, Lally was arrested and sent to the Bastille prison, spending 19 months there without being interrogated. He wished a military court martial to judge his conduct. However, French opinion in all classes of society abhorred and blamed him for all the defeats of the Seven Years War. For the government and the Compagnie des Indes, he was thus the perfect scapegoat. Accused of high treason, his trial began in December 1764 with 160 charges against him and nearly 200 witnesses in procedures that dragged on for a year and a half. On 6 May 1766, he was found guilty and beheaded three days later. By then, there were acrimonious disputes between those who wanted him dead and those that thought it was a parody of justice. In Voltaire's opinion, Lally's trial culminated in 'a murder using the sword of justice.'[1]

---

1 Chassaigne, *Lally*, chapters 14 to 18; Voltaire, *Fragments sur l'Inde*, p.156; O'Callaghan, *History of the Irish Brigades*, pp.505-579. Lally's trial was later reviewed and charges against

The Comte de Lally, circa 1766. He proved unequal to the admittedly difficult task of repulsing the British, surrendered Pondicherry in January 1761 and, back in France, was beheaded for treason in 1766. This print shows him in prison wearing his mantle of the Order of Saint-Louis. (Private collection, author's photo.)

Fate of India's French Garrison

The British treated the French officers relatively correctly according to the usual practices in European armies when it came to officers and gentlemen. Lally and many officers were shipped back to France, but many others waited in India. One of the officers surrendering at Pondicherry on 15 January 1761 that was kept in India related that the 'officers who were prisoners of war were authorised to find a residence, of their own choice, on the coast of Coromandel.' They remained for several months or even years until sent to Europe. After a while, being captive was not especially pleasing and some accepted offers of Indian princes to serve in their armies.[2]

The treatment of French NCOs and soldiers that became prisoners of war following the fall of Pondicherry is one of the regrettable aspects that was seemingly unknown, or, worse, ignored by the British authorities. Many of those humble NCOs and men in India had a terrible fate at the hand of the British Honourable East India Company personnel. According to one prisoner, *Sergent* René Madec of the company's troops, the 'unfortunate prisoners of our nation were submitted by the victors, in the prisons of Madras, to unimaginably bad treatments. Many perished; others, to escape the same fate…accepted to serve in the British corps in Bengal.' With some 105 other prisoners, Madec enlisted in a unit in Bengal led by one Martin-Lion, a French marine he had known at Masulipatam. Years passed, Madec and his comrades fought bravely with the Indo-British troops in 1763-1764 against the troops of Shuja-ud-doulah's, nabob of Oude and one of the most powerful princes of India. He was one of the first Indian princes to foresee and oppose the total British domination of India. Madec later opined that 'without the help of the French [soldiers in British service], not only would they [British] have failed to take Bengal; they would not have tried to conquer it.' The nabob was impressed by the military qualities of his French opponents and henceforth sought to recruit them. Many French soldiers had secretly vowed to abscond from near slavery conditions. Their chance came in what was later remembered as the 'first sepoy mutiny' in mid-August 1764 during which some 250 French and two British soldiers, who were owed 22

him were found to be excessive, especially regarding treason. His memory was rehabilitated in 1780.

2 Voltaire, *Fragments sur l'Inde*, pp.132-133; '[Lettres et souvenirs de Du Tour de Noirfosse, officier de l'armée des Indes', *Carnet de la Sabretache*, Vol.IX (1901), p.595. Du Tour de Noirfosse (1732-1818) could not stand such confinement and sought to get back to France although he was approached by Bassalet Sing (or Jung) to command his sepoys against the British. His adventurous escape in 1762 led him to Muscat in the Persian Gulf, Bagdad, Aleppo and Cyprus landing at Marseille in March 1763.

Pondicherry in 1769. Part of the city was still in ruins following its destruction by the British after its capitulation. Some new buildings are also seen and many more were built during the 1770s. A: artillery workshop; B: general store; C and D: new and ruined Capuchin missionary convent; E: a house; FF: ruins of the citadel; G: flag pole; HH: ruins of government house; HI: observatory; K: well. Print in Gentil's *Voyage*. (Author's photo)

months of pay, ran off to Benares led by Madec to join Shuja-ud-doulah. The following years and decades would see Indian princes hiring Madec and many others to train their armies in European ways of war.[3]

What then became of the French prisoners of war that refused to enlist as soldiers of the British Honourable East India Company? Madec's writings quoted above mention being submitted to unspeakably horrid treatment by the British victors. *Colonel* Gentil also stated that the French prisoners were all forced to enlist in their army. Not all did.

Service records with narratives of enlisted men are few. The record of *Caporal* François Chauffray of the Compagnie des Indes' artillery initially seems like another application for a pension, but reading on more pages reveals a tale of horrors. Taken prisoner of war at Pondicherry on 16 January 1761, he was treated outrageously by the British. Sent to Trichinopoly, he was 'thrown in a ditch 22 feet deep full of water where I remained 29 consecutive months in the most awful misery after which I was transferred to Madras where I remained three months.' One is amazed that he survived physically and mentally. He was, with other surviving French prisoners of war, sent to France in 1763 on a British ship arriving at Le Havre in June 1764.[4]

3 Émile Barbé, *Le nabab René Madec* (Paris: Alcan 1894), pp.24-31. The quotations are from Madec's own writings; Gentil presented Madec to Shuja-ud-doulah as per his *Mémoires*, p.458. See also Fortescue, *A History of the British Army,* Vol.3, chapter V; Sheford Tidwell, *Swords for Hire European Mercenaries in Eighteen Century India* (London: Murray, 1971), pp.10-13. Madec's (1736-1784) opinion on the assistance provided by French soldiers in the British submission of Bengal may seem exaggerated, but it comes from an extraordinary soldier of the Compagnie des Indes army who rose from private in 1752 to successfully lead his own troops from 1764 to many victories and be honoured with the title of nabob in 1769. Back in France in 1779, he was knighted in the Order of Saint-Louis and ennobled by King Louis XVI.

4 AC, E, 76, service record of François Chauffray; Gentil, *Mémoires*, p.215. Other survivors likely had terrible tales of inhumane treatments, but we must recall that most of them were illiterate and that French public opinion simply wanted to forget the humiliations of the Seven Years War.

French Military Adventurers with Indian Princes

As it turned out, it was not quite over for the French in India. The 1763 Treaty of Paris returned the old lodges of Pondicherry (which had been systematically demolished by the British during their occupation of the city), Chandernagor, Carical and Mahé. The vision of a French empire was certainly defunct. On the other hand, the British Honourable East India Company certainly did not rule all of India either.

We have related above the forced enlistments or else the horrible treatments that awaited French soldiers that became prisoners of the British in 1761. Many managed to escape such a fate by deserting from the British or escaping from their compounds. Hyder Ali welcomed about a thousand in Mysore, most of whom joined his army, and the memoirs of his son draws a corner of the veil insofar as those French officers and soldiers that simply ran off into the countryside

> The ruin of Pondicherry filled [Mysore's Hyder Ali's] court with Frenchmen. They formed his main force; he went to [review] their battalions as a simple ordinary man, rendered a just homage to the precision of their manoeuvres, talked to them about vengeance and promised them nothing less than to bring them back victorious to their cities, from the smoking ruins of those of the British.[5]

This was in the south. Up north, Shuja-ud-doulah welcomed *Colonel* Gentil, of the Compagnie des Indes' troops, with several officers in 1765. This nabob was especially pleased that he could talk with Gentil without needing an interpreter. Many French soldiers and adventurers were also in his area. Shuja-ud-doulah asked Gentil if he could form a corps of 400 French soldiers for his army; he organised a battalion of 600 French fusiliers.[6]

Meanwhile, René Madec and about a thousand French, German, British and Indian sepoy military adventurers had gone on to serve in the forces of nabobs of the Great Mughal from 1765. Madec went on to serve the emperor himself at Delhi in 1772 with the rank of nabob thus becoming one of the most influential Frenchmen at the imperial court.[7]

---

5 Antoine Fantin-Desodoards (trans.), *Révolutions de l'Inde pendant le dix-huitième siècle ou mémoires de Typoo-Zaeb*, (Paris: Bridal, 1796), Vol.2, p.24; Guénin, 'Documents inédits', p.83.

6 Gentil, *Mémoires*, pp.6, 203, 262. More French military adventurers obviously came to Oude later on. In 1775, Gentil's French contingent numbered about 700 men. He went back to France in 1776, was received by King Louis XVI who thanked him for his services, both military and diplomatic, and awarded him the Order of Saint-Louis. He passed away in 1784. Much of his impressive collection went to the royal collection and is now in the Bibliothèque Nationale as can be seen by its courtesy through many illustrations in this book.

7 Madec went back to Pondicherry in 1777, was at its 1778 siege and fall to the British and went back to France in 1779 where he learned he had been promoted from *sergent* to *colonel* and awarded the Order of Saint-Louis for his military and diplomatic services in India. For details, see: Barbé, *Le nabab René Madec.* A short biography is also in Henry Lachouque, *Les vagabonds de la gloire* (Paris: Copernic, 1980), pp.31-54.

Left: *Colonel* Jean-Baptise-Joseph Gentil. Born in 1726, he came to India in 1752 as an officer in the troops of the Compagnie des Indes in which he served with distinction until the surrender of Chandernagor in 1757 and went on in the service of several Indian princes, later presented Indian ambassadors to King Louis XVI in 1778. He died in 1799. His posthumous *Mémoire sur l'Indoustan* is an outstanding source. This print after his portrait show him in the uniform of the company's troops in the style of the later 1760s with epaulettes. (Author's photo)

Right: Military adventurer René Madec, c. 1770. Print after portrait. (Author's photo)

While it is outside the parameters of this study, there can be no doubt that those former soldiers of the Compagnie des Indes certainly negatively affected the ambitions of the British Honourable East India Company. For a time, the troops of Meer Cossim (or Mir Kassim), nabob of Bengal, were also involved. Although the nabobs were somewhat unlucky in the field against the British during the 1760s and early 1770s, the overwhelming rule of India by the Honourable East India Company had to be postponed until the nineteenth century.[8]

Last Years of the Company's Troops in India 1765-1772

The 1763 Treaty of Paris gave back to France Pondicherry and some of its lodges in India. In early 1765, officials and troops of the Compagnie des Indes landed in Pondicherry that was now a largely devastated city. Lally had

8 See Fortescue, *A History of the British Army*, Vol.3 for an account of the 1760s-1790s campaigns.

destroyed Fort St David and much of Madras in 1758 so, in turn, Pondicherry was razed in April 1761. The British had notably destroyed the fortifications, the public buildings and some of the infrastructure. Much would have to be rebuilt, but amongst the first priorities was to have a secure environment. Some 500 soldiers of the company came from Lorient and about 400 sepoys were recruited. Commandant Law de Lauriston was now the governor and he reported in 1766 that his French soldiers had 'at least 130 invalids, the majority being disabled for service' while the sepoys would still need a lot of training. By 1770 the European soldiers were organised into a battalion of 10 companies of 56 men led by 40 officers, plus two companies of artillery totalling 100 men. The sepoys had six companies of 100 men each. About half were posted in Pondicherry and the rest at Chandernagor and Carical.[9]

The Compagnie des Indes closed its books in France during 1770 and the Ministry of the Navy of the royal government became responsible for the French posts in India. In distant Pondicherry and other lodges, the company's French and sepoy troops remained on guard with the same organisation for another two years. The royal order of 31 December 1772 created the Régiment de Pondicherry, which was organised in the following year as were the sepoys in 1774 by a royal ordinance signed in Versailles on 12 November 1773.[10]

9 Voltaire, *Fragments sur l'Inde*, p.132; S.P. Sen, *The French in India* (Calcutta: Firma, 1958), pp.63-64. Quotations of Law de Lauriston in this work are taken from the Pondicherry Archives, ms. 100; Reneld, *Les Cipahis de l'Inde* (Paris: Lavauzelle, 1891).

10 AC, D2C, 130, De par le Roy…Corps de Sipahis, 12 November 1773; Reneld, *Les Cipahis de l'Inde*; Sen, *The French in India*, p.64. Following India and Pakistan's independence from Great Britain in 1947, a plebiscite revealed that the overwhelming majority of the population of the French territories wished to join India which was done on 1 November 1954. The corps of sepoys had become a constabulary force that became the police thereafter.

13

Africa

The coast of West Africa was known to French traders since the Middle Ages. Early records mention two ships from Dieppe reaching the mouth of the Senegal River in December 1364 and conducting lucrative trading with the local inhabitants. More French merchants followed during many decades thereafter.

Senegal

A French Senegal trading company was created as early as 1626 and a trading 'factory' was set up in 1638 at Bieurt. Fort Saint-Louis was founded in 1659. The Dutch fort of Arguin was taken by the French on 29 August 1666, but not occupied. In early November 1677, the Comte d'Estrées' squadron captured Gorée and Arguin from the Dutch. D'Estrées did not leave troops there and destroyed the forts. Merchant captain Jean-Baptiste Ducasse, who would later go on to have a distinguished naval career, happened to be in the area from late November and foiled a Dutch attempt to retake Gorée. He then raided a few nearby African kingdoms that had killed some Frenchmen and sided with the Dutch. An army of 'thousands' of African warriors was defeated with many killed and towns destroyed by Ducasse. In 1678, he built the post of Albreda on the Gambia Rivier. The 1678 peace treaty ceded Gorée and Arguin to France and the Senegal company eventually rebuilt the forts. The capital of French Senegal was moved from Gorée to Saint-Louis in 1688.[1]

In early 1693, British ships from Gambia captured and ravaged both Saint-Louis and Gorée before sailing away. Retribution came in July 1696 when a French squadron under the Comte de Gennes attacked, captured and blew up Fort St James in Gambia. Exploration of the interior via the Senegal River led to the establishment of Fort Saint-Joseph in 1700 in the Galam area, some 300 leagues from the sea.

1 Jean-Baptiste Labat, *Nouvelle relation de l'Afrique occidentale* (Paris: Giffard, 1728), Vol.4, pp.110-126.

Map of Senegal, 1726. The fortified posts garrisoned by soldiers of the Compagnie des Indes are circled in black. The most important were Gorée and Saint-Louis, the capital. The penetration eastward of French explorer/traders went into the interior via the Senegal River as far as Galam (or Saint-Joseph). This map by G. Delisle is replete with notes on African kingdoms. (Dutch National Archives. AMH-7674-NA)

War broke out in Europe; on 18 April 1701, a British ship unsuccessfully attacked Saint-Louis. There were more small raids such as the Dutch raid on recently fortified Saint-Louis in November 1702, which attack was repulsed by the small garrison of 30 men and a substantial number of auxiliary Africans with allied warriors of the Issiny kingdom. Two years later, French ships took a British fort in Sierra Leone and Fort St James in Gambia. For all that, the monopoly companies were hardly reaping great profits as a result of warfare and, in 1705, the French in Senegal and the British in Gambia signed a neutrality agreement for that area. More forts that were really trading lodges were built, such as Saint-François in 1714, Portendick in 1717, Farabana in 1733, Bissau in 1735 and Podor in 1743.[2]

On the whole, although there might occasionally be some deadly incidents, Senegal was a stable territory with regards to relations with African populations and kingdoms. The most serious event occurred from the 1720s at Arguin, in the northern part of the Compagnie des Indes' concession, which was situated in present day Mauritania. The population there was termed as 'Trarza Maures' (Moors) of North African culture and Islamic faith; the hinterland was the western end of the Sahara desert. The Dutch, who claimed to be in the service of Brandenburg, plotted with local leaders

2 Robert Cornevin, *Histoire de l'Afrique* (Paris: Payot, 1966), pp.334-354, 364; *Mercure Galant*, June 1696, pp.222-231.

View of Fort Nassau on the hill seen from Orange Castle, Island of Goree, early 1670s. This contemporary Dutch print shows the interior of Orange Castle with unmounted cannons and rather neglected masonry walls. Such conditions would have helped the French when they attacked in November 1677. (Anne S.K. Brown Military Collection)

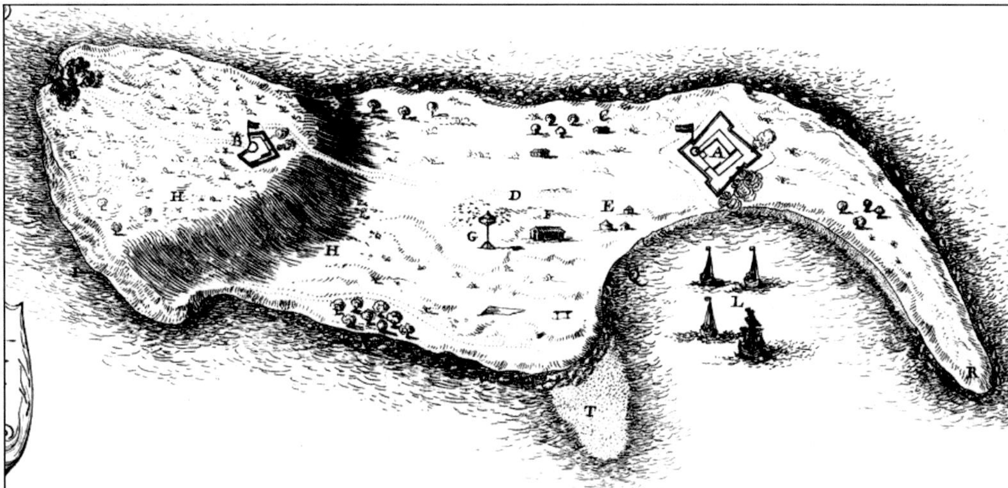

Plan of the island of Gorée, November 1677. This shows the aspect of the island when taken by French from the Dutch on 1 November 1677. Fortifications consisted only of Fort Nassau (A) and Orange Castle (B). C was a forge, D a road, E was quarters of the Africans, F a large storehouse. (Bibliothèque Nationale de France, Paris)

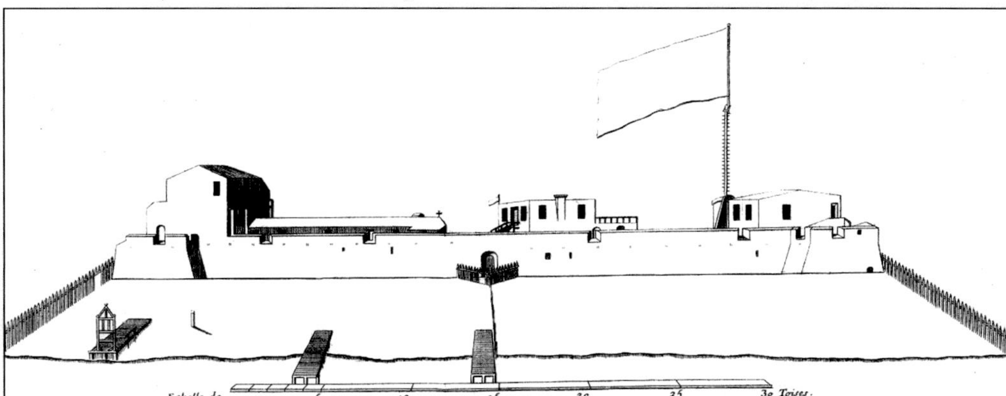

The fort at Saint-Louis, Senegal, 1720s. Plan from Labat's 1728 *Nouvelle relation de l'Afrique occidentale*. (Author's photo)

which led to their occupation of Arguin, and were also active in the vicinity of the French at Portendic, a post established three years earlier.

The Compagnie des Indes reacted by sending out a squadron of five ships from Lorient led by Périer de Salverte that arrived at Arguin on 26 February 1721. The Dutch garrison evacuated into the interior to join a party of Trarza Moors while Périer took possession of the fort and left a garrison of 40 men there under a director named Duval. Soon thereafter, a Dutch ship bearing a new governor arrived at Arguin and immediately met with Trarza Emir

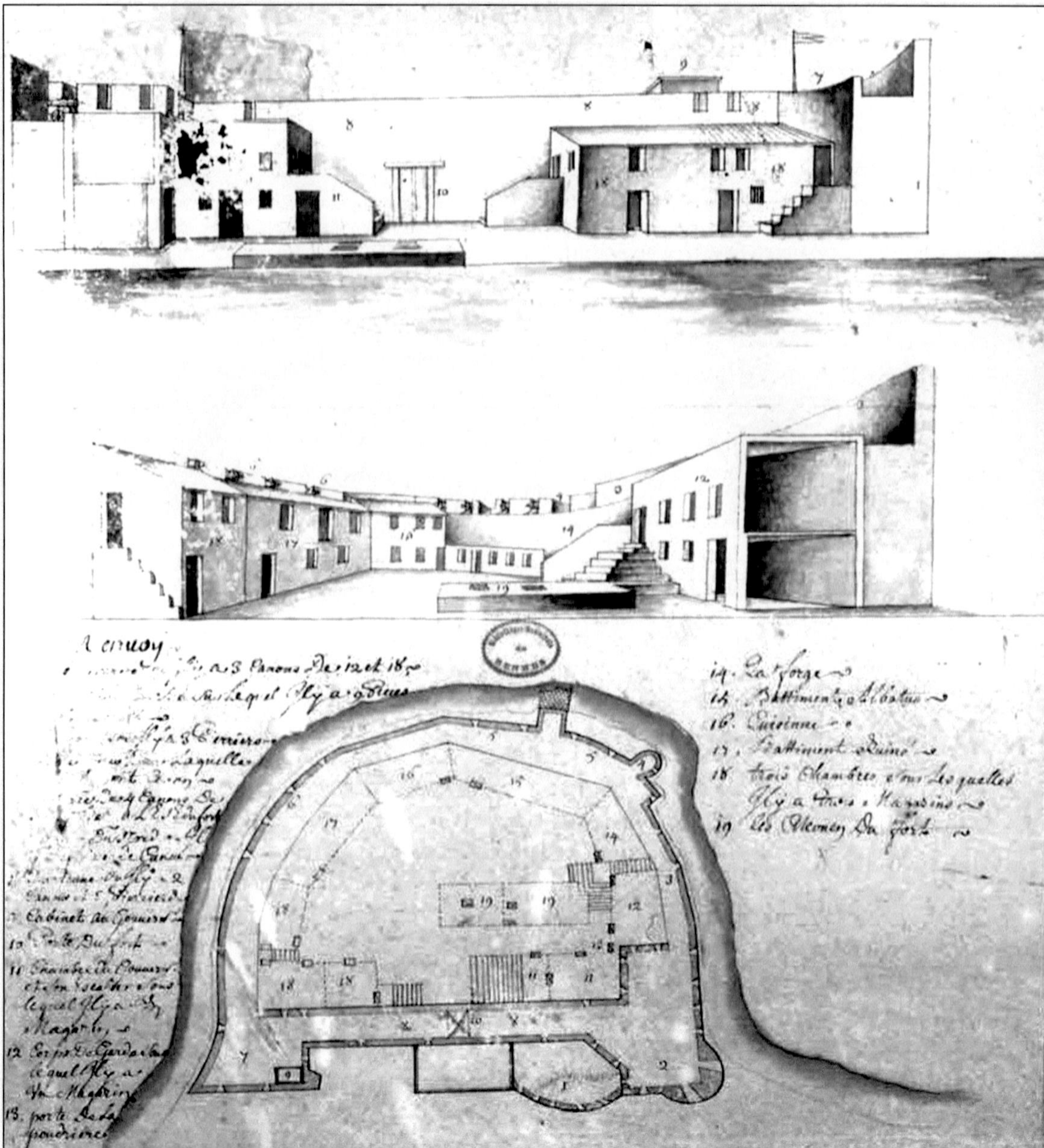

Plan of Fort Arguin (or Darguin) and elevation of its interior, 1724. Taken by the French from the Dutch in 1677 and again on 20 February 1721, this fort was the only substantial post of the Compagnie des Indes on the coast of present-day Mauritania, north of Senegal in West Africa. At upper left is a large French standard. Plan by De Souville. (Bibliothèque de Rennes. Ms0296)

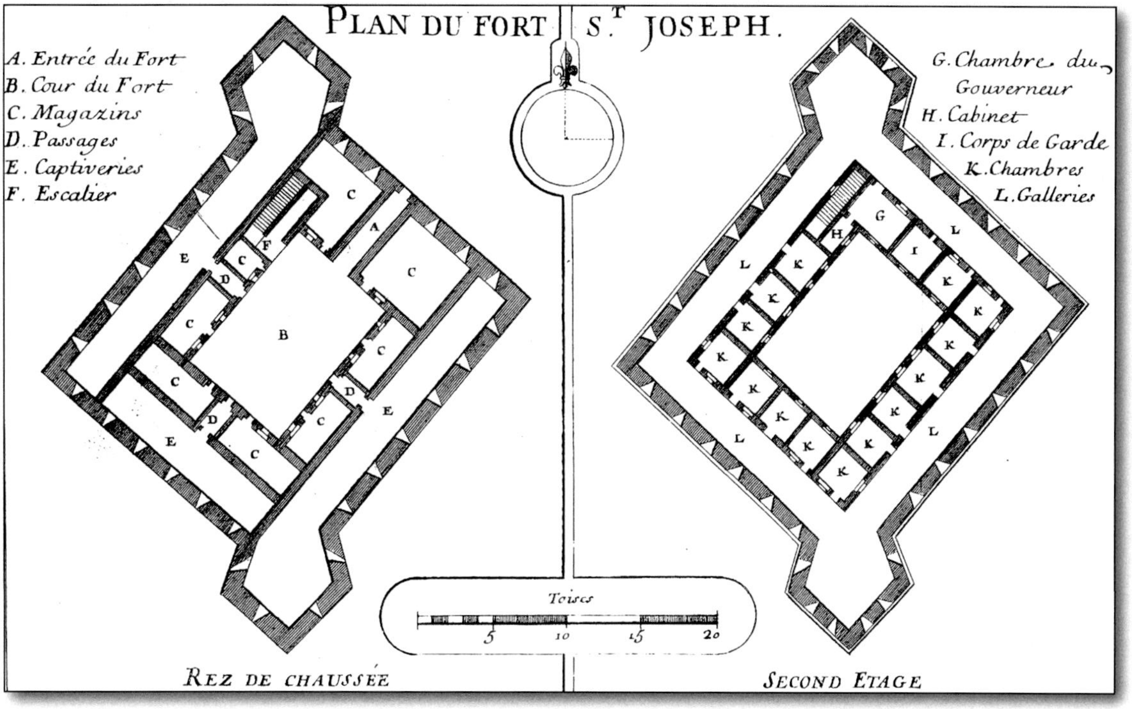

Plan of Fort Saint-Joseph (Galam), Senegal, 1728. This fort was built as a two-story castle-like strong house with two bastion corners. The ground floor (left) had the only narrow entrance, a courtyard and magazines. The second floor (right) had the guardhouse (I), rooms for the governor (G), civil personal and soldiers (K) bordered by an outside gallery. Plan from Labat's 1728 *Nouvelle relation de l'Afrique occidentale*. (Author's photo)

Ali Chandora. The emir was very upset at Duval who had even ordered his soldiers to shoot at any Moor that approached the fort. Accordingly, the Trarza warriors set up a blockade of the fort in which a smallpox epidemic broke out. By July, only 12 Frenchmen were left in Arguin. On 25 October, some 1,500 Trarza warriors laid siege to the fort with Dutch assistance; a few starving survivors surrendered on 11 January 1722.[3]

In response, the Compagnie des Indes sent out another expedition under Froger de La Rigaudière that landed some 400 men at Arguin on 17 February 1723. Dutch governor Jean de Beers rejected the summons to surrender the fort, which he claimed to hold for the Elector of Brandenburg. In any case, the siege soon had to be abandoned due to lack of drinking water. To make matters worse, the small French garrison at Portendic was starving. It was finally evacuated and the fort blown up. The Compagnie des Indes was nevertheless very determined to secure the area and another expedition led by Périer de Salverte with three companies of soldiers landed at Arguin on 14 February 1724, occupied the area and notably its water wells, invested the fort and started bombardment on 17 February. The Dutch capitulated after three shots and the fort was evacuated by the Dutch three days later.

3 Duval had sneaked out of Arguin to get reinforcements at Saint-Louis. Only 16 soldiers could be spared and they were killed with Duval by Trarza warriors who intercepted his boat going back to Arguin.

Portendic was also later occupied by Périer de Salverte's expedition. The area was now secured. Diplomatic negotiations with the Dutch resulted in their formal agreement that Portendic was French. The fort there was rebuilt and its commercial activities there were immediately very successful while those at Arguin considerably decreased. Arguin was abandoned in 1733 as was Bissao for the same reason. Business profits came foremost.[4]

The slave trade was an important part of European activities in Africa, and Gorée in Senegal has since become one of the most famous historic sites associated to that horrible chapter of human history. Senegal was also a very important outlet of gum by African traders, then a much sought after import, for which the Compagnie des Indes had a lucrative near-monopoly in Europe. Gum was produced by trees found from north of Saint-Louis to the area of Arguin. Other export items included hides, bees wax, ivory, cotton, gold dust, ostrich feathers, ambergris, indigo and civet. Gold dust was also widely traded by Africans at Ouidah on the Guinea coast (see below) and could be worth some 2,500 livres a pound in the early eighteenth century.[5]

African Garrisons

Data on the garrisons before the Compagnie des Indes took over the operations in Senegal from 1719 seems rather scarce. Some 30 soldiers were sent to Saint-Louis in 1701 to garrison its new fort. In 1720, there was an officer with 35 soldiers at Saint-Louis and four soldiers at Galam, which were likely to be originally troops of the Compagnie du Sénégal now merged into the Compagnie des Indes.[6]

A royal order dated 5 October 1722 allowed the Compagnie des Indes to raise a company of infantry to serve 'in its forts and concessions in Senegal' led by a *capitaine* with a *lieutenant*, a *sous-lieutenant*, an *enseigne*, two *sergents*, two *caporaux*, two *anspesades*, 43 fusiliers and one drummer. The Compagnie des Indes was allowed to deploy these troops on land or at sea. The administrative conditions were generally the same as those of the depot company in Lorient.[7]

Because the garrison was divided into several small detachments, the troops do not appear to have been organised into a company. As seen below, its establishment of enlisted men varied considerably and was much higher than what was prescribed in the 1722 order. Instead, it seems that detached squads of 30 men or less were favoured. Some of these squad might have also detached a few men to smaller posts.

4 Much of the above are relations are from Labat, *Nouvelle relation de l'Afrique occidentale*, Vol.1; Maurice Delafosse, 'Afrique occidentale française', in Hanotaux and Martneau (eds), *Histoire des colonies françaises et de l'expansion de la France dans le monde*, Vol.IV, pp.10-34.

5 Anon., *Histoire universelle* (Amsterdam and Leipzig, 1766), Vol.26, p.87; J.J. Crooks, 'A statement of events in Senegal and Goree 1758-1784', *The United Service Magazine*, Vol.52 (1916), p.309; Chevalier de Beauchêne, *Aventures du Chevalier de Beauchêne* (Paris: Librairie Commerciale et Artistique, 1969), Vol.2, pp.194-195.

6 Bernard Faij, *L'aventure coloniale* (Paris: Perrin, 1962), p.95.

7 AC, F3, 62, De par le Roy, 5 October 1722.

There were relatively few officers (19 between 1724 and 1758 of whom six died) and of these, there was usually only one *capitaine* or senior officer commanding in the territory. An engineer was also on the staff. Overall command was in the powers of the governor. The European components of the garrison were as follows:

- 1725: 148 soldiers (48 at Saint-Louis, 23 at Galam, 46 at Arguin, 25 at Gorée) plus five officers.
- 1734: 86 soldiers (26 at Saint-Louis, 16 at Galam, 32 at Gorée).
- 1736: 76 soldiers (14 at Saint-Louis, 20 at Galam, 39 at Gorée).
- 1741: 112 soldiers.
- 1745: 250 including 149 that arrived in April.
- 1750: 150 soldiers (40 at Saint-Louis, 30 at Podor, 30 at Galam, 40 at Gorée).
- 1756: 200 soldiers with five officers that arrived in March.[8]

Records indicate that 1,007 NCOs and fusiliers were sent between July 1724 and March 1758. Some 282 died between theses dates, but mortality was probably higher because 10 years were not computed nor were later years. Overall, it seems that about one third of the garrison in Senegal died.

There were in addition a few gunners and bombardiers. Their duty was to look after matters relating to ordnance and provide training to some soldiers and African auxiliaries. From 1727 to 1758, three bombardiers, six master gunners and seven gunners served in Senegal. On average at any one time, there were five gunners present serving mostly at Gorée, which had elaborate fortifications and thus more cannon.[9]

While the regular garrison was sufficient to provide local defence at the main fortified posts such as Saint-Louis and Gorée against unfriendly African warriors from adjacent territories, it was another matter when faced with a British or Dutch naval squadron. The fortifications built by the trading companies of any European nations in Africa were not generally designed to face bombardments and

French infantry fusilier, circa 1740. A soldier of the Compagnie des Indes posted in Senegal would have likely had this aspect when wearing the undress light grey linen jacket and breeches in warm weather beneath the grey-white coat with blue cuffs and brass buttons. (Anne S.K. Brown Military Collection, author's photo)

8 André Delcourt, *La France et les établissements français au Sénégal entre 1713 et 1763* (Paris: IFAN, 1952), pp.117, 243, 403; Jean-Bernard Lacroix, *Les Français au Sénégal au temps de la Compagnie des Indes de 1719 à 1758* (Vincennes: Service historique de la Marine, 1986), pp.103, 109-111, 145-147

9 Lacroix, *Les Français au Sénégal*, pp.141-142, 174-175; 223; Delcourt, *La France et les établissements français au Sénégal*, p.117.

African soldier/warrior at Ile Saint-Louis, Senegal, eighteenth century. This soldier bidding farewell to his family was obviously employed to the Compagnie des Indes' service. He is armed with a musket, a lance and a machete-like cutlass. Print after Grasset de Saint-Sauveur. (Los Angeles County Museum of Art, Costume Council Fund ma-56016)

assaults by European troops as seen by the 17th century raids and counter raids evoked above.

The garrison had African auxiliary soldiers usually called 'Laptots' that designated men-at-arms or sailors, the 'Laptots captifs' being those that were on permanent service and the 'Laptots libres' being those called occasionally on duty. In 1736, there were 236 'Laptots' of which 94 were 'captifs' and 142 were 'libres' in the personnel of the Compagnie des Indes. A surviving 1765 document regarding a corps of 'Laptots' organised that year at Goree gives a glimpse on how they might have been organised previously. The officers were French and, for armament, a quarter of the men had muskets, bayonets and sabres and the others carried a lance seven-and-a-half feet long. They were dressed in linen jackets and sailor's style trousers.[10]

British Invasion 1758

For the Compagnie des Indes, its rule in Western Africa came to an end in 1758. A British Royal Navy squadron led by Commodore Henry Marsh arrived at the mouth of Senegal River at two in the afternoon of 23 April 1758 and, by 26 April, its large ships could not go further on the river due to low water level at a bar except for the 'small vessels and boats' with the sloop *Swan*. They were soon met by 'seven vessels, three of which were armed with ten guns each, [that] made a show of attacking our small craft, and kept a kind of running fire, but were soon repulsed and obliged to retire up the river'.[11] The French account by Governor de La Brue, which was not meant for readers of the *London Gazette*, gives more details. His only gunboat was the *Aigle* to which had been added five other small boats with 300 'elite' men on board that managed to force a British 'galiote' (flat bottomed boat or bomb ketch) to run aground on the shore, that the Engineer Paradis commanding a six-gun boat prevented British efforts to rescue the 'galiote' and also abandon another British boat that had run aground. But ammunition ran short, Paradis was wounded in action and some African auxiliaries panicked and ran off. The

10 Delcourt, *La France et les établissements français au Sénégal*, p.403; Albert Depréaux, 'Les Laptots de Gorée 1765', *Carnet de la Sabretache*, March 1931, pp.129-131. The linen uniform had yellow trimmings and is illustrated from a contemporary document. The unit was ordered disbanded as per AC, B, 126, minister to M. de la Gastière, Versailles, 5 March 1767.

11 *London Gazette*, 10 June 1758.

British thus landed, secured ground by building field fortifications and now had four guns on shore that were used against African auxiliaries who attacked. On 27 April, the British managed to sail up thanks to another 'galiote' leading 13 boats.

A French council of war meeting revealed that the ammunition left would only provide a hundred shots for the 12 and 9 pounder guns in Saint-Louis. The allied Africans warriors that had come to help in the defence had vanished. There 'remained 25 employees, 70 soldiers and 47 artisans including the sick. Of all our Africans, we could only count on 87 'gourmets' soldiers which made in all 240 men, [including the] sick and disabled.' The British 'marines and seamen, to the number of 700, landed and got the artillery on shore; and next day (the 30th) when they were ready for proceeding to attack Fort Lewis [Fort Saint-Louis], which is on a small island about twelve miles up the river from the bar.' At that point, articles of capitulations were proposed and agreed to on 1 May 1758. The next day, the British marines took possession of Fort Saint-Louis where 'were found 232 French officers and soldiers' and 92 cannons. The number of soldiers was much exaggerated and obviously included French civilians and African soldiers. 'All the white people' belonging to the Compagnie des Indes were to be sent to France while the free Africans were not 'to be molested in their religion or effects, and to have liberty to retire if they chose it.'[12]

The British squadron then headed for Gorée arriving on 24 May 1758 off that small island. Governor Saint-Jean reported that the garrison consisted of seven officers and 210 soldiers with 160 Africans. Gorée was the best-fortified post in Senegal as was soon proven when Royal Navy ships approached; the artillery duel resulted in several ships damaged and about 60 sailors as casualties including about 20 killed. Commodore Marsh decided to sail for England and did not write to the newspapers about Gorée. But the failure was reported to the government who, not wishing to remain defeated, ordered a new and stronger expedition against Gorée to be led by Commodore Augustus Keppel. The fleet consisted of 11 Royal Navy warships with two tenders and seven merchant ships carrying 700 men of the 76th Regiment of Foot and supplies. It sailed from Kinsale, Ireland, on 11 November 1758. The weather and sea conditions were terrible and two warships were lost as well as a merchant ship.

At length, Gorée was reached in the evening of 28 December 1758 and was attacked early the next morning by the ships that opened fire on 'the forts and batteries…which were soon reduced to desire to capitulate' according to Keppel's press report. It was actually more involved according to Reverend Lindsay who was in the stern gallery of the British 64-gun *Fougueux* during 'the whole of the action' which impressed him and he could see hundreds of Africans 'lining the opposite shore'. One was seen armed with a musket and a sabre and another with a bow and a lance. The French coastal batteries returned fire and while the lower Fort Saint-François made a good target,

12 *London Gazette*, 10 June 1758; L. Joie, 'Les établissements français sur la côte occidentale d'Afrique de1758 à 1809', *Revue française d'histoire d'outre-mer*, Vol.51 (1964), pp.25-26 reproduces the French report.

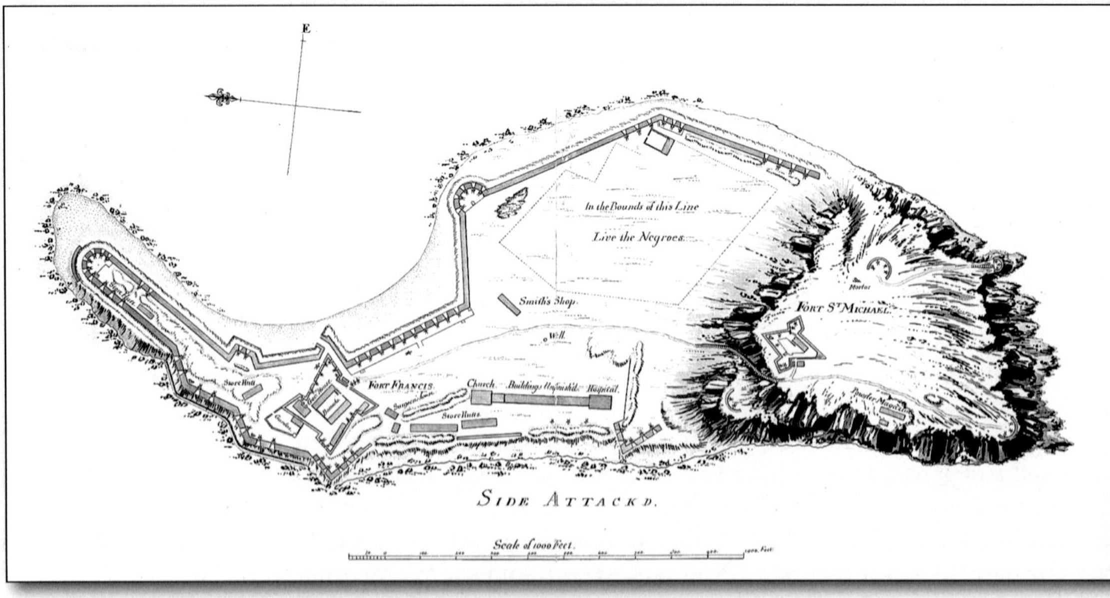

Gorée, 'Taken Decr/ 29th 1758, by a Squadron of His Majesty's Ships, Commanded by the Hon/le Aug/s Keppel'. This plan taken on the spot is the most accurate of the actual fortifications and other structures actually existing on the island. The bird's eye view published in Labat's 1728 *Nouvelle relation* copied and printed in the Netherlands during1746 after 'designs' by H. Compagnon that was copied again and published in London by T. Jefferys in 1759 shows features that were never built and others not shown that were. Plan after Cleeve Pleydell. (British Library, London)

the upper Fort Saint-Michel was hardly reachable. The initial British fire 'was remarkably brisk, but not well aimed, insomuch…[that] many went entirely over the island.' These were bombs fired from overcharged mortars in a bomb ketch and, noticing this, Keppel immediately ordered corrections. The British bombardment thereafter became more accurate and first terrified the many Africans helping serve the guns followed by French gunners and soldiers that abandoned the position. Governor Saint-Jean threatened 'every man to his quarters on pain of death' to no avail. It was clear he had to surrender and proposed terms, but the conditions asked by the French were rejected by Keppel and he 'began a fresh attack; it was however, but of a very short duration, when the island, fort, garrison, etc. surrendered at discretion to His Majesty's squadron' on the same day, 29 December 1758. According to Lindsay, the governor was obliged to drop the 'regimental colours' over the walls, as a signal of surrender.' The number of French prisoners of war came to about 270 or 300, part of which were employees rather than soldiers, with in addition 'Blacks in arms, a great number.' Some 94 cannons, three mortars and 11 swivel guns were found with ammunition. The British had about 20 men killed and 70 wounded which gives an idea of the initial good shooting of the French shore batteries while the French reported only one African killed 'by a piece of a shell' and three wounded.[13]

13 *London Gazette*, 29 January 1759; John Lindsay, *A Voyage to the Coast of Africa in 1758 containing A Succinct Account of the Expedition to, and the Taking of, the Island of Gore, by a squadron commanded by the Honourable Augustus Keppel* (London: Paterson, 1759), pp.42-

As can be seen, it can be misleading to rely solely on official dispatches published in newspapers. Many have since concluded that hardly a shot had been fired and that the French meekly surrendered quickly. No mention appears of the repulse of the first British attack on Gorée. The resistance was indeed short during the second attack but, judging from the British casualties, obviously intense. Accounts on both sides infer the abandonment of African soldiers and allied warriors. They too could see numerous sails of British warships arriving off their shores: that African soldiers actually stood and fought against such odds was admirable; that allied warriors withdrew was simply because African kingdoms were not at war with Europeans fighting amongst themselves.

The Guinea Coast

From the end of the sixteenth century, the kingdoms of Savi and Allava on the coast were in contact with European merchants and engaged in the slave and gold dust trade. According to Beauchêne, gold dust was exchanged pound for pound with European goods and noted that 'all Africans' wore gold rings on their hands, feet and 'even in their hair'.[14] Back in France, a hundred pounds of gold dust could be worth 250,000 livres gained at minimal expenses and risks compared to the slave trade, hence the interest of the Compagnie des Indes.

Eventually, Europeans obtained from local kingdoms permission to have permanent forts on the coast. In 1671, the French and the British each built fortified lodges next to each other at the coastal town of Ouidah and were joined the Portuguese and the Dutch . The kingdom was also called Adjudah, Juda or Ouidah whose capital was Savi further north. The French fortified lodge was formerly known as Fort Saint-Louis de Gregory, but was commonly called Ouidah or Juda (spelt several ways). 1717 and 1718 bills for its expenses mentions that its European personnel consisted of Director Bouchel, a sub-director, two clerks, a chaplain, a lieutenant of the fort and four *sergents* or supervisors. The African staff consisted of 40 men that were 'provided with linen' presumably as clothing.[15]

No European soldiers, or else very small temporary detachments, were posted there at the time of the Compagnie des Indes. Ouidah was basically always considered a neutral zone in case of wars between European nations. There were African armed guards seen by corsair Jean Doublet, who called

46, 54; Thomas Keppel, *The Life of Augustus Viscount Keppel* (London: Colburn, 1842), Vol.1, pp.268-278.

14 Beauchêne, *Aventures du Chevalier de Beauchêne*, Vol.2, pp.190

15 Cornevin, *Histoire de l'Afrique*, p.284; AC, F1A, 20, Dépenses et entretient du fort et comptoir de Juda, 1717; AC, F1A, 22, Dépenses et entretient du fort et comptoir de Juda, 1718. A small fort was built at a missionary post at Assini in 1701 with a garrison of Compagnies franches de la Marine of the king's warship *Joly*. Dutch troops from Elmina attacked on 13 November 1702 and were disastrously defeated by the marines and their African auxiliary soldiers. The mission failed and was abandoned in 1705 as per Delafosse, *Afrique occidentale française*, pp.44-45.

at Ouidah in 1704. At its guardhouse were 'ten or twelve Africans with their muskets' that were possibly some of the 40 men noted above. The Canadian buccaneer Beauchêne was at Ouidah in 1711 and related that its French governor, M. de Chamois, 'gave himself the trouble of teaching the military arts to many African, with which he sought to assist his ally, the king of Juda, who was harassed by his neighbours, but he needed officers to lead his Africans who otherwise were always bad troops.' One of Beauchêne's companions named Roland did accept the governor's offer. According to a watercolour dated 1725, the African guards wore white linen loincloths and were armed partly with muskets and partly with lances. That year, the Chevalier des Marchais reported that Ouidah now had a very small garrison of 15 European soldiers (two *sergents*, two gunners, a drummer and 10 fusiliers) and 30 African auxiliary soldiers.[16]

The four European countries that had outposts on the coast had very favourable conditions from the African king at Savi until 1727. A great war later engulfed the region and the kingdom of Dahomey's army conquered the kingdom of Juda marching into Savi. Sometime later, the African town of Juda at Ouidah was destroyed and a Dahomey town built on its ashes. King of Dahomey Agbadja did not attack the Europeans, but informed their personnel that the lodges had to surrender or they would be destroyed and the heads of all Europeans cut off. The French director, the Sieur Derigouin, was entrusted with the negations for all European lodges and he managed to convince King Agbadja that it was in his interest to keep the lodges at Ouidah functioning while those at Savi were abandoned. Thereafter, these agreements remained in force.[17]

16 Charles Bréard (ed.) *Journal du corsaire Jean Doublet de Honfleur* (Paris: Charavay, 1887), p.254; watercolour of the 'Comptoirs' in the 1724-1726 journal of Compagnie des Indes' ship's captain the Chevalier des Marchais at BNF, Ms. fr. 24 223, fol. 147; Beauchêne, *Aventures du Chevalier de Beauchêne*, Vol.2, pp.194-195. In 1719, Beauchêne encountered in Nantes his buccaneer companion Roland who had remained at Ouidah to train Africans. He came back to France with 80 pounds of gold dust, which amounted to a value of 200,000 livres, a notable sum with which he intended to comfortably settle in his native Paris. Beauchêne was in more humble circumstances at the time, but had once saved Roland's life so, in true Brothers of the Coast fashion, gratefully generous Roland gave him a pound of gold dust on the spot. As per Beauchêne, *Aventures du Chevalier de Beauchêne*, Vol.2, pp.174, 194.

17 Delafosse, *Afrique occidentale française*, pp.47-48; ADR, Co, 632, Houdoyer du Petitval at Fort Saint-Louis de Grégory, Ouidah, to the Ile de Bourbon council, 12 February 1729. Some 2,000 Africans were reported killed at the capture of Juda.

14

Louisiana and Other Territories

Louisiana was an immense territory spanning northwards from the Gulf of Mexico to just south of the Great Lakes in Canada. Most of its early settlements were in the area of the Gulf Coast at Mobile and at New Orleans, this last being near the entrance of the great Mississippi River that flowed from the north and that had been discovered by Robert Cavelier de La Salle in 1682. In typical fashion of the times, he took possession of the whole area for France and named it Louisiana after the name of its Sun King Louis XIV. After La Salle's disastrous settlement attempt in 1685, Pierre Le Moyne d'Iberville, and his brother Bienville created the first permanent settlements from 1699 on the Gulf Coast. Much further north in what was called the 'Pays des Illinois' (the Illinois Country) or Upper Louisiana, missionaries and settlers from Canada had founded small hamlets in the area where the Mississippi and Missouri rivers met. Much of the area beyond the shores of the rivers were unknown to Europeans, especially further west. Far to the east were the British Atlantic seaboard colonies.[1]

The neighbours on the Gulf Coast were the Spanish, and they were much closer. East of Mobile was their fort of Pensacola in Spanish Florida. Further to the north-east was the French Fort Toulouse that faced the British Carolinas further east. If one went west from the French fort at Natchitoches, he would soon come to the area of the Presidio of Las Aldeas in Spanish Texas.[2]

1 In the French command, political and church authority structure, Louisiana was in the protocolary general government of 'Nouvelle-France' (New France) covering North America that, from 1714, included Canada, Isle Royale and Louisiana. In practice, the governors of all three territories reported to the minister of the navy in France (and also the monopoly trade companies for Louisiana from 1712 until 1731).

2 In its expansion period regarding Louisiana, the Compagnie des Indes sent Bernard de La Harpe a ship for a reconnaissance of the Texas shore in the area of present-day Galveston, but the settlement scheme there was not pursued. It was really in Spain's territory and a presidio was eventually established there in 1755. See Marc de Villiers du Terrage and Paul Rivet, 'Les Indiens du Texas et les expéditions françaises de 1720 et 1721', *Journal de la Société des Américanistes*, Vol.11 (1919), pp.403-442. This paper reproduces the original reports.

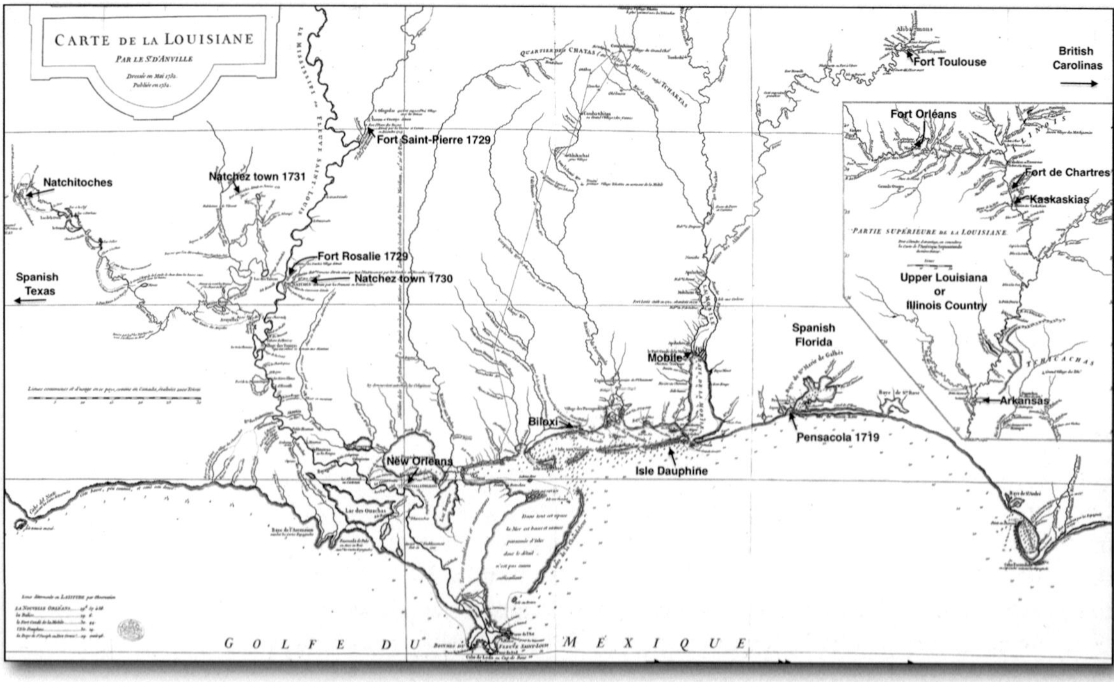

Map of lower Louisiana on the Gulf Coast with an inset of Upper Louisiana (or Illinois). Compiled by D'Anville in 1732 and published 20 years later, it shows the territory when governed by the Compagnie des Indes. Overlaid with the names of various locations. Those with dates mean a military engagement that year. We add that Fort Orléans on the Missouri River was only occupied from 1723 to 1726 by a small garrison. (British Library, London; digital overlays by the author)

Originally garrisoned by metropolitan royal Compagnies franches de la Marine soldiers from 1699 to 1704 and then by two territorial Compagnies franches de la Marine companies posted there permanently as Louisiana's garrison, the territory's administration had been ceded by the crown in 1712 to financier Antoine Crozat's monopoly Compagnie de la Lousiane. The two garrison companies of 50 men each there had been augmented to four in 1715 and to eight in 1716. On 27 October 1717, Crozat's privilege was taken over by John Law's Compagnie d'Occident (Western Company), which, in optimism, doubled the number of men per company to 100 each during 1718.

War having broken out with Spain, the company augmented again the garrison on 11 February 1719 by reorganising it into 20 companies of 50 men each, which now called for a theoretical 1,000 soldiers and 60 officers. In fact, not enough recruits were sent. In August 1721, a total of 623 soldiers were reported posted throughout the territory. The emphasis had been given to establishing forts or garrisoning those existing. Troops were posted at: Old Biloxi 69 soldiers; Fort Louis (Mobile) 97; Fort Condé (Mobile) 110; Dauphine Island 21; Alibamons (Fort Toulouse) 47; New Orleans 49; Natchez (Fort Rosalie) 23; Vasoux (Fort Saint-Pierre) 48; Nachitoches 50; Arkansas 34; Fort de Chartres 60; Pensacola 15. [3]

3 AC, B, 42, Ordonnance pour l'augmentation de quatre compagnies à la Louisiane, 1 March 1716; Ordonnance de la Compagnie [d'Occident] pour le règlement des troupes quelle a

Pensacola 1719

The last post on the list was Pensacola in western Florida. Established by the Spanish in 1697, it was a sentinel to prevent the French of going further east into Florida. News that the War of the Quadruple Alliance had been declared reached Louisiana on 19 April 1719 and Governor Jean-Baptiste Le Moyne de Bienville decided to immediately attack Pensacola. A force of 60 soldiers with about 80 Louisiana and Canadian volunteers was organised under the command of the governor's brother, Alexandre Le Moyne de Chateauguay. The soldiers and volunteers sailed from Mobile on three frigates of the Compagnie des Indes while about 300 allied First Nations warriors went by land. The frigates arrived on 12 May off Rosas Island near Pensacola. The Spanish fortifications consisted of a small fort on the island of Santa Rosa and a larger one at Pensacola on the mainland where the governor had his quarters. A French party landed furtively on Rosas island, captured a few Spanish sentries, put on the Spanish uniforms and captured the small fort by surprise. They then went on to attack the fort at Pensacola using the same stratagem and 'surprised the sentinels, the guard house, and at last the fort, to the governor [commander] himself, who was taken in bed; so that they were all made prisoners, without any bloodshed' according to Le Page du Pratz. A garrison of 60 soldiers under Chateauguay remained as its garrison.[4]

The Spanish prisoners were taken to Havana according to the terms of the capitulation. Governor and *Capitán General* Gregorio Guaso Calderon at Havana was not amused and, contrary to the usual conventions of war, he ordered the two French ships bringing the Spanish garrison taken at Pensacola seized and their French crews thrown in prison. He then mustered a fleet led by Alfonso Carrascosa de la Torre, detached 100 to 150 regular soldiers of Havana's garrison to join 300 marines of the Barlovento Squadron from Veracruz, Mexico, some French deserters and privateers. The force was said by the French to total some 1,200 men and all sailed out of Havana on 8 August with orders to recapture Pensacola.[5]

Once at Pensacola, there was some exchange of fire between the Spanish ships and the forts at Pensacola while Chateauguay appealed for reinforcements. Carrascosa summoned a surrender giving Chateauguay two days to answer. A couple of days later, a dispatch came from Bienville stating that he did not have enough men to send a French relief force. When that was learned, most of the French soldiers deserted to the Spanish. Carrascosa

augmentée, 11 February 1719; Giraud, *Histoire de la Louisiane française*, Vol.3, p.309; AG, A1, 2592, Soldats en garnison…, 10 August 1721.

4 Le Page du Pratz, *The History of Louisiana* (London: Becket, 1774), pp.111-113; Dumont de Montigny, *Mémoires historiques sur la Louisiane* (Paris: Bauche, 1753), pp.9-12. The 300 First Nation warriors were apparently not present nor involved and would have departed when learning of the capture of Pensacola.

5 Conde de Clonard, *Historia organica de la infanteria y caballeria espanolia* (Madrid: D.B. Gonzalez, 1857), Vol.7, p.428; Jack D.L. Holmes, 'Dauphin Island in the Franco-Spanish War' in John Francis McDermott (ed.), *Frenchmen and French Ways in the Mississippi Valley* (Urbana: University of Illinois, 1969), pp.113-116.

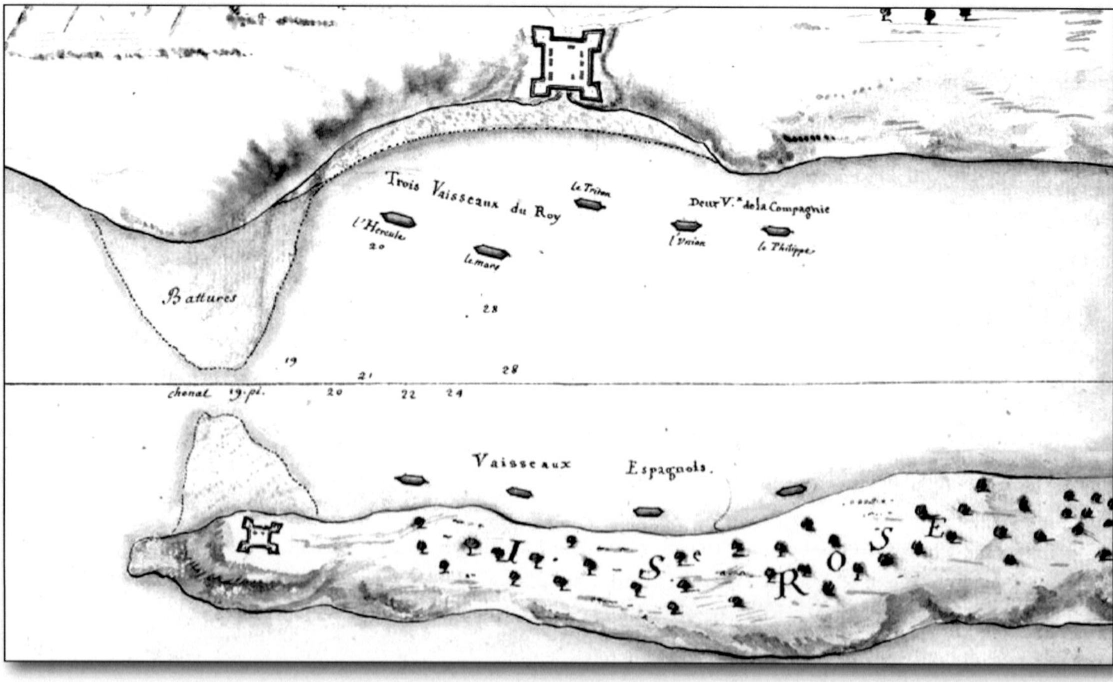

Plan of Pensacola's forts and harbour during the French attack, September 1719. Three French navy warships (*Hercule, Mars, Triton*) with two Compagnie des Indes ships face the main fort (top). The small fort on Santa Rosa island has four Spanish ships nearby (bottom). The narrow entrance was between mostly submerged sandbanks and rocks. The small numbers indicate the depth in feet. (Bibliothèque National de France, Paris)

agreed to grant the honours of war to Chateauguay and his remaining 20 men, and the Spanish standard was once again hoisted over Pensacola.

The Spanish commander then sailed west in a warship and attacked Dauphine Island which only had a shore battery for its defence. However, the Spanish could not land troops due to shooting from armed settlers and soldiers and the nearby anchored ship *Philippe* turned into a floating battery. Landing from a ship on Dauphine Island was difficult and most attempts were repulsed by hidden defenders led by Joseph Le Moyne de Sérigny. The one that succeeded by a small party of 35 men was on Maringouin (mosquito) Island further north on 17 August. It resulted in some looting until they were intercepted by a small force of Canadians and allied warriors led by *Capitaine* Villainville. In their flight, most Spaniards and French deserters were lost or captured. A second small Spanish ship arrived and, on 21 August, both engaged the battery and the *Philippe*, but the French fire soon proved superior, the guns being 'served by Canadians, people that are naturally warriors and good hunters' according to de Montigny. The Spanish withdrew. However, Carrascosa did not give up and went on to Mobile Bay where their two landing attempts were foiled by the French defenders. Bowing to events, the Spanish sailed back to Pensacola on 25-26 August.[6]

6 Of the raiders on Maringouin Island, seven were killed, nine, drowned and 18 French deserters taken by the Indians. One was hanged at Dauphine Island as an example; the 17 others were

On 1 September 1719, three French royal warships with two Compagnie des Indes ships led by *Capitaine de Frégate* Desnos de Champmelin arrived at Dauphine Island with up to 800 soldiers on board. De Bienville resolved to attack Pensacola with 400 French soldiers, 150 Louisiana and Canadian volunteers, about 300 indigenous allied warriors, and marines from the ships. They arrived at Pensacola early on 14 September when the Spanish, after a skirmish with the warriors, retreated to their forts. On 17 September, Champmelin proceeded on a general attack. The French land forces moved closer waiting for the order of an assault. There were first two hours of bombardments on the main fort, which lasted three hours for the small fort on Santa Rosa Island. The Spanish garrison numbered about 600 soldiers and there were also seven Spanish ships in the harbour, but very much outgunned compared to the attacking French ships. The French flagship even had three 48-pounder cannon, then the heaviest artillery calibre in the French Navy, and these guns cut the mainmast of the strongest opposing ship and scattered the others. After about five hours, the Spanish ran out of ammunition.

The Spanish then capitulated after giving an honourable resistance to the French force. The French reported only six casualties, the Spanish some 100 men. When Carrascosa, the Spanish commander, surrendered his sword, Champmelin gave it back saying that 'he knew how to distinguish [between] a brave officer, and one who was not' according to du Pratz. The fate of the 47 French deserters found in Pensacola was less gallant: 12 were hanged and the rest condemned to be slave labourers on Compagnie des Indes' plantations. The Spanish garrison and inhabitants, said to be some 1,200 souls, were all evacuated to Cuba, the fort and the town later destroyed. Only four houses were kept and a French guard of about 15 soldiers remained there. Peace was meanwhile convened in Europe and Pensacola was returned to Spain.[7]

Spanish Defeat in Nebraska, 1720

While the treaty of peace ending the Quadruple Alliance War was signed at The Hague in the Netherlands on 17 February 1720, this news was not received at Santa Fe, New Mexico, until many months later. In any event, mirroring Madrid's concern about France's expanding settlements in Louisiana, the viceroy of New Spain in Mexico City, Baltazar de Zuniga, Marques de Valero, instructed the governor of New Mexico, Antonio Valverde y Cosio, to send a Spanish expedition much further north to establish a 'Presidio' (which was usually a combination fortified military post and religious mission) west of the French settlements in Illinois. This would create some concern to the

---

taken to Mobile where Bienville turned them over to the warriors who killed them as per Holmes, 'Dauphin Island in the Franco-Spanish War', p.120.

7 Pratz, *The History of Louisiana*, pp.113-117; Montigny, *Mémoires historiques*, Vol.3, pp.13-28; Jean-François Bretet de la Clue (Francis Escoffier and Jay Higginbotham, eds), *A Voyage to Dauphin Island in 1720* (Mobile: Museum of the City of Mobile, 1973), pp.64-65; Giraud, *Histoire de la Louisiane française*, Vol.3, pp.300-303; Holmes, 'Dauphin Island in the Franco-Spanish War', pp 117-122. The French abandoned the site of Pensacola in 1722, the Spanish came back to rebuild it from 1726.

First Nations trading with the French in that area that Spanish power could reach them. It would also be a warning to the French.

Governor Valverde accordingly sent a first exploratory expedition of 60 troopers of the leather coated 'cuera' cavalry that garrisoned northern New Spain (now Texas, New Mexico, Arizona) with 465 allied Pueblo indigenous warriors to the north. They came back to Santa Fe with evidence that French traders and explorers were in contact with First Nations further to the north and northeast. In mid-June 1720, another expedition from Santa Fe led by Lieutenant Governor Pedro de Villasur headed north to Taos. It consisted of 48 troopers, three civilians (including a French expatriate translator), a missionary and 60 mounted Pueblo warriors led by chief Joseph Naranjo. From Taos the expedition headed eastward then turned north-eastwards travelling through present-day Kansas and eastern Nebraska to reach the Platte River (Rio de Jesus Maria to the Spanish). By then, it had travelled some 1,500 kms (900 miles). Villasur crossed the river on 7 and 8 August and headed east, soon meeting a large Pawnee encampment when reaching the confluent of the Loup River (Rio de San Lorenzo). The Pawnee chiefs did not want to speak with the Spanish officers, seemingly because they had been told that the expedition had treated rather severely the indigenous groups they had encountered on the way. Villasur had been told of a European man living amongst the Pawnee First Nation, most probably a French trader, but his message in French to him was never answered. Sensing a delicate situation in the presence of numerous warriors, the expedition moved some distance away and set up its camp on 12 August on a field with tall grass (near present day Columbus, Nebraska).[8]

At dawn on 13 August 1720, a large band of Pawnee and allied Oto warriors attacked the Spanish camp. It seems no guards had been posted. Vallasur and his men were surprised, most were killed on the spot in a short time, apparently mainly by musket shots. In all 34 troopers, Villasur, the translator and the missionary were killed as well as 11 Pueblo warriors. Most of the other Pueblo warriors escaped, but few Spaniards. In one stroke, a third of the garrison of New Mexico was wiped out making 32 widows and many orphaned children in this disaster. Furthermore, it was a major impediment to Spanish prestige amongst the First Nations; a strong party of the feared and near-invincible regular 'cuera' cavalry had been annihilated by First Nations warriors with, possibly, gun-toting French traders.

A major mystery remains of this event: were French soldiers and/or traders from Illinois actually present at the battle? A large indigenous hide painting made sometime after the battle show 37 figures wearing European costume of various colours and armed with muskets fighting alongside the First Nations warriors. It also shows the Spanish soldiers dressed in the

---

8 The Spanish forces in northern New Spain were posted in 'Presidios' from the Gulf of Mexico to the Pacific established from the end of the 16th century. See notably Max L. Morehead, *The Presidio: Bastion of the Spanish Borderlands* (Norman: University of Oklahoma Press, 1975) and our own 'Leather Jacket Soldiers: the Cuera cavalry of the American south-west', *Military Illustrated*, No. 54 (November 1992), pp.36-42 for the material culture from primary sources in Spanish Mexican and American archives and museums.

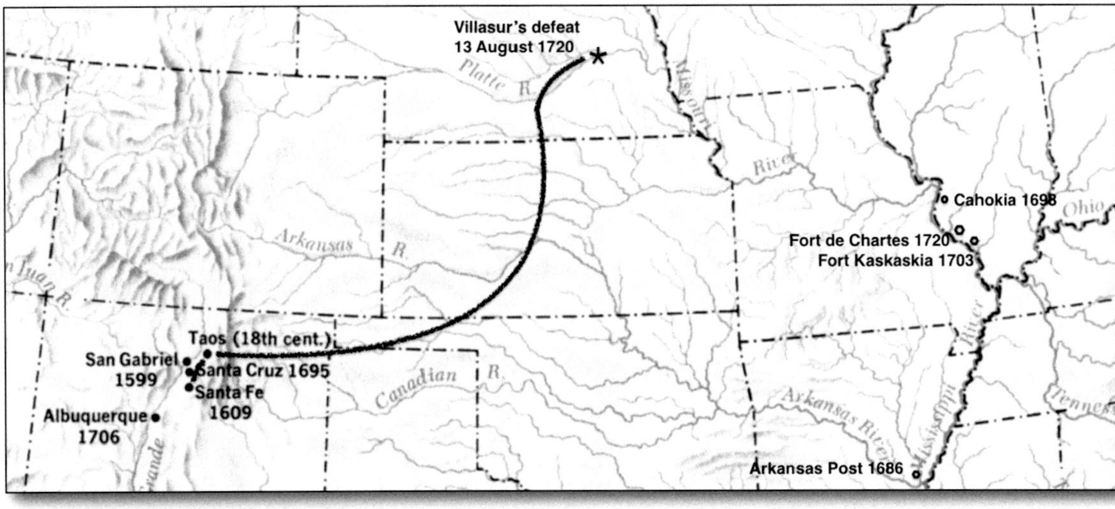

Map showing a suggested route of Villasur's expedition, 1720. The Spanish force left Santa Fe, New Mexico, in June crossing Kansas by a quite hypothetical suggested route to Nebraska's Platte River that was forded in early August. By then, it had travelled some 1,500 kms (900 miles). (National Park Service of the United States of America; Digital overlays by the author)

Annihilation of Villasur's expedition, 13 August 1720. This detail from a large hide painting made after the engagement shows a last stand by a group of Spanish 'Cuera' cavalry soldiers, correctly clothed and armed in their peculiar dress, being overwhelmed with indigenous warriors. Some figures dressed in Europeans costume are also shown (notably lower right) always armed with muskets were most probably meant to represent French or Canadian traders who often lived amongst indigenous groups. (New Mexico Museum, Palace of the Governors, Albuquerque)

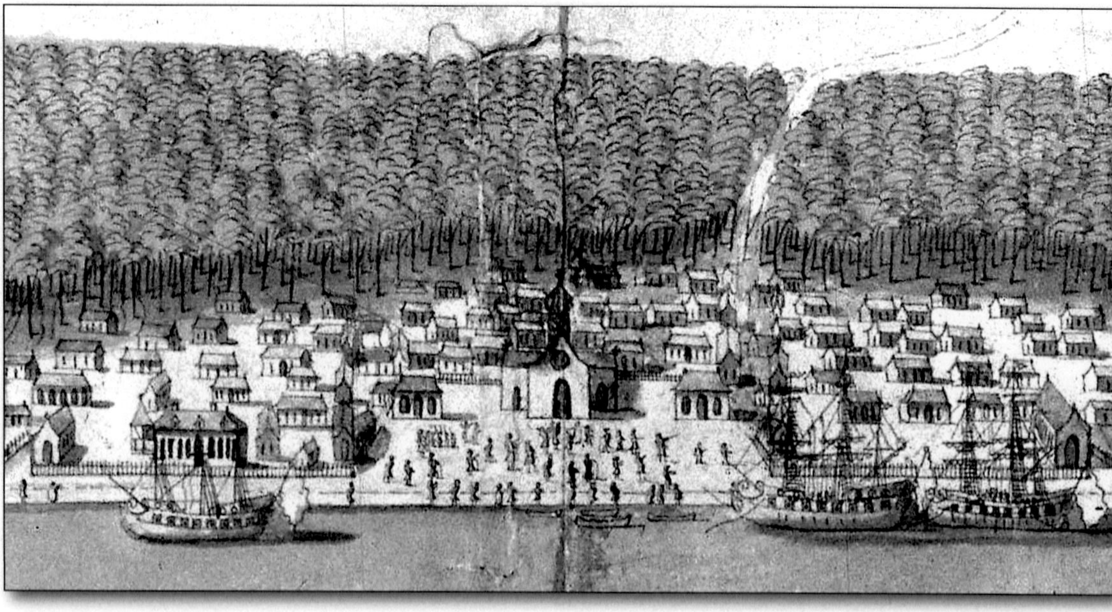

New Orleans, 1726. The centre of the newly-founded city shown includes a few extremely small figures representing soldiers of the Compagnie des Indes armed with muskets. No fortifications were to be seen at that time. (Archives Nationales Outre-Mer, DFC71A)

correct styles worn by the 'cuera' cavalry as well as accurately depicting their leather jackets, shields and weapons.

The hasty interpretation that French Compagnie des Indes soldiers were present can be dismissed. *Capitaine* Pierre Dugué de Boisbriand at Fort Kaskaskia in Illinois was amongst the first to hear with surprise of the Spanish disaster from allied warriors and reported this news to New Orleans. Had some troops of the Illinois garrisons been fighting in this victorious action, he would have proudly reported it to the governor that would have been relayed to Versailles and the French media. No such reports are known to exist, which is overwhelming evidence that regular soldiers were not involved.

This does not mean that no Europeans were present fighting the Spanish. It was well known that 'Frenchmen accustomed to the Illinois who trade with the indigenous people of Missouri say with assurance that it is a very beautiful and fertile country'. It was common practice for them to live for a time within the indigenous groups, some never or very rarely coming back to the French settlements. Therefore, it would be extremely probable that some French/Canadian *coureurs-de-bois* and *voyageurs* living with the Pawnees and other First Nations fought the Spanish with the warriors (see chapter 21 for the Louisiana Militia in Illinois). In any event, the Spanish did not venture this far again for many years.[9]

9 Charles Bennett, 'The Segester Hide Paintings Revelations About the Southwest's Colonial Past', *Terra*, Vol.30, No. 4 (Summer 1992), pp.22-31; Marc de Villiers, 'Le massacre de l'expédition espagnole du Missouri', *Journal de la Société des Américanistes*, Vol.13 (1921), pp.239-255. Especially valuable as it reproduces amongst several sources the translation from French to Spanish of part of a soldier's journal found on the battlefield by a warrior that gave it to Boisbriand. *Mercure Galant*, February 1719, p.216; AC, C13A, 6, Bienville to Council, 20 July 1721. On the First Nations, see also: Russell M. Magnaghi, 'Plains Indians in New

Tensions and War with Indigenous First Nations

In 1722-1723, tensions with the Natchez First Nation situated at about 280 kilomatres north of New Orleans resulted in some settlers in the Natchez area. It seems to have originated in disrespectful treatment of some Natchez indigenous persons by settlers at the Sainte-Catherine land concession. The whole concept of Europeans seizing and conceding First Nation land to themselves infuriated many Natchez warriors and, from October 1722, that concession and then others became targets by harassment. For instance, hidden warriors would shoot at African slaves toiling in the field or at carts transporting supplies and also at settlers. To increase security, some settlers were armed and attached to squads of soldiers patrolling out of Fort Rosalie. Many settlers also sought refuge in the fort at the time. A force of 60 men that arrived from New Orleans later that month achieved nothing worthwhile before going back. The situation did not improve during the following year while Fort Rosalie only had 23 soldiers and was not esteemed capable of repulsing a substantial attack. Finally, at the end of September 1723, Governor Bienville led an expedition made up of 200 troops and inhabitant volunteers joined by allied First Nations warriors (who had white armbands for distinguishing friend from foe) joined on the way by French and Canadian traders made up a force of some 600 men. It arrived in the area during October1723. After some skirmishing, the hostile Natchez warriors were impressed and calm returned, for a while.[10]

Swiss Mercenary *Soldats-Ouvriers*

In 1720 meanwhile, a Swiss mercenary *Soldat-Ouvriers* (soldier-worker) company of 210 men led by five officers was hired by the Compagnie des Indes from *Capitaine* Merveilleux. They were to accomplish engineering-pioneering work as well as to serve as soldiers if the need arose. This Swiss company was autonomous from the other French troops. A first contingent arrived in early 1721 and was reviewed on 7 February. Unfortunately, it suffered dreadful losses in an epidemic. By 4 May, 55 men had died and only 30 were left. The second contingent sailed for Louisiana on April 1721. On the whole all these Swiss soldiers were displeased with their new home and many wanted to desert and leave. The chance came for 30 of them in May 1722 when they boarded a small ship taking them from Biloxi to New Orleans. Once under way, they mutinied and forced the captain of the vessel to take them to Havana. The Spanish authorities in Cuba, no doubt fearing diplomatic repercussions, refused them permission to land, whereupon the Swiss headed for the British colonies and reached the Carolinas. Only two officers and a *sergent* remained. Other Swiss recruits arrived from France

---

Mexico: The Genizaro Experience', *Great Plain Quarterly*, Vol.10, No. 2 (Spring 1990), pp.86-95.

10 Giraud, *Histoire de la Louisiane française*, Vol.4, pp.292-295.

Fort de Chartres, Louisiana, 1720s. Built from 1718, it was described in 1723 by inspecting officer Diron D'Artaguiette as being 'square in shape, two bastions which command all the curtain [walls]'. Each side was 58.52 m (192 ft). This scene reconstructs some of the typical activities at such an outpost. (Fort de Chartres State Historic Site, Illinois, USA, author's photo)

and a strength of 80 men was reported in 1724. That year, the company office in Paris received a dispatch in March that deemed the remnants of the Swiss company as 'useless' and expensive, recommending to disband it. It was indeed ordered disbanded on 26 July 1725.[11]

The establishment of the French companies was also reduced to eight companies in December 1725 so that postings were in mostly small detachments from 1726: La Balise: 20 men; New Orleans 130; Biloxi 7; Natchitoches 25; Natchez (Fort Rosalie) 35; Yazous (Fort Saint-Pierre) 15; Ouabache (Fort Ouiatenon) 30; Illinois (Fort de Chartres) 30; Les Mines (Arkansas) 10; Missouris (Fort Orléans 8; Mobile 85; Alibamons (Fort Toulouse) 15. Total 400 men plus 24 officers.[12]

Drama at Fort Rosalie 1729

Resentment nevertheless ran deep for years especially in the Natchez First Nation and they were not alone in having doubts about seeing more and more Europeans. On 28 November 1729, Natchez warriors suddenly

11 AC, B, 43, Project de capitulation pour la compagnie suisse de la Compagnie des Indes dans la Louisiane, 4 January 1720; AG, A1, 2592, notes on the Swiss, Biloxi, 4 May 1721; Giraud, *Histoire de la Louisiane française*, Vol.4, 302-303; AC, C13A, 7, De la Chaise to company directors, New Orleans, 6 September 1723, received in Paris 8 March 1724; AC B, 43, État général…Louisiane, 1725; AC, B, 43, Ordonnance…Compagnie des Indes, 26 July 1725.

12 AC, B, 43, État des postes, Paris, 12 December 1725; Morris S. Arnold, 'French Soldiers in Colonial Arkansas', *Arkansas Historical Society*, Vol.80, No. 4, (Winter 2021), pp.408-409.

attacked Fort Rosalie and its settlement. Surprise was total. The place was quickly reduced to ashes, some 235 settlers with the garrison and Commandant Chepart perished and many others captured with their slaves.

At the beginning of December, the disaster's news reached Governor Étienne de Périer in New Orleans. This horrid event hit the city's population like a thunderbolt and immediately spread panic amongst the colonists. They further learned later that the small Fort Saint-Pierre had also been overwhelmed. Government authorities were also extremely perturbed by this event, much fearing that this might be only the beginning of a much larger general uprising by the First Nations everywhere in Louisiana. Fear by all colonists of all origins and classes of society was heightened further as everyone now realised that the regular garrison at New Orleans was very weak and of dubious quality. The only really decent fortifications were at Mobile, which was not seen as being immediately under threat compared to New Orleans that had no fortifications and could thus be open to any hostile infiltration or attack. Another concern was a shortage of weapons available. And to make matters worse, there was no militia.[13]

Attack and massacre at Fort Rosalie, Louisiana, 29 November 1729. That day, Natchez warriors unexpectedly attacked Fort Rosalie and its settlement reducing the place to ashes and killing some 235 settlers as well enslaving many others. This event led to the Compagnie des Indes giving up its monopoly and administrative role in Louisiana. Print after Sahib in the 1883 *Nouvelle histoire des voyages*. (British Library, London)

The Natchez War

Governor Périer believed that the best defence was an offensive. He was preparing an expeditionary force to go up against the Natchez. The command of this force was entrusted to the Chevalier de Loubois, an experienced officer. By mid-January, about 200 men were assembling under his command at the Tunicas northwest of New Orleans. It was a mixed force of regulars, volunteers of the New Orleans and German Coast, newly formed militia and

13 Le Page du Pratz, *The History of Louisiana*, pp.90-91; Bernard Lugan, *Histoire de la Louisiane française* (Paris: Perrin, 1994), pp.116-119. The number of settlers killed at Natchez is unsure and varies from 238 to 183 in studies and survivor's accounts seen by Lugan. Dumont de Montigny, *Regard sur le monde atlantique* (Québec: Septentrion, 2008), p.241 mentions that only one soldier escaped by hiding in baker's oven. The population was then about 1,000 in New Orleans and 2,000 in its area as per A. Baillardel and A. Prioult, *Le Chevalier de Pradel* (Paris: Librairie orientale et américaine, 1928), p.46.

also 15 free Africans who had been issued with weapons including muskets. The French force was joined by about 600 allied warriors, mostly Choctaws. By 12 February, it attacked the Natchez who were in a strongly built fortified village. Loubois had no artillery so a blockade was the only option. Sporadic but vigorous fighting occurred until 26 February when most of the Natchez managed to escape their stronghold. However, two men, 54 women and children with 150 African slaves who had been taken prisoners were recovered, so the expedition had some success. It was also a failure to some extent due to shortages of supplies, ammunition and muskets.[14]

Calls for help had been sent to France with the news of the uprising and, in August 1730, ships arrived at New Orleans with 60 very bad recruits for the Louisiana troops, not enough weapons and supplies, but also with three companies totalling 150 good marines of the Compagnies franches de la Marine. The captain of one of the ships later reported that 'all the inhabitants of the colony were very alarmed', that the regular troops of the Compagnie des Indes that were left were 'not good enough' and that the artillery asked for from France had not been sent. Nevertheless, Périer was encouraged and organised another expedition to definitively 'punish' the Natchez. In December, the marines with French navy sailors totalling 200 men went up to Natchez followed in early January 1731 by Governor Périer with 200 of the better soldiers of the Compagnie des Indes and 150 volunteer militiamen under *Capitaine* de Bénac, commander of the militia, some African volunteers and about 150 allied warriors. The force then went up the Ouachita River to the area where the Natchez had fled and built a new fort, which was reached by the French expedition on 20 January. With colours unfurled and drums beating, the French troops moved up to the fort, but remained out of musket range and invested it. Skirmishing followed, but inside the fort the Natchez were much surprised that the French would follow them that far away. The next day, a mortar was brought up and a European style siege started; the Natchez attempted a sortie unsuccessfully and they hoisted a white French flag on 24 January while a Natchez warrior came out with two peace pipes and released the 19 remaining African prisoners they held. The weather had turned very rainy and the Natchez tried to escape during the night, but this time, only about 200 got away. The 387 other Natchez were made prisoners, their fort was destroyed and the expedition made a glorious entry into New Orleans on 5 February. Casualties had been very light; the militiamen and Africans had evidently been engaged because militia *Capitaine* de Laye was wounded and an African killed.[15]

---

14 Pierre-François-Xavier de Charlevoix, *Histoire et description général de la Nouvelle-France* (Paris: Giffart, 1744), Vol.4, pp.264-269; Roland C. McConnell, *Negro Troops of antebellum Louisiana* (Baton Rouge: Louisiana State University Press, 1968), p.7; Baillardel and Prioult, *Le Chevalier de Pradel*, p.72; Fort Rosalie (or Natchez) was rebuilt as an earthwork with a strong garrison of three officers and 90 regulars of the Compagnie des Indes.

15 AC, C13A, 13, Relation de la défaite des Natchez par Monsieur de Périer, 1731; Charlevoix, *Histoire et description*, Vol.4, pp.277-289; Dumont de Montigny, *Regard sur le monde atlantique*, pp.260-261; Charles Gayaré, *Histoire de la Louisiane* (New Orleans: Magne & Weisse, 1846), Vol.1, p.277; McConnell, *Negro Troops*, p.10. The Compagnie des Indes soldiers were formed into a temporary company of grenadiers and two of fusiliers; the number

The Natchez War did not quite end until November 1731. The year was generally marked by warfare between various First Nations that resulted in the pre-eminence of those favourable to the French. But settlements could still be at risk. On the Red River, the French post at Natchitoches and its Fort Saint-Jean-Baptiste was attacked by about 250 hostile warriors, some of them Natchez, on 5 October 1731; its garrison of 34 soldiers with 15 Spanish soldiers, 24 allied warriors and the settlers managed to repulse them. A blockade ensued that was countered by several sorties resulting in the withdrawal of the hostile warriors by 5 November.[16]

In France, meanwhile, the government realised that the Louisiana administration of the Compagnie des Indes had been very questionable in terms of leaving it almost defenceless militarily, failing to invest sufficiently in bringing more settlers while its diplomacy with the First Nations was largely ineffective. For its part, the Compagnie des Indes just wanted to get out of this troublesome and unprofitable territory and, on 22 January 1731, simply begged the royal government to take it over. King Louis XV ruled that from 1 July 1731, Louisiana would become a royal domain like other French territories in America. This must have been a great relief to Louisiana settlers in particular. Governor Périer was replaced by the more experienced Bienville who was appointed for a second term. The three companies of marines stayed to reinforce what was left of the Compagnie des Indes troops while more were being organised in France.[17]

Canada and China

The Compagnie des Indes had agents and small stations, offices or lodges in other territories. In the case of Canada and China, the company had sizeable lodges where trade was conducted. No garrisons were needed, but there were armed constabulary corps in Canada and small detachments of the company's troops in China.

The Canadian Beaver Privilege 1720-1760

While the Compagnie des Indes did not have garrisons in Canada, a territory administered by the royal government, it did have some armed 'guards' to protect its privilege regarding the export of beaver pelts. Since the early seventeenth century, many monopoly enterprises had tried to control the

---

of Africans is not given. The captured Natchez were shipped to Saint-Domingue (Haiti) and sold as slaves.

16 Charlevoix, *Histoire et description*, Vol.4, pp.293; Lous R. Nardini, *My Historic Natchitoches, Louisiana, and its environment* (Natchitoches: Self Published, 1963), pp.44-46, 49-50. Nardini confuses militiamen with regular soldiers. The commander mentioned he could only arm 16 men, who may have been inhabitants.

17 Heinrich, *La Louisiane sous la Compagnie des Indes*, pp.253-254; AC, B, 57, Ordonnance pour régler le nombre des troupes de la Louisiane, 11 November 1732. This royal order created 13 Compagnies franches de la Marine as permanent garrison troops of Louisiana that, with the 4th Company of the Swiss Régiment de Karrer, would be the colony's military establishment for a total of 800 men.

lucrative Canadian beaver trade in and out of its territory without much long term success. In 1717, the beaver trade was made free within the country while its export to France was granted to the Compagnie d'Occident, which was merged into the Compagnie des Indes in 1719 and its beaver privilege confirmed by a royal edict the following year. In 1722, the Compagnie des Indes' ship *Driade* sailed from Québec with a cargo of 120,000 pounds (in weight) of beaver pelts.[18]

This meant that beaver pelts could be bought and sold at leisure while they were in New France until they would be exported to France. Canadian traders wishing to do so had to bring the furs to the Compagnie des Indes' offices (or lodges) and storehouses at Montréal, Trois-Rivières and Québec where they were paid a set price depending on quality. The monopoly only applied to exporting beaver pelts. Other pelts remained on the open market except for those coming from the royal monopoly area called the *Domaine du Roi* (King's Domain) that extended from the Saguenay River to Labrador's Atlantic coast. From the 1720s, the Compagnie des Indes' staff at Québec included its agent, a comptroller, a receiver, an inspector of beaver pelts and a clerk as well as a receiver in Trois-Rivières and Montréal. The Trois-Rivières office did not have much business and was closed in June 1749 while the Montréal office, which was Canada's hub of the fur trade, expanded. There, the Compagnie des Indes received the majority of beaver pelts, packed them into 120 lbs bales, marked and sealed them for their voyage to France. It was a lucrative trade and represented about 70 percent of Canada's exports to France. Figures varied, but it might represent about a million and a half livres a year while the Compagnie des Indes' business expenses in Canada were roughly 10 percent of that sum.[19]

As with any monopoly trade system, smuggling was widespread in Canada. Therefore, part of the Canadian staff in Québec and Montréal included a variable number of armed 'Gardes de la Compagnie des Indes' each led by a *brigadier*. There were also a few 'Gardes du Domaine du Roi' in Québec harbour inspecting ships and cargoes. These guard units were constabulary organisations somewhat akin to customs and border guards. In October 1729, Intendant Hocquart approved an agreement between the Compagnie des Indes and the Domaine du Roi directing that both guard units would be led by *Capitaine* Dufoucher of the Gardes du Domaine and consist of a *brigadier* and four guards in Québec while the Gardes de la

18 Dufresne de Francheville, *Histoire de la Compagnie des Indes*, pp.104-106; Haudrere, *La Compagnie des Indes au XVIIIe siècle*, Vol.3, pp.902-903; AC, C11A, 44, Vaudreuil and Bégon to the Conseil de la Marine, 17 October 1722. The Compagnie des Indes usually paid 4 livres (currency) per pound of the best beaver furs on which it levied a 25 percent service and freight tax. In France, a pound of quality beaver pelt sold for 7 1/2 livres (currency). Lower quality was worth 2 livres. There was fluctuation in prices, but a shipment could be worth up to a million livres in France.

19 AC, B, 43, Instructions pour le Sieur Barthelémy Coton, Paris, 9 May 1725 and Mémoire de la Compagnie des Indes, Paris, 2 May 1726; P.-G. Roy (ed.), *Inventaire des Ordonnances des Intendants de la Nouvelle-France* (Beaucheville: L'Éclaireur, 1919), Vol.3, p.131; Marcel Trudel, *Initiation à la Nouvelle-France* (Montréal: Holt, Rinehart & Winston, 1968), pp.207-211.

The Compagnie des Indes office (or lodge) at Montréal, Canada, c. 1750. Needing larger facilities for receiving beaver pelts exported to France as well as European and Asian goods for New France, the company bought the property of former Montréal Governor de Ramezay in 1745. It included the chateau, which was expanded in 1756, as well as secondary buildings and a large garden and orchard. Unlike lodges in Africa and Asia, fortifications were not needed apart from fences. The company had its own brigade of armed guardsmen in Canada to insure security and prevent smuggling. (Model by Michel Bergeron, Chateau de Ramezay Museum, Montréal, author's photo)

Compagnie des Indes in Montréal grew to eight guards led by its *brigadier* and they even had their own guardhouse.[20]

For guardsmen of the Compagnie des Indes in Montréal, it was a much more dangerous occupation. They were facing though and often battle-tested *voyageurs* and *coureurs-de-bois*, woodsmen smuggling beaver pelts and other goods to and from British colonies further south. The guards initially requested squads of Compagnies franches de la Marine soldiers to assist them, a duty that was not 'to the taste of a soldier' commented Governor-General de Beauharnais in 1727. Most of the smugglers were caught south of Montréal and there might be stiff resistance. One case brought to court in August 1730 concerned four *voyageurs* that had 'beaten up' guards of the Compagnie des Indes before being apprehended. The guilty could be fined, imprisoned, his property seized, or worse. There appears to be no precise description of these guards apart from a 1749 document mentioning muskets, pistols, swords and bandoliers as worn by constabulary troops in France. All Compagnie des Indes business in Canada became redundant with the capitulation of Montréal to British forces on 8 September 1760.[21]

---

20 AC, C11A, 51, Nous soussigné François Étienne Cygnet, 18 October 1729; Roy (ed.), *Inventaire des Ordonnances des Intendants*, Vol.3, p.40. There previously were some 'Gardes du Castor' employed by the 'Compagnie de la Colonie'. A statement of 14 November 1705 mentions Sieur Leboeuf, *capitaine* 'des gardes', Sieur Saint-Paul, *lieutenant* and a guard named Hervé as per Vol.1, p.6.

21 Roy (ed.), *Inventaire des Ordonnances des Intendants*, Vol.1, pp.265, 267, 288; AC, C11A, 49, Beauharnais to minister, 27 October 1727; Archives nationales du Québec à Montréal, Pièces

Denis Bossinot de Pomphily, circa 1730. A former naval officer, he was a senior official of the company in Montréal where this portrait was possibly made by an unknown artist. He wears a red coat with gold buttons and embroidery. At right, in the background, the stern of a ship, most likely of the Compagnie des Indes, can be hazily seen. (Château de Ramezay Museum, Montréal, author's photo)

China

The most distant outpost of the Compagnie des Indes to reach was at Canton in the province of 'Quang-Tong', part of the Empire of China. It was only accessible by sailing up the Canton River from the China Sea after passing Macao, the only territory in the empire conceded (in the sixteenth century) to a foreign power, Portugal, although it was really governed as a condominium with the Chinese authorities. There had been several French China companies since 1660 that were often near bankruptcy until their trade privilege was assumed by the Compagnie des Indes in 1719, which brought more stability and the China trade flourished.

Canton was the only port in the Chinese Empire where foreign ships were allowed to anchor. That city held a trade fair that lasted seven months during which Dutch, British, Portuguese and French merchants participated having lodges called 'hans' or 'factories' on the harbour in a very intense and lucrative trade with businessmen coming from all parts of the Far East. The Chinese government strictly imposed import and export taxes and this process started by a visit from Chinese customs officials to any foreign ship arriving.

Foreigners were not allowed to go within the city of Canton and were required to reside at Macao when the fair closed for the season. Their personal security and that of their merchandise was efficiently looked after by the local Chinese police and the small squad of European soldiers that the foreign hans were allowed to maintain on the spot. In the case of the Compagnie des Indes, this consisted in a detachment of about 15 to 30 French soldiers. For instance, one *caporal* and 14 soldiers boarded the *Duc de Penthièvre* for China on 19 November 1754; one *sergent*, one *caporal* and 16 soldiers by the *Duc de Chartres* on 20 November 1754; one *sergent*, one *caporal* and 12 soldiers by the *Pondicherry* on 15 January 1755. All received four months' pay in advance.[22]

judiciaries, Boîte 06-MT1-1/121, Compagnie des Indes vs Landreville, Vaudry, Rivest et Dubreil, voyageurs accusés d'avoir cassé la gueule a des Gardes de la Compagnie des Indes, 11 juillet and 20 août 1730; AC, C11A, 121, Mémoire concernant la régime pour la perception des droits, 4 June 1749. This memoir mentions that the bandolier of the Gardes du Domaine should have a plate engraved with the heraldic 'Arms of the King' and the words 'Gardes du Domaine' for recognition. This would seem to indicate that there was no particular livery or uniform.

22 AC, D2C, 187, Rôle des noms…pour aller en Chine, 19 November 1754, 20 November 1754 and 15 January 1755.

Lodges of European trade companies at Canton, China, mid-eighteenth century. The French lodge of the Compagnie des Indes is identified by the white standard (second from right). It maintained a squad of its soldiers at the lodge. The lodges were built in European style by Chinese businessmen who rented them to the companies. Detail from a remarkable model of the harbour made of ivory with added colouring. (Peabody Essex Museum, Salem, Massachusetts, USA, author's photo)

Joseph Develaër, circa 1750. Develaër (1709-1785) was a merchant who became a senior official at the Compagnie des Indes' lodge in Canton, China. Surprisingly, he wears the medal of a knight of Portugal's Order of Christ (seen at the bottom of the portrait), which also suggests a military role. This honour would have been awarded for services for or with the Portuguese at nearby Macau, possibly against Chinese pirates. He came back to France and was made count de Lude in 1752. His coat is blue with gold buttons and his waistcoat red. (Musée de la Compagnie des Indes, Lorient / Ville de Vitré D VIT 2011, photo Stephen Wood)

These soldiers were advised to be very disciplined while in Canton. They were subject to Chinese law that was rigorously applied by the police. A brawl with a Chinese person in a tavern could be forgiven providing no blood was shed. If blood was shed, it was taken seriously and would incur a heavy fine. If death resulted, be it involuntary or by wilful murder, the culprit was summarily executed swiftly. As a result of the closure of the Compagnie des Indes in France, its China privilege came to an end, its lodge was closed and its personnel including the soldiers left Canton in 1771.[23]

23 Boudriot, *Compagnie des Indes*, p.254 after the memoirs of P.Blancard; AC, C1, 11, Canton council to the company, 19 January 1771.

15

Military Organisation and Establishments

The military forces of France's monopoly trading companies can be divided into two time periods. The first period spans from about 1600 to 1719. As seen above, there were between those dates many East India companies as well as some for Africa, others for the Far East with a few for America whose modest number troops usually consisted of independent companies. Those monopoly companies existing in 1719 were all consolidated into the new and all-encompassing Compagnie des Indes. This second era, which saw the emergence of the company's sizeable multiethnic armies in India, ended in 1770.

From 1600 to 1719

There is modest data regarding soldiers taken into the service of these early monopoly companies. Since soldiers were expensive for fledgling investor-stockholders hoping for an eventual substantial profit, military men were a necessary expense in some cases, but such expenses had to be as low as possible. The soldiers hired might serve as marines on an outward voyage, then double as settlers and militiamen in a nascent establishment overseas. This was a pattern in the early settlements in America and on Madagascar. These were areas that were to have settlers from France to create territories that would eventually have large French populations. This had some positive results in America, especially in Canada and in the West Indies to a lesser extent, but a total failure in Madagascar. As seen in the chapter on early Madagascar, a peak of sorts may have been achieved in 1656 with up to 350 soldiers (although many seem to have been also settlers) at Fort Dauphin. In 1666, four infantry companies were detached from royal regiments to Fort Dauphin. What surviving soldiers that were there had evacuated by 1674. As for Ile de Bourbon, it had no garrison.

The lodges established in India from 1668 did have soldiers, sometimes in numbers. This was initially due to the considerable backing from King

French Fusilier, late 1660s-early 1670s. A substantial number of soldiers sent to the East Indies were armed with flintlock muskets as well as matchlock muskets and were issued European style clothing. Plate after Derek FitzJames. (Private collection, author's photo.)

Louis XIV who had set up the Compagnie des Indes orientales (East India Company) in August 1664. Its first lodge in India was established at Surat in 1668. Some 400 soldiers detached from the Régiment Royal-Marine were on board Viceroy de La Haye's fleet 'of Persia' that only arrived at Surat in October 1671. There also was La Haye's guard company, some officers detached from the King's Musketeers of the royal guard and a company of cadets. The soldiers from this diminishing contingent, with perhaps 100 more arriving later, were the basis of the troops of the Compagnie des Indes orientales at Pondicherry from 1673. In 1675, its garrison consisted of 100 French soldiers and 200 locally recruited Indo-Portuguese Christian topasses that usually formed part of a company. There were also Indian auxiliary soldiers that could be an early form of what became known as sepoys. The garrison seems to have hovered at about 100 Europeans thereafter. The Siam expedition of 1688-1689 mustered up to 600 soldiers of the king's navy. Some 200 marines arrived at Pondicherry in late 1689, some from the Siam expedition, and remained there. It had two companies when the Dutch attacked and took it in 1693. Following Pondicherry's return to France and reoccupation in September 1699, the garrison consisted of two companies of marines, three of the Compagnie des Indes orientales in 1701, five in 1706, reduced to four in 1709 and three in 1713. By then, the East India business was nearly bankrupt and was eventually absorbed into the Compagnie des Indes in 1719.[1]

Governors, Generals and Staff Officers

From the seventeenth century well into the eighteenth, military matters in overseas territories would be managed by a governor or Governor-General with assistance from the local council and senior officers including an engineer. By the later 1740s, however, it was clear that France's territories in India were becoming outstandingly important. To meet the challenges brought by the opportunities opened with the gradual collapse of the Mughal empire, more troops were needed and raised amongst sepoy Indian soldiers.

1 Much of this paragraph is from Kaepelin, *La Compagnie des Indes orientales* and Martin, *Mémoires*, Vol.1. The company of cadets was most likely found from gentlemen aspiring to obtain officer's commissions.

On paper in France, the military establishment and its command structure remained generally the same in all territories, but reality in India dictated that Governor-General Dupleix make important decisions quickly. Dupleix had remarkable geostrategic and political views to expand the Compagnie des Indes' influence so as to gain more territory, revenues and influence in southern and central India.

A senior command organisation therefore became necessary in India. The number of troops, especially the sepoys, was multiplying and something like a permanent staff of senior officers was needed to manage what was becoming an army. European field artillery and cavalry units with expanded medical and administrative services were organised in India to meet the needs of corps in the field. The company's troops being organised as independent infantry companies, the rank of *capitaine* was the highest most officers could hope for. Yet a talented officer such as Bussy was theoretically only a *capitaine* commanding a corps of thousands of French and Indian soldiers in the Deccan from 1751. In fact, Bussy also had important diplomatic mandates as well as being a de-facto general. That year, Dupleix asked the Compagnie des Indes to formally promote him to *lieutenant-colonel*, which was finally approved two years later. By 1753, there were at least 3,000 European soldiers and some 10,000 sepoys in French service. Dupleix was asking the company to send a *brigadier* with several *lieutenant-colonels*, promote Bussy to the rank of *colonel* and himself to *maréchal de camp* (major general) to manage the military properly. Dupleix had successfully repulsed the British at Pondicherry in 1748, yet he was not a military officer. His request caused some outrage amongst military circles in Versailles and Paris; his request was denied, but the idea of a senior commander with staff officers was not forgotten.[2]

With the reinforcements involving royal army units that were sent from France to India arriving in 1757-1758, the royal government imposed a command structure that combined the posts of Governor-General and commander in chief of all military forces in French India, be they of the Compagnie des Indes or of the royal army. The Comte de Lally held this appointment and he came with a number of staff officers. They included three aides-de-camp, a *maréchal-de-camp* with his aide-de-camp, a *brigadier* of infantry, an *aide-maréchal-général-des-logis* (assistant quartermaster-general), an *aide-major-général d'infanterie, an aide-maréchal-général-des-logis de cavalerie*, a *colonel* and a *lieutenant-colonel* of infantry, a *officier-partisan*, a *commissaire des guerres* with a *commissaire en second* (administrative non-combatant officers), a surgeon-major, a surgeon *aide-major*, and an *ingénieur-géographe*. All these officers belonged to the metropolitan army. They were expected to work in conjunction with the Compagnie des Indes' officers and officials.[3]

2 Prosper Cultu, *Dupleix* (Paris: Hachette, 1901), pp.306-307.

3 BNF, Réglement pour le traitement des officiers généraux, & autres employés du corps de troupes destiné à passer aux Indes Orientales, 10 November 1756.

Military Officers of the Compagnie des Indes

The men seeking commissions to officer rank were selected by the company, submitted to royal approval and, if all agreed, the commission was delivered to the individual. About 1,150 officers were commissioned by the company during its existence, an average of about 22 yearly. Being in the company's service did not, however, equate to holding a commission in the royal army or the king's navy. Royal orders specified that the king's troops always had precedence. As in the king's navy, these commissions had no monetary value and could not be bought or sold. The prospective young gentlemen had surely heard of the deadly tropical fevers in Africa and Asia, but they also knew that some survived and had come back home with substantial amounts of money in their pockets, which was a strong incentive. The officers were generally young men from gentry or noble families of modest means that were hoping to make their fortune as well as see and live in exotic, far away countries. They were to be Roman Catholics, have a fairly good education and genteel manners. Good family connections helped.

Before being commissioned as an *enseigne*, there was schooling to be attended to at Lorient as a gentleman cadet. The depot company had an establishment of 24 cadets attached to it. The curriculum included sciences, hydrography, art, drawing, literature and probably also basic tactics and dancing to round out the perfect young gentleman. As in the royal troops, the length of time spent as a cadet could vary. In the case of young Gaston Brochard de Puymorin, he became a cadet at Lorient in 1739 and was commissioned *enseigne* in 1740. He may have been a strong candidate because he distinguished himself at Tanjore, Madras, the victorious 1748 defence of Pondichery as a grenadier *lieutenant* and several more battles including the capture of Gingee. Bussy decorated him as a knight in the Order of Saint-Louis in April 1750.[4]

For nearly all, the highest rank was *capitaine*, which was worth a rather modest 1,080 livres a year. There was no pension plan as in the royal forces. The best that could be hoped for the elderly was approval of an application for some money to the destitute, but this was seemingly not often granted. *Capitaine* Bouteville was exceptionally awarded a 400 livres pension when he was 78 years old. The widow of engineer *Capitaine* Paradis killed at the 1748 siege of Pondicherry had to settle for a one time only payment of 2,000 rupees.[5]

In India, the monthly pay came to 175 rupees for an *enseigne*, 200 to a *lieutenant*, 400 to a *capitaine* and 800 to 1,000 to a commandant. In 1754, due to considerable inflation in prices of food and rents, Dupleix

4 Martineau, *Dupleix*, Vol.1, p.33; Giraud, *Histoire de la Louisiane française*, Vol.4, pp.44-45; AC, E, 343, Brochard, Gaston, chevalier de Puymorin, capitaine des troupes de la Compagnie des Indes à Pondichéry. While not covering cadets of the East India companies, Léon Hennet, *Les Compagnies de Cadets Gentilhommes et les Écoles Militaires* (Paris: Baudouin, 1889), remains a very good source on this topic.

5 Cultru, *Dupleix*, p.303.

Left: French Infantry officer, 1740s-early 1750s. The more debonair officers of the Compagnie des Indes would likely have appeared much as in this drawing by Augustin de Saint-Aubin. (National Gallery of Canada, Ottawa)

Right: A young officer-cadet, circa 1730. An officer-cadet of the Compagnie des Indes at Lorient would have had a general similar appearance. His uniform was a white coat with blue cuffs, coat lining, waistcoat, breeches and blue or white stocking, gilded buttons with a gold-laced hat. Print after Watteau. (Private collection, author's photo.)

recommended raising the officer's pay by 90 rupees and assume the rent for *capitaines*, 65 to *lieutenants*, 50 to *sous-lieutenants* and 45 to *enseignes*. However, there could be bonus-like 'gratifications' as well as prize money. Even better, local princes in India might add some money to the basic pay to French troops serving in their areas. In 1751, the pay of a contingent of European troops going to Golconde was augmented by 1,000 rupees to a *capitaine*, 600 to *lieutenants*, 500 to *sous-lieutenants*, 300 to *enseignes*, and 25 to enlisted men besides gifts. When Bussy's troops reached Hyderabad that year, he was given a gratification of 300,000 rupees, Kirjean had 250,000, Vincens 200,000 and even the translator de Larche 100,000 while the troops' pay was doubled. This princely largesse was qualified as a 'road to fortune' so it must have made a positive difference to the troops' pocketbooks. On the other hand, there also were periods when coffers were empty and there could then be delays in pay.[6]

The rapid expansion of the military establishment in mid-eighteenth century India meant that commissions, be they as new officers or as promotions, simply had to be delivered immediately to have enough officers to train and command new European and sepoy corps. About a year could pass from the recommendation going from Pondicherry to Lorient then to Paris and Versailles for final approval and a signed commission going back to the prospective officer in India. In both the royal and the Compagnie des Indes' overseas territories, governors resorted to 'expectative' local commissions until the officially approved document arrived.

The problem arising in India was that an army was being raised. By 1750, there were 15 *capitaines*, 17 *lieutenants*, 19 *sous-lieutenants* and 27 *enseignes* for a total of 78 officers, without commissions for the rank they actually occupied. In one case, the demand had been lost somewhere in the bureaucracy since 1743! This was not an especially positive factor for morale and hampered efforts to promote those officers 'that had the most merit'. To solve the problem, Dupleix asked for and obtained approval in France on 24 October 1750, to have blank commissions that could be given immediately.[7]

All of the above-concerned gentlemen born in France. By comparison many officers of the royal troops of the Ministry of the Navy posted in North America and the West Indies were born overseas. In Canada, education to cadets leading to an officer's commission in the Compagnies franches de la Marine was offered as early as 1685 and 1730 for the West Indies. This was the result of territories populated by French settlers. The aims of the various French East India and African monopoly companies were to create trade, commerce and other profit-making activities, rather than settlement. There was an exception: the Iles de France and de Bourbon. The latter island in particular had a sizeable Créole population, as children of Europeans born overseas were then called. A few sons of gentlemen surely aspired to become officers, but not many seem to have succeeded in such ambitions; only in 1759 were five young men of Ile de Bourbon commissioned into the Compagnie des Inde's troops.[8]

---

6 BNF, Ms Français 8971, Recueil de pièces sur l'Inde; BNF, NAF, 9146, Dupleix to council in Paris, 15 February 1754; Fréville, 'Une armée coloniale au XVIIIe siècle Dupleix aux Indes', *Revue des questions historiques*, October 1904, p.419; Vaissière, *Dupleix*, pp.143-144.

7 AC, E7, Personal record of *Capitaine* Urbain d'Argy, Plan…24 October 1750. The names of the officers were (as best as could be read: *Capitaines*: D'Argy, d'Auteuil, Baldie, de Bussy, Dancy, St. Martin, Floissac, Law, Mainville, du Passage, Piscou Du Lude, Prévost de la Touche, de St. Jean. *Lieutenants*: Bellemares de St. Cyr, Cochinat, D'hivy, Gassonville le fils, du Jauddaye, Maulin, Pichaud, Puymoiny, du Rocher de Lavigne, St. Denis de Virvaine, de St. Georges, Villeon de Quillon. *Sous-lieutenants*: de Caix, D'or, Du Guez, Jainville, Vincent, Pradeau, Sehonamille, Vérry. *Enseignes*: Aymand, aZam, Bassecourt, Boulaine, Calquises, Chalond, Couziol, Dublin, Dumesnil, Du Rouvray, Duval, Gavangez, Gaumont, Gubrie, Jason de St. Maurice, Kaly, La Randisse, Lauzun, Le Guis, Mendoce, Mirvault, de Mouy, Plonsquelet, St. Mons, Thibault, Vay Sandek, Yon.

8 ADR, Co 500, Conseil supérieur de l'Ile de France to the Conseil supérieur de l'Ile de Bourbon, 6 June 1759.

Swiss Troops of the Compagnie des Indes 1720-1725

Oddly enough, when the Compagnie des Indes was formed in 1719, the largest establishment of troops it inherited was in Louisiana. Since 11 February 1719, its garrison was to have 1,000 soldiers led by 60 officers. India had about 375 Europeans and 150 topasses. Senegal had about 40 Europeans and some 40 African soldiers. Ile de France and Ile de Bourbon had no garrisons at all. The total then came to about 1,400 European soldiers, 190 Asians or Africans and perhaps 80 officers.[9]

To have a quick solution for providing dependable troops and skilled workers, the Compagnie des Indes called on mercenary Swiss officers to raise companies that were to be sent to Louisiana and Ile de France. These Swiss soldiers were also to be skilled workers and artisans for construction work. On 4 January 1720, a 'Capitulation' (agreement) had been made between the company and *Capitaine* Wonwunderlick de Merveilleux to raise 210 men (including six officers) to serve in Louisiana and ready to be shipped out in September 1720.A similar agreement for a company of 210 men for Ile de France was also made on 27 February 1720 with *Capitaine* Beugnot, *Capitaine* Schmidig being in actual command. This company seems to have taken longer to raise. It sailed on 31 June 1721. Once at Ile de France, the Swiss soldier-workers were quite disappointed and unhappy with their new homes at Port-Louis and they were sent back to France the following year. Please see 'Ile de France and Ile de Bourbon Garrisons 1721-1763' in Chapter 16 for more details.[10]

Meanwhile, Merveilleux's Swiss Company arrived in Louisiana in 1721. Please see chapter 14 for its peculiar story. It was ordered disbanded on 26 July 1725. Thus ended the Swiss soldier-worker experiment that turned out to be a near disaster for all concerned. The Compagnie des Indes did not form Swiss units thereafter.[11]

Depot Company at Lorient 1721-1772

The nascent Compagnie des Indes kept whatever was standing guard in its overseas territories in 1719. In France itself, it was not until the royal order of

9 Ordonnance de la Compagnie [d'Occident] pour le règlement des troupes quelle a augmentée, 11 February 1719

10 AC, B, 43, Project de Capitulation pour la Compagnie Suisse de la Compagnie des Indes dans la Louisiane, 4 January 1720; AG, A3, 76, Capitulation faite avec le Sr. Bugnot pour une Compagnie Suisse de la Compagnie des Indes aux Indes, 27 February 1720; Marcelle Lagesse, *L'Ile de France avant La Bourdonnais* 1721-1735 (Port-Louis, Mauritius: Mauritius Archives Publications, 1972), p.11; APL, 1P 256b, 8, Compte...des recète et dépenses...21 Mars...23 May..., and Substance de la Compagnie de Beugnot; Lagesse, *L'Ile de France avant La Bourdonnais*, p.18; Albert Lougnon, *L'Ile Bourbon sous la Régence* (Paris: Larose, 1956), p.226. It sailed for Ile de France with 20 women and 30 children. Sadly, it seems a pandemic struck these Swiss. Only 67 men of whom 32 were fit remained by 1722.

11 AG, A1, 2542, Biloxi, Les Suisses..., 4 May 1721; AC, B, 43, Etat général des dépenses... pendant l'année 1725 and Ordonnance pour le licenciement de la compagnie suisse, 26 July 1725; Giraud, *Histoire de la Louisiane française*, Vol.3, p.278.

1 October 1721 creating 'a company of infantry at the service and paid by the Compagnie des Indes' that steps were taken to regulate more closely troops that, while not part of the royal army or navy, rendered essential services in France as marines and to the overseas garrisons. To continue to do so more efficiently, the Compagnie des Indes needed a permanent depot at Lorient in France. The royal order's preamble stated that:

> His Majesty being informed that the Compagnie des Indes has a large number of ships at the port of Lorient and great warehouses in the park of the said port, filled with all the merchandise necessary to its commerce, whose conservation [and safety] is important; His Majesty has judged that it would be convenient for the said company to have a company of infantry at its service, and in the pay of the said Compagnie des Indes, for the guard of the said port of Lorient, and to furnish detachments that are necessary in the colonies of its concessions.[12]

The King, who was then 12 years old, of course followed the advice of the Duc d'Orleans who presided the Regency Council that ordered the company to have five officers and 98 enlisted men. The pay and other expense were assumed by the Compagnie des Indes. This depot company was not, at times, sufficiently numerous to accomplish its routine guard and police duties in the city of Lorient. This was solved from 1729 when the royal authorities posted a company of invalids permanently in Lorient.[13]

The port of Lorient was the designated port for 'merchants and merchandise arriving from the Orient' to quote a 1689 letter signed by the Madame de Sévigné who visited what was then mainly a shipyard. It really prospered from 1719 when the Compagnie des Indes made it its main naval and military base in France. A report of 1731 mentioned that it was evolving 'day after day' into a 'large and beautiful town' that had 1,000 workmen in its shipyard, 3,000 sailors on its ships at sea and that over 800 soldiers having been trained there were presently posted in the company's overseas territories. Lorient was growing into a city of 14,000 souls and, in 1733, the rather too elegant M. de Rigby, then director of the company, had a luxurious lifestyle with retainers dressed in a green livery richly laced at the seams who wore solid silver bandolier plates engraved with the company's coat of arms, and employed a dozen sailors for his boat and three dozen servants to attend him. While this lavish-minded director was soon replaced by a less carefree administrator, Lorient continued to prosper with fine stone buildings and mansions replacing the previous humble constructions.[14]

In 1721, the depot company was initially known as 'Plantin's company', the name of its commanding captain. He was succeeded by *Capitaine* Romé

12 BMG, Ordonnance du Roy. Pour la Levée d'une Compagnie d'Infanterie au service de la Compagnie des Indes, 1 October 1721.

13 Giraud, *Histoire de la Louisiane française*, Vol.4, p.45

14 APL. 1P 300, 46, 29 June 1731; Armel de Wismes, *La vie quotidienne dans les ports bretons aux XVIIe et XVIIIe siècles* (Paris: Hachette, 1973), pp.139-140. One is tempted to conclude that the green uniform was the livery of the company, but it could simply be that of the director. As it turned out, M. de Rigby was denounced and his administrative career ended in the Bastille royal prison.

in September 1731. From June 1740, it became *Lieutenant-Colonel* Bessan's company until 1766 when that officer was replaced by La Périgne.[15]

The enlisted men of the company that might desert were to suffer the same punishments as deserters of the royal army. In effect, they were subject to the same code of military discipline. This was made clear by a royal order of 5 February 1722 regarding infantry and ship's officers, soldiers and employees of the Compagnie des Indes at Lorient whose behaviour and 'refusal to obey' was deemed 'entirely contrary to the service of His Majesty' and, if strict discipline was not immediately applied, would result in cancelled commissions for officers and senior employees with, for enlisted men and soldiers, punishment for sedition. Thereafter, the personnel at Lorient, be it military, naval or civil, understood that all had to be up to the standards wished by the royal government.[16]

Governance of the Compagnie des Indes' troops at Lorient did not seem to have caused much concern in the following decades. As in the royal forces, desertion was a recurring problem for the company in Lorient. A royal order of 26 January 1727 specified that deserters from the Compagnie des Indes troops were liable to the same penalties for that crime as were those deserting from the royal army.

One of the age-old tactics of professional deserters was to cash in another enlistment bounty. This occurred in 1736 when several newly enlisted soldiers proved to have previously deserted the Compagnies franches de la Marine. After 1722, royal orders were not often seen because the routine services of the Compagnie des Indes troops were to enlist and train soldiers that were then detached as marines on board the company's larger ships. The ratio of marines to sailors on board appears to have been about one soldier to five sailors. Of the ships that sailed for India in 1762, seven had 279 soldiers and 1,047 sailors on board. The actual number of men in the Lorient depot company fluctuated mostly upwards during the following years. On 20 October 1740, a royal order officially allowed a major increase in its establishment to 'ensure the security' of the port of Lorient and to provide recruits for the 22 companies of 100 men each serving in Africa and Asia. The King allowed the company at Lorient to henceforth have 11 officers and 300 enlisted men. Their pay and other conditions remained as before.[17]

---

15 BMG, Ordonnance du Roy. Pour la Levée d'une Compagnie d'Infanterie au service de la Compagnie des Indes, 1 October 1721. The details of the infantry company's composition and monthly pay are: a *capitaine* (90 livres), a *lieutenant* (60 livres), a *sous-lieutenant* (50 livres), two *enseignes* (40 livres each), four *sergents* (19 livres 10 sols each), four *caporaux* (13 livres 10 sols each), four *anspesades* (12 livres each), 84 fusiliers (9 livres each) and two drummers (13 livres 10 sols each). APL. IP 300, 46, 29 June 1731 unsigned letter; APL, 1P 305, 48, Louis XV to Bessan, 26 February 1741.

16 BMG, Ordonnance du Roy. Pour ordonner aux officiers et soldats de la Compagnie d'Infanterie au service de la Compagnie des Indes, 5 February 1722. The text also includes naval officers and civil employees.

17 BNF, Ordonnance du Roy. Portent que les déserteurs des Troupes de la Compagnie des Indes…, 27 January 1727; Haudrère, *La compagnie française des Indes au XVIIIe siècle 1719-1795*, Vol.3, p.854; AM, A1, 77, Ordonnance du Roy. Portant augmentation de la Compagnie de Fusiliers entretenue au Port de L'Orient, 20 October 1740. The details of the infantry company's composition and monthly pay are: a *capitaine* commandant, a *capitaine-*

In 1745, James Ray, a volunteer under 'his R.H. the Duke of Cumberland' during the Scottish Highland's uprising mentioned in his 1749 book: *A Compleat History of the Rebellion, From its first Rise in 1745, To its total Suppression at the glorious Battle of Culloden, in April 1746* that an officer of the French Navy 'raised a Company of one hundred Men, under the Pretence that they were for the East India Company's Service, which they styled Grassins de Mer, and were handsomely cloathed in Blue faced with Red.' He further related having seen them as prisoners of war following their capture at sea. However, there is no official record so far encountered of such a unit in the Compagnie des Indes troops, nor those of the navy nor the army.[18]

British Attack on Lorient 1746

By the mid-1740s, the War of Austrian Succession pitted France against Great Britain and, seeing thriving Lorient, some British officials and officers decided that time had come to strike a powerful economic blow by destroying France's base for oriental trade. A fleet was gathered, six infantry regiments went on board led by Lieutenant General James St Clair that landed on 1 October 1746 at Loch, a somewhat isolated place between Pouldu and Talut. It was important for the British force to avoid the highly fortified citadel and batteries at Port-Louis, which guarded the naval access to Lorient. Loch may have been rather distant, but was far safer. Opposition to a landing there could only come from mustered coastguard militiamen and what few regular troops there might be in the area.[19]

As it was, about 800 mostly hastily mustered coastguard militiamen with some 400 dragoons of the Régiment l'Hôpital in that area withdrew without resistance estimating that about 5,000 redcoats had landed. The appearance of nearly 50 enemy ships landing regiments clearly signalled that this was more than an occasional corsair's small raid. The next day, when the British reached the village of Ploemeur, a party of armed peasants opened fire from a concealed position upon Frampton's 30th and Richbell's 39th regiments, which, never having been in action, broke and ran in disorder with the

en-second, a *lieutenant-en-premier*, a *lieutenant-en-second*, a *sous-lieutenant*, six *enseignes*, 14 *sergents*, 14 *caporaux*, 14 *anspesades*, 250 fusiliers and eight fifers and drummers. The order mistakenly mentioned the Guinea Coast, which had no European garrison, when Senegal was meant. Jean-Yves Le Lan, 'Les départs des navires de la Compagnie des Indes de Lorient pour l'Océan Indien de 1760 à 1764', <https://www.histoire-genealogie.com/Les-departs-des-navires-de-la?lang=fr> (accessed 11 October 2023).

18 James Ray, *A Compleat History of the Rebellion, From its first Rise in 1745, To its total Suppression at the glorious Battle of Culloden, in April 1746* (Bristol, 1752), pp.18-19. *Grassins de Mer* (sea-service Grassins) was after the land army's renowned light corps the 'Volontaires de Grassin'.

19 Since the later Middle Ages, inhabitants of villages and hamlets along the coasts of France were obliged to serve in the coastguard militia while town dwellers everywhere in the nation were to be part of the Bourgeois Militia some of which were remarkably well armed and uniformed. The militias were massively reorganised from the late 1680s eventually restructured into the National Guard from the 1790s. For more details, please see: René Chartrand, *The Armies and Wars of the Sun King Volume 4: The War of Spanish Succession, Artillery, Engineers and Militias* (Warwick: Helion, 2021).

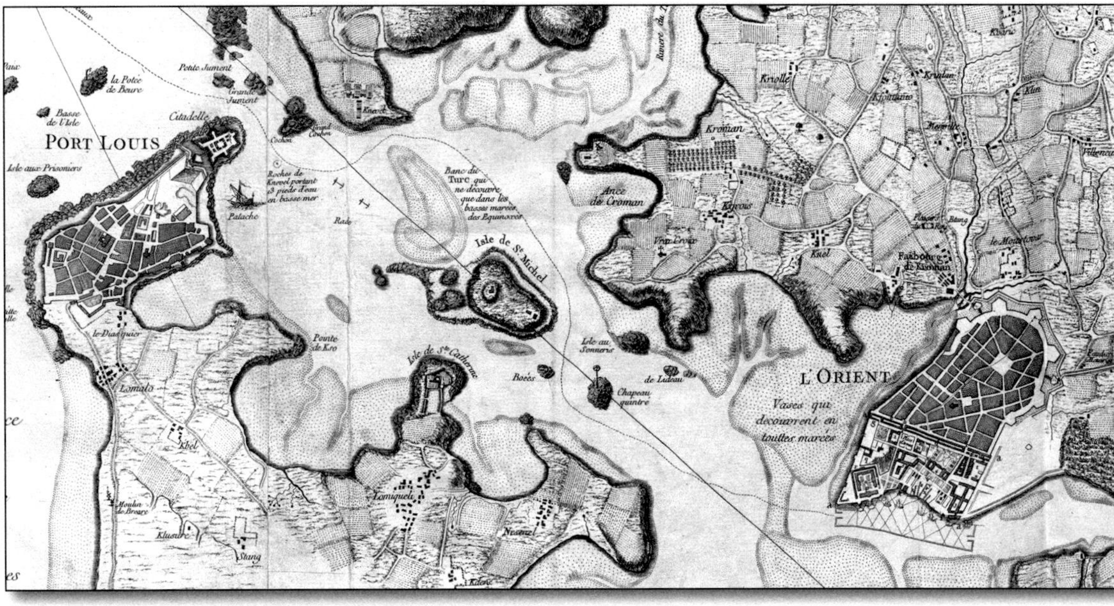

Map of the area of Lorient and Port Louis, mid-eighteenth century. Lorient's harbour was guarded by the citadel at Port Louis (at left). Passed the citadel, ships still had a hazardous journey to get to the town of Lorient because of low lying sand bars, invisible at high tide, as well as some rocky reefs. Detail of a map by Georges-Louis Le Rouge. (British Library, London)

Guidon bearer of dragoons, mid-eighteenth century. This was the general aspect of dragoon units at that time including the 400 dragoons belonging to the Régiment l'Hôpital that participated in the victorious defence of Lorient in October 1746. Its uniform consisted of a red coat with red cuffs, blue waistcoat, white metal button, white buttonhole lace, white stockings, silver laced hat with black cockade, red cap with blue turn-up, red cloak, blue housings edged with white lace, buffs accoutrements with white stitching according to the 1748 army register. The guidon was blue with gold sun, lilies and fringes. (Private collection, author's photo.)

exception of the grenadier company of Frampton's, which stood its ground. More British troops arrived and the defending peasants fled. Ploemeur, including even its church, was then utterly looted and savagely destroyed by British troops.[20]

---

20 The British force consisted of St Clair's 1st, Harrison's 15th, Bragg's 28th, Frampton's 30th, Richbell's 39th, and Murray's 43rd (later 42nd) infantry regiments that may have numbered about 4,800 men. The fleet under Admiral Lestock had 13 warships and 33 transports as per Anon., *British Minor Expeditions 1746 to 1814* (London: HMSO, 1884), p.7; Fortescue, *A History of the British Army,* Vol.2, p.156. The

By 3 October, the British were approaching Lorient, which confirmed to the French that it was their target. The summons sent by St Clair threatened to burn down the city and slaughter its inhabitants 'by the sword' unless he received its keys. Had the British proposals been less sanguinary and their troop's behaviour somewhat better at Ploemeur, there might have been grounds for a capitulation if the safety of inhabitants and their property had been agreed to. It was now clear to Lorient's officials that nothing of the sort was likely to be granted although the military ardour of some officials did not seem very high. Ironically, it was the soldiers of the depot company and the city's inhabitants that were more warlike. Some 4,000 inhabitants went to work erecting field fortifications in record time.

The regular troops in garrison consisted of about 400 men of the company's depot and 400 dragoons of l'Hôpital's regiment. Some 600 shipyard and harbour workers formed a seven-company volunteer battalion for full time service. The city's Bourgeois Militia was partly mobilised also with all other men ready to muster. Nearby towns also mustered their Bourgeois militias to reinforce Lorient. From 2 October, hundreds of militiamen from Hennebont, Rennes and other towns streamed into the city as well as the 600 cavalrymen of the Régiment de Heudicourt's a couple of days later. There may have been about 6,000 men ready to defend the city, but it must be recalled that only about 1,400 were professional soldiers and nothing could immediately be expected from the fortress at Port-Louis.

One advantage the garrison of Lorient had was its numerous reserves of naval ordnance to arm its ships, many of these cannons being of heavier calibres, such as 18-, 24- and 36-pounders, than those of the British. They were mounted on carriages and about 100 guns now appeared on Lorient's field fortifications served by hundreds of soldiers and sailors already trained to serve artillery. By 4 October, it was clear Lorient would not surrender. Two days later, a British siege battery of four 12 pounders with a 9-inch mortar opened fire on the town causing little damage while vigorous and well-aimed counter fire from the city's batteries 'entirely desolated' the British gunners according to one of the besieged. During the afternoon, a 300 men detachment of the company's soldiers and dragoons made a quick sortie resulting in the British troops compelled to seek cover in their trenches due to the city's accurate cannon fire. The day before, a large party of coastguard militiamen had attacked the small village of Guidel where a rearguard of British troops was posted; it made a stand huddled in the village church. Since the militiamen's raid's aims had been achieved; they decided not to set fire to the church for humane and religious reasons and withdrew.

As days passed, the situation of St Clair and his troops looked increasingly worrisome. The British bombardments were not very effective largely due to robust counter fire. Although about 4,000 shots had been fired on Lorient by 7 October, only about 15 persons, mostly civilians, had been killed or wounded and 20 houses damaged. That day, some 2,000 militiamen from Concarneau arrived in Lorient. There was 'by then in the city 14 to 15,000

Marquis de l'Hôpital Sainte-Mesme had been the proprietary colonel of his regiment since October 1739.

men including 600 cavalry troopers and dragoons', besides the company's soldiers. Morale was reported very high and there was plenty of ammunition and arms in the city. Late in the evening of 7 October, the besieged – some of whom were still prepared to negotiate an end to the siege – noted that the British batteries were amazingly quiet.

At about eight at night, the British had discreetly abandoned their camp and hastily marched back to their fleet. They were followed, but not attacked and left Loch on 12 October for the Quiberon Bay area where they sacked and burned down a few villages in the next days. St Clair summoned the coast fortress at Belle-Isle to surrender; it simply answered with artillery salvos so the fleet sailed for England on 23 October. The British lost about a hundred killed or wounded with many more sick and some further losses due to bad weather on the way back.

In reviewing this operation, one notes that Lorient was improperly invested for an effective siege by the British in that it was never cut off from outside; men and supplies entered seemingly without opposition. Lines of communications between the British force outside of Lorient and its fleet far away at Loch were insecure due to harassment and ambushes from well concealed coastguard militiamen. While Lieutenant General St Clair had created what we now call a 'public relations disaster' by his summons as well as letting rather questionable treatment be inflicted upon defenceless French inhabitants by tacitly condoning a pillage-and-rape attitude by his soldiers, he further seems to have been quite indecisive when faced with stiff opposition. The French defenders, who suffered only a handful of military casualties in Lorient, probably would have come to terms if the garrison had been granted the honours of wars and property respected. Officials in the city were, most of all, businessmen hoping to make a deal. Some of the lack of vigour for a pursuit by French commanders, especially the Marquis de l'Hôpital and the Comte de Volvire, might be due to that factor. As for St Clair and the naval commander Admiral Lestock, their performance ensured that their career advancements and hopes of substantial prize money by sacking Lorient vanished.[21]

Lorient's Garrison 1750s-1772

While there were alarms and some raids on the French coast during the 1750s, Lorient was not attacked again and continued to provide soldiers for overseas garrisons in India and marines for its ships during and after the

21 Besides the above cited, this account is largely based on several contemporary memoirs reproduced in: C. du Chalard, 'Le siege de Lorient et la procession de la victoire', *Revue de Bretagne et de la Vendée*, Vol.7 (1863), pp.169-183; Charles Bougouin, *Descente des Anglais en Bretagne et siege de Lorient en 1746* (Nantes: Société archéologique, 1870); Joseph-Emmanuel Laboria, *Notice sur la défense des côtes maritimes de France* (Paris: Corréard, 1840), pp.48-62; Anon., 'Journal de ce qui s'est passé sur les côtes de Bretagne aux mois de septembre, octobre et novembre 1746 à l'occasion de la descente des Anglais', *Bullletins et mémoires de la Société archéologique du département d'Ille-et-Vilaine*, Vol.43 (1918), pp.420-484.

end of the Seven Years War. There were no further changes in the military organisation until a royal order of 1 March 1767 reduced the strength of the Lorient company to 241 men including nine officers. It could be augmented to up to 300 men if necessary. The company was divided into two half companies. The company's colour was carried by the half company whose *capitaine* was senior in precedence. It was disbanded at Lorient on 30 December 1772 being replaced the same day by two garrison companies of 106 men each including three officers.[22]

22 APL, 1P 304, 20, Ordonnance du roi, 1 March 1767; APL, 1P, 305, 157, Les syndics et directors de la Compagnie, 1 March 1767; AC, A, 18, Ordonnance…portant suppression de la compagnie…du port de Lorient, 30 December 1772.

Top: Regimental colour of the Royal-Marine Regiment. Some 400 men of this regiment were part of La Haye's 1670 expedition to India. (Anne S.K. Brown Military Collection, author's photo)

Above: Troops and ships in battle, India, late seventeenth century. The top half of this detail from an Indian wall hanging shows what appears to be engagements between French and Dutch ships according to their much stylised standards. They are in a river, which could indicate the Ganges where some French ships held out until the war ended in 1697-1698. The lower group of soldiers in European dress might be Dutch or French or even British, Portuguese or Danish. The styles shown were the same for all European soldiers although this painting does not show specific coat colours for the various groups. (Metropolitan Museum of Art, New York. Harris Brisbane Dick Fund and Louis V. Bell Fund. 2014.88)

Above: Soldier of the Navy, 1680s. Many soldiers sent to Siam 1687 may have worn a grey-white coat lined and cuffed with blue, blue serge breeches and stockings, white metal buttons, hat edged with false silver. Once there, the torrid weather dictated that clothing made of linen was preferable and the coats and stockings issued in 1688, may have been of made of linen or other light material produced locally. Watercolour sketch by Eugène Lelièpvre after Valmont's manuscripts at the Bibliothèque Nationale de France. (Private collection, author's photo)

Dutch siege of Pondicherry, August 1693. The naive watercolour by a Jesuit missionary shows the numerous Dutch fleet, the town with its walls and turrets, Dutch batteries and trenches, and Dutch troops in square battle formation. Print after watercolour. (Author's photo)

Left: A marine of the metropolitan Compagnies franches de la Marine, end of the seventeenth to early eighteenth centuries. A detachment formed the garrison of Pondicherry in 1699. His uniform is according to the regulations of 1689. The men's pewter buttons and false silver hat lace were changed to yellow metal in the early eighteenth century. Watercolour by Eugène Lelièpvre. (Private collection, author's photo)

Centre: Soldier of Crozat's and Law's Louisiana monopoly companies, 1716-1719. The uniform shown basically remained the same except for the waistcoat, which was changed to blue from the time when soldiers in Louisiana were part of the Compagnies des Indes' troops. Print after Eugène Lelièpvre. (Private collection, author's photo)

Right: A rare depiction of a topas, late seventeenth century. Some of these Metis men of Portuguese and Indian unions who dressed as Europeans were employed as regular soldiers by the Compagnies des Indes. This illustration shows a pipe-smoking man dressed in European costume and armed with an Indian sabre as can be seen by its guard, apparently made of bone or ivory. From the Shah-nameh manuscript by Firdausi. (Library of Congress, Washington)

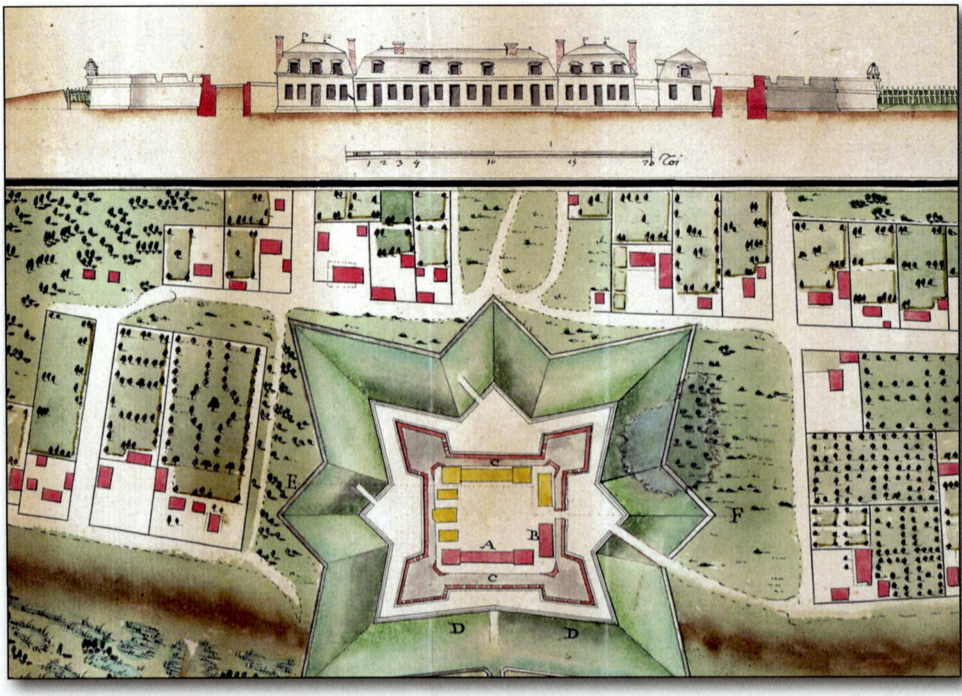

Plan and elevation of Fort Condé and the town of Mobile, Louisiana, as proposed in 1725. The design was approved and the fort was gradually built, especially in the early 1730s. It was the most extensive French fort on the Gulf Coast. Its curtain walls were of brick and sand that were quite resilient during bombardments. Signed on 25 March 1725 by Engineer Adrien de Pager. (Archives Nationales Outre-Mer, 04DFC124C)

European trading lodges at Ouidah on the Guinea Coast, 1725. The French lodge of the Compagnie des Indes is at the upper centre marked A. B: meeting room, C and D: director's and sub-director's quarters, E: storehouse, F and g: employee's and servant's quarters, h and 16: France's standard, j: forge, l: kitchen, m: commodities, n: magazine, o: vegetable gardens, p: gate, q: main gate, 14: the French director in a palanquin escorted by African guards. At left is the Portuguese lodge, the British lodge is at upper right with the Dutch lodge below. At top left and centre are quarters for African princes, their wives and warriors; at top right lodgings for slaves arriving from the interior. Watercolour by the Chevalier Des Marchais' 1724-1726 in 'Journal du Voiage de Guinée et de Cayenne'. (Bibliothèque Nationale de France, Paris, Ms. fr. 24223)

The siege and assault of an Indian fortress, eighteenth century. This illustration from the Pādishahnāmah manuscript shows the siege operations carried out by Indian armies in some detail. Senior officers are at the bottom foreground. Gunners are shown serving their cannon, which are Indian, some having an animal's head as the muzzle. Shield-carrying infantrymen, most wearing chain mail shirts and steel helmets, try an assault through a breech in the city's walls. Some defenders are similarly dressed, others wear turbans and robes. Although the Pādishahnāmah is a biography of Emperor Shah Jahan's life (ruled 1627-1666), it was made later. (Library of Congress, Washington. Gift of Lessing J. Rosenwald)

Armour of a Mughal cavalryman, eighteenth century. This warrior is equipped to fight on horseback. He wears an expensive coat of mail that has over 11,500 individuals riveted links making it likely that is wearer was a nobleman. The head is protected by a mail 'kula zirah' over which a helmet was likely worn. His long-bladed sword with a gold-plated guard covering the whole hand is a 'pata', a weapon peculiar to India. The steel blade of this example was made in Europe and imported by Indian swordsmiths. During 1751, such a warrior was seen in battle by a French soldier holding the reins of his white horse with his teeth while slaying some 20 enemy Indian cavalrymen with his sabre before being overcome. (Former Higgins Armory Collection, Worcester Art Museum, Worcester, Massachusetts, author's photo)

Indian warriors or sepoys in battle, eighteenth century. Note the elephant trampling an unfortunate opponent, which was one of the deadly dangers of Indian battlefields. Unsigned painting from Rajasthan. (Los Angeles County Museum of Art. Gift of Jane Greennough. ma-142185)

An Indian prince or general on his elephant seated in his palanquin or 'howdha', first half of the eighteenth century. Elephants were seen in Indian forces since ancient times and still common during the eighteenth century, be they in armies allied with the French or the British. A senior army general would see the battle much better on his elephant, but it was a risky proposition if defeated. Two of his attendants wear red robes and the driver has a red turban; the red colour was associated with the Mughal Empire as were the green (sometimes red) triangular flags having a figure embroidered in gold with a gold fringe. (National Gallery of Canada, Ottawa)

An Indian prince amongst his army, middle or later half of the eighteenth century. This very fine unsigned painting is said to have been made in the Deccan. The foot soldiers near him have varied arms and costumes, those with spears or pikes might be peons. The pale green triangular flags might indicate a connection or approbation of the Mughal empire. A top of the painting are a multitude of small figures, the detail of some being given in another plate. (Anne S.K. Brown Military Collection)

Detail of a painting showing an Indian prince amongst his army, middle or later half of the eighteenth century. This plate reproduces part of the top of the painting. It shows possibly sepoy cavalry in red coats with pale green facings and turbans charging with, or being pursued by cavalrymen wearing helmets and chainmail. In the distance, one field gun is retreating (at left) facing a seven-gun field battery. Its indistinct gunners are being joined by files of sepoys wearing red coats with dark red (or violet) turbans and trousers. At top left, a large triangular pale green Mughal colour hoisted on an elephant. No European figures are visible. Red uniforms in India could be seen worn by sepoys and European troops of French, British, Dutch and Danish garrisons as well as in some princely armies. (Anne S.K. Brown Military Collection)

A view of the shoreline of Pondicherry, circa 1750-1755. In the background, the government's Roman style neoclassical buildings that were also the residence of the governor general. In front, a lively assemblage of city residents and Compagnie des Indes troops. Amongst the figures in uniform, (from left) a small squad of topasses preceded by sepoy officers, a member from Kirjean's volunteers in blue, a mounted life guard of Bussy and an 'Étranger' of Bussy's troops in red. Painting by Eugène Lelièpvre. (Musée des Troupes de la Marine, Fréjus, France. Photo courtesy Marc Morillon)

A Sepoy officer in the service of the Compagnie des Indes, 1730s-1760s. He is armed with a fine quality Talwar sabre and has a 'katari' dagger at his waist. A servant attend his robe and one of his soldiers is nearby. Unsigned watercolour by an Indian artist. Print from Depréaux's *Uniformes*. (Author's photo)

A senior officer's or courtier's robe, called a 'Jama', seventeenth century. This example is of fine cotton decorated with hand painted pink flowers and bordered with applied gold leaf. It was probably made and worn in the Deccan. (Metropolitan Museum of Art, New York. Rogers Fund, 1929. 29.135)

An 'Indian Warrior'. This watercolour depicts a veteran sepoy soldier whose basic dress was basically as seen in the seventeenth and eighteenth centuries. It was faithfully created in the early twentieth century by Alfred Crowdy Lovett (1863-1919). He was also possibly the most outstanding artist depicting the Indian army of his times as well as a distinguished officer during the Great War. (Anne S.K. Brown Military Collection)

Left: Fusilier, troops of the Compagnie des Indes, East Indies, circa 1738-1748. This blue uniform with red cuffs was officially approved in 1738 for companies posted in India and the islands of Bourbon and Ile de France. The ample cut of the coat may have been made until about the middle or later 1740s. Watercolour by Michel Pétard. (National Historic Sites, Parks Canada)

Right: Dragoon, Company of the Militia Dragoons of the Ile de Bourbon Militia, 1740s. This elite company wore a green coat with red cuffs. Watercolour by Michel Pétard. (Anne S.K. Brown Military Collection, photo by the artist)

French soldiers of Commandant Bussy's contingent in the Deccan, At left, a fusilier of *Capitaine* Kirjean's elite company in July 1751; at centre, a gunner, and at right, a dragoon, both wearing uniforms issued at Hyderabad in June 1753. Print after Lucien Rousselot in *Le Passepoil*, 1931. (Author's photo)

Volunteer, Compagnie des Volontaires, Bussy's troops in the Deccan. This elite company led by *Capitaine* Kirjean wore, from June 1753, a blue uniform with red lapels and cuffs and featuring a white aiguillette with a cap trimmed with fur in front. Print after Lucien Rousselot, 1931. (Author's photo)

Fusilier, Compagnies des Indes troops in the Deccan, June 1753. This red uniform trimmed with green was issued to the 'Corps de Troupe' that had three companies. The white epaulettes identified the first company. Watercolour by Michel Pétard. (Anne S.K. Brown Military Collection, photo by the artist)

Great Mughal Shah Alem II reviews a French company, circa1759-1761. The troops are shown dressed in totally red coats without cuffs or collars, very dark blue breeches and stockings and unlaced black hats. The senior officer alone has gold buttons and buttonhole lace on the breast of his coat while his black tricorn is also gold-laced. The style of the uniforms is of the 1750s. The rectangular colour is all violet . The approximate date and circumstances of the event are unsure. The French officer is said to be *Colonel* Gentil, but he was presented to the Great Mughal only in 1765 at the earliest. Much more likely, it is Commandant Law de Lauriston and his corps in north-central India that was the only French contingent serving with Shah Alem (who became Great Mughal in May 1760) and his army from April 1759 to 1761. The dark brown accoutrements are unusual in that they are slung over the right instead of the left shoulder, possibly because no swords are shown for the enlisted men. (Bibliothèque Nationale de France, Paris, Colonel Gentil bequest, Manuscrits Français 24219)

Shuja-ud-doulah, nabob of Oude, one of the most powerful princes of India, with European officers, early 1760s. The three European officers are most probably the engineer Polier, artillery officer Claude Martin and *Colonel* Jean-Baptiste Gentil, all of whom entered the service the nabob during the 1760s. They all wear European dress that are not necessarily uniforms although Gentil has fringed epaulettes. As Gentil related, the nabob was a very good target shot and holds a very long-barrelled Indian musket which appears to be a matchlock. Gouache by Dip Chand in the album 'Indes. Costumes et mœurs'. (Bibliothèque Nationale de France, Paris, Colonel Gentil bequest, RH n° 274-2).

Left: Soldier of the Compagnie des Indes in India, 1760. This figure wearing an ornate Antiquity style cap (its latin motto has 'Ubique' [everywhere] and another illegible word that might be 'gallica' [gallic]), a red coat with a yellow collar, green lapels and cuffs, a white aiguillette and epaulette is from a watercolour titled 'Troupes servant dans l'inde' (Troops serving in India) and dated 1760. It is certainly a confirmation of the colourful uniforms worn in India. It is inserted with two other plates dated 1772 proposing a simpler grey linen uniform with caps for overseas troops in AM, G, 239. This good copy of it was made in 1860. (Anne S.K. Brown Military Collection)

Right: Fusilier, troops of the Compagnie des Indes, 1758-1770. This attractive uniform was not actually worn in India until 1765. Watercolour by Michel Pétard. (Anne S.K. Brown Military Collection, author's photo)

Right: Gunner, Royal-Artillerie Regiment, 1758-1761. The gunners had a blue coat with red collar, cuffs, lining, waistcoat and breeches, brass buttons (three to each cuff, six to each pocket, two rows of small buttons set in pairs on waistcoat and three to each waistcoat pocket), false gold hat lace. Gunners were armed with a brass-hilted hanger. Watercolour by Eugène Lelièpvre. (Private collection, author's photo)

Right: Fusilier, Régiment de Lally., 1758-1761. According to the 1758-1761 *État Militaire de France*, its uniform was a red coat with 'clear' (meaning pale) green cuffs, white lining, clear green waistcoat, white breeches, brass buttons (three at each coat cuff and pocket, 12 in front of the coat and two rows of 12 buttons in front of the waistcoat), false gold laced hat. Watercolour by Robert Marrion. (Private collection, author's photo)

Bottom left: Regimental colours of the Régiment de Lally. (Private collection, author's photo)

Bottom right: Regimental colours of the Régiment de Lorraine. (Anne S.K. Brown Military Collection, author's photo)

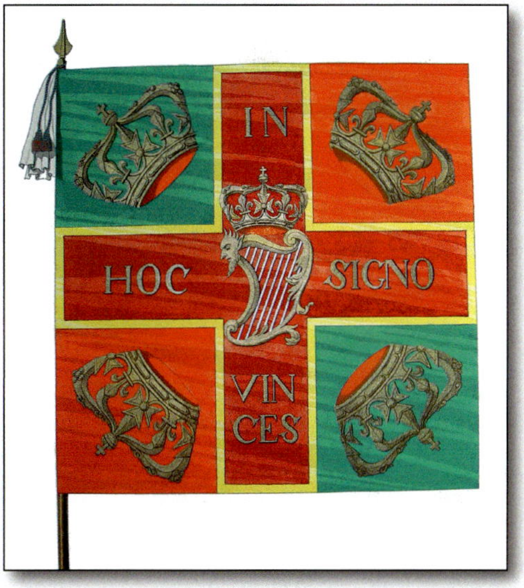

Top Left: Fusilier, Régiment de Cambrésis, 1760-1763. This regiment served at Ile de France during those years. Its uniform was grey-white with red cuffs, collar and waistcoat, brass buttons (six to each cuff, nine to each pocket), false gold hat lace. The Model 1754 infantry musket may have been used by the regiment. It was much the same as the Model 1728 except that the rear buckle for the musket sling was attached to the trigger guard. Watercolour by Derek FitzJames. (Private collection, author's photo)

Top right: Fusilier, Compagnies franches de la Marine, 1754. This twentieth-century copy of a figure from the now vanished 1754 'Tarascon' uniform manuscript shows the distinctive blue collar of the metropolitan marines and also white anchors on the turned back coat skirts. A note confirms the gaiters to be grey in this instance. Copy by Lucien Rousselot. (Private collection, photo courtesy of Jean Boudriot

Right: Regimental colour of the Régiment de Cambrésis. (Anne S.K. Brown Military Collection, author's photo)

16

Lifestyles of the Troops at Home and Overseas

Officers and men of the French East India Companies were faced, when posted overseas, with considerable lifestyle adaptations from what they had known Europe. Conversely, they brought with them European ways and technology into very diverse civilisations in faraway countries.

Recruiting and Training Soldiers

As with the troops belonging to the royal army and navy, the Compagnie des Indes had personnel or, in some cases, hired private agents to convince men that the career of arms in exotic places such as India was a marvellous experience. The enlistment period was six years, the pay was better than in the royal army, one would go to extraordinary far-away countries to which potential recruits could never even dream of traveling to see; once there, serious chances for substantial self-enrichment would be encountered. At least, this would have been some of the 'facts' uttered by finely dressed recruiting officers and *sergents* wielding money to mostly young men from usually very humble backgrounds looking for adventure and some wealth. Some 24,000 men are recorded as having enlisted in the company's troops between 1721 and 1772.[1]

Although recruiters might be found in any French tavern, it was the province of Brittany that provided nearly half of the recruits. This was surely due to Lorient being in that province. Next was the Paris area with about 16.5 percent. As seen above, recruiting techniques were generally similar in all European armed forces and young men might be enticed after a good many drinks, the prospect of a cash enlistment bonus, and the general levity

1 The enlistment records are in AC, D2A, 3 to 32, 36, 41 for which see calendar in André Corvisier, *Les contrôles de troupes de l'Ancien Régime* (Paris: Ministère des Armées, 1970), Vol.3, pp.573-577; André Corvisier, 'Les soldats de la Compagnie des Indes en 1755-1756', *Revue d'histoire économique et sociale* (January-March 1968), pp.1-34.

A recruiting party with a new recruit about to sign his enlistment, circa 1750. Such a scene of military recruiters enticing a young man with promises of life as a maharaja with plenty of drinks in a local inn was common in western Europe. Many of the soldiers of the Compagnie des Indes were enlisted this way between 1720 and 1770. Print from Hennebert's *Nos Soldats*. (Author's photo)

of recruiters hailing their wonderful life in the company's troops, to mark or sign an enlistment document. Following this, the newly enlisted men were gathered in Paris and Rennes (Normandy) in recruit groups that then travelled to Lorient.[2]

Average enlistment age was 23 years eight months, the youngest recorded being 16 and the eldest 49 years old. Nearly three out of four (73.5 percent) were recruited from ages 17 to 26, which represented a fairly young contingent. Over 90 percent were natives of France, the foreigners enlisted being from western European countries. The average height of the recruits was 1.62 metres. The smallest recorded was 1.40 metres and the tallest 1.81 metres.

The number of officers and men sent by the Compagnie des Indes to India reached a peak during the early 1750s. Foreigners could also be called upon and, in 1753, the rather well known German mercenary officer Jean-Chretien Fischer was retained by the company to recruit in that country and eastern France, with the result of that about 1,000 of his recruits were described as 'Germans', which included hussars, as part of the 1753-1754 recruits. They were not told they would serve in India… (see chapter 18).[3]

2 Brice Guignard, 'Les soldats de Pondichéry 1700-1761', *Centre d'information et de documentation de l'inde francophone*, Lettre No. 12/13 (25 January 2010), also at: <http://cidif2.go1.cc>; Haudrère, *La compagnie française des Indes*, Vol.4, pp.1277-1278.

3 Édouard de Ribaucourt, *La vie militaire et les exploits de J.-C. Fischer* (Paris: Librairie Universelle, 1929), pp.65-67. Fischer was to recruit 900 men by the agreement of 7 September

The numbers of European soldiers and officers sent to serve in India during 1750-1761 were:[4]

- 1750-1751: 301 men including *sergents*
- 1751-1752: 613 men
- 1752-1753: 1,442 men, 16 officers
- 1753-1754: 1,993 men, 46 officers
- 1755: 425 men, 8 officers
- 1756: 239 men, 2 officers
- 1757: unknown for the men, 3 officers
- 1758: 459 men, 1 officer
- 1759: 51 men, unknown for officers
- 1760: 57 men, 2 officers
- 1761: 83 men, 5 officers

This came to at least 5,744 officers, NCOs and soldiers sent to India during that decade.

There were also recruits for Senegal, Ile de France, Ile de Bourbon and the depot at Lorient. For instance, six officers and 103 soldiers were sent to Ile de France in 1761. To better manage the increased number of recruits, *Capitaine* François Boucher of the Ile de France and Bourbon companies was sent to France in 1751 and 'fixed his office in Paris' for recruiting operations in 1752. By late 1756, he mentioned having sent over 7,000 men to India and other territories. On the whole, about 46 percent of the recruits went to India, 42.5 percent to deadly Senegal and 11.5 percent to Ile de France and Ile de Bourbon.[5]

Although about one in four recruits could sign his name, the others left only a mark on the enlistment papers and account must be taken three men out of 10 coming from areas such as Brittany that did sign their names. A fair ponderation would indicate that two out of five recruits had some level of literacy. About one in six knew a trade, a quarter of these being related to agriculture. It was once in Lorient that they actually signed their formal enlistment and were incorporated into the depot company. The training period at Lorient could be quite variable. According to 1755-1756 ledgers, half of the recruits boarded a ship that sailed out of France after about two and a half months. The other half was much more variable; some left after only a month while a few others might leave only two years later. On average, the recruit was posted at Lorient for six months or more before sailing.[6]

1753.

4 Figures for 1750-1754 from Anon., *Mémoire pour la Compagnie des Indes contre le Sieur Dupleix*, pp.98-102. Figures for 1755-1761 most kindly compiled for the author by Bruno Helias from the archives in Lorient.

5 AC, E, 43, Record of *Capitaine* François Boucher 1752-1758; Bruno Hélias, 'L'uniforme des troupes de la Compagnie des Indes lors de la guerre de Sept-Ans', *Carnet de la Sabretache*, nouvelle série No. 116, 2e trimester 1995, p.50.

6 Corvisier, 'Les soldats de la Compagnie des Indes en 1755-1756', pp.1-34; Cultru, *Dupleix*, pp.301-303.

A plate from the army's infantry drill of 1750. This was an essential part of the recruit's training for the company's troops at Lorient. The unit shown is the Gardes-Françaises, but apart from minor details such as not having buttonhole lace, the appearance of Besson's company at Lorient would have been much the same as shown in this print by Eisen including accoutrements and weapons. (Anne S.K. Brown Military Collection, author's photo)

Basic training was generally similar to that of the marines of the king's navy and royal garrisons in America. It essentially consisted of the royal army's field exercises and manoeuvres. The infantry arms drill followed suit and that from 1703-1704 was used until updated in 1750, 1754 and 1755. Possibly the most visible change between 1703 and 1754 concerned the battle line going from four ranks deep to three ranks, a practice that had been unofficially adopted in many units. Whether drill updates were actually followed in 1750s India is a moot point. However, the very fact that troops overseas had drill practices was certainly an advantage when faced with far more numerous African warriors or Indian armies.

Then as now, drills and manoeuvres made for impressive and orderly units marching about in martial-looking lines that were admired by local princes and their subjects. This was increasingly seen in India during the early 1740s, not only from the European troops, but also by the increasingly numerous sepoy units in its service that were armed and drilled like French soldiers. Some Indian princes' armies also formed lines of battle, but they proved utterly ineffective when faced with by French soldiers and French-trained sepoys. The first major and outstanding result of this training, which was to have vast consequences of the history of India, came at Adyar/Sao

Tomé on 4 November 1746 and confirmed at Ambour on 3 August 1749 as related above.[7]

The quality of the recruits that reached India and the Indian Ocean islands appears to have been quite variable according to the comments of governors and other officials that saw them on arrival. After the long sea voyage, up to half might be sick and were sent to hospital on arrival. In 1727, a soldier enlisted at 16 years old was dismissed after he was actually found to be 13 while another was 45 when enlisted, which was somewhat too old. In 1752, Dupleix complained that 600 recruits were 'a gathering of knaves that a hundred good soldiers will beat' in combat. Many recruits arriving in India during early 1753 were 'children armed with old muskets who did not know how to use them' and Dupleix opined that recruiters should be 'punished to have furnished 1,400 men [who were in fact] mere children and knaves.' As it turned out, a 'captain recruiter' at Bicèrte (France) answered that there are 'honest men everywhere' including at the local jail where he convinced prisoners to enlist. Some had only committed petty offences while others were men convicted for attempted murders, robberies and drunkenness, some having been sentenced to be marked with a fleur de lys, a punishment usually reserved for the worse culprits. When these types of recruits arrived in chains at Lorient, there was no great wish to train them and they were put in jail until they boarded a ship departing as soon as possible. During the sea voyage, many refused to drill or be trained and so, in some cases, had to be kept in chains. Once arrived, the recruits were armed, clothed and assigned to their units in which they might yet learn to be good soldiers.[8]

Deserters

Desertion was seen in all the company's garrisons in France and overseas, but no overall statistics appear to have been compiled. Once in Lorient, about one in ten deserted (which was the usual average in the royal army), one in twenty recruits were rejected as physically unsuitable, while one in thirty – those who had some money – paid to be released from their enlistment. The administrative correspondence and local court records mention various individual cases.

Possibly the most famous deserter in India was Joseph Louis de Volton, a soldier skilled in medical care, who vanished in 1739 and made his way to Delhi where he became the Mughal emperor's physician. This amazing elevation earned him a royal pardon two years later. More commonly, French deserters might be enlisted in British or Dutch service. For most of the others who were caught in the act, capital punishment or a sentence to the royal galleys was more likely although there were also pardons announced every once in a while. We should add that desertion was a two-way street. For

7 John A. Houlding, *French Arms Drill of the 18th Century* (Bloomfield, ON: Museum Restoration Service, 1988, pp.24-26. This fine study includes all plates of the 1703 and 1755 drills and the original texts (with English translations) for all drills cited.

8 Cultru, *Dupleix*, pp.301-303; Martineau, *Dupleix*, Vol.3, pp.50-52.

instance, in India, British deserters could be enlisted in the company's French troops as well as in an 'Étrangers' (foreign) company. But in peacetime, there was an agreement between the French and the British to return the deserters found in their jurisdictions.[9]

Viruses and Mortality Overseas

Service in Africa and India came with a high mortality rate. The statistics for the garrison of Pondicherry in peacetime show that some 80 percent of the soldiers died before the end of their six-year enlistment and 53 percent died in the first three years. The causes can be attributed to oriental viruses and also alcohol abuse, said to be due to the strong liquor called 'araque' that was much more 'violent' than French brandy, and was the cause that half of the garrison of Pondicherry perished every year according to a 1748 memoir: this was exaggerated, but also instructive as to the perception people had.

The garrisons in Senegal were seemingly at the deadliest postings. The mortality rate was higher even if a very few soldiers served there beyond seven years. They were the lucky survivors. The West African coast was a graveyard to many Europeans that were posted there, and it seems that Senegal was the worst place for a soldier. Civilians too frequently perished from the deadly viruses, but not as much as soldiers. From 1725 to 1753, the garrison represented about 20 percent of the European population, but had about 40 percent of the deaths, nearly all of which were caused by sickness.[10]

Medical Care

For health care, the company's establishments included surgeon-majors, surgeons and assistant surgeons in its sizeable lodges or forts, which usually had small infirmaries. Main centres such as Lorient and Pondicherry had an hospital and so did Saint-Louis in Senegal from 1734. Troops on campaign in India had some medical staff and might even have a field hospital such as in Bussy's army in the Deccan. The nursing personnel was predominantly Indian or African outside of France and Louisiana.

The level of care in hospitals was lauded in India where it was said that the Compagnie des Indes took such a 'paternal care' of its patients that they could have no 'further desires' for food, medicines, treatments and attention. This was due to the company's Doctor Bourdier, assisted from about 1758 by the royal army's *Médecin-major* Girard, both having great knowledge and honesty. The same could not be said of the royal army Intendant Dubois regarding ambulances and portable beds that he never furnished during the 1758 siege of Madras, using instead his largely Indian staff to bring loot he had gathered in that city's sacking to Pondicherry. The wounded

9 Guignard, 'Les soldats de Pondichéry 1700-1761'; Martineau, *Dupleix*, Vol.3, pp.53-55.

10 Jean-Bernard Lacroix, *Les Français au Sénégal au temps de la Compagnie des Indes de 1719 à 1758* (Vincennes: Service historique de la Marine, 1986), pp.109, 119.

soldiers were thus abandoned in the camp when the siege was raised to the 'discretion of the British who, happily, treated them with decent humanity'.[11]

The company's soldier's souls overseas were attended by chaplains seemingly in much the same way as in the metropolitan army. In India, they were mostly Jesuit and Capuchin missionaries. The Jesuits in particular had a 'love and hate' relationship with the authorities at Pondicherry regarding protocol and fiscal viewpoints amongst matters raised, but they, like other religious orders having missions overseas, seem to have correctly attended the faithful side of soldier's souls as more or less permanent military chaplains. Some left remarkable records of their forays into remote parts of India and the Far East.[12]

A Jesuit missionary and chaplain in India, first half of the eighteenth century. In that country, they wore an orange coloured cotton habit, sandals with wooden soles and carried a brass water jug due to the heat. Print in Vol. 7 of *Lettres édifiantes*. (Author's photo)

Wedlock or Not

As in the royal army, marriage was not especially encouraged. However, before 1720, it was not especially repressed either. The previous year, 48 out of 149 soldiers in Pondicherry were married, often to Indian girls. In the following years, chaplains were forbidden to perform weddings unless the brides were French girls, which were rather scarce in India although the official concern was that the Indian climate did not suit their health. Soldiers who wished to marry were to be assigned to serve at Ile de France and Ile de Bourbon as these were territories where French settlers were welcome.

Garrisons in India and Africa protected business interests only; there was no desire to populate those countries with French settlers. On 3 September 1743, it was decided by the company's council in Paris that any man in the service of the company in Lorient or overseas could not marry without having first received permission for the local ruling council. Those who contravened this ruling were dismissed from the company's service without possibility of later regaining their post.[13]

11 Albert Depréaux, 'Troupes coloniales d'autrefois, Mémoire sur les troupes de l'Inde [c. 1763]', *Revue de l'histoire des colonies françaises*, XVI (1928), p.432. Following the 1761 capitulation of Pondicherry, Intendant Dubois was mysteriously assassinated.

12 Notably in Anon., *Lettres édifiantes et curieuses*, Vols. 7 and 8.

13 Guignard, 'Les soldats de Pondichéry (1700-1761)', unpaginated; APL, 1P 305, 48, Extrait du régistre général des deliberations, 3 September 1743. There were exceptions made for foreign recruits. Wives and children were allowed in limited numbers for the 1720 Swiss companies and Fischer's 1753-1754 German levy.

Food and Drink

The Compagnie des Indes provided food and drink that was generally equivalent to what soldiers of the royal army received in France. The basic daily ration consisted of a pound (500 grams) of bread or the equivalent in rice or biscuits; 250 to 300 grams of meat; 150 to 200 grams of salted bacon four days of the week and 150 to 300 grams of dried peas or another dry vegetable. Fish such as dry cod was not usually mentioned. For drink, three quarters of a pint (75 centilitres) of wine or 30 centilitres of spirits (rum, brandy, etc). In terms of nutrient balance, the rations listed could be now considered as too rich in lipids and proteins with too few carbohydrates. The above food and drink would provide about 3,500 to 4,000 calories daily, enough for men exerting physically demanding activities such as long marches with weapons and equipment or as labourers on constructing fortifications.[14]

Soldiers who served as marines on board the company ships had a somewhat different daily ration, which was identical for sailors. It consisted of 18 ounces (550 grams) of biscuit or a pound and a half of fresh bread; five ounces (177 grams) of salted bacon on Sundays, Tuesdays and Thursdays; four ounces (125 grams) of dried cod with olive oil and vinegar on Wednesdays, Fridays and Saturdays. The cod might be replaced by four ounces (125 grams) of cheese or seven ounces (215 grams) of dried vegetables. Two ounces of rice might be added at dinner. The wine or spirits (usually cognac) ration was the same as above. Each man was further allowed three pints of water (2.8 litres) a day.[15]

On land or at sea, the men had, in principle, three mealtimes a day: at sea, breakfast consisted of biscuit; lunch was the main meal with bread, meat of fish, dried vegetables or cheese; diner was as breakfast with dried vegetables and rice. A quarter pint of wine was given at each meal. On land or at sea, Compagnie des Indes and royal Compagnies franches de la Marine soldiers had an iron pot for a mess of seven men. The squad cooked meals on land although this could vary greatly in garrisons that would have more centralised kitchens. This was always the case on ships. Without going into further details, NCOs had more generous rations as did officers who also had more elaborate dining arrangements.[16]

Tropical Cuisine

Troops posted in tropical establishments certainly had rations that were largely or wholly based on local produce. One of the challenges of the early soldiers and settlers at Fort Dauphin in Madagascar was the difficulty of obtaining beef, vegetables and fruit from the indigenous population in periods when ships from France did not arrive or their own crops might not supply enough produce. Ile de France and Ile de Bourbon also had

14 Haudrère, *La compagnie française des Indes au XVIIIe siècle*, Vol.3, pp.790-791.

15 Boudriot, Compagnie des Indes, p.139.

16 Boudriot, *Compagnie des* Indes, pp.139-140, 144.

their challenges to serve meals that were up to regulations because, at times, no ships showed up so that the daily ration might be, at least in 1725, a loaf of bread of a pound and a half with some dried fish or meat, fresh if possible.[17]

In India, 'the most common food is rice' that could be consumed with a broth, or with a meat sauce, or with fish or vegetables amongst ingredients added to the rice dish. Wine came all the way from France; some might be spoiled after many months at sea and there never was enough, even for celebrating Holy Mass at times. Water was the common drink along with juices and good fresh water was not always found easily in coastal India. Alcoholic drinks were made from various concoctions such as with palm tree leaves or bark that were strong enough to be set aflame. There was also a strongly alcoholic linseed wine. All these drinks were 'infamous liquors' according to a Jesuit chaplain and missionary at Pondicherry. All or any of the above could have been the 'araque' or 'Arak', the negative effects of which on soldiers are mentioned by their officers in India.[18]

Rations issued to soldiers in coastal India was subcontracted locally and was said to consist of questionable rice that was only half cooked to save on wood as well as giving the impression that it was more filling when expanding in the stomach; meat was of the very worse quality while inspectors of the rations were seemingly often bribed. Food poisoning was common. Some soldiers disposed of their rations, notably on campaign when they preferred to eat whatever they could forage or steal and cook themselves.[19]

As warfare increasingly moved into the interior of India from the late 1740s, the diet would change. The journal of a French soldier in Bussy's corps in Hyderabad during April 1751 mentions that the allied prince of the Deccan supplied rations to its officers and men that were quite different to what they had in Pondicherry. It consisted of a flat bread that 'our soldier associated with the Spanish manteca' that would be what we now call naan bread. The main course was a stew made with chicken or mutton, very well flavoured with 'all sorts of spices' on a rice 'Plao' now called pilaf. It was a version of curry. There were also some sugared sweets for desert 'all of which we found to be very good'. This naturally did not last for very long as the troops marched west to Aurengabad on more basic rations with deserts being less likely. But, on the whole, food supplies seem to have been adequate for most of the 1750s.[20]

The tragic exception occurred during the siege of Pondicherry in 1760-1761. Concern over having enough food for the troops gradually became serious in late 1760 as the French forces retreated into Pondicherry thus decreasing their access to reserves from adjoining territories. Although hoped for, supplies from a French fleet arriving in the harbour was unlikely. In the early autumn of 1760, the city's council computed at 2,741 European

17 Lougnon, *L'Ile Bourbon sous la Régence*, p.226.

18 Anon., *Lettres édifiantes et curieuses*, Vol.7, pp.49-50.

19 Depréaux, 'Troupes coloniales d'autrefois, Mémoire sur les troupes de l'Inde [c. 1763]', pp.430-431.

20 Depréaux, 'Les uniformes de la Compagnie des Indes…', p.164.

soldiers and men able to bear arms; there were also a few dismounted cavalrymen and 40 of Lally's guardsmen as well as unspecified numbers of sailors and hospitalised men. Food was already in short supply in the city when an inspection by the Chevalier de Mesme revealed that some 1,200 daily rations were over the number actually needed. This naturally aroused Lally's furore, which made things go from bad to worse. The result was that on 28 November, daily rations had to be cut by half. Henceforth, one ration was issued to two men. It was halved again on 7 January 1761.

By then, just about every cat, rat and bird in the city had been hunted down, and perhaps other animals too. The last of the beef used to transport artillery and ammunition to the ramparts were eaten. Soldiers and officers were receiving only nine ounces of a nourishing powder that passed for flour. Coconut trees were cut so as to extract the somewhat cabbage-like fibres as well as to distil a coconut brandy of sorts. This last was consumed more than it should have been by discouraged soldiers. Because of the loss of proteins and other shortages, mortality rose amongst the sick and wounded. Lally even considered drying up the moats that were the city's best defence against an assault so as to catch the fish within, a rather wild idea as they would turn rotten in half a day due to the torrid weather. As a result, all the men that were still somewhat fit to serve had the visible symptoms of malnutrition; skin-and-bones bodies except for expanded bellies; they now tired at the least effort.[21]

Lodgings

The soldier's 'home' was always frugal. In the field, they had canvass tents that would give shelter to about 10 men although there could be many variations. In Lorient and most garrisons in America, soldiers could be assigned quarters in civilian houses, which was not especially popular with inhabitants and was also seen as bad for discipline. Nevertheless, military barracks were not usually built until the second third of the eighteenth century. Like in all French barracks, each wooden bed was to theoretically accommodate three soldiers, two sleeping while the third was awake on guard duty, which did not always happen so there might actually be three in the same bed. If there were too few or no beds, hammocks might be substituted. If there was no accommodation available in forts, especially in Africa and India where the possibility of quartering European troops with civilians was very limited, the men built huts of sorts near the fortifications or used tents as their lodgings. This was the case at Ile de France and Ile de Bourbon until the 1730s when Governor-General La Bourdonais had barracks built of stone. In Pondicherry, soldier's lodgings appear to have been somewhat temporary affairs until the mid-1720s when a large barracks (whose second story doubled as a storehouse) was erected in the Saint-Louis citadel. Plans

21 Chassaigne, *Lally*, pp.202, 211, 217-218.

of that period in India and the islands show that barracks were built within the forts and fortified lodges.[22]

On campaign the troops had tents in principle, although this might not always be the case. The other option was then to quarter the troops in inhabitant's homes. This could be done for all troops in towns. In the countryside, a modest village could only accommodate officers while enlisted men would build huts (when tents were not provided) or sleep under the stars if there was good weather. This might do for a short period of time, but a report mentioned that about a hundred soldiers died of sickness after three months out in the open field without tents.[23]

Europeans and Topas Garrisons of India 1723-1770

Until 1757, the European garrisons of fusiliers and gunners also had a number of topasses in each company, although there could exceptions to this, especially after 1750. In 1723, there were 80 Europeans and 40 topasses in each of the four companies, but this could vary. On the whole, there were two Europeans for every topas until 1738 when the four companies in India were augmented to 100 Europeans so the ratio became three European for one topas decreasing at six to one in the 1750s.[24]

Except for occasional detachments of the king's marines, all were troops of the Compagnie des Indes until 1758 when the royal army's Lorraine and Lally regiments with Royal-Artillerie detachment and staff officers arrived in Pondicherry.

The figures below in time periods of several years can be interpreted as averages.[25]

1723-1729
Pondicherry: 12 officers, 33 NCOs, 144 fusiliers, 14 gunners, 114 topasses.
Chandernagor: 3 officers, 10 NCOs, 55 fusiliers, 4 gunners, 30 topasses.
Mahé: 3 officers, 14 NCOs, 78 fusiliers, 5 gunners, 8 topasses.
Total: 374 Europeans, 152 topasses.

1730-1739
Pondicherry: 23 officers, 40 NCOs, 240 fusiliers, 18 gunners, 130 topasses.
Chandernagor: 9 officers, 28 NCOs, 190 fusiliers, 5 gunners, 96 topasses.
Mahé: 8 officers, 30 NCOs, 190 fusiliers, 11 gunners, 30 topasses.
Total: 792 Europeans, 256 topasses.

22 Haudrère, *La compagnie française des Indes au XVIIIe siècle*, Vol.3, pp.789-790; a few plans are reproduced in this chapter.

23 Depréaux, 'Troupes coloniales d'autrefois, Mémoire sur les troupes de l'Inde [c. 1763]', pp.430-432.

24 AC, C2, 28, Extrait du régistre général de la Compagnie des Indes, 2 June 1738; Martineau, *Dupleix*, Vol.1, p.33.

25 After the compilation in Haudrère, *La compagnie française des Indes*,Vol.4, p.1,279.

1740-1749
Pondicherry: 24 officers, 97 NCOs, 412 fusiliers, 16 gunners, 152 topasses.
Chandernagor: 5 officers, 20 NCOs, 95 fusiliers, 5 gunners, 26 topasses.
Mahé: 9 officers, 27 NCOs, 176 fusiliers, 12 gunners, 80 topasses.
Total: 898 Europeans, 293 topasses.

1750-1756
Pondicherry: 84 officers, 450 NCOs, 1,798 fusiliers, 14 gunners, 227 topasses.
Chandernagor: 15 officers, 28 NCOs, 154 fusiliers, 5 gunners, 170 topasses.
Mahé: 11 officers, 49 NCOs, 250 fusiliers, 14 gunners, 115 topasses.
German troops at Pondicherry: 16 officers, 45 NCOs, 322 soldiers.
Total: 3,259 Europeans, 512 topasses.[26]

1757-1759
Compagnie des Indes: 167 officers, 3,300 NCOs and soldiers.
Royal army: 159 officers, 3,100 NCOs and soldiers.
Total: 6,750 Europeans.

Part of these garrisons were actually detached to various outlying forts. This was especially the case during the 1750s when sizeable contingents were sent for years as far as Aurangabad in the Decan or the southeastern coast. There was even a small expedition to the Maldives in 1754.[27]

A royal order of 6 December 1756 'concerning the troops attached to the service of the Compagnie des Indes' specified that all the European infantry would be divided in independent companies each having four officers and 70 NCOs and men. Ten companies could form a battalion of 40 officers and 700 men that included a company of grenadiers and nine of fusiliers. This order appears to have been the origin of the Batallion de l'Inde formed in early 1758 at Pondicherry. Other companies in India do not appear to have been formed into battalions due to this order.[28]

Following the return of Pondicherry and other factories to French rule in 1765, the European garrison until 1770 had an average of:[29]

Pondicherry: 28 officers, 60 NCOs, 352 fusiliers, 20 gunners.
Chandernagor: 6 officers, 12 NCOs, 60 fusiliers.
Mahé: 8 officers, 20 NCOs, 103 fusiliers, 12 gunners.
Total: 691 Europeans.

26 Example at a given date return of troops in Pondicherry and its dependencies, 1 October 1755. French: 2,281 (including 84 officers), German: 383 (including 16 officers), Sepoys: 3,418 (including 113 officers), topasses and *Caffres*: 260. Total: 6,345. BNF, Ms Français 8971.

27 BNF, NAF 9146, Bussy to council, 17 February 1754. The Maldives islands detachment was modest at 25 European soldiers and 60 topasses.

28 AC, F3, 238, Ordonnance du Roi Pour les troupes attachées au service de la Compagnie des Indes, 6 December 1756. Each company was ordered to have: one *capitaine*, one *lieutenant*, one *lieutenant-en-second* 'performing the functions of Aide-Major', one *enseigne*, four *sergents*, four *caporaux*, four *anspessades*, 56 fusiliers and 2 drummers.

29 Haudrère, *La compagnie française des Indes*,, Vol.4, p.1,279.

Bussy's Army in the Deccan

On 15 January 1751, Bussy left Pondicherry with 300 European soldiers, 100 *Caffres* and topasses, and 2,000 sepoys. The European troops were divided into Kerjean's company, the grenadier company, the volunteer's company and the artillery company. They arrived at Hyderabad in April and at Aurengabad on 18 June. By December 1751 they had been reinforced to 500 Europeans and 5,000 sepoys.[30]

By June 1753, Bussy's army had a small personal mounted bodyguard attending Bussy, a corps of dragoons, a company of Étrangers, Kirjean's volunteers, three French companies, one of artillery and one of topasses.

On 4 November 1754, Bussy's army included a dozen of his guards, the horse grenadiers (which may have been the former dragoons) and the other companies. Some 14 *Caffres* were also mentioned.

Besides Bussy's field army, these territories henceforth required a few garrisons. By mid-1754, they had the following establishments:

- Rajibendrie (Rajimendrie, Rajamundry): 12 European artillerymen. 150 sepoys, 100 'ordinary government Peons', 10 cavalrymen, two employees and one officer.
- Chicacol (Chikacola, Cicacole): same as above.
- Caffincotté (Cossimcoten): five European artillerymen. 50 sepoys, 100 peons and one chief.

Ganjan (Gaudjam) and Vichiapour had similar establishments. The peons would have served more as constables than as soldiers. The total or these garrison came to: 39 artillerymen, 450 sepoys, 500 peons, two officers and three chiefs (presumably senior NCOs) for a force of 994.[31]

On 1 September 1756, Bussy's army consisted of: 83 officers, 653 European soldiers (that included Bussy's guards and the horse grenadiers), 65 *Caffres* and Abyssinians, 652 Indian men attached to the artillery, 145 Germans of Brandt's brigade, 47 German hussars, 400 Abyssinians, 4,000 sepoys and 300 Indian cavalry for a total of 6,045.[32]

Ile de France and Ile de Bourbon Garrisons 1721-1763

The earliest garrison of Ile de France was the Swiss Company of *Capitaine* Beugnot that sailed from Lorient on 31 June 1721. It was to have 210 men and assume the construction of fortifications and other infrastructure so that its military duties were to represent one third of their time. They were actually

30 Depréaux, 'Les uniformes de la Compagnie des Indes d'après un journal inédit de la campagne du Décan 1751-1755', pp.163, 167-168, 171-173, 178.

31 *Réponse du Sieur Dupleix*, p.283. The expenses of this force came to about 751,135 rupees. Bussy's Deccan army cost another 1,800,000 rupees for a total of 2,551,135 rupees. Tax revenues came to 3,100,000 rupees so that there was a profit of 548,865.

32 Martineau, *Bussy*, p.215.

commanded by *Capitaine* Schmidig and soon were very disappointed with their new homes at Port-Louis. By mid-1722, they were on the verge of mutiny, threatening to abscond in the woods rather than be compelled to work. In effect, it was a mutiny and they were sent back to France the following year. Many had died, most likely from fevers, and out of 67 left, only 32 were fit for service. To make matters worse, there was no garrison on Ile de Bourbon and it had been raided by pirates.[33]

The news of the raid and of the doubtful suitability of the Swiss soldiers had reached Lorient and two companies of 50 French soldiers each were created to garrison Ile de Bourbon; some 60 soldiers were sent at once. Two more French companies were also created to replace the Swiss at Ile de France. Time was the essence to recruit those four companies so the Compagnie des Indes obtained a royal order dated 16 March 1723 stating that half of the soldiers would be volunteer soldiers from the Picardie, Piedmont, Richelieu and Artois regiments of the royal army. They were to train the other half that were mostly recruits. The same day, the royal government ordered that seven companies would garrison the islands. On 9 November, each company was to have four officers and 60 NCOs and men for a total of 28 officers and 420 by an order of the Compagnie des Indes.[34]

The seven companies were later reduced to four, one of 75 men at Ile de France and three of 86 men each at Ile de Bourbon by 1734. In 1735, La Bourdonnais became governor and a fifth company was added. During 1738, the five companies of 80 men each were augmented to 100 men with an additional *enseigne*. There were still 300 soldiers in 1755, but recruits were rarer and, in May 1759, its troops were reorganised into three companies of 70 men each led by 15 officers.[35]

On 11 and 12 July 1760, the ships *Comte d'Artois*, *Berryer* and *Massiac* arrived at Ile de France with the Régiment de Cambrésis on board under the command of the Chevalier de La Galissonière. The authorities in France felt the islands needed more troops if they were to put up a successful defence in case of a British attack. There were suggestions that the regiment could be sent on to reinforce Lally's troops in India, but this was not acted upon, no doubt because that would have been contrary to the government's instruction. One can also wonder if the regiment would ever have arrived at

33 AG, A3, 76, Capitulation faite avec le Sr. Bugnot pour une Compagnie Suisse de la Compagnie des Indes aux Indes, 27 February 1720; APL, 1P 256b, 8, Compte…des recèttes et dépenses…21 Mars…23 May…de la Compagnie de Beugnot; Lagesse, *L'Ile de France avant La Bourdonnais*, p.18; Lougnon, *L'Ile Bourbon sous la Régence*, p.226. It sailed for Ile de France with 20 women and 30 children.

34 AM, A1, 61, Ordonnance du Roy pour la levée et le paiement de quatre compagnies d'infanterie…Isles de Bourbon et de France, 16 March 1723; ADR, Co 1186, Les Directeurs de la Compagnie des Indes, 9 November 1723. Each company had a *capitaine*, a *lieutenant*, a *sous-lieutenant*, an *enseign*, two *sergents*, two *caporaux*, two *anspessades*, two cadets, 50 fusiliers and two drummers.

35 AC, C2, 28, Extrait du régistre général de la Compagnie des Indes, 2 June 1738; ADR, Co 162, Les syndics et directeurs, Paris, 23 August 1755; ADR, Co 1197, État Actuel…garnison…Ile de Bourbon, May 1759.

Pondicherry with the Royal Navy totally dominating India's seacoast. The Régiment de Cambrésis remained at Ile de France until 1763.[36]

As the population of Africans in bondage rose in the islands, some escaped seeking freedom in the nearly inaccessible mountains. As in the West Indies and Brazil, they were termed 'maroons' because they raided plantations to obtain weapons and other supplies. European soldiers were not suited to pursue them in the wilderness so, during his tenure as governor general, La Bourdonnais decided to organise a small *Maréchaussée* armed constabulary company of 10 'archers' in about 1739 later raised to 24. They were Africans from Madagascar who obviously were elite warriors in the wilderness. They received weapons, clothing, pay and were free men. Deployed to raid into the mountains, a detachment of only five archers attacked a maroon camp managing to capture one of their leaders with his two wives. By 1740, 20 maroons and 25 wives had been captured at Ile de France. However, the problem was only partly solved since the unit continued to be in service thereafter.[37]

36 The ships left France with 17 companies of Cambrésis on board on 26 and 27 March 1760 as per: APL, 2P10, IV, Armements au long cours. Rôles des bureaux (1760); Chassaingne, *Lally*, pp.143, 183, 225. Susane, *Histoire de l'infanterie française*, Vol.5, pp.311-312.

37 Gennes, *Mémoire pour le sieur de La Bourdonnais*, pp.10-11; Crepin, *Mahé de La Bourdonnais*, pp.78-79; ADR, Co 262, Conseil supérieur de l'Ile de France to Conseil supérieur de l'Ile de Bourbon, 16 May 1741.

17

Asiatic Soldiers

It should always be borne in mind that the great majority of the soldiers in the service of the Compagnie des Indes were born and raised in India. At the peak of French dominion and influence India during the mid-eighteenth century, there were some five sepoy soldiers to one European soldier. Although 1737 is usually the date given for the first corps of sepoys in French service, it must be recalled that as early as 1676, only three years after the establishment of the Compagnie des Indes orientales' lodge at Pondicherry, Indian men-at-arms had been enlisted by the company. These Indian men-at-arms were not termed sepoys although they certainly could have been.

As is well known, the non-Muslim population of India was divided in system of castes since ancient times, which defined all classes of society. In terms of military service, historic India had an enormous difference regarding the profession of arms as practiced in Europe where, any man could bear arms, be it as a professional soldier or as a militiaman. In India, only men born of certain castes or into families of 'military generations' could be warriors or soldiers and carry arms. Other castes did not, and some had a philosophy and lifestyle based on the virtues of peace and non-violence. In Bengal for instance, the non-military classes included intellectuals, traders and artisans as well as well as so-called untouchable castes. This rendered 'any form of levy en masse impossible, or any form of Militia service' according to a later veteran British officer of the Indian Army.[1]

Given the large population of India, there were enough young men in the warrior castes to raise the large armies seen throughout the country. The caste system could be considerably different depending on the area in the country. The Muslim minority was not, in theory, subject to this caste division of society, but ancient traditions could be strong in many areas. There were

1 J.F. MacMunn, *The Armies of India, painted by A.C. Lovett* (London: A. & C. Black, 1911), pp.129-131. On Indian philosophy and non-violence, we recommend the excellent and extensive History of Philosophy site sponsored by the University of Munich and King's College, London at: <https://historyofphilosophy.net/non-violence>, (accessed 12 October 2023).

also exceptions in that certain Hindu sects developed into powerful military societies.[2]

Early Sepoys

According to a mid-eighteenth century memorandum on sepoys employed by the Compagnie des Indes, they originated in the mid-sixteenth century during the reign of Mughal Emperor Humayun who raised them as companies of infantry armed with muskets, then a novelty, because such firearms were very scarce in the country. Soon thereafter, some were recruited by the Portuguese to support their European soldiers standing guard in Goa and other bases they had on the Indian Ocean.[3]

Possibly as early as the 1670s, the French employed what would later be known as *Cipahis* (sepoys in English). The amazing capture of Valdaour by Martin on 24 September 1676 included 60 allied Indian soldiers out of a corps of some 300. Some few appear to have continued to serve in Pondicherry thereafter, but it was the Indo-Portuguese topasses that eventually formed part of the European companies in the French lodges.[4]

The first *Cipahis* designated under that name may have entered the service of the Compagnie des Indes during 1737, probably initially numbering only a few squads. Facing the Maratha threat to Pondicherry and other lodges, Governor-General Dumas expanded the force to over a thousand men from 1739. By May 1740, when the huge Maratha army was practically at the city's gates, Dumas had recruited some 4,500 sepoys in French pay, most of them Muslims. Traditionally, sepoys were enlisted in distinct units for a period of time during periods of tensions and then disbanded when calm returned. This partly happened after the Marathas left in May 1741, but many were kept to garrison Pondicherry. In October, a detachment of about 500 sepoys was part of La Bourdonnais' force that relieved Mahé.[5]

Once taken into service, the sepoys were immediately disciplined, armed, trained to drill and manoeuvre like and with French soldiers. In effect, the concept was that they be instructed to a level whereas they could efficiently

---

2 Marie Guillaume Pierre Aubineau-Duplessis, *Manuel du Cipaye contenant quelques réflexions sur leparti que l'on pourrait tirer du militaire indien…* (Pondicherry: Unknown Publisher, 1784), p.14.

3 'Mémoire sur la Milice des Cipayes' in Albert Depréaux, 'Troupes coloniales d'autrefois', *Revue de l'histoire des colonies françaises*, XVI (1928), pp.411-417. This Mémoire is unsigned, but its author was a veteran obviously very familiar with sepoys. Ferrera Martins, *Historia do Exercito Portugues* (Lisbon: Inquérito, 1945), p.115; J. N. Da Fonseca, *An Historical and Archaeological Sketch of the City of Goa* (Bombay: Thacker and Company, 1878), p.39. In 1708, there were seven companies of sepoys at Goa.

4 Martin, *Mémoires*, Vol.2, pp.39, 62, Kaeppelin, *Compagnie des Indes orientales*, pp.159-160; Pourouchotman, 'Nos Cipahis de l'Inde', p.580.

5 Bruce Lenman, 'The Weapons of War in 18th century India', *JSAHR*, XLVI (1968), p.33 mentions that the first sepoys in French service were raised at Mahé between 1721 and 1729. This is not mentioned in Alfred Martineau, *Les origines de Mahé de Malabar* (Paris: Champion, 1917) considered the most complete study on early Mahé, which shows detailed establishments of European and topasses. It is possible that Indian soldiers were hired more or less temporarily and thus not appear on the establishment, but this is a moot point.

A sepoy soldier in the service of the Compagnie des Indes, mid-eighteenth century. (Print after Lucien Rousselot. Private collection, author's photo)

fight shoulder to shoulder with their French comrades. Their units had to manoeuvre like the French troops they were brigaded with; thus, both sepoys and French soldiers knew that survival and success on a battlefield depended on their united efforts. Sepoys did not understand French, but they learned well enough the commands to manoeuvre efficiently as shown by their future exploits using linear tactics in battle. Each unit had amongst its Indian and French officers and *sergents* a few who were bilingual. It was estimated that after six weeks of training, a sepoy soldier could understand sufficiently to drill and manoeuvre efficiently.[6]

When Dupleix replaced Dumas as Governor-General in 1742, he took steps to have a substantial number of sepoys serving permanently in garrison. They were recruited amongst the best and bravest. In the following years, the sepoys evolved into a flexible organisation that was not necessarily the same everywhere. There was a French infantry major acting as an inspector of sepoys, assisted by a commissary officer. The choice of sepoy officers by the governors at Pondicherry and senior officers was not always perfect, favouritism sometimes being exerted rather than the capacity of the pretenders to these ranks. Some of them were hardly 'out of their cribs' when it was 'old and brave sepoys of the Malabar Coast' that should have been chosen according to our memorialist. However, it should be also considered that appointment of officers in European armies had widespread and similar flaws.[7]

Some French senior commanders might put sepoys in very exposed positions; thus one could not be 'surprised if these troops sometimes abandoned their posts'. [8] While Sepoys were remarkably patient about ration shortages, they were less so when it came to delays in being paid and this was another cause for desertion Their companies might be incomplete and a group of Sepoys carrying 25 colours that should have 2,500 men behind

6 Aubineau-Duplessis, *Manuel du Cipaye*, pp.21-23. This manual has its pp.27-262 devoted to drill and manoeuvre based on the 1776 French regulations.

7 'Mémoire sur la Milice des Cipayes', p.422. The author mentions that Madame Dupleix had obtained commissions for some of her servants. The metropolitan army was also rather pathetic as shown in Lee Kennett, *The French Armies of the Seven Years War* (Durham, NC: Duke Universty, 1967), chapter 6 and many French histories such as Reboul, *L'Armée* (Paris: Seheur, 1931) and Émile Léonard, *L'Armée et ses problems au XVIIIe siècle* (Paris: Plon, 1958).

8 'Mémoire sur la Milice des Cipayes', p.418.

them might in fact have about half that number. On the whole, however, they were deemed dependable, very steady and essential troops. This was certainly due in part to their Indian and French officers as long as they did not needlessly expose them to danger and always led by example. If well led by their officers and *sergents*, they could be as effective and steady in volley fire as European troops. Although armed with French muskets, the bayonets that came with these muskets might be less useful when they engaged in hand-to-hand combat in a charge or assault. They preferred drawing their Indian sabres and daggers in such combats, weapons which they knew since their childhood and far less cumbersome to them than a musket with its bayonet. However, many battle accounts show that sepoys used bayonets quite efficiently.

Some 500 sepoys were part of the force that accepted the surrender of Madras in September 1746 and there were 700 at Commandant Paradis' astounding and historic victory at Adyar/Sao Tomé in November of that year. They henceforth fought in every battle, siege and skirmish involving French troops in India until 1761. The amazing and frankly admirable and glorious heritage of the sepoys in the service of France in India during those years is a rich subject that is yet to be chronicled in detail.[9]

The memorialist mentioned that sepoys of the Compagnie des Indes were organised in companies of 100 men each led by a *soubadar* (captain), an *alfer* (ensign), two *sergents*, four *caporaux* and two 'tam-tams' that were a type of Indian drum with two drumsticks having a round end. Each company had a colour, but it was not carried by its *alfer*. He further commented that other Europeans employing sepoys had not changed anything to this Portuguese organisation.[10]

Although overwhelmingly infantrymen, some sepoys were cavalrymen. The largely locally raised troops that the British called 'Irregular Forces' should also be mentioned. They were mostly cavalry units that were paid by European monopoly companies, attached to their contingents and could be considered sepoys at times. The French sepoy cavalry appears to have been such, and a trooper came with his own horse, weapons and clothing for which he was paid 25 rupees monthly. This was the 'Siladar' system of Mughal armies. In wartime, these troops might be part of the regular forces as part of a sepoy company or acting independently in their province and some also served in peacetime, notably as a mounted armed constabulary alongside sepoy and peon units providing aid to civil power.[11]

9 Reneld, *Les Cipahis de l'Inde*, is a small booklet that appears to be the only book-like publication that is solely devoted to the sepoys.

10 'Mémoire sur la Milice des Cipayes', pp.411-417.

11 Martineau, *Dupleix*, Vol.3, pp.69-70; B.N. Majumbar, 'History of the Irregular Forces of India 1600-1918', *Bulletin of The Military Historical Society*, Vol.17, No. 67 (February 1967), pp.76-78; MacMunn, *The Armies of India*, pp.12-14.

Organisation and Indian Command

The sepoys command system featured a higher level of organisation consisting of a few French officers attached to supervise them. These officers were mainly concerned with overall command, training and logistics. French *sergents*, at least initially, were also likely to be attached to sepoy units from time to time to instil European-style drill and manoeuvres in linear tactics, which proved so decisive from 1746.

Sepoy companies were tactically commanded by Indian officers. Their rank of *soubadar* was a far more independent entrepreneur situation; they recruited and supervised their men-at-arms according to Indian ways and means, adopting certain European military practices to satisfy their employer, the Compagnie des Indes. At the same time, Indian officers had substantial bargaining powers as seen in the correspondence of Dupleix and Bussy insofar as the interior management of their units, recruiting and conducting their own practices of military justice. An unhappy sepoy *soubadar* might mention that he would simply leave with his men and offer his services to other Europeans or Indian princes. This was a transposition of certain features of Mughal armies, also reminiscent of European fifteenth- and sixteenth-century armies, in which 'freelance' *soubadars* were really chief officers responsible of groups of soldiers/warriors that were attached for a fee to a prince's army. These practices were a prerogative of sepoy senior Indian officers. They formed a line that governor generals such as Dumas and Dupleix did not wish to cross.

A detailed list dated in June 1753 of some 5,700 sepoys, which formed the major part of Bussy's army at Hyderabad, shows they were divided into eight corps led by Indian officers/leaders. The strength of the corps was not the same for all and could as small as one company of 100 sepoys to a corps of nearly 1,500. Taking the corps of Abdoul Rhaman, one finds that it included 13 *soubadars* whose seniority depended on their rate of pay (which was not uniform), 47 other officers, 80 *sergents*, 91 *caporaux*, 838 private sepoys and 76 cavalrymen. Bussy only had about 400 European soldiers at that time so there were 14 sepoys for every French soldier in his army.[12]

One notes that sepoy troops organisation was much more standard in the Carnatic. At Pondicherry on 29 June 1753, there were 15 companies each of 100 men including three officers, while four companies had between 46 and 72 NCOs and sepoys. There also were some 100 sepoy cavalrymen.[13]

Sepoy pay varied. In the Carnatic, a *soubadar* would have 100 rupees while a private sepoy received 9 to 10 rupees a month although this could go up to 12 rupees at times. A *soubadar* in the Deccan would have a minimum of 175 rupees and a private sepoy 17 rupees.[14]

---

12 Martineau, *Bussy*, pp.118-119. The corps were: Abdoul Rhaman 1,145 sepoys at 34,081 rupees; Mamoud kh 919 at 27,765; Aboubaker 454 at 14,090; Ecker kh. 551 at 9,360; Lar kh. at 548; Romani kh. 549 at 8,901; Aboukaber 100 at 1,510; Ibrahim kh. 1,434 at 36,361.

13 Anon., *Mémoire pour la Compagnie des Indes contre le Sieur Dupleix*, pp.135-139. The 15 companies each had a *capitaine*, two *enseignes*, four *sergents*, six *caporaux* and 87 sepoys.

14 Martineau, *Dupleix*, Vol.3, p.65.

Sepoy Lifestyle

Sepoy service was 'very considerable' in garrisons because they were far more acclimatised to the torrid Indian climate and lifestyle than Europeans; they were thus responsible for many of the daily chores associated with garrison service, especially in daytime when the 'prodigious heat bothered Europeans' that often also caused many to be sick. Sepoys were always on guard at a governor general's residence and a company escorted him went he went out. They also supervised workers and some were trained to serve artillery. The number of sepoys in service could fluctuate considerably since a portion of them could be dismissed from the service in peaceful times. There always seems to have been a sufficient pool of men to call upon when expanding the force although their quality might be questionable, the more experienced having often been recruited to serve in other European garrisons on the coast. Another factor concerned sepoy *soubadars* that might recruit men of a lower caste, who they could pay less, to pocket the difference. In such cases, the professional sepoys forced to serve with pariahs would desert to join elsewhere, especially if offered better pay by their opponents, often taking their weapons with them. In general, however, sepoys were faithful to whom they served. The best sepoys were said to come from Mahé and its area on the Malabar coast, Patan, Arcot and Nagard.[15]

It could be added that, according to Law de Lauriston's memoirs, once a sepoy had been enlisted, issued 'his red jacket and his musket, he believes he has become a totally new man, he sees himself European…'[16]

Sepoys were not issued rations like French soldiers, topasses or *Caffres*, but had to purchase their own although, as in all armies, some might pilfer vegetables or poultry from hapless farmers. Lodging was also elective as they do not seem to have had barracks like French soldiers. They also slept under the stars since they were not issued tents until 1753 and we suspect many did not have them after that date. A veteran officer of sepoys related that, unlike European soldiers, sepoys did not mind sleeping fully dressed on sand. It was recommended that five tents per company were necessary for the 'preservation of their weapons and ammunition, and to serve as rallying points.'[17]

All sepoys were not necessarily examples of discipline and order. A common problem was the rather relaxed way they maintained their muskets, whose locks might not have a flint and even its cock broken when on garrison duties. They seem to have had muskets in good order when going into battle. Sepoy marching through the countryside on campaign could be a plague to poor villagers in their path; some few unruly sepoys might well erupt into little farms and steal whatever they could, even cattle. Local officials would

15 BNF, Ms Français 8971, Parallele des dépense militaires…, January to March1755; Aubineau-Duplessis, *Manuel du Cipaye*, p.14. The budget dropped from 98,997 to 34,970 rupees for Pondicherry and its area. Sepoy cavalry went from 805 to 200. This was raised considerably from 1756.

16 Law de Lauriston, *Mémoire*, p.310.

17 'Mémoire sur la Milice des Cipayes', p, 421; Aubineau-Duplessis, *Manuel du Cipaye*, p.9..

complain to French and sepoy officers, but culprits were difficult to identify and the suspects would always insist that it was not them but enemy sepoys.

Some Indian sepoy *soubadars* were also interested in gains and a favourite practice was reporting more men at inspections than were actually there so as to pocket the extra pay. There was nothing especially Indian about this practice also seen in every army in Europe. Called, *passe-volant* in France, it had been much lessened during the reign of the Sun King and Dupleix would cashier officers who tolerated it. But it was no easy task. *Capitaine* Hibault, who led four companies of sepoys, reported to Dupleix that in spite of all his efforts, one of his Indian *soubadars* named Babro went so far as threaten to leave with his men if they could not keep stolen cattle. The usual cure was to pay more money to the sepoys who would then be back on duty with renewed courage – or so reported another French officer, *Capitaine* Goupil. It must also be added that there were times when sepoys were owed substantial arrears in pay. Some might leave, but it is obvious most stayed with their French comrades.[18]

Alcoholism, which substantially plagued all European soldiers, was not an outstanding problem with sepoys, or for that matter, any other type of unit made up of Indian soldiers. The majority of Indians of all classes, castes and religions habitually drank water and tea. This sobriety, needless to add, was a very positive factor with regards to the interior discipline of sepoy units.[19]

Sepoys had their own Indian martial music played by small groups of musicians whose instruments consisted mainly of small tambourines, cymbals, trumpets and flutes. The two 'tam-tams' per company were for military manoeuvres, but could also occasionally be with the musicians.[20]

Some sepoys may have had female companions with, in some cases, children as camp followers, but documentation regarding their family life seems very elusive. Muster rolls or regulations regarding marriages or camp followers have not been encountered. However, Indian artwork occasionally shows women with sepoys as well as considerable numbers of camp followers in the wake of armies.

Much More Sepoys Than Europeans

In the mid-eighteenth century, there were, according to the memorialist, about 5,000 sepoys in the service of the Compagnie des Indes and most of them were detached to various places. He was obviously referring only to sepoys deployed in the Carnatic and along the Coromandel coast. The garrisons at Pondicherry and its wider area mustered 3,418 sepoys on 1

18 Fréville, 'Une armée coloniale au XVIIIe siècle Dupleix aux Indes', p.434-437; 'Mémoire sur la Milice des Cipayes', pp.419-420.

19 Tambi Pourouchotman, 'Nos Cipahis de l'Inde', *Armée, Marine, Colonies* (1927), p.581. There was also *Kallo* (or *Toddi*), an alcohol made from palm or coconut tree sap that had to be consumed quickly and cool before sunrise after which it became bitter. Made and sold by *chanars*, it was inexpensive but impractical. Jean-Jacques Chabrélie, *L'Inde française ou collection de designs lithographiés* (Paris: Chabrélie, 1827), Vol.1, unpaginated.

20 Law de Lauriston, *Mémoire*, p.575.

October 1755, not including Nellore that had another 1,200. There were also those with Bussy's in the Deccan, which, in June 1753, amounted to some 5,701 sepoys just in the city of Hyderabad. In September 1756, Bussy's sepoys numbered about 4,952 of which 300 were cavalrymen and 652 were attached to the artillery. By adding hundreds of sepoys posted on the Malabar coast and elsewhere, their number could reach 11,000 men in India.[21]

Sepoys normally made up about three quarters of the Compagnie des Indes' troops in the field, the rest being European soldiers. When formed in line, they were placed at the left of the French troops and were said to be steady and courageous soldiers, especially if their European comrades showed such qualities. Their firepower in an engagement could be equal to European troops when well led. In combat formation, which, the memorialist noted, 'in India is always [deployed] on a plain, sepoys were to be placed to the left and right [flanks] of a European corps while supported by a detachment of Europeans at each of their wing, and to place at least one cannon in front of each sepoy corps, protected by sepoy grenadiers.' They were much encouraged and flattered to have a cannon at the head of their formations.[22]

The number of sepoys in French service decreased quickly in the later 1750s. Defeats resulting in territorial losses meant that less revenue was collected for a French treasury that was already in deficit. Lally's army had about 5,000 sepoys at the abortive 1758 siege of Madras; by January 1761, only 1,200 were left at the siege and fall of Pondicherry. A few hundreds more would have been at Mahé, Gingee and a few smaller outposts, but, on the whole, there would have been none left in French service by the end of the year.

Following the return of Pondichery, Chandernagor, Mahé, Carical and Yanaon to France in the 1763 Treaty of Paris and the arrival of French Compagnie des Indes personnel and garrisons from 1765, companies of sepoys were also established. Their command structure was more European than previously with each company having a European *capitaine* and *lieutenant* with two sepoy officers. The company of *Capitaine* de Prédigue, which had 36 men including four officers, was on guard at Pondicherry by 1 May 1765 with more companies recruiting. Later that year, Governor Law de Lauriston praised sepoys for their outstanding services in the previous wars and argued that many more should be raised to properly ensure the safety of the lodges as well as to maintain a certain diplomatic image of France as a major European power. However, expansion of the garrisons in India was hardly popular in the Paris offices of the near bankrupt Compagnie des Indes. At the time, his sepoys had very old muskets compared to the French soldiers who had new ones. By March 1768, the 'Sepoys in the Company's service' numbered 125 men including five officers.

Thereafter, the numbers of sepoys rose quickly probably due to the company's demise and the royal government assuming the responsibility of the lodges in India. By early 1772, there were 11 companies of sepoys at Pondicherry, 300 sepoys at Chandernagor, 126 at Mahé, 100 at Carical and 50 at Yanaon for a total of 1,076 officers and men. They formed up to two thirds

21 BNF, Ms Français 8971, Tableau général..., 1 October 1755; Martineau, *Bussy*, pp.118-119, 215.

22 'Mémoire sur la Milice des Cipayes', p.420.

of the troops in French India. This increase was clearly too much for the authorities in Paris who ordered a reduction to 300 sepoys on 23 February 1772. By the end of the year, the Pondicherry commanders reported having 450 at Pondicherry and 50 at Carical. Clearly, the reduction wished for had been too drastic and a royal order of 12 November 1773 reorganised the companies into a battalion of 11 companies numbering 593 men including 44 officers. France's sepoys saw many more distinguished services during the American War of Independence and are perpetuated today by the Pondicherry Police.[23]

A *Caffre* warrior, eighteenth century. Print after Maréchal's 1788 *Costumes*… (Bibliothèque Nationale de France, Paris)

Topasses

In 1724, the garrison of Pondicherry had about 300 topasses. In 1727, the four companies in garrison each had an establishment of 120 men. Part of these men were actually topasses. They had no officers, but mustered two *caporaux*, 38 infantry soldiers and a *capitaine d'armes* (*sergent* who was responsible for the company's weapons). Furthermore, there was a master bombardier, a master gunner and 18 gunner 'aides' (assistants) who were topasses. Topasses thus then made up about half the strength of each company.[24]

While they overwhelmingly served in continental India, some might be detached further afield. A detachment of 72 topasses sent for construction work at Ile de Bourbon was ordered back to Pondicherry in 1738 and 60 were detached to the Maldives in 1754. From the early 1740s, the proportion of topasses in the European companies gradually lessened, no doubt due to the addition of the more numerous sepoys being taken in the pay of the Compagnie des Indes. On 1 October 1755, the garrisons of the Coromandel coast had 262 topasses (including about 35 *Caffres*) and mostly vanished from the military records thereafter. This may also be due to their perceived lacklustre performance in combat according to some French commanders.[25]

23 AC, D2C, 130, Cayer contenant toutes les pièces concernant la composition du corps des Cipayes [1772], De par le Roy…Corps de Sipahis, 12 November 1773; Reneld, *Les Cipahis de l'Inde*. The 1773 order specified 10 fusilier companies and one of grenadiers. A uniform was imposed consisting of a blue short-tailed coat with yellow collar, cuffs and lapels, white metal buttons stamped with an anchor, white waistcoat, white breeches going to above the knees and edged with blue, white turban.

24 E. Lennel de la Farelle (ed.), *Mémoire et correspondence du chevalier et du général de la Farelle* (Paris and Nancy: Berger-Levrault, 1896), pp.306-307.

25 AC, C2, 28, Extrait du régistre général de la Compagnie des Indes, Paris, 2 June 1738; BNF, Ms Français 8971, Tableau général…, 1 October 1755. A topas drummer per company was

Peons

Documents occasionally mention 'Peons' (or 'pions') escorting Indian princes or senior European officials. Their name originated from the Portuguese word *peao* indicating a man on foot or a footman. In the early eighteenth century, the governor at Pondicherry was said to have some 300 'Gardes à pied' (foot guards) 'named Peons who [also] serve in other functions.' They were more like personal security guards and armed constables than soldiers. They guarded the lodgings of their master and attended him as guards as well as in other various ways. They could also be found in lodges outside of Pondicherry and in addition, some 500 were part of the forces posted in territories under French administration in 1753-1754. They were divided in several classes, the higher ones being those who frequently had contacts with the master. They carried a baton or mace of about five feet long with a silver pommel of three or four inches, those of inferior rank having smaller ones. Their costume was usually the common Indian dress of white cotton although some might have a jacket in the livery colours of their master. The had a wide shoulder belt, seemingly usually red or dark blue, with a silver or yellow metal plate attached upon which was engraved the initials of seal of their master.[26]

Peons in Pondicherry, eighteenth century. These police-type guards attached to senior officers were armed with a baton or a spear when parading with troops. They wore Indian costume with the distinctive red shoulder belt edged with yellow and a with a yellow metal plate. The figure at left has a blue jacket edged with yellow. Print in Chabrelie's 1835 *L'Inde française*. (Bibliothèque Nationale de France, Paris)

mentioned on the establishment of the sepoy battalion authorised raised on 12 November 1773 according to AC, D2C, 130.

26 Abbé Guyon, *Histoire des Indes orientales* (Paris: Jean Desaint & Charles Saillant, 1744), Vol.3, p.253; J.-J. Chabrelie, *L'Inde française* (Paris: Chabrelie, 1835), Vol.2, unpaginated.

18

Other Units: European Cavalry, Foreign Units, Volunteers, Engineers and Gunners

Besides European infantry soldiers, the French East India companies also employed specialists such as engineers and gunners in France and overseas. There were also various types of units serving in India such as European cavalry units including even German hussars as well of mostly British deserters and volunteers. In its heydays during the mid-eighteenth century, the company's troops in India truly had the components of a regular army.

Governor General's Guards

Having a modest detachment of guardsmen to attend provincial governor generals and senior royal army generals was a long-standing feature in metropolitan France. Louis XIV instituted this practice from the 1660s for overseas territories. For instance, Governor-General de La Haye's company of guards was seen on 18 March 1672. The Compagnie des Indes did not follow the royal example in its territories except for the Governor-General in India sometime during the first half of the eighteenth century. Due to the need to 'respond' to the elaborate oriental grandeur practices, the Governor-General at Pondicherry was attended by a personal guard of originally 12 troopers led by a *capitaine* and later having 24 troopers by 1752. These '24 guards of M. Dupleix' were described as mounted on good horses, well dressed and led by their officers at a parade in 1752. This unit appears to have been disbanded or merged into Lally's company of guardsmen in 1758.[1]

1 Anon., *Relation d'un voyage fait aux Indes orientales* (Paris: Michallet, 1677), p.78; Prévost d'Exiles, *Histoire générale des voyages* (Paris: Didot, 1751), Vol.XXXVI, pp.328; BNF, Ms Français, 8971, folio 109, "Relation des principaux événements arrivés aux Indes dans la province du Carnate…de juillet 1749. Jusqu'au 17 Octobre 1752."

Accused by Godeheu of excessive spending for this guard company, Dupleix vigorously answered that there were:

> [N]ever more the eight guardsmen at the expense of the Compagnie [des Indes]; these guards were always on campaign and never near the governor, without being mounted; those that I sent you were three invalids, not mounted, and absolutely unable to serve, the others were with the army. Of what use could be these poor invalids to you, sir, who had a company of forty men dressed superbly at great expense.

This last was a reference to Godeheu's escort of La Tour's dragoons (see below). Dupleix went on to question the duties that his successor had assigned to his guardsmen, which gives a rare insight on the duties of guardsmen:

> They have attended you from the time of your arrival, and whatever the heat [of the weather], they always followed or proceeded you, dispersed to a certain distance the Indians that wished to speak to you and even escorted you within the sanctuary of churches; they furnished two sentinels at the door of your hall, three for the gates of your office, of M. your brother's [office] and that of your secretary.[2]

Certainly, for the same reasons regarding diplomacy in India, Bussy also had a small mounted guard seen at Hyderabad in April 1751 (and described as having 12 troopers in 1753) when leading the troops in the Deccan. They were escorting Bussy when his troops went from Hyderabad to Bengal during the Fall of 1756 and possibly disbanded in 1757.[3]

The Comte de Lally was entitled to a company of 30 guardsmen including three officers due to his rank as a senior general officer of the French army. This was especially appropriate as Lally was also appointed Governor-General of India. They arrived with Lally in 1758 and attended him at the siege of Madras, his defeat at Wandewash and the siege and surrender of Pondicherry in January 1761 when four of his troopers escorted him. The troop was obviously much reduced and perhaps mostly dispersed by then.[4]

The Governor-General of Ile de France and Ile de Bourbon did not have a company of guards. However, he could be attended by the militia's elite company of mounted Gendarmes, which was superbly appointed (see Chapter 21 on Militia).

---

2 Dupleix, *Réponse du sieur Dupleix a la lettre du sieur Godeheu*, p.30. Dupleix's letter was written on 20 May 1755 while sailing to France on board the *Duc d'Orléans*.

3 'Relation du siege de Pondichéry', *Gazette*, 1749, pp.230-231, 236, 238-241, 244-245, 248-249; Martineau, *Bussy*, p.19; Albert Depréaux, 'Les uniformes de l'Armée de la Compagnie des Indes…', pp.161, 171-178.

4 BNF, Réglement pour le traitement des officiers généraux, & autres employés du corps de troupes destiné à passer aux Indes Orientales, 10 November 1756; Orme, *Military transactions*, Vol.2, No. 2, p.723. Lally's four troopers 'of his own guard' were accompanied by '15 English hussars…'

Dragoons and Grenadiers à Cheval (Horse Grenadiers)

The first dragoon unit organised in French India appears to be a troop under the command of *Capitaine* Combault d'Auteuil. Dragoons at this time were mounted infantrymen that could fight as fusiliers on foot or as troopers if engaged mounted. When it was raised is uncertain, but it was present at the siege and capture of Madras in September 1746 and saw distinguished action during the siege of Pondicherry in August and October 1748. There were '60 French dragoons' seen escorting Governor-General Dupleix at Pondicherry on 28 September 1749. This was very likely the same unit mentioned with Bussy's army at the capture of Gingee in September 1750 and near Hyderabad in the Deccan during April 1751. The dragoons were in many actions in the Deccan campaigns and later seen at Aurengabad in June 1753. The dragoons appear to have been transformed into a company of Grenadiers à cheval (Horse Grenadiers) sometime in 1754.[5]

Horse grenadiers were considered elite dragoons. Bussy must have upgraded the unit to make it known that it was made up of some of the best battle-tested mounted soldiers of his contingent. He may also have wanted to distinguish his men from the dragoons being raised in Pondicherry by Governor-General Godeheu at that time (see below). In February 1755, it was posted at Golconde where Claude-Thomas Du Tour de Noirfosse joined it as a *lieutenant* and his detachments were at 'several war actions' under Bussy's orders. The Grenadiers à cheval were with Bussy's army in September 1756 that went to Bengal and were later at Pondicherry in 1760. When the city was about to be besieged by the British, the cavalry, useless in siege operations, was sent to Gingee, whch that served as a base to harass the Indian contingents allied to the British. The unit was surely dissolved at the time of the British occupation of Gingee over three months after the fall of Pondicherry in January 1761.[6]

Another company of dragoons was organised in Pondicherry during September 1754 at the behest of Governor-General Godeheu to serve with the army and also provide his escort. It had 40 dragoons led by *Capitaine* de La Tour de Saint-Igest and *Lieutenant* du Tour de Noirfosse. Nine dragoons under a senior *sergent* remained in Pondicherry as an escort to Godeheu while the others served with the army in the Carnatic. It had 24 dragoons at Pondicherry in February 1756. This company was said to have been 'superbly clothed at great expense' with its officers 'dressed magnificently in the latest' fashion. A reinforcement of one *capitaine*, one *lieutenant*, two NCOs and 38 dragoons for this company was sent from Lorient to India in May 1757 arriving in Pondicherry in 1758. A few cavalry officers also arrived including *Lieutenant* Dégras who became its *capitaine* on 1 September 1759. A cavalry company was seemingly raised in 1758 led by *Capitaine* Aumont, which was incorporated into *Capitaine* Dégras' dragoon company on 10

5 Vaissière, *Dupleix*, p.130; Depréaux, 'Les uniformes de la Compagnie des Indes…', pp.171, 178.

6 'Lettres et souvenirs de Du Tour de Noirfosse, officier de l'armée des Indes', p.591; Martineau, *Bussy*, p.216; Barbé, *Le nabab René Madec*, p.27; Le Bail, *René Madec*, p.80.

February 1760. Dégras' dragoons were sent to Thiagar in October 1760 and probably dissolved there after the fall of Pondicherry in January 1761. Only three officers and 12 private troopers of European cavalry were mustered at Pondicherry on 15 January 1761. These 15 cavalrymen may have been the remnants of Lally's guard.[7]

German Temporary Units

The German recruits provided by Jean-Chrétien Fischer that arrived in India were armed, clothed and incorporated into the company's French troops. However, some were grouped into temporary German 'Brigades' probably in 1754, the 1st led by M. Fischer and the 2nd by the Baron de Wust (or Wuhl). This may have been done because some of these recruits only knew their native German language. According to Godeheu, the baron was accused of inconsiderate statements in front of his men in October 1754 and may have been relieved of duty; in January 1755, some German officers plotted to desert with some of their men. According to musters of troops at Pondicherry and its dependencies, the 1 October 1755 muster lists separately 383 'German troops' (including 16 officers and 17 *sergents*) from the French and sepoy soldiers. The following year, 145 German infantrymen of 'Brandt's brigade', with 47 German hussars, had been sent to reinforce Bussy's force. In 1758, the 'German troopers and foot' were part of the force that attacked Fort St David.[8]

German Hussars

Amongst the German recruits and troops provided to the Compagnie des Indes by Jean-Chrétien Fischer that were sent to India was a company of hussars. They were part of a group assembled at Belfort on France's eastern border in October 1753 that arrived at Lorient in December. It sailed from Lorient for India on 31 December aboard the company's ship *Duc de Bourgogne*. After a stop at Ile de France where it was to take aboard 150 horses for the unit, it arrived at Pondicherry on 1 August 1754. Two weeks later, 50

---

7 'Lettres et souvenirs de Du Tour de Noirfosse, officier de l'armée des Indes', pp.586-587; AC, D2C, 187, [signalement] Pondicherry, 24 February 1756; Dupleix, *Réponse du sieur Dupleix a la lettre du sieur Godeheu*, p.30; Martineau, *Bussy*, p.216; AC, E, 114, service record of Capt. Dégras in the service of the Compagnie des Indes; see Appendice on 1757 reinforcement. 'State of the French Forces…at Pondicherry', 15 January 1761, *The Daily Advertiser*, London, 22 July 1761; Le Bail, *René Madec*, p.80. Biography from the papers of the Madec family.

8 BNF, Ms Français 8971, Tableau général des troupes, Pondicherry 1 October 1755; Martineau, *Bussy*, p.215; Ananda, *Diary*, Vol.11, p.141. We thank Robert A. Selig for kindly bringing to our attention his research on the Baron de Wust, 'former commandant of hussars and of a German brigade, in the East Indies' according to the title page of his *L'Art militaire du partisan* (La Haye, 1768) that has otherwise very little (pp.22-23) on his time in India nor in his service record (AC, E, 393). He styled himself 'General Johann Georg Baron von Wust, King of East India' (1721-1791), but he was neither a baron nor a general or king as related by Dr Selig in the German historical journal *DAMALS*, Spring 2000.

serving on foot were sent to Trichinipoly. A few weeks after their arrival at Pondicherry, some hussars were disappointed by India and they apparently protested by refusing to drill, which was something of a mutiny. Order was eventually restored and 50 dismounted hussars were sent northwards to Masulipatam in October 1754. When it was mounted the following month, some of its men did not know how to ride a horse! A review return made there on 6 November 1755 mentions 59 hussars including three NCOs led by *Capitaine* Deis and *Lieutenant* Meyer.[9]

At an uncertain date, but possibly in June 1756, the hussar company was part of reinforcements sent to join Bussy's army, which had arrived on 3 June at Hyderabad in the Deccan. A strong force of mostly Maratha cavalry surrounded the city. On 30 June, a party of hussars under *Lieutenant* Meyer was badly mauled in a small but robust fight against Indian cavalrymen resulting in Mayer and three troopers being killed and 28 troopers wounded. Most or all hussars obviously recovered and may have taken parts in sorties and skirmishes thereafter until the Marathas gave up the siege on 28 August. On 1 September, the company was 47 strong and probably was with Bussy's army that now marched into Bengal. It later went to Pondicherry as Lally bought horses for the 'company of hussars' and had 30 hussars with his army in August 1758 at the siege of Fort St David. He also mentioned 'two companies of hussars' with his forces at Arcot on 24 February 1759 and, ultimately at Wandewash on 22 January 1760.[10]

Volontaires de Bourbon

When, in January 1741, the Marathas approached the vicinity of Pondicherry, Governor-General Dumas' appeal for reinforcements from the islands resulted in about 80 to 100 young creole men of Ile de Bourbon coming forth as volunteers 'with zeal and swiftness', who sailed for India in late March with regular troops. They were the first of several Volontaires de Bourbon corps that became renowned for valour. Meanwhile, the threat against Pondicherry abated during the following months so that when La Bourdonnais arrived there with ships and more troops on 27 September, it was the lodge of Mahé that had been blockaded since a year and a half by local Indian princes that needed reinforcements. The Volontaires de Bourbon were apparently with the relief troops led by La Bourdonnais

9 BNF, Fonds Français 385, Journal du voyage de M. Godeheu, fait en 1754, Hussard; AC, D2C, 41, Volontaires embarqués par [Jean-Chrétien] Fischer pour la Compagnie des Indes, 1 May 1754; Ribaucourt, *La vie militaire et les exploits de J.-C. Fischer*, pp.66-67; Anon., *Memoire pour la Compagnie des Indes contre le Sieur Dupleix* (Paris. M. Lambert, 1763), p.101; AC, D2C, 187, Review return of the 'Hussars de la Compagnie de Deis' at Masulipatan, 6 November 1755. The three NCOs were named But, Marvaux and Zarlet; there were 46 horses.

10 Martineau, *Bussy*, pp.206-207, 215; Gentil, *Mémoire…*, p.97 mentions that Bussy's army had '300 hussards' in mid-1756, which was obviously a false rumour; Duval d'Eprémesnil, *Mémoire*, pp.166-167, 309; Orme, *A History of the Military Transactions*, Vol 2, pp.581, 587; AC, E, 343, record of Capt. Gaston Brochard, chevalier de Puymorin of the troops of the Compagnie des Indes, certificate of 15 January 1761.

that landed there in late November and took part in the victorious attack that secured Mahé on 5 December 1741. They were called to India again and 80 volunteers led by six officers arrived at Mahé in January 1752 and at Pondicherry the following month. In September, they were sent to join Bussy's army in the Deccan where they were described as a 'fine looking company of 80 creoles from the Iles de France et de Bourbon' in September 1752. Their services in central India are somewhat shrouded because they are not clearly identified although they were possibly the 'volontaires' (or some of them) mentioned in various sources that took part in countless events and actions. They went back to Ile de Bourbon in April 1755.[11]

With war officially declared the following year, volunteers from Ile de Bourbon were again sought; some 75 were enlisted in late June and early July 1757 when they sailed for India on board the Chevalier de Soupire's squadron of d'Aché's fleet arriving in Pondicherry in September. The Volontaires de Bourbon that went to India during 1757 were granted encouraging inducements for their service. Upon his return home, each volunteer was allowed 10,000 rupees of merchandise free of any taxes or impositions, could embark two slave servants free of charge to accompany him during his service, and his plantation's coffee crop would be taken in preference to others by the Compagnie's store. Furthermore, volunteers that served in India were allowed the rank of *enseigne* from the day they carried arms. Lally was very satisfied with the Volontares de Bourbon and promoted three or four to effective officer's rank. As 'many more volunteers as could be' were sought in 1758-1759 with two recruiting officers being active at both Ile de France and Bourbon. However, some volunteers also appear to have returned to the islands in late 1759 'after distinguished services they have given to the Compagnie [des Indes]' in India according to the council of Pondicherry. Most of all perhaps, it was at that time that their redoubtable reputation for being excellent target shots, somewhat like modern 'snipers', was solidly established to this day in French military annals. Some stayed in India and were part of the garrison of Pondicherry, 40 'Volunteers of Bourbon' being listed in the city's capitulation on 15 January. In February 1761, four officers and 34 volunteers received their pay at Pondicherry.[12]

---

11 ADR, Co, 360, La Bourdonnais to the Conseil supérieur de l'Ile de Bourbon, 3 April 1743; ADR, Co, 92, Directors of the Compagnie des Indes to Conseil supérieur de Bourbon, Paris, 15 February 1743. Most volunteers were coffee planters and their service in India until about mid-1742 had an effect on the crop.ADR, Co, 618, Conseil de Mahé au Conseil de Bourbon, 7 January 1752; Martineau, p.70; ADR, Co, 619, Conseil de Pondicherry to Conseil de Bourbon, 19 February 1752; ADR, Co. 449, Conseil de l'Ile de France to Conseil de Bourbon, 9 April 1755; BNF, Ms Français, 8971, 'Relation des principaux événements arrivés aux Indes dans la province du Carnate…de juillet 1749. Jusqu'au 17 Octobre 1752.'; Jean-Jacques Duval d'Eprémesnil, *Mémoire à consulter et consultation, pour le sieur Duval Dumanoir, & M. Duval d'Espremenil, avocat du roi au Châtelet; héritiers du feû sieur Duval de Leyrit, gouverneur de Pondichéry. Avec les lettres que les sieurs Duval de Leyrit & de Lally se sont écrites dans l'Inde, pour servir de pièces justificatives* (Paris: Lambert, 1766), pp.308-309, 320.

12 Dussieux and Soulié (eds), *Mémoires du Duc de Luynes*, Vol.XV, pp.375-376; AC, D2C, 41, Conditions pour messieurs les Volontaires de Bourbon…, Saint-Denis, 16 June 1757; Albert Lougnon, *Classement et inventaire du fond de la Compagnie des Indes (série Co) 1665-1767* (Saint-Denis: Archives départementales de La Réunion, 1956), p.362; ADR, Co, 629, Conseil

Volontaires Portugais

The Compagnie des Indes recruited Portuguese adventurers that inhabited the Indian coast, many probably originating from Portugal's sizeable European colony at Goa. They appeared in the French forces in the mid-eighteenth century. Their services appear presently to be largely unknown, but must have nevertheless been quite useful as they served until the final years. In January 1752, the 'Compagnie Portugaise' mustered one *capitaine*, two *sergents*, three *caporaux*, one clerk, 41 soldiers and one drummer; one *caporal* led its 18 topas soldiers. The separate listing of the Metis topasses shows that the volunteers were considered to be Europeans. They were part of Bussy's army in the Deccan, entering Aurengabad numbering 60 men on 11 June 1753 under the command of *Capitaine* Louis de Norognha. This company was disbanded on 22 July 1755.[13]

Another Portuguese company was later raised at Pondicherry. In September 1758, the company of 'Volontaires Portugais de Pondichéry' had two officers and 41 men increasing to three officers and 45 men from November. From January 1759, it was part of Lally's troops at Arcot numbering three officers and 50 men that had decreased to only 22 men in July. More volunteers were enlisted thereafter and, in January 1760, the corps had one company of grenadiers, two companies of fusiliers (under *Capitaines* De Britto and Thelés) and one company of topasses for a total of five officers and 194 men decreasing to 154 in July.[14]

Caffres

The *Caffres* (or Cafres) were often mentioned in documents as very hardy warriors who were attached to the French forces in India from 1746. Their origin is somewhat shrouded. Their original homeland appears to have been the South African province of Natal whose east coast faced the Indian Ocean. Some reached India and one had risen to be governor of the fortress of Valdaour (just north-west of Pondicherry) by the mid-17th century. The name of *Caffres* came to designate any African man from, for instance, Madagascar, Ethiopia or other parts of East Africa. How they came to the French Ile de Bourbon or Ile de France was most likely mainly through the slave trade. They were imported there in increasing numbers from the early 1730s.[15]

In 1746, La Bourdonnais saw the military potential of the *Caffres* that had been enlisted to serve mainly as sailors on his fleet. They had a warrior's ethos that could be turned into being trained soldiers, which many of them must have preferred. He had them clothed and supervised their training including

de Pondicherry to Conseil de Bourbon, 15 October 1759; AC, D2C, 41, Etat de paye de la Compagnie des Volontaires de Bourbon, Pondicherry, 6 February 1761.

13 Martineau, *Dupleix*, Vol.3, p.53; Gentil, *Mémoires*, p.60.

14 AC, D2C, 41, Volontaires Portugais de Pondicherry, revues d'inspection, 1758-1760; Duval d'Eprémesnil, *Mémoire,* pp.308-309.

15 Sylvain Maréchal, *Costumes civil actuels de tous les peoples connus...accompagnés d'une notice historique sur leurs coutumes, moeurs, religions, &c.* (Paris: Fayard, 1788), Vol.4, pp.1-6; Martin, *Mémoires*, Vol.2, p.59.

handling of European weapons, learning French drill and manoeuvres and having them fire blank volleys to accustom them to gunfire. He saw them as being especially suited as assault troops and actually instructed them himself on how to best scale a curtain wall and instal *pétard* explosive devises. He also trained the best of the *Caffres* to use 'a machine of his invention' that propelled grappling hooks up to about 30 yards to board an enemy vessel. When he reached Madras in September, he had about 600 *Caffres* serving on his ships of whom 400 were landed as soldiers. Their reputation as merciless warriors during an assault was also known to the British and may have been a factor in the reasons to surrender Madras. About 300 remained in India. They soon distinguished themselves by their valour and the French commented it was difficult to restrain them from fighting. They were technically somewhat still in bondage; however four were granted total freedom for their bravery in 1746.[16]

A detachment of 32 *Caffre* soldiers formed part of Bussy's column that went into the Deccan in 1751. They were undoubtedly involved in many actions and skirmishes in the next years. There were still at least 14 *Caffres* with Bussy when his little army came back to Pondicherry in a grand parade, 'some mounted on elephants and others marching on foot' on 4 November 1754.[17]

By 1755, the number of both topasses and *Caffres* had decreased to perhaps 35 serving in Pondicherry, Gingee, Carical, Chillumbrum, Alumparva and Cherinbam. Their warlike reputation nevertheless remained. During later 1758, Lally asked d'Aché for reinforcements of 700 men from Ile de France including 400 to 600 *Caffres*; 160 European soldiers and 140 *Caffres* actually arrived. D'Aché further landed 400 marines and 200 additional *Caffres* at Pondicherry to reinforce Lally's army before he sailed away. About 200 African slaves from Ile de Bourbon were authorised to serve on d'Aché's fleet in June 1759, but these were hardly the trained *Caffres* that were required. Those with Lally's army seem to have largely vanished thereafter.[18]

Étrangers (Foreigners)

A company of 'Étrangers' (foreigners) was part the French contingent at the defeat of Nasir Jang in December 1750. They were under an officer named Kane and most probably raised from British deserters that had fled to Pondicherry. During May 1748 at Fort St David, Private Miller wrote that

16 Gennes, *Mémoire pour le sieur de La Bourdonnais*, pp.44, 61; Crepin, *Mahé de La Bourbonnais*, pp.305-306, 315, 321, 477.

17 Albert Depréaux, 'Les uniformes de l'Armée de la Compagnie des Indes…', pp.155, 178; Martineau, *Dupleix*, Vol.4, p.35.

18 BNF, 8971, État général des troupes, 1 October 1755; Duval de Leyrit, *Mémoire*, pp.268-269, 282, 320, 413, 546; Alfred Martineau (ed.), *Correspondence du Conseil superieur de Pondichéry et de la Compagnie des Indes* (Pondicherry, undated.), Vol.5, p 394; ADR, Co 500, Superior council of Ile to France to the superior council of Ile de Bourbon, 20 June 1759. By early October 1760, Lally reported 800 European soldiers and 700 sepoys was 'all the army' he had at Pondicherry.

'our men have been going over to the French by 6 or 8 every night'.[19] A group of '55 English soldiers [that were] deserters' was mentioned in September 1752 as being sent to Golconde just west of Hyderabad, which was probably the same unit found in Bussy's European force in the Deccan. Dupleix was not especially keen on recruiting deserters, but also reasoned in 1751 that enlisting them was 'a man less' in the enemy force. These deserters were fearful of facing British forces since that likely meant execution if captured. It may be why they appear to have served mostly in central India with Bussy's army, where British troops were not widely deployed. There were 'quantities of foreign deserters' at Hyderabad according to a French soldier of Bussy's corps. They arrived 'naked' and miserable. They were 'Portuguese, Scots, Irish, Germans and Dutch who joined us and which we distributed in the companies' notably that of Massé 'that was nearly all of topas[ses]' otherwise. In Bengal, there were few French troops in 1756 and to compensate, numerous British deserters from Clive's army were welcomed. In March 1757, out of 237 soldiers at Chandernagor, 117 were British deserters: part of them served in a company of grenadiers of 50 men, an artillery company of 30 men and one of sailors. They vanished during the siege of Chandernagor, some managing to join Law de Lauriston's corps that eventually went from Cossimbazar as far Delhi. This shows that foreign deserters could be found individually in French companies as well as distinct foreign companies. Some or all may have eventually gone to Pondicherry and perhaps incorporated into another 'Compagnie Étrangère' raised there. Such a company was part of the abortive relief force sent to Masulipatam in June 1759, but arrived four days after its capitulation. The force had many misfortunes on the way back and this company may have dissolved thereafter. By the Autumn of 1760 when Coote's Indo-British army was closing in on Pondicherry, British deserters in French forces would have likely absconded into central India where some were later mentioned in the service of Indian princes.[20]

Engineers and Fortifications

The various monopoly trading companies employed engineers both in France and overseas. They basically consisted of two types of engineers. The first type were those serving overseas. Their rank and status was usually expressed by holding a commission, usually of the rank of *capitaine* for a senior engineer, of an infantry company whose daily command duties was seconded to a subaltern officer so that he could perform his engineering duties. The senior engineer was also part of the governor general's staff.

19 Miller, 'The diary of James Miller', p.222.

20 BNF, Ms Français 8971, Victoire sur Nezerzingue par l'armée française commandée par M. de La Touche le 16 décembre 1750; Martineau, *Dupleix*, Vol.3, pp.53-54. One named Murray may have been an officer of 'Étrangers'. He might be Daniel Murray listed as a Compagnie des Indes officer in India in 1753 and 1756 as per Haudrère, *La Compagnie française des Indes*, Vol.4, p.1206; Depréaux, 'Les uniformes de la Compagnie des Indes…', p.164; Hill, *Three Frenchmen in Bengal*, pp.23-24, 38; Barbé, *Le nabab René Madec*, p.16.

The second type were the naval *Ingénieurs-constructeurs* (engineer-builders) who specialised in designing and building ships usually in France and are not part of this study as they concern the fleets of the French East India companies – a substantial topic by itself.

The engineer's organisation generally followed that of the engineering services in the royal Ministry of the Navy. The company's engineers overseas were somewhat like the Ingénieurs du Roi (King's Engineers) of the Ministry of the Navy whose work also involved the design and building of military, civil and even religious buildings. Indeed Ingénieurs du Roi might be detached to serve in the French East India companies and it appears that quite a few remained in their service as officers in their troops.[21]

Engineers were involved with troops campaigning in the field and siege warfare, either with a defending garrison or with an army besieging an enemy fortification. Their specialised knowledge made them critically important officers on the governor's staff of any territory, especially as they needed to adapt European engineering practices in countries that had very different conditions than what they had learned in France.[22]

There were many instances of engineers in royal army service being seconded for service of the Compagnie des Indes. An example was Charpentier de Cossygny, chief engineer at Besançon, acting as such in the company's service from 1753 at Iles de France and de Bourbon. Dubreuil also served as an Ingénieur du Roi seconded to the service of the company at those islands.[23]

The most important military work built overseas was the citadel of Saint-Louis at Pondicherry, India. For this rather elaborate work, Ingénieur du Roi de Nyon was detached to India and arrived in Pondicherry during 1701. He was busy with many projects and first had some temporary fortifications built. By 1705, those on the seaside were replaced by two bastions, then bomb proof casemates were built followed by other structures eventually all linked by curtain walls that completed this citadel built on a star plan featuring five bastions surrounded by a wet moat and glacis. It was inaugurated on 25 August 1706. A Roman Catholic church and barracks were added within during the 1720s and a splendid new government palace in the early 1750s. Everything was razed by the British fallowing the 1761 surrender of the city.[24]

---

21 The best source for the engineer's work of the various French monopoly companies are plans and memoirs preserved at the Archives Nationales Outre-Mer, at Aix-n-Provence in the Dépot des Fortifications des Colonies series. Anne Blanchard, *Dictionnaire des ingénieurs militaire 1691-1791* (Montpellier: Centre d'histoire militaire et d'études de défense nationale, 1981) outlines the service of every engineer recorded in royal service and is thus an inestimable source. It does not list engineers in the various monopoly companies unless they were assigned to a territory.

22 Michel Thévenin, *Changer le système de la guerre. Le siege en Nouvelle-France 1755-1760* (Québec: Université Laval, 2020). This remarkable study, which stems from a PhD thesis, discusses the engineering challenges during the Seven Years War in North America. We have not encountered any equivalent study for the East Indies (where formidable Indian fortifications could be encountered); it would certainly be a fascinating and useful topic to consider.

23 Chevalier de La Rozière, *Lettre justificative de M. le chevalier de La Rozière,... ingénieur pour la Compagnie des Indes aux îles de France et de Bourbon, à M. de Charpentier Cossigny* (Paris: Unknown Publisher, 1755), pp.3-6.

24 Yvonne Robert Gaebelé, *Une parisienne aux Indes au XVIIe siècle* (Pondicherry and Paris: Société de l'histoire de l'Inde française, 1937), pp.190, 214-218.

Left: The 'Porte Royale' (Royal Gate of Fort Saint-Louis, the citadel of Pondicherry, 1709. It was a suitably impressive work with the royal coat of arms above the main entry gate with a clock above. Although this elevation is dated 15 February 1709, the year 1705 is indicated in Latin. (Archives Nationales Outre-Mer, 26DFC10terC)

Below: Plan and elevation of the barracks and storehouses in Fort Saint-Louis, Pondicherry, 1725. The plan at the centre shows the ground floor which consisted of the private soldiers' barracks (A) with sergeant's rooms (B). Next to the barracks were rooms that were built on the ground floor within the curtain walls for storage (G), kitchens (H), soldier's mess (I), stairway and ramps to top of the curtain wall and the basement (K, LM, N), water wells (E) in the alley or street (F) were between the barracks and the curtain wall. The barrack's gate (M) faced the fort's interior parade ground. (Archives Nationales Outre-Mer, 29DFC20B)

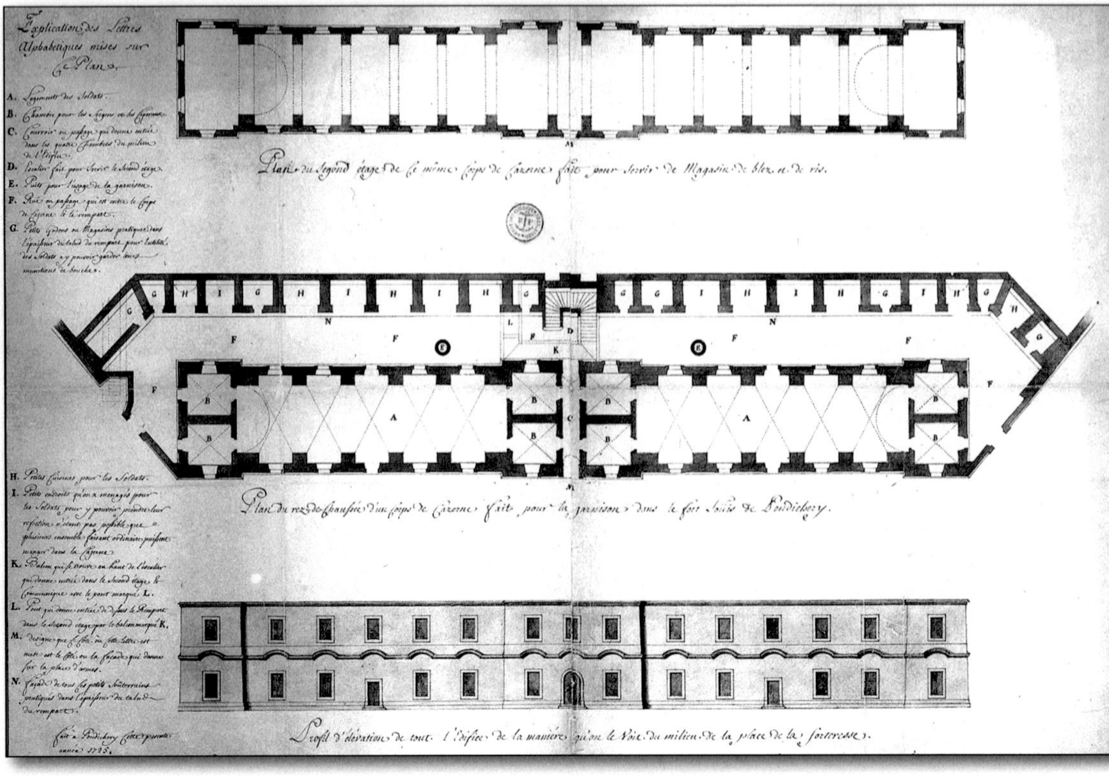

The city of Pondicherry did not initially have protective fortifications outside of the company's compound. The advent of the Saint-Louis citadel combined with the rapid growth of the city dictated that basic protective fortifications were necessary as seen by a plan of the 1720s. By 1748, the size of the city had doubled and fortifications had also been built. They consisted of bastioned walls surrounded by a wet moat with glacis outside. A redoubt was also built on St Thomas Island commanding the entrance of the Ariancoupan River just south of the city. This remained generally the same up to the 1760-1761 siege.

Other fortifications built by the French elsewhere in India were less elaborate. In general, they were to provide some security for the lodges and usually consisted of a bastioned fort on a square or a rectangular plan, a good example being Fort Orleans at Chandernagor, Bengal. Other works in the form of sizeable redoubts were sometimes added as at Mahé, on the Malabar coast. Some lodges had very modest protective elements, for instance, at Dacca.

In most cases, the fortifications occupied by Indo-French troops were of Indian military architecture and some were formidable. Some minor European feature such as a bastion or ravelin here and there might have been added, for instance at Masulipatam. On the whole, these massive and extensive Indian fortifications formed daunting defences. Some, such as Gingee, were considered near to impregnable if properly guarded. The abortive French sieges of Trichinopoly are a confirmation of this factor.

At Ile de Bourbon and Ile de France, the lodges were basically built as fortified administrative and commercial structures. The 1732 plan by Engineer Sornay for the lodge at Saint-Paul, Ile de Bourbon, show a sizeable battery facing the shore (built in 1734) with the lodge's buildings being protected by a crenelated wall, and outside dry ditch and glacis. Ten years later, the plan of the lodge at Saint-Denis, Ile de Bourbon, revealed a wall with two small bastions at the lodge with an large outside battery facing the sea and another battery to provide crossfire.

Governor-General La Bourdonnais sought to strengthen the defences of both islands and especially Ile de France. It had the two best harbours in

Redoubt built at Fort Matlaye, Malabar coast, 1753. This view of its eastern side shows the white standard of France. Matlaye, which is north of Mahé, was taken on 23 January 1752, destroyed and rebuilt on a rectangular plan by the French. The redoubt's walls were faced with red bricks. Plan by Dupassage. (Archives Nationales Outre-Mer, 25DFC191B)

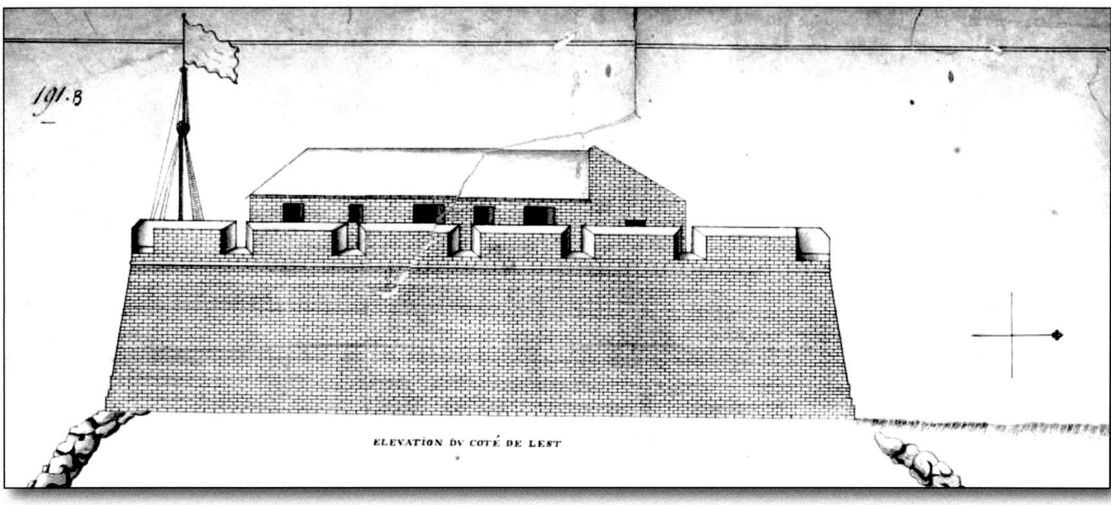

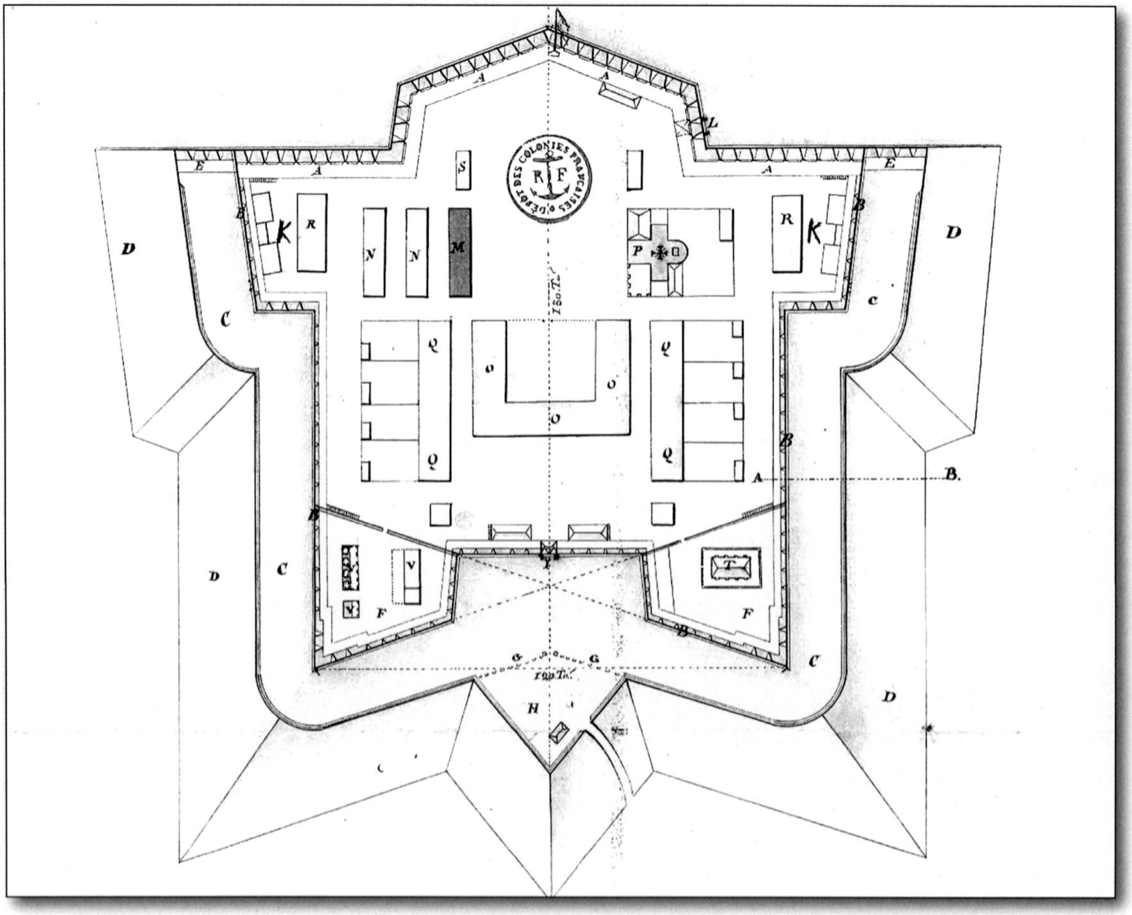

Fortified lodge of the Compagnie des Indes at Saint-Paul, Ile de Bourbon, 1732. This plan by engineer Sornay shows the main defence features facing the sea (top) with a battery of 43 guns. At each end was a lower battery of three guns each. The upper half-bastions each had three guns to cover the ditch and the two lower half-bastions (bottom) each had four guns. The lodge was also a place to do business and could accommodate some 300 persons including soldiers. There is also a copy of this plan at the departmental archives of La Réunion (series Co, 1171). (Archives Nationales Outre-Mer, 23DFC0018B)

the islands being both safe and large, but they hardly had any substantial fortifications. In the mid-eighteenth century, the approach to the harbour of the capital of the islands, Port-Louis, also called Port Nord-Ouest, was guarded by seven batteries including a large one to act as a small citadel ordered built by La Bourdonnais from 1741 on Ile des Tonnelliers. It consisted of a very strong redoubt with artillery on two levels built on a star plan featuring glacis and a ditch outside its curtain walls and artillery platforms. Its centre had a rectangular cavalier whose guns formed an elevated battery surmounted by a tower for signals and the white standard of France. This redoubt was nearly impossible to attack by surprise. Its land side was covered by marshes; its seaside had coral reefs just below the water's surface as far as three kilometres outwards that prevented ships from approaching it.[25]

25 Crepin, *Mahé de La Bourbonnais*, pp.85-87

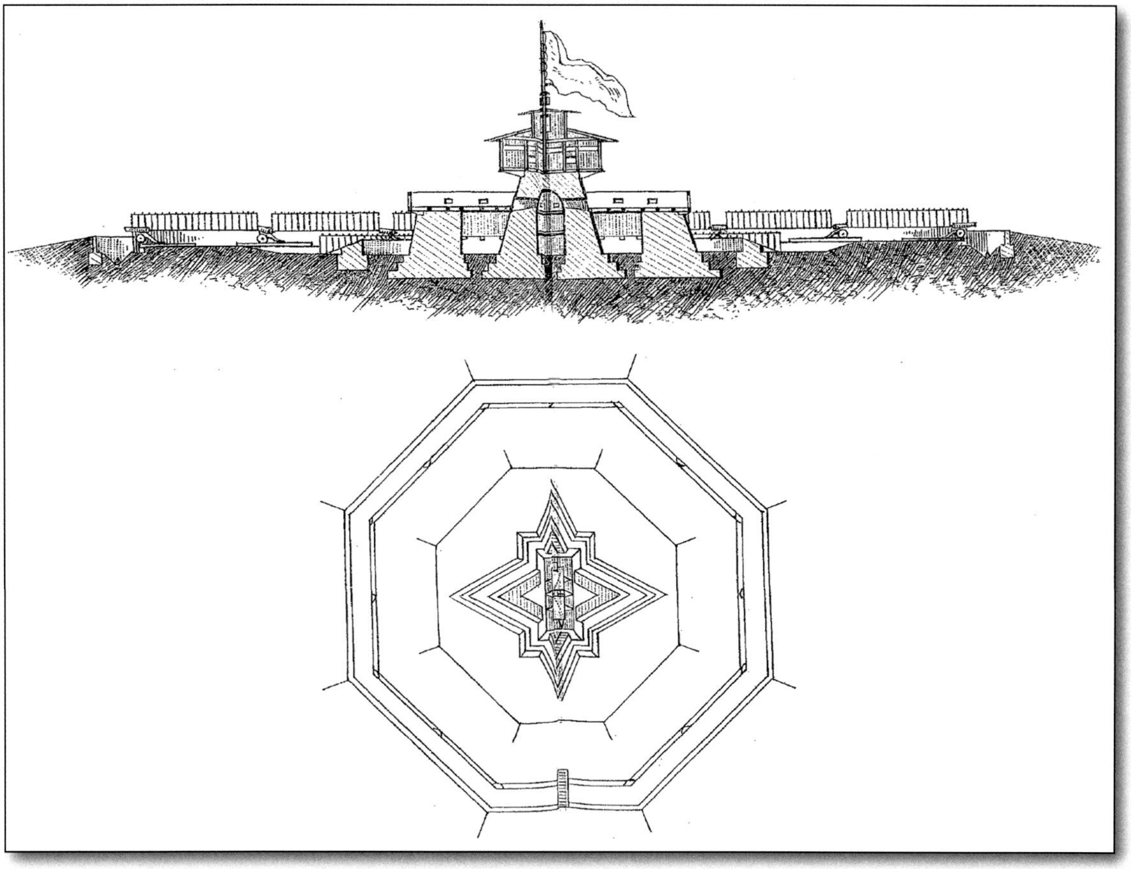

Redoubt of Tonneliers Island, Port Nord-Ouest, Ile de France, mid-eighteenth century. Built on a star plan from 1741 to guard the port's entrance at the behest of Governor General La Bourdonnais, it was the most elaborate defence work on the island featuring glacis, a ditch and a central keep also acting as a cavalier surmounted by a pole for signals and the large white standard of France. Print after Poyen. (Private collection, author's photo)

Across the island, Port Bourbon, also called Grand Port or Port Sud-Est, had three batteries guarding its entrance and also had field fortifications covering the landward access. Later on, in 1761, another type of fortification was built due to fears that the British might invade the island. As in the West Indies, a 'Réduit' was built in a site difficult to access where the population could seek refuge and have some safety. It featured field fortifications capable of repulsing an assault. Ile de France had fairly similar defences.[26]

The French fortified lodges in Senegal were in the usual plan of a wall enclosing the lodgings for mostly Europeans and warehouses. The plan could be square with two corner bastions, a long rectangle with four bastions for the larger fort at Saint-Louis or a half circle with batteries and turrets as at Arguin. Gorée had the most elaborate fortifications with its two main forts that were originally built by the Dutch and expanded by the French from 1677.

26 Gennes, *Mémoire pour le sieur de La Bourdonnais*, pp.12-13, 19, 28

When Louisiana came into the fold of the Compagnie des Indes in 1719, France was in the peak of a financial frenzy with a booming stock market rising out of control with shares promising enormous profits regarding this nearly 'virgin' territory. Full of inherent optimism, company settlers and troops went to Louisiana's Gulf Coast; the company also obtained the services of four royal army king's engineers to build up the infrastructure. They arrived that year led Leblond de La Tour, the senior of the group, who died soon thereafter. Meanwhile, the stock market collapsed and sobriety became the order of the day, the company being barely saved. War with Spain did not help matters either, with Louisiana having Spanish territories as neighbours, so a sizeable fortification was necessary. Much of what then existed in Louisiana consisted of wooden stockaded forts usually built on a square or rectangular plan with two or four bastions. There were also a few shore batteries. The material and manpower to build masonry fortifications was simply not available. Fort Condé built at Mobile in the mid-1720s was the first major fortification and its walls were built of sand faced with bricks. New Orleans, the capital, had a powder magazine and not much else to defend it until the 1729-1730 Natchez War. A year later, the company gave back its privileges and bowed out of Louisiana. The engineers and their staff there were amalgamated into the territory's royal service.[27]

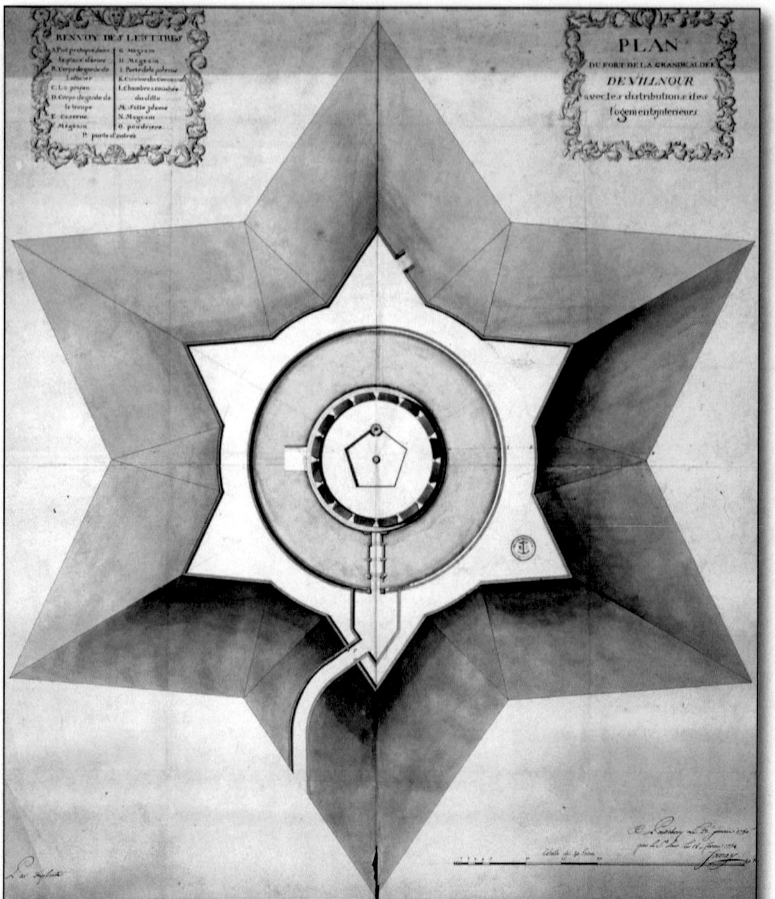

Plan of the fort built at Villnour, 18 February 1754. This work consisted of a round fort armed with 16 cannon surrounded by a moat full of water and an outside six pointed glacis. Signed by Fornay. (Archives Nationales Outre-Mer, 26DFC67A)

The basic barrack accommodations for Compagnie des Indes soldiers were generally the same as for the royal army and the Compagnies franches de la Marine posted overseas. Barrack rooms had variable numbers of beds, one bed being assigned to three infantrymen. Guardhouses at the gates would also have wooden platforms for sentries to rest that could be considered beds of sorts.[28]

27 Gilles-Antoine Langlois, 'Les "mousquetaires" du Mississippi', in Laurent Vidal and Émilie D'Orgeix (eds), *Les villes françaises du Nouveau Monde* (Paris: Somogy, 1999), pp.147-151; Willard B. Robinson, 'Maritime Frontier Engineering: The Defence of New Orleans', *Louisiana History*, Vol.18, No. 1 (Winter 1977), pp.5-16.

28 Haudrère, *La compagnie française des Indes au XVIIIe siècle*, Vol.3, p.790

Gunners and Artillery Units

The various French East India companies needed and employed individual gunners to serve in its ships and its forts overseas. The official establishment as defined in France did not mention specific artillery units. The deployment of gunners on ships was obviously mostly similar to those in the king's navy with master gunners supervising squads of sailors to man the guns. On land in Africa and Asia, European master gunners would supervise some soldiers in the basics of serving artillery at fortified lodges, shore batteries and other fortifications. An example is Master Gunner Pierre Fanton sent to Pondicherry in 1739 with orders from the Paris council to its authorities to assist him to train men as gunners and also provide their replacements so that there would always be a sufficient number available.[29]

Grouping men into an artillery unit in India became necessary for troops that were increasingly deployed in the field from the early 1740s. A company of 120 gunners was also raised at Lorient by the Compagnie des Indes during 1740 or 1741 and embarked on a fleet bound for India. It was under the command of *Capitaine* Louis Joseph Philippe, Comte de Rostaing, who was detached from the royal army's Corps Royal de l'Artillerie. He was a talented 25-year-old officer who came from a family of gunners, had been schooled at the artillery academy in Metz and had served in three sieges and a battle during the Polish Succession War of 1733-1735. He eventually became renowned for inventions relating to artillery. The fleet, under the command of La Bourdonnais, called at Ile de France, arrived at Pondichery on 30 September 1741 and went on to relieve Mahé in late November and early December. It is unclear as to what happened to the company thereafter although it can be assumed it remained in Pondicherry or was broken up so that its artillerymen could serve as cadres. Rostaing went back to Ile de France to organise an artillery school there and also set up a saltpetre refinery and a black powder mill on that island so as not to be totally dependent on explosives sent from France.[30]

At the 1748 siege of Pondicherry, the garrison's company of artillery 'very much distinguished itself' led by *Capitaine* Dancy and *Lieutenants* Rangal, d'Or and Grandmaison. It most likely provided the detachments of artillerymen to troops operating elsewhere in the Carnatic and, from 1751, Bussy's contingent in the Deccan that formed an artillery company.[31]

Finding many gunners quickly was a constant challenge in India. In some instances, a corps had to be organised in record time. An example was news reaching Dupleix on 31 July 1752 that an Indo-British force led by Major Kinnear to was marching towards the fortress of Gingee. He immediately ordered Commandant Kirjean to muster a force to intercept the enemy.

29 AC, C2, 28, Extrait du Régistre Général des Délibérations de la Compagnie des Indes, 14 July 1739.

30 Rostaing, 'Expedition de La Bourbonnais dans la mer des Indes en 1746', *Revue maritime et coloniale*, 1880, pp.73, 427-429

31 BNF, Ms Français 8971, 'Relation du siège de Pondichéry par les Anglois en 1748', fol. 143; Depréaux, 'Les uniformes de la Compagnie des Indes…', pp.163, 168.

Kirjean needed gunners right away to serve six field guns. Two Compagnie des Indes ships had just arrived at Pondicherry and, on 6 August, he ordered 70 sailors trained as gunners to go to the citadel where they were uniformed and armed. Three days later they served the guns at the defeat of Major Kinnear. An artillery company had also been formed in the Coromandel in which served *Caporal* François Chauffray who was wounded seven times in as many battles.[32]

Sepoys and possibly other types of Indian auxiliaries were also serving guns. They were often termed 'lascars' or 'gun lascars' by the British. Some 652 were attached to the artillery in Bussy's army on 1 September 1756.[33]

By a royal order of 10 November 1756, the detachment of 150 gunners of the metropolitan Royal-Artillerie sent to India would be formed on arrival into a 'corps of three hundred men in three companies of a hundred men each' by incorporating 150 men, presumably of the Compagnie des Indes' artillery. By the time they arrived at Pondicherry in 1758, the situation had changed and the two units remained separate. By 6 February 1759, the artillery in India had lost a third of its officers so the Comte de Lally appointed *Lieutenant* Brice Aux Couteaux Conti de Fercourt of the Régiment de Lorraine and previously in Royal-Artillerie to be *capitaine* of the 'artillery troops attached to the Compagnie des Indes.' The gunners were involved in all the great battles and many smaller engagements until the surrender of Pondicherry. On 15 January 1761, some 83 officers and gunners of Royal-Artillerie and 94 officers and gunners of the Compagnie des Indes' artillery surrendered at Pondicherry.[34]

32 BNF, Ms Français, 8971, 'Relation des principaux événements arrivés aux Indes dans la province du Carnate…de juillet 1749. Jusqu'au 17 Octobre 1752.'; AC, E, 76, service record of François Chauffray.

33 Martineau, *Bussy*, p.215; 'A short history of the China Gun Lascars', *JSAHR*, Vol.101 (Summer 2023), pp.115-116.

34 AC, F3, 238, Ordonnance du Roi concernant le corps de troupes que Sa Majesté destine à faire passer aux Indes, 10 November 1756; AC, E, 181, service record of Brice Aux Couteaux Conti de Fercourt; 'State of the French Forces…at Pondicherry', 15 January 1761, *The Daily Advertiser*, London, 22 July 1761.

19

Portable Weapons, Accoutrements, and Ordnance

The early weapons used by the personnel of the French East India companies during the seventeenth century were identical, or nearly so, to those of soldiers in France.

Firearms

Lists of the weapons loaded on board ships of the 'Persia Squadron' in 1670 gives an indication of the types of weapons. These included:

- 600 good flintlock muskets 'with bayonets to insert in the barrel' and 1,000 ramrods
- 600 good reserve matchlock muskets
- 50 dozen bayonets for matchlock muskets
- 15 flintlock muskets [most likely of superior quality]
- 600 pistols[1]

In 1674, a shipment to India on board *Le Rubis* included: 400 matchlocks muskets; 100 *mousquetons* (carbines) and 200 pistols. François Martin's memoirs mentions his French soldiers' matchlock muskets as well as flintlock muskets with plug bayonets and pistols at the capture of Valdaour in September 1676 and also later. In 1681, he used a flintlock musket for hunting. These muskets came from France as he distinguished them from the matchlock muskets '*du pays*' ('of the country' – that is to say, Indian-made) used by his auxiliary Indian soldiers.[2]

1 AC, B, 1, État des armes, munitions…voyage du Sr. de La Haye dans les Indes, 3 December 1669; AC, B, 2, Extrait de l'Estat de munitions embarquées sur les vaisseaux de l'escadre de Perse…, 1670.

2 AC, B, 6, Mémoire de ce qui pourra être chargé dans le *Rubis* pour le voyages aux Indes d'Orient, 12 February 1674; Martineau (ed.), *Mémoires de François Martin*, Vol.2, pp.73, 86, 253, 289.

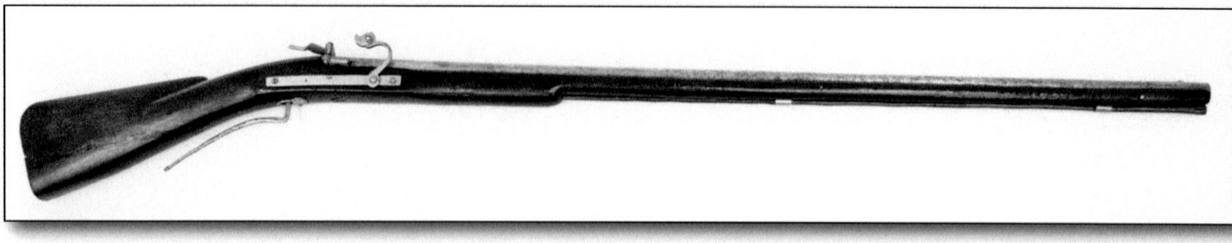

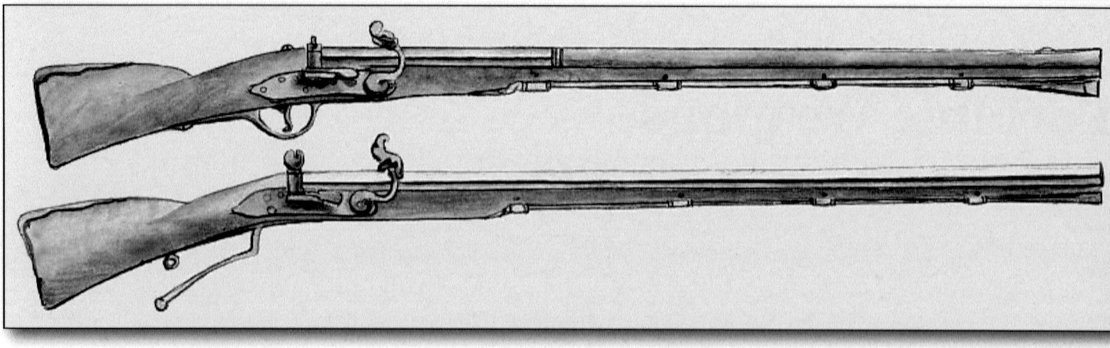

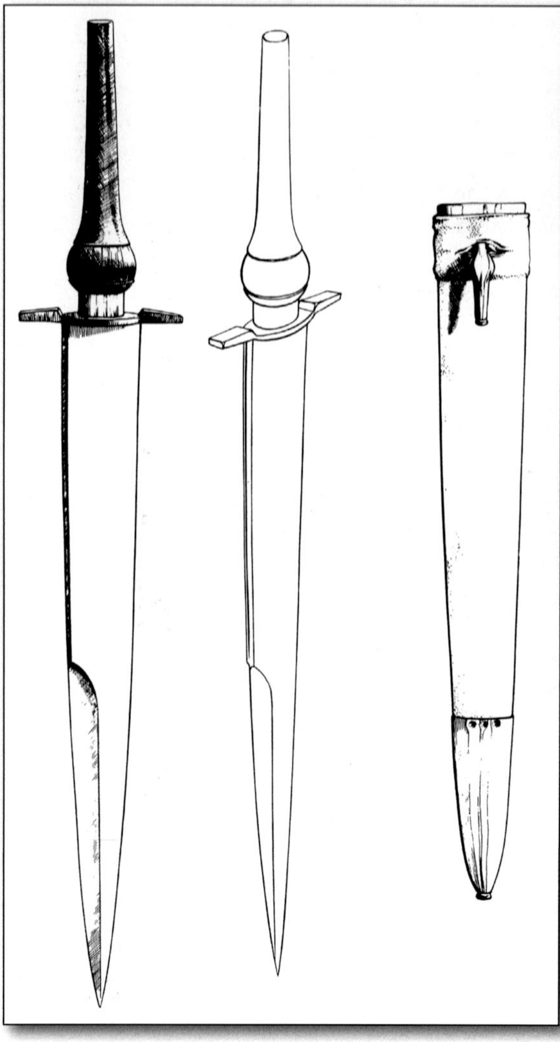

Top: Infantry matchlock musket, mid-seventeenth century. (National Historic Sites, Parks Canada)

Middle: Infantry matchlock muskets, second half of the seventeenth century. The one at top had the trigger guard associated with the later seventeenth century. (Smithsonian Institution Libraries, Washington)

Left: Infantry 'plug' bayonet with its scabbard, middle to late seventeenth century. Drawing by Michel Pétard. (National Historic Sites, Parks Canada)

From the 1720s, small arms of the Compagnie des Indes essentially came from Saint-Étienne, especially from the Carrier workshops. Some were also bought from Charleville and Maubeuge. The gunsmith firms in all three towns supplied the small arms for the metropolitan army and it is safe to assume that the company purchased identical weapons that conformed to royal army models, for instance, infantry muskets of the 1717, 1728 and 1746 models or cavalry pistols of the 1733 model.[3]

An agreement dated 12 May 1751 between the Compagnie des Indes and arms manufacturers P. Girard and Robert Saint-Périeux & Company at St. Étienne for two thirds and the firm of Siméon and Sauvade at Charleville for one third of the small arms ordered by the company. The document specified broadly the more technical details of each type of firearm, which appears to be the only one so far known giving such information (see footnote). As expected, the technical specifications generally conformed to those used for the weapons supplied to the metropolitan army and navy. The most visible difference concerned putting brass furnishings and brass barrel bands for all the company's weapons. The strictly military weapons intended for troops were the grenadier musket (calibre 16) and the rampart musket (calibre 14). There were no carbines. The ship's pistols were to be identical to cavalry pistols. Therefore, mounted troops, which were mostly dragoons and horse grenadiers in India who could also serve and fight on foot, were likely to have grenadier muskets and naval or cavalry pistols.[4]

While some of the 1751 contract weapons probably reached India, there was a shortage of muskets by 1758 for the company's troops, European and sepoys. Some 'old muskets' in the Pondicherry arsenal were repaired later that year, those taken at Sadras that had a suitable calibre were being selected and authorities sought to buy those that were in private stores. Lally meanwhile complained that his troops should get new muskets.[5]

---

3 Gérard Le Bouedec, 'Les approvisionnements de la Compagnie des Indes 1737-1770', *Histoire, économie et société*, Vol.1, No. 3 (1982), pp.377-412; A. Legrand and F. Marec, *Inventaire des archives de la Compagnie des Indes (sous-série 1P)* (Paris: Imprimerie de la Marine, 1978), pp.xx, 64. The eighteenth century army models are described and illustrated in Didier Bianchi, *French Military Small Arms Volume 1 Flintlock Longarms* (Woonsocket: Mowbray, 2015). Weapons of the Compagnie des Indes are not, as far as we have seen, studied nor mentioned in arms book in French or English. Marine and metropolitan army edged weapons, portable firearms and accoutrements are presented in our *French Military Arms and Armour in America 1503-1783* (Woonsocket: Mowbray, 2016) and *Armies and Wars of the Sun King 1643-1715* (Warwick: Helion, 2020), Vols. 2 and 3.

4 APL, 1P 305, 69, Extrait du régistre général des deliberations de la Compagnie des Indes, 12 May 1751. The specifications are, briefly: Grenadier (meaning with a sling) musket: barrel three feet eight inches long, calibre 16, flat lock plate, cast brass furnishings, iron ramrod, bayonet (price: 16 livres); Half buccaneer musket: barrel three feet six inches long, calibre 16, brass furnishings, wooden ramrod (9 livres 10 sols); Trade musket, same as Half buccaneer, probably with barrel bands (9 livres); Fusil de bord (ship's musket) same as Grenadier musket (16 livres); Rampart musket: barrel three feet eight inches long, reinforced breech, calibre 14, cast brass furnishings, iron ramrod (19 livres); Ship's pistols: same as cavalry, brass furnishings and iron hooks (16 livres 10 sols).

5 Duval de Leyrit, *Mémoire*, pp.229, 246-247.

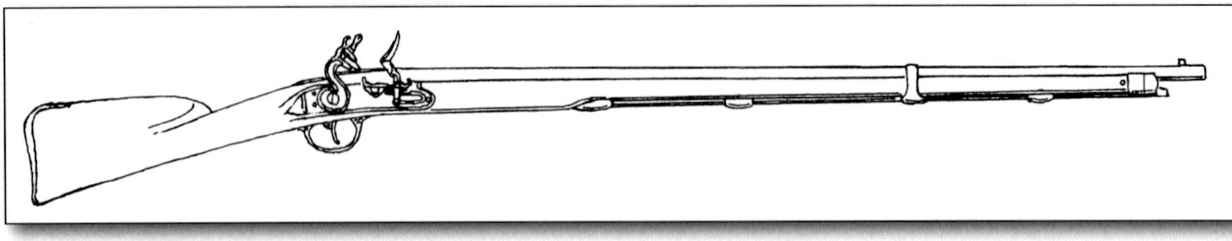

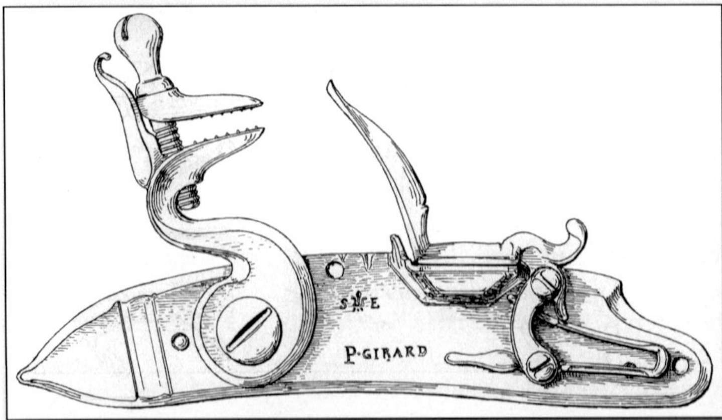

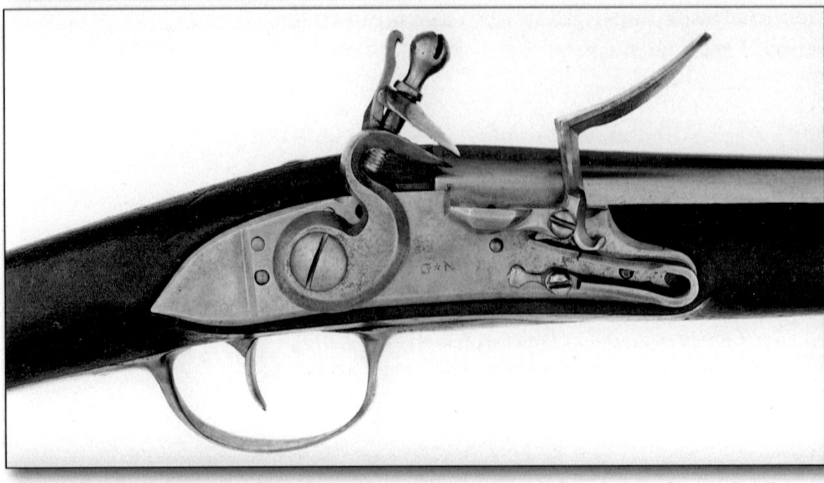

From the top: Model 1717 army musket. Furnishings were of steel. Print after Jandot. (Private collection, author's photo)

Model 1717 army musket lock. Note the bridle at the spring. Stamped to Saint-Étienne and the gunsmith Pierre Girard (probably the elder active since the early 1700s). Print after Jandot. (Private collection, author's photo)

Model 1728 army musket. This pattern introduced steel barrel bands. This example was made in Saint-Étienne. The 1751 contract between the Compagnies des Indes and the arsenals of Saint-Étienne specified a generally similar musket except for brass furnishings. (National Historic Sites, Parks Canada)

Lock plate of the Model 1728 army musket. The mark G N is to Grange Neuve, a Saint-Étienne gunsmith. The small crowned S E above identifies Saint-Étienne. (National Historic Sites, Parks Canada)

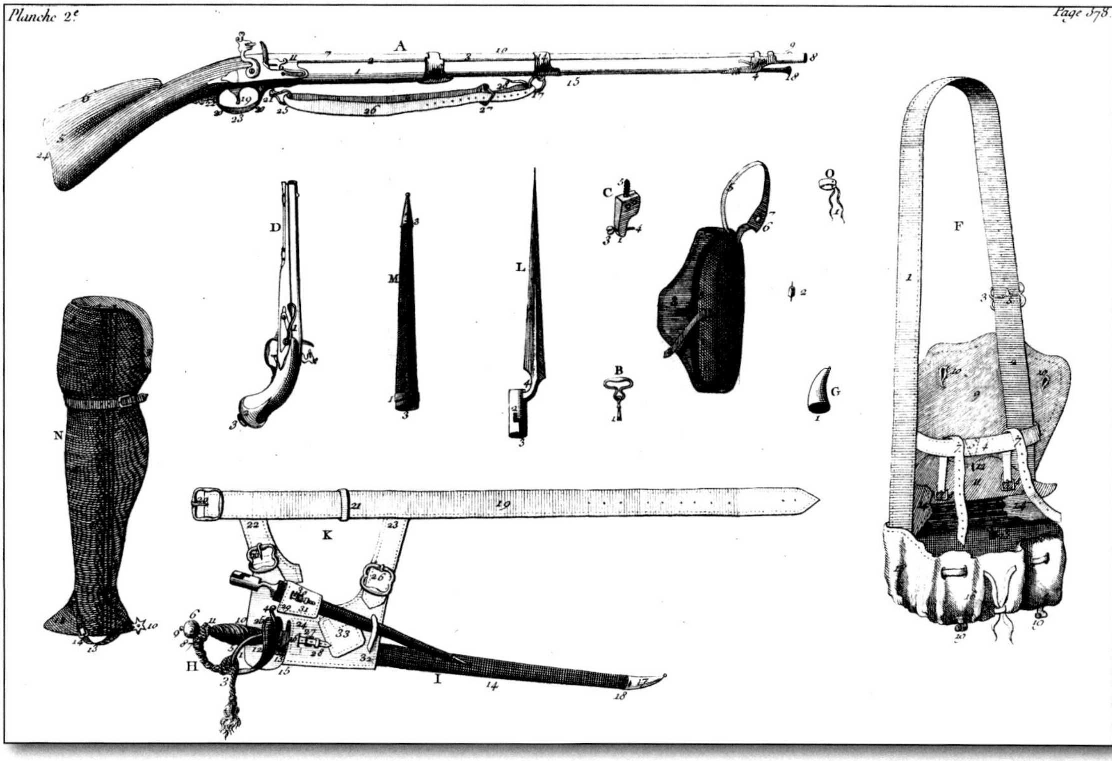

Dragoon's arms and equipment, 1750s. Plate in La Porterie's 1754 *Institutions militaires pour la cavalerie et les dragons*. (Private collection, author's photo)

Edged Weapons

The 1670 'Persia Fleet' had on board: 300 cutlasses; 300 swords; 30 halberds; 50 partisans; 200 pikes. The pikes may have been for sailors as there is no evidence of pikemen as being part of the troops and no pikemen's helmets and breastplates are listed. The 1674 shipment to India included 100 pikes and 200 halberds or partisans. From the seventeenth century until the end of the Seven Years War, infantry *sergents* had by regulation to be armed with halberds and a sword, infantry officers with a half pike (also called spontoon), a sword and also wear a gilded brass gorget when on duty. There were many exceptions to this for troops in the field, especially overseas when all officers and *sergents* used firearms instead of polearms during campaigns. No evidence has so far been seen that there were peculiar patterns of edged weapons for any of the French East India companies. These would thus have been of the same types as those that armed royal forces.[6]

Accoutrements

Accoutrements of soldiers of the early East India companies would also have been identical to those of troops in France, as confirmed by those carried by

6 AC, B, 1, Estat des Armes, 3 December 1669; See notably: Michel Pétard, *Des sabres et des épées* (Nantes: Éditions du Canonnier, 1999), Vol.1 Cavalry and Vol.3 Foot troops.

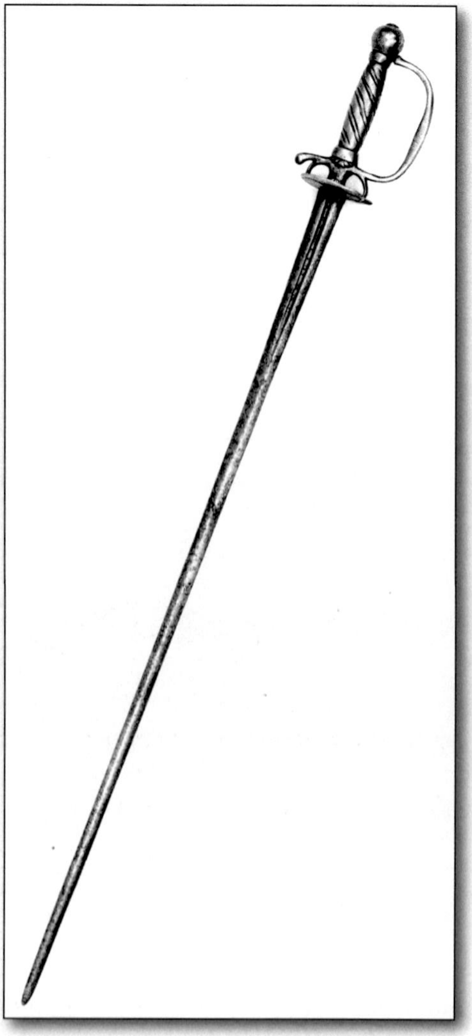

Above: Infantry sergeant's sword, 1750s. Iron hilt and white metal wire grip. (National Historic Sites, Parks Canada)

Infantry soldier's sword, late-seventeenth century to mid-eighteenth century. Brass hilt. (National Historic Sites, Parks Canada)

the 1670 'Persia Fleet': 400 bandoliers; 290 dozen charges for bandoliers; 600 shoulder sword belts with their scabbards.

The accoutrements used by the soldiers of the 1719 Compagnie des Indes were apparently similar to those of the Compagnies franches de la Marine except for omitting the navy's anchor badge put on the flap of the 'gargoussier' cartridge box attached to the buff waist belt. No insignia or indeed other details are presently known regarding this type of cartridge box as used by the company's soldiers, but it probably had a wooden form pierced with nine holes like those of the marines. These 'gargousiers' are frequently mentioned from the 1720s to the late 1740s and some were still issued at Ile de Bourbon as late as 1754 for a few *ouvriers* (military artisans).[7]

7 ADR, Co 1210, État du signalement de deux caporaux…19 September 1732; ADR, Co 1221,,Pour la date du 11 juillet 1754

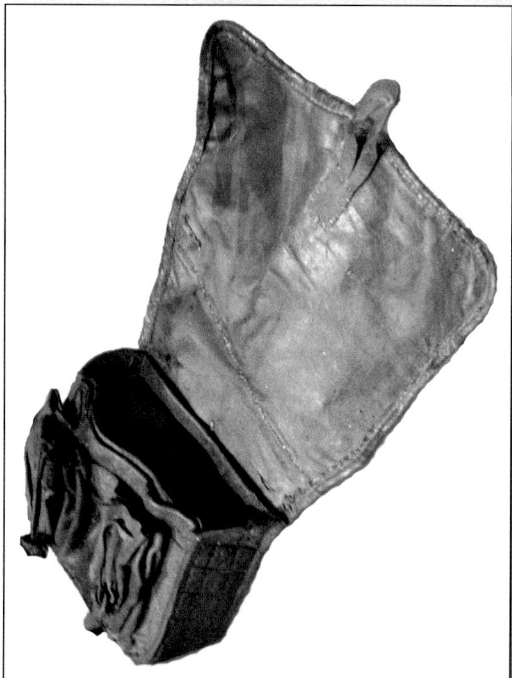

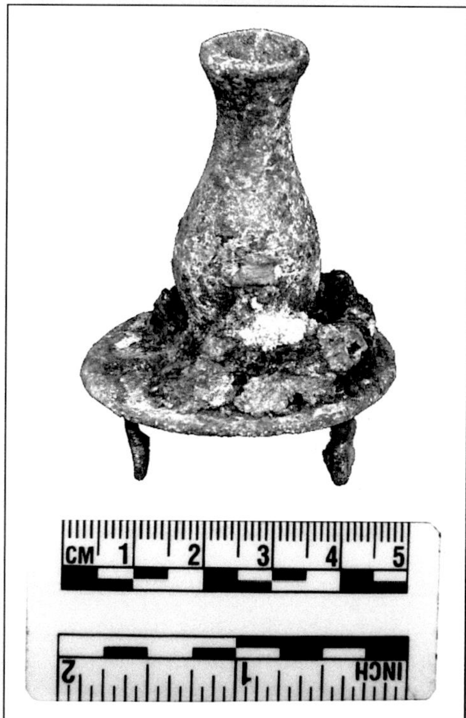

Top left: Infantry cartridge box, used 1690s to 1736 by line Infantry, and until the late 1740s for shipboard marines and Compagnie des Indes troops. This was the 'gargoussier' type worn on the waist belt. Its wooden block usually had nine holes. Drawing by Michel Pétard. (National Historic Sites, Parks Canada)

Bottom left: Infantry cartridge box, mid-eighteenth century. This is the 'giberne' type which had a buff shoulder belt. Brown leather. The cover flap is shown open. (Musée de l'Armée, Paris, author's photo)

Top right: French military powder horn, first half of the eighteenth century. Horn with brass fittings. (Private collection, photo courtesy Simon Gilbert)

Bottom right:: Brass spout from a soldier's powder horn, first half of the eighteenth century. This artefact was found on the site of Fort Rosalie near Natchez, then in French Louisiana. While it could date from the era of the 1720s and thus associated to the capture of the fort by Natchez warriors in 1729, the fort was reconstructed soon thereafter and remained a garrisoned post until 1763. (National Parks Service of the United States of America)

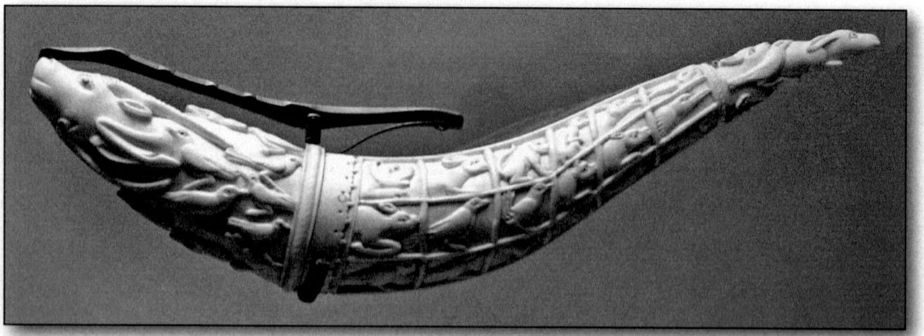

Top: Indian priming powder flask, eighteenth century. This example, which would have been suitable for an Indian soldier, is made of carved ivory and had an iron stopper. (Musée Guimet, Paris, author's photo)

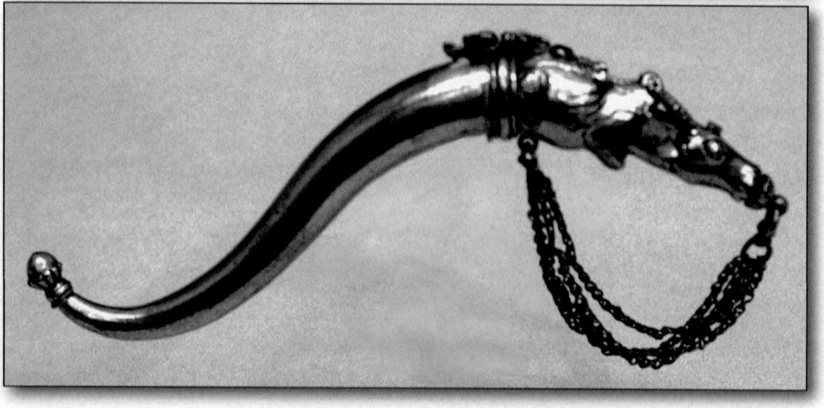

Bottom: A luxurious priming powder flask, eighteenth century. Made in India, probably in Rajasthan, this silver flask highlighted with gilding and semiprecious stones would be carried by an officer of noble lineage. It is in the form of a 'makasa', a mythical fantastic creature shown catching an antelope in his powerful, lionlike jaws. (Virginia Museum of Fine Art, Richmond, USA. Adolph D. and Wilkins C. Williams Fund, author's photo)

From the end of the 1740s, the Compagnies franches de la Marine in France were equipped with the 'giberne' type of cartridge boxes, which was carried with a buff shoulder belt. It would seem that the Compagnie des Indes troops at Lorient also changed from the 'gargoussier' to the 'giberne' at about that time or thereafter. It was routinely mentioned in 1761 as containing 18 to 20 cartridges each. They were issued to a detachment of 120 men guarding Lorient divided in four squads of 30 men, each squad also having ten tools such as shovels or picks.[8]

There could be exceptions. An Indian illustration shows enlisted men of Law de Lauriston's corps wearing dark brown 'giberne' type cartridge boxes with dark brown shoulder belts slung over the right shoulder, probably because they did not have swords (see colour illustration and plate).

Sepoy Weapons

Some early Indian soldiers recruited locally by officials of the French monopoly companies in the seventeenth century came with their Indian-style matchlock muskets as noted by François Martin at Pondicherry during the 1670s. These being considered rather inefficient by Europeans, it can be fairly certain that European muskets would be supplied eventually, especially as they were trained in French drill. From the late 1730s, Indian auxiliary soldiers became much more numerous and now known as sepoys. Since they manoeuvred in battle with the company's European troops, they had

8 M.J. Hébert, *Les ports militaires de France* (Paris: Challamel, 1867), p.35. See also: Michel Pétard, *Equipments militaires de 1600 à 1870* (Saint-Julien-de-Concelles: Self-Published, 1984), Vol.1.

Two young Indian noblemen practicing fencing with wooden-bladed swords, mid-eighteenth century. For most Indian men-at-arms, the sword was considered the primary and most noble weapon. From the album 'Dames et seigneurs…' (Bibliothèque Nationale de France, Paris. Col. Gentil bequest. OD-43-PET)

the same training and firearms as European soldiers. There may have been a few variations, but, on the whole, they were issued with French muskets and bayonets like their French comrades. In June 1753, some 1,400 sepoys were reported 'armed with our [French] flintlock muskets and in our pay' when entering Aurengabad. Data on their accoutrements appears very slim. They were most likely locally made versions of those carried by the French soldiers because they had to manoeuvre like their comrades.[9]

Sepoy Edged Weapons

Traditionally, Indian men-at-arms considered the sword to be their most important weapon as well as a sign of their social status and caste. It was considered a disgrace to have a blunt blade.

Every sepoy had a sword with a curved blade, which was actually a sabre. The Talwar type sabre was the most widespread in India. These could be made in several places; Bondelkante province had iron, sulphur and diamond mines so that many sabre blades were made at its city of Choterpour. A Talwar had a fairly wide, moderately curved, steel blade and came in various lengths and qualities. Its hilt had a short, heavy quillon and disk pommel that was all metallic, steel or brass, with, usually, a knuckle bow to protect the fingers. As plain as some Talwar sabres could be, others belonging to princes had fortunes of precious jewels and diamonds decorating their hilts with blades enhanced with gold and silver inlays.[10]

9 Martin, *Mémoires*, Vol.2, pp.57-59, 85; Gentil, *Mémoires*, p.60; Lenman, 'The Weapons of War in 18th century India', pp.33-36.

10 Stone, *Glossary*, pp.601-602; Richard L. Burton, *The Book of the Sword* (London: Chato and Windus, 1884) pp.130-133; Law de Lauriston, *Mémoires*, p.262. He was in Choterpour in June 1758.

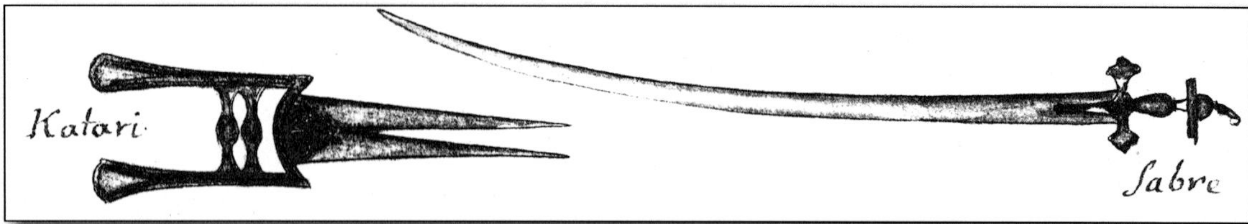
Katari
Sabre

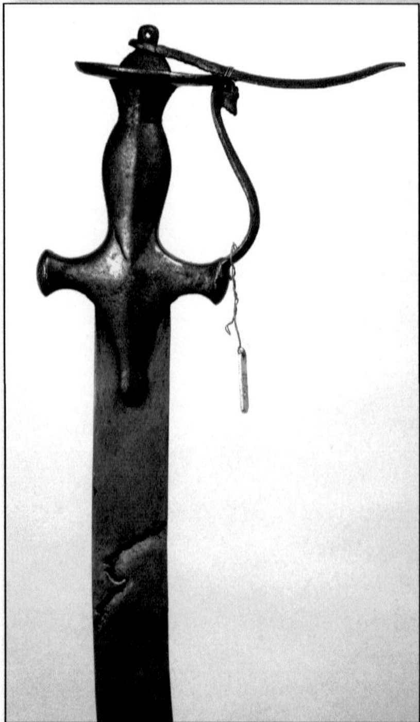

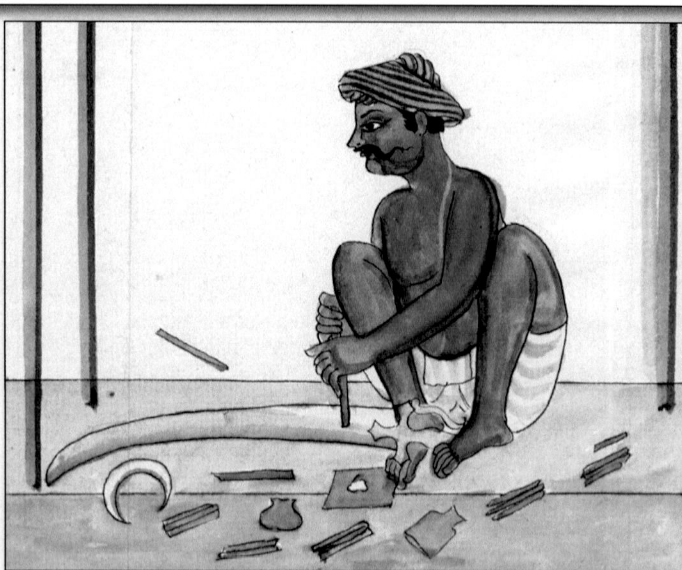

Clockwise from top: A Compagnie des Indes sepoy's 'Katari' dagger and Talwar sabre, 1730s-1760s. Unsigned watercolour by an Indian artist. Print from Depréaux's *Uniformes*.... (Author's photo)

Indian sabre's guard, eighteenth century. This plain Talwar type of sabre would have been common amongst ordinary warriors and sepoys. All steel with some silver filigree for enhancement. (Metropolitan Museum of Art, New York. Bequest of George C. Stone, 1935 36.25.1596_001)

A swordsmith finishing a Talwar type sabre, mid-eighteenth century. The Talwar shown is common type with a brass guard carried by sepoys Indian warrior's steel spearhead, seventeenth-eighteenth centuries. From Tanjore, south India. (Bibliothèque Nationale de France, Paris. Col. Gentil bequest)

The jewel-ornamented hilt of a fine Talwar type sabre of a senior officer or a noble person in southern India, eighteenth century. The lavish gold and silver hilt is encrusted with rubies, emeralds and diamonds set into nearly pure gold. It may have been a mainly ceremonial sword, but its relatively plain blade suggests that it could also been useful on campaign. (Virginia Museum of Fine Art, Richmond, Virginia, author's photo)

Indian officer's Shamshir type sabre with its scabbard and belt, dated to 1748-1749. Made in northern India. The highly curved Shamshir steel blade with gilt inscriptions has an ivory grip, enhanced with silver and blue enamel guard and pommel. Brown scabbard and gold laced belt with silver and blue mountings. (Museum of Art, New York. (Metropolitan Museum of Art, New York. Bequest of George C. Stone, 1935. DP160357)

Another type of sabre widely found in India was the Shamshir (Shamsher). It was especially popular amongst cavalrymen. It had Persian origins and, in India, could often have a Talwar-style hilt as well as its more traditional hilt with a single cross guard, a light and plain grip often covered with bone such as ivory ending at its curved top with a pommel projecting on one side. Its main distinctive feature was its long and highly curved blade; there was also a Turkish variation. The high quality Shamshir sabres always featured watered steel blades. It was said that 'whoever was struck on the head by these Indian blades was cleft to the waist, or if the cut was on the body, he was divided into two parts.'[11]

A sword much seen in the Deccan was the Dhoup that had a straight blade. Its guard had a disk-shaped pommel with a spike and a broad finger guard. A related type was the Firangi (or Faring) meaning foreign. This was because it had originally a long European blade imported in India by the Portuguese.

Just about every man-at-arms from prince to private soldier in India including a sepoy was armed with a Katar style dagger, possibly the earliest such weapon in the country. It was an all-metal very sturdy weapon. The most common type had a handle featuring two parallel bars connected by two, sometimes more, cross pieces, its base fastened to a wide and flat double-edged and elongated triangular steel or iron blade narrowing to a point. It came in all sizes, about 30 centimetres being a more or less common length although some few could be at about a metre long. Variations and exceptions were practically countless apart from the basic type given above. Many had in addition metal guards to protect the back of the hand. For instance, the sides of the blade of some of the better Katars could open making it three-pointed. It was tucked into the waist belt or sash.[12]

11 Stone, *Glossary*, pp.550-552; Irvine, *The Army of the Indian Moghuls*, p.76 quoting the *Majasir-ul-Umara*, Vol.3, 152. In Europe, this type of sword was known as a scimitar, which became popular in the later eighteenth century especially amongst general officers in its ivory grip version without a knuckle bow.

12 Stone, *Glossary*, pp.344-345, 347.

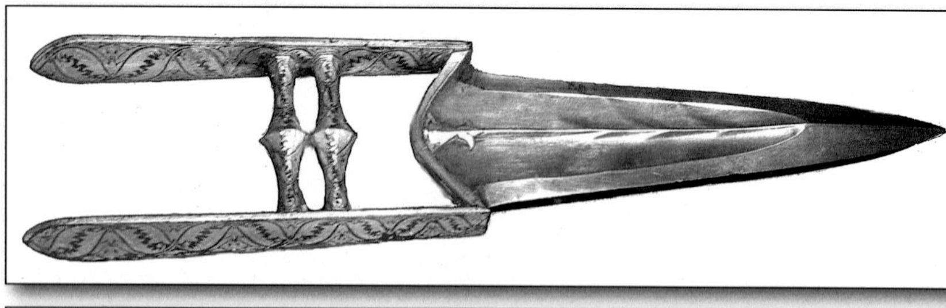

From top: Indian 'Katari' dagger, eighteenth century. Also called a 'Punch' dagger, this type commonly armed Indian men-at-arms. This example has a brass handle with a steel blade. (Former Higgins Armory Collection, Worcester Art Museum, Worcester, Massachusetts, USA, author's photo)

Indian officer's 'Katari' dagger, seventeenth and eighteenth centuries. Steel enhanced with gold. Leather scabbard with gilt tip. 48.36 cm long. (Metropolitan Museum of Art, New York. (Metropolitan Museum of Art, New York. Bequest of George C. Stone, 1935. DP158187)

An 'Ayudha katti' (war knife), eighteenth century. Its dark red wooden handle is decorated with gold. (British Museum, London)

Some peons and, at times, sepoys and other types of Indian troops, would also be armed with pikes or spears that had iron points. These were seen especially at parades and processions where pageantry reigned. There were indeed a multitude of other edged weapons carried by Indian men-at-arms (see illustrations for a few examples). Sepoys might wield them for hand-to-hand fighting to repel an assault in a fortification. However, in the field, it was thanks to their training in the linear tactics with French muskets and bayonets as well as their unflinching steadiness, reported in many battles, that the company's sepoys proved far superior to the masses of warriors in the armies of Indian princes and equal to their British opponents.

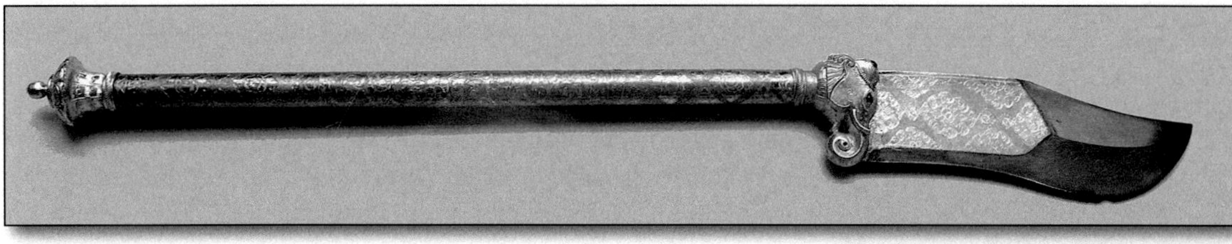

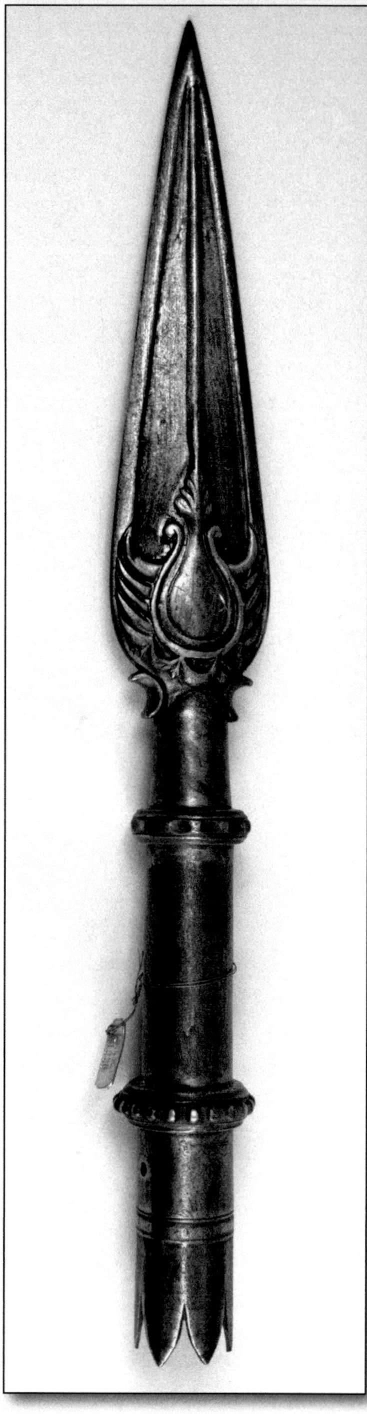

Above: A 'Bhuj' (knife axe), eighteenth century. This item came from the Sind region. Its long blade is slightly blued and decorated with gold. The handle's gold cap can be unscrewed to pull out a concealed narrow blade inside. (British Museum, London)

Right: Spear or pike head, eighteenth century. From Tanjore, southern India. Courtesy Metropolitan Museum of Art, New York. (Metropolitan Museum of Art, New York. Bequest of George C. Stone, 1935)

Ordnance

The French East India companies needed cannon and mortars to arm their vessels, forts and troops in the field. Up until the 1719-1770 Compagnie des Indes, the ordnance was purchased or taken from opponents. Thereafter, the company obtained custom-made brass cannons that were cast bearing its coat of arms and other insignia. On the whole and as seen below, the variety was considerable otherwise.

East India Companies' Cannon

The cannons used by the various French trade monopoly companies to arm their ships and fortifications overseas were usually made in France and could be of iron or brass. The basic patterns and calibres were the same as in the royal army and navy. There were numerous calibres with quaint names from the sixteenth century until the early 1660s when King Louis XIV imposed fewer simpler models. The naval cannons in brass from 1661 were 4-, 6-, 8-, 12-, 18-, 24- and 36-pounder. For iron naval cannons, there were from 1661 4-, 6-, 8-, 12- and 18-pounders to which 24-poundes were added in 1669 and 36-pounders from 1692. A royal edict of 1699, renewed in 1728, exempted the monopoly trading companies from paying taxes on ordnance they purchased.[13]

Before the 1719 Compagnie des Indes, the previous companies appear to have purchased their ordnance from the same makers as for the royal armed forces. Indeed, some of the early cannon sent

13 Ernest Picart, *L'artillerie française au XVIIIe siècle* (Paris: Berger-Levrault, 1906), Bouedec, 'Les approvisionemments…', p.390. Some very heavy iron 48-pounders were also cast for the navy in the 1690s, but their weight was too impractical onboard ship and they armed coastal forts in France.

to India may have been royal guns. In 1669, the king ordered 10 brass and 20 iron cannon with 24 ship's carriages and six field carriages be embarked on the Persia squadron. In 1674, twenty 10-pounder cannon were loaded on the ship *Rubis* going to 'India of the Orient'. The Compagnie des Indes Orientales primarily needed iron guns; if they also acquired brass cannon, these do not seem to have been cast with insignias of the various companies – at least, no such guns appear to have survived.[14]

From 1719 to 1770, the Compagnie des Indes assumed its obligation to provide ordnance for its multinational obligations on land and sea. The basic patterns and calibres for the company's ordnance were naturally the same as those used by the royal armed forces: 4-, 6-, 8-, 12-, 18-, 24- and 36-pounders in the navy; 4-, 8-, 12-, 16-, 24- and 33-pounders in the army.[15] The company did not order calibres above 24-pounders. Its overwhelming need was for iron cannons. In August 1723, the company requested that an artillery specialist with a *caporal* of the Bombardiers de la Marine travel from Rochefort to the iron forges in Périgord and Angoumois to proof the cannons it had ordered.

Over time, what evolved was the procurement of iron ordnance within France and also outside of it. Some guns were bought in England, the Netherlands and especially Sweden. They were obviously made to the pre-1766 French artillery specifications for the navy. During March 1756, the company reported receiving at Lorient '360 cannons of various calibres from Sweden shipped in several vessels.' That country was an important exporter of good quality iron and the company had an agent in Stockholm since 1738 whose main purchases were cannons. Such a large purchase from a neutral country was probably due to French ironworks being overwhelmed by royal government orders. However, some were also ordered by the company in France. In February 1756, the iron forges at Douai were contracted to make 78 cannon and 18 mortars; more were purchased from ironworks at La Nouée in 1762.[16]

For brass cannon, the coat of arms of the company and the company's name was cast on the guns indicating that these were obtained by specific purchase orders. This book's illustrations show several of these now rare cannons that have survived. They were made by the same firms that produced brass ordnance for the royal army, but, as seen above, had clearly visible insignias that proudly identified the Compagnie des Indes. The calibres of these expensive brass cannons appear to have been small, going from 1-pounders to 4-pounders.

---

14 AC, B, 2, Extrait de l'Estat des munitions, 1670; AC, B, 6, Mémoire de ce qui pourra estre chargé dans le Rubis, 12 December 1674.

15 Picart, *L'artillerie française au XVIIIe siècle*, pp. 44-45, 54-56. The 33-pounder, a mainstay of the Sun King's artillery nicknamed the 'Canon de France', was abolished in the army by the advent of the Vallière artillery system in October 1732.

16 AR, 1A, 8, De Morville, Meudon, 1 August 1723; APL, 1P 278c, 11, cannon and mortars from Douai, 18 February 1756 and cannon from Sweden, 6 March 1756; APL, 1P, 299c, 33, cannon cast at La Nouée, 12 October 1762; Boudriot, *Compagnie des Indes*, p.30; Le Bouedec, 'Les approvisionemments…', pp.387, 403. The Stockholm agent was Bédoire and Petersen who also exported anchors, chains and iron parts for shipbuilding. Some products received from any producer that were altered or improved at Lorient might have the letters C.D.I. (Compagnie des Indes) while some might be marked with their ultimate destinations with I.B (Ile de Bourbon) or I.F (Ile de France).

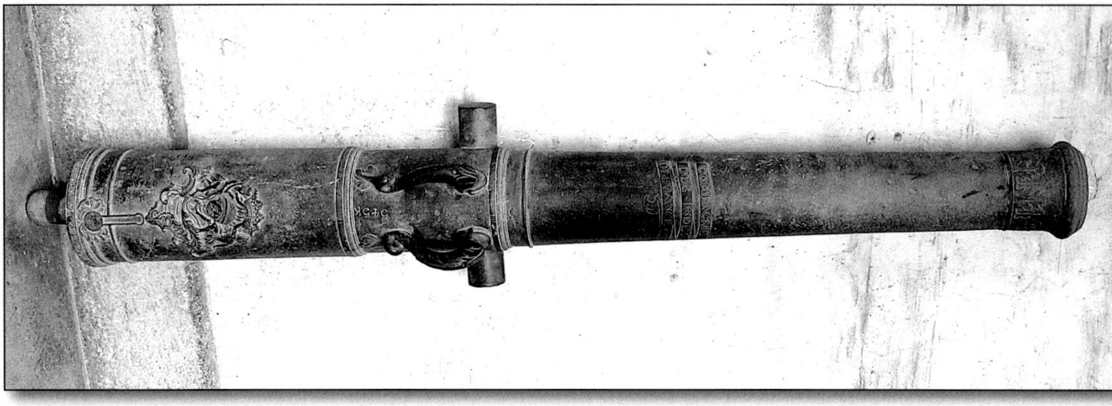

Brass 4-pounder cannon of the Compagnie des Indes, cast at Douai in 1755. It is 237 centimetres long, has an 84 millimetre bore at its mouth and weights 547 kilograms. (Musée de l'Armée, Paris, author's photo)

Left: Inscription 'Compagnie des Indes de France' cast on the 4-pounder cannon. (Musée de l'Armée, Paris, author's photo)

Centre: Detail showing the coat of arms of the 1719-1770 Compagnie des Indes on the 4-pounder cannon. (Musée de l'Armée, Paris, author's photo)

Right: Inscription and coat of arms on a Compagnie des Indes cannon. (Rotunda Museum, Woolwich, UK, author's photo)

Overseas, the French East India companies had to provide their forts with ordnance. An ongoing practice for European nations was to leave the older guns of a ship, which could still be useful in an overseas fortification. This, in time, could result in much variety. Another source of variety were the guns found in captured forts. For instance, amongst the ordnance in the fortress of Gingee in India, one could find in September 1750, an iron 24-pounder from Europe, an obviously quite old brass 36-pounder emblazoned with the French coat of arm and a brass 48-pounder with the coat of arms of the Dutch East India Company. This sampling was probably typical of what could be seen mounted on the ramparts of all the European forts overseas.

Field Artillery in India

Warfare in India was often fought in the field. Indian armies had, as seen in the campaign accounts, large numbers of heavy guns being slowly dragged by masses of bullocks with hundred if not thousands of labouring 'coolies' apart from the gunners and lascars attending these pieces of ordnance. They consequently made the movement of armies very slow, especially as the roads were then awful in India. Things were not much better on a battlefield since the Indian artillery had not technically progressed greatly since the sixteenth century. They were slow to load and fire and were not very mobile.

From the 1740s, the Compagnie des Indes had increasing needs for light-calibre cannon and mortars in India. Warfare in that country was increasingly carried out by field forces that operated farther out from the company's main centres on the coast. By the mid-eighteenth century, mobility of artillery had become a major tactical challenge and the main European military powers were devising ways to lighten ordnance without compromising on efficiency and speed up its deployment when in action. This light ordnance could be quite varied and sometimes supplied by an allied Indian prince. In April 1751, Commandant Bussy's field force was at Hyderabad and he was shown some 3,000 guns by Nabob Salabat Jing who invited him to choose what he needed; 24 were chosen: four French brass 8-pounders; four French brass 4-pounders; a fine-looking French brass culverin 6-pounder that was strewn with lilies, marked with a crowned letter 'L' with two dolphins as handles and a chameleon holding its head as its muzzle ornament. The rest of the cannons chosen were 3- and 4-pounders to be used as 'minute' guns.[17]

Rostaing Guns

As it turned out, one observer of ordnance as used in India was the inventive Comte de Rostaing who served in Ile de France and India during 1746-1755. During those years, he devised a very light cannon based on the Compagnie des Indes' brass 1-pounder anti-personnel brass light cannon for ships. He also designed its light carriage that could be taken apart and assembled again fairly easily. Because of their great lightness, these pieces could be drawn by only one horse and follow all the operations of light or fast-moving troops. It was also possible to pull this light cannon upon a steep hill, which an ordinary carriage could not do, and it could even be carried by hand without major difficulties.

17 Depréaux, 'Les uniformes de la Compagnie des Indes…', p.165; one brass Compagnie des Indes 2 ¾-pdr cast in Douai by Jean-François Bérenger in 1755 was eventually found by the British at Seringapatam in Mysore and sent to the Tower of London as per H.L. Blackmore, *The Armouries of the Tower of London The Ordnance* (London: HMSO, 1976), pp.120-121. Another French gun that stayed at Gingee was a brass 24-pounder strewn with lilies with the coat of arm of the Duc de Beaufort, master general of ordnance in the 1660s as per BNF, 8971.

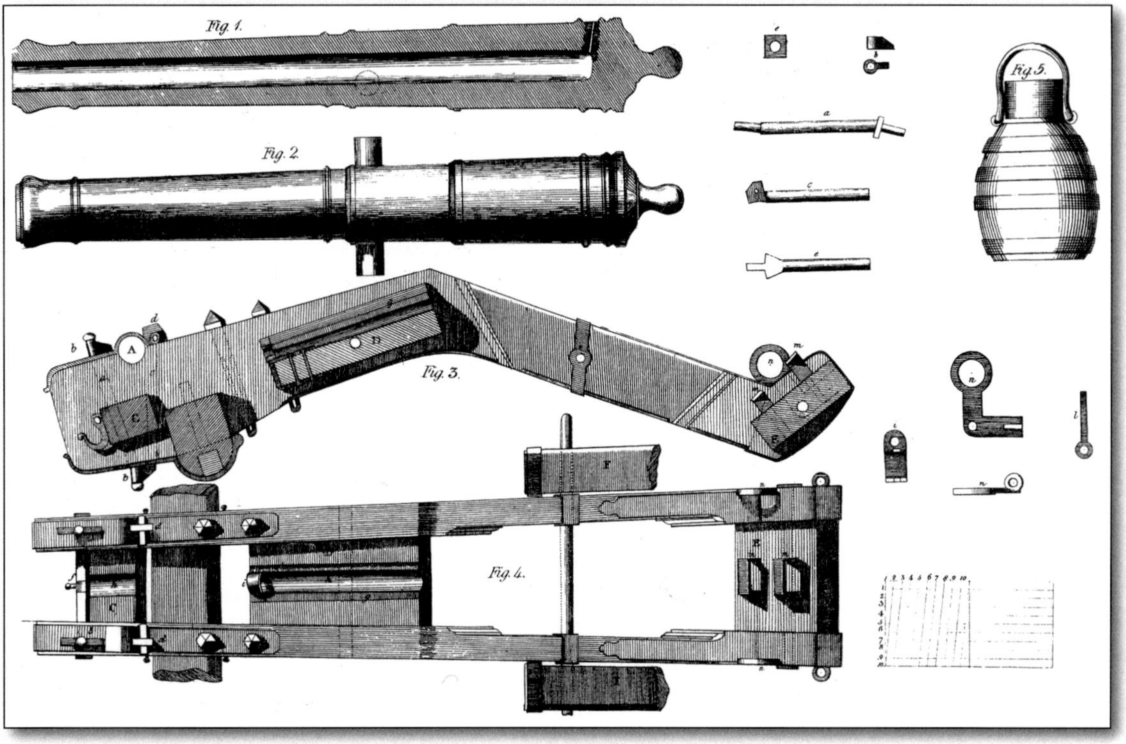

Top: Brass 1-pounder Compagnie des Indes light cannon, cast in 1732. It was found on the bottom of the harbour at Fortress Louisbourg (Canada) where Compagnie des Indes ships occasionally called. (Canadian War Museum, Ottawa, author's photo)

Bottom: Rostaing light cannon with its carriage, middle to late eighteenth century. This plate from De Scheel's 1792 artillery manual of Gribeauval's system reprinted in 1800 for American artillery shows a light 1-pounder first mooted by the Chevalier de Rostaing when in India and Ile de France in the mid-eighteenth century. It was later noted by General Gribeauval and included in his artillery system adopted by the French army from the 1760s. Fig. 1 and 2: Profile and plan of a one pounder brass light cannon. Fig. 3 and 4: Profile and plan of the carriage. Fig. 5: water bucket. Other smaller items are: a. Turning Key Bolt, b: Key, c: Hurter, d: Joint of the Cap Square, g: Groove for the Coin, h: Cavity for the play of the Pointing Vice, I: Pin to confine the Vice to the Coin. (Private collection, author's photo)

These light rapid-fire cannon were obviously some of the 'minute guns' mentioned in contemporary documents of campaigns in India as 'those that fire several shots within a minute.' In 1747, some brass 2-pounders could fire up to 21 shots a minute; others, to fire 12 shots a minute, were cast at Pondicherry. One can imagine with some horror what the effect could be when several of these cannons peppered grapeshot or cannonballs at such a fast rate in the compact masses of opposing Indian armies: particularly as they could be easily moved during the battle to concentrate on the best targets. Indeed, the mobility of these light cannons could be impressive. Law de Lauriston's small column left Bengal in 1757 with its two 2-pounder, two 3-pounder and six 1-pounder light cannon criss-crossing north-central India as far as Delhi for over three years.[18]

Rostaing went back to France in 1756. His light cannon was tried out by the French metropolitan army towards the end of the Seven Years War and thereafter remained in service. Each gun was served by eight gunners led by a *caporal* and a *sergent*. In 1767 and 1772, a few of these cannon were attached to the garrisons of Ile de France and Ile de Bourbon. In France, they became a main field weapon of the mountain artillery.[19]

18 Law de Lauriston, *Mémoire*, p.316.

19 Fréville, 'Une armée coloniale au XVIIIe siècle Dupleix aux Indes', p.425; Rostaing, 'Expedition de La Bourbonnais dans la mer des Indes en 1746', pp.427-429; Cultru, *Dupleix*, p.308 quoting 1747 Pondicherry Superior Council documents; AC, A, 17, De par le Roy… Légion de l'Ile de France…, 1 November 1767; AM, A1, 110, Ordonnance du roi portant établissements de deux pieces de Canon à la Rostaing à la suite de chacun des Regiments créés pour la garde des Iles de France et de Bourbon, 30 December 1772.

20

Uniforms

Governors, Senior and Staff Officers

The various monopoly companies had no dress regulations for its governors, governors generals, senior and staff officers. Even in the royal service, uniforms for army generals were only introduced from 1744, and from 1756-1757 for governors and staff officers. Before then, senior royal officers dressed as gentlemen or else wore the uniform of a unit they belonged to. Those of the Compagnie des Indes did the same during the whole period the company existed; they were not royal officers and no obliged to follow royal dress regulations. A gentleman's dress could be luxurious on special occasions. When posted at Chandernagor in Bengal during 1737, Dupleix had a coat and waistcoat of cinnamon-coloured material embroidered with gold worth 400 rupees. In 1752, gentlemen at a ball in Pondicherry, undoubtedly many of them senior officers, 'were superbly dressed, suffocating from the heat under the weight of the richest laces and materials' for their gentlemen's costume or uniform of their unit.[1]

Engineers in the service of the Compagnie des Indes had no known prescribed distinct uniform. A 1750 portrait of infantry *Capitaine* Antoine Barthélemy de Vire Duliron de Montivers, who was a fortifications engineer, shows him wearing a blue coat with blue cuffs and lining, scarlet collar, gold buttons and 'brandebourg' style gold lace at the buttonholes, scarlet waistcoat edged with gold lace, gold buttons and lace as on the coat, blue breeches, gold-laced hat and a gilt-hilted sword. While not identical to the uniform of the company's troops in India, it does have the same general hues except for blue cuffs rather than scarlet.[2]

1 Farelle (ed.), *Mémoire et correspondence du chevalier et du général de la Farelle*, p.301; BNF, Ms 8971, Relation des principal événements…July 1749 to 17 October 1752. 400 rupees was the basic monthly pay of an infantry *capitaine*.

2 Portrait by François-Dagobert Jouvenet, dated 1750 at the Musée de la Compagnie des Indes, Lorient. Duliron de Montivers served in Senegal from 1741-1748, at Pondicherry from 1752 to 1767.

Early East India Companies Soldiers

There is very little evidence found so far that gives details on the dress of these somewhat forlorn soldiers of the early French East India companies. What has been found is not detailed, but at least confirms that some European style military dress was worn.

Infantrymen, 1640s. Print after Lostelneau's 1647 drill book. (Private collection, author's photo)

The four infantry companies detached from the army and sent to Madagascar in 1666 had 'ammunition [regulation] clothing',[3] and the 400 soldiers from the Régiment Royal-Marine detached from the navy to the 1670 Persia Squadron would have been clothed too. Being a 'royal' regiment, it would be tempting to state they wore a grey-white coat lined and cuffed with royal blue, which was the royal colour, but there is no evidence on the hues of clothing before 1692 for this regiment whose detachment in the East Indies had long vanished by then.

In March 1674, bales of material were distributed by Viceroy de La Haye to the soldiers and sailors 'of the whole garrison' at besieged Sao-Tomé so that 'habits' (suits of clothing) would be made for them. The material must have been unsuitable because, in June, the soldiers were 'very badly dressed' and La Haye issued *justaucorps* (coats) from France made of woollen cloth to all. An early February 1674 shipment to India on the *Rubis* for the company's troops included 500 coats and 500 hats. Thereafter, the soldier's clothing seems to have been procured in India. This certainly made sense since that country was a great producer and exporter of many types of usually light-weight textiles suitable in a warm climate. In 1678, François Martin was particularly interested in linen dyed blue. Perhaps this might have been the origin of the blue uniform seen in eighteenth century India although this remains a mere possibility. Another possibility is the grey-white and blue uniform of the king's marines, as was seen from 1716 in Louisiana and adopted from 1721 by the Compagnie des Indes.[4]

---

3 AC, C11A, 113, Fonds faits pour les troupes et les officiers pour l'Ile Dauphine [1666].

4 AC, C11A, 113, Fonds faicts pour les troupes et officiers pour l'Isle Dauphine, 1666; Kaeppelin, *La Compagnie des Indes Orientales*, p.30; Martineau (ed.), *Mémoires de François Martin*, Vol.2, pp.175, 597, 634; Ac, B, 6, Mémoire de ce qui pourra être chargé dans le *Rubis* pour le voyages aux Indes d'Orient, 12 February 1674. The *Rubis* appears to have safely reached Sao-Tomé.

Top: Infantry officers and soldiers marching, circa 1685-1690. The officers are shown carrying their spontoons and wearing swords held by a shoulder bandolier. They have the sash, which was white, around the waist. The enlisted men wear uniforms and hold their matchlock muskets over the shoulder. Their swords are in scabbards held by waist-belts, a new arrangement introduced from 1684. The shoulder belt holds a bullet bag. From a large brass medallion by Jean Régnaud and Pierre Le Nègre. (Musée du Louvre, Paris)

Below left: Infantry officer, 1690s. Although some officers wore regimental uniforms, it was not formally ordered in the royal armed forces before 1729. White waist sashes were worn by French officers until about 1700. They were armed with pontoons and swords. Watercolour by Eugène Titeu. (Anne S.K. Brown Military Collection)

Below right: Infantry soldier, 1690. By that time enlisted soldiers of all units in the royal armed forces had uniform. This would have been also the case of soldiers belonging to the French East India companies although the hues of their uniforms are not generally known until the 1720s. Watercolour by Eugène Titeu. (Anne S.K. Brown Military Collection)

Compagnie des Indes Troops at Lorient 1721-1758

When the various monopoly companies were merged in 1719, the new Compagnie des Indes inherited a variety of territories with garrisons on three continents. The company at Lorient created from October 1721 acted as the recruit's depot, training centre, port garrison and shipping out centre of soldiers posted overseas as well as those serving as marines on the company's ships. These duties being nearly identical to the Compagnies franches de la Marine of the royal government, their uniform was chosen to be the one worn by the troops of the Compagnie des Indes.

Thus, from that time until 1758, the Compagnie des Indes soldier's uniform consisted of a grey-white or white cloth coat with blue cloth cuffs and blue serge lining trimmed with 36 large brass buttons; blue waistcoa t and breeches lined with linen with 36 small brass buttons. The number of buttons was probably reduced during the later 1740s as was the case in the royal army and marines. The cravats may have been initially white, but by 1746, they were black. Blue collars appear to have been added to the coat in the late 1740s or early 1750s. Hat were laced with false gold for the men. The forge caps were white, probably with a blue turn-up.

Previous page:

Left: Infantry fusilier, 1740s. Watercolour by Eugène Titeu. (Anne S.K. Brown Military Collection)

Right: Infantry sergeant, 1740s. Sergeants were armed with halberds and swords. Their uniforms were usually the same as the soldiers, but of better quality material. Their rank insignia was gold lace at the buttonholes of the coat's cuffs or else a gold lace edging the the top of the cuffs. Watercolour by Michel Pétard. (National Historic Sites, Parks Canada)

The new soldiers incorporated into the depot company at Lorient were issued clothing consisting of a coat, a waistcoat, cloth breeches, a hat, a pair of stockings, two cravats, two shirts, a pair of shoes, a linen frock, linen trousers, a pair of linen gaiters, a musket, a bayonet, a cartridge box and a waist belt. The coat was issued every second year, the rest of the clothing yearly. When embarking on a ship for a voyage, such as the *Jupiter* sailing for Pondicherry in October 1726, each soldier further received two shirts, a pair of shoes, a waistcoat and breeches of 'Métis' linen.[5]

Sergents were distinguished by gold buttons, gold hat lace and, most probably, gold lace at the cuffs.

As for drummers or other musicians, no documents have so far been seen describing their dress nor any regarding the appearance of their instruments and accoutrements. The uniform of the soldier's did have blue cuffs, waistcoats, breeches and stockings and that hue was the main colour of the king's livery. Furthermore, that livery was worn by drummers of Crozat's company in Louisiana in 1716 with, surely, royal permission because only certain royal troops were allowed to wear it in the army. On the other hand, although we found many documents on uniforms, not a single one described the uniform of drummers from 1719 to 1770.[6]

The uniform for officers would have followed the practice in the royal army and marines in that its colours would be the same as the soldiers, but made of superior quality materials. From 1729, lace was not allowed on the coats of the royal troops and this would have been also followed by the Compagnie des Indes' officers. Thus, in 1752, a young *enseigne* entering the company's service was informed that his uniform should be 'a white coat, blue cuffs, gilded brass buttons, boot cuffs, a blue Swedish style collar and a blue waistcoat'. The question of having lace on the waistcoat was raised in 1756, but some officers objected and the company concluded that there would not be any lace.[7]

5 APL, 1P, 4, Façon d'habit de soldat, 9 July 1746, 11 May 1748, 13 May 1750; AC, D2C, 187, Compagnie de Plantin, Etat de signalement de 50 soldats embarqués sur le vaisseau *le Jupiter*, 9 October 1726 (the coat was not issued to recruits).

6 Unless one had royal permission, only the king's royal household servants, musicians in certain regiments and the marines were allowed to wear blue as their livery before the French Revolution.

7 APL, 1P, 280c, 49, Godeheu to the Chevalier de Pujot, 16 June 1752; APL, 1P, 278, 12, Lettres du bureau, 16 August 1756; Hélias, 'L'uniforme des troupes de la Compagnie des Indes lors de la guerre de Sept-Ans', pp.50-52.

Above: The king's grand livery lace, circa 1716. It decorated the drummer's coats of the Louisiana companies until about 1719. This wide lace consisted of a strip of the ordinary white chain on red or crimson-red livery lace edging both side of the narrow white central lace with red or crimson-red small elongated triangles. Sketch by Eugène Lelièpvre. (Private collection, author's photo)

Left: Drummer wearing a coat decorated with the king's great livery lace, 1717. This drummer of the navy's Gardes du Pavillon Amiral (Guards of the Admiral's Standard) wears the blue coat with red cuffs of the royal livery with the lace thereon. Drummers of the Louisiana companies were issued with this type of coat, no doubt with special permission. The drum was blue with yellow lilies. Print after Vassé. (Private collection, author's photo)

The 'For All Troops' Uniform of the Compagnies des Indes, 15 March 1758

As seen below, the uniforms worn by the company's troops posted in India, Ile de France and Ile de Bourbon were of very different colours that those described above, which were worn in Lorient, Senegal and Louisiana. On 7 October 1755, the company's Paris council decreed that henceforth, their uniforms would be of the same colours as those worn in France so as to have a standard dress for all. Grey-white Lodève cloth coats with blue cuffs, linen lining, guigham waistcoats were to be henceforth worn in India and the islands. The coats were further to have shorter skirts, without pockets and folds in the skirts with a hidden pocket.[8] Guigham (also guingam, guigam, guingan, and other variants) was a blue or mixed blue and white light material that had the further advantage of costing much less so that its deduction from the soldier's pay was less so the company did not risk losing money if a soldier deserted or died before his payments ended.

This met with considerable opposition by the Pondicherry council who answered on 3 February 1757 that while it would 'conform to the instructions' when the Lodève cloth would arrive, it would add waistcoats of 'blue guigam

8 APL, 1P, 305, 69, Deliberations de la Compagnie des Indes, 7 October 1755.

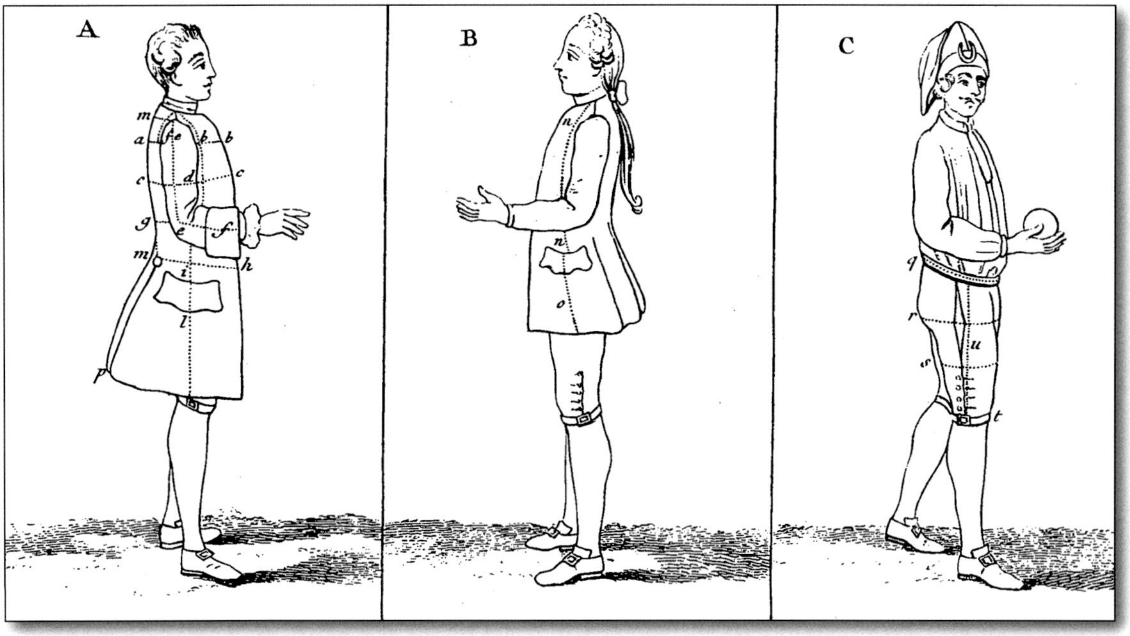

Mid-eighteenth century European measurements for a coat, a waistcoat and breeches, the figure at right also showing a forage cap and a shirt. Up until about the 1770s, the basic cuts of tailor's patterns for military uniforms generally followed those for civilian men's costume, whether made in France or overseas. Garsault's *L'Art de tailleur*. (Author's photo)

pinnace without stripes' while stressing to the company in France that a blue uniform was 'best in these countries' as it lasted longer and did not get as dirty as white.[9]

Once it received this answer, the Compagnie des Indes council in France had some serious second thoughts about its troops' uniforms. On 15 March 1758, it issued the following uniform regulation:

> That the uniform of all its troops, those in India as well as those in the islands and at Lorient will be of royal blue, with red cloth lapels and cuffs, flat pewter buttons…, white laced buttonholes and blue serge lining.
>
> The waistcoat will be of red tricot [a light knit cloth] and lined with grey linen.
>
> The breeches will be of royal blue tricot also lined with grey linen.
>
> The buttonholes of the coat and the waistcoat will be of white wool, will only go down to the waist belt; and there will be three on the coat's cuffs.
>
> The coat will have in front slit pockets with pocket flaps, and the real pocket will be in the opening that separates the front from the back of the coat.
>
> The coats will have collars like those of the present uniform…
>
> The *serjents* will have a fine silver lace on the cuff and pocket flaps; *caporaux* three white wool double laces, and the *anspessades* single laces on the cuffs.
>
> Regarding the officers they will obliged to wear the same colours and to have made the coats, cuffs and lapels in wool, the linings and waistcoats as they wish.
>
> The use of royal blue wool stockings will be continued for soldiers; but the hats will be edged with white goat's hair according to the model presented by the Compagnie [des Indes].

9 *Correspondance du Conseil supérieur de Pondichéry et de la Compagnie des Indes…*, Vol.5, p.175.

> There will be further issues of white moleton gilets [short-waisted waistcoats] that will be issued every year on 15 October and withdrawn in the following month of April.[10]

All ranks are mentioned in this detailed regulation except the drummers whose traditional distinctive dress, as seen in all armies, remains unknown.

Later documents mentioned further details, notably in 1762 when the hats of *sergents* were to have silver lace and the men's white lace. The 1758 uniform is unlikely to have been worn in overseas before the end of the Seven Years War, except perhaps at Ile de France and Ile de Bourbon, the only territories that did not fall to the British. The French army's registers published in 1762 and 1763 confirmed its uniform as: 'blue coat, lining and breeches; red cuffs and lapels; white buttons and buttonhole lace; hat edged with white sheep's hair.' From 1765, the company's troops garrisoned at Pondicherry and Chandernagor would have worn this uniform as did the marines on board the company's ships. Silver buttons, silver hat lace, white lace, blue and red material were sent to Pondicherry in 1765 and 1766 to 'complement' the troops' uniforms. It was noted at the time that the quality of the uniforms was important to prevent desertion as well as to impress Indian officials of the good standing of the company's soldiers. Even after the company ceased its operations in 1770, the company at Lorient was on duty in this uniform until disbanded on 30 December 1772.

Officers wore the 1758 uniform made of superior quality materials with silver buttons and buttonhole lace. Following the adoption of epaulettes as a rank insignia in the French royal army, silver epaulettes were added from December 1762.[11]

India: A Galaxy of Uniforms and Hues

Military dress of European troops of the Compagnie des Indes stationed in India and the Indian Ocean islands were radically different dress from the troops in France, Senegal and Louisiana.

Little is known of the colours of the uniforms in India until the 1720s. Recruits and reinforcements arriving from France would have had their grey-

10 ADR, Co 1190, Extrait du Régistre general des deliberations de la Compagnie des Indes, 15 March 1758. This uniform was worn at Lorient until the disbandment of the depot garrison company on 30 December 1772 replaced the same day by two new companies with similar duties under royal authority via the ministry of the navy as per AC, A, 18. Its uniform was: a blue coat with blue cuffs lined white, white waistcoat and breeches, white lace edging the hat, 10 buttons down the front of the coat, three buttons on each cuff and pocket, three small buttons under each cuff, all buttons of white metal stamped with an anchor.

11 APL, 1P 283c, 110, Compagnie des Indes to Codron, 20 October 1762 ordering 12 *sergent*'s and 300 fusilier's hats; *État Militaire de France pour l'année 1762* (Paris, 1762), p.371 and 1763, p.302; *Correspondance du conseil supérieur de Pondichéry et de la Compagnie*, Vol.6, pp.356-358; AC, A, 18, Ordonnance…portant suppression de la compagnie…du port de Lorient, 30 December 1772; for the specific ranks shown by epaulettes, see: Ordonnance du Roi concernant l'infanterie française du 10 décembre 1762 (Lyon, 1763), p.43; Règlement arrêté par le Roi pour l'habillement et l'équipement de ses troupes du 25 avril 1767 (Paris, 1767), pp.6-7.

white and blue cloth uniform and their undress linen clothing somewhat worn after a voyage that might have taken many months until Pondicherry was reached. Once landed there, they perceived that many hues could be used to clothe soldiers in India. In 1721 the Pondicherry Council, obviously concerned with the company's profits, decided that the garrison would be dressed 'with lemon yellow cloth that the Compagnie has in its stores…that risks becoming a total loss if we keep them any longer.'[12]

The usual colour of the uniform in India at that time actually seems to have been red, which was also the favoured hue chosen for Dutch, Danish and British soldiers in their respective East India companies' service. In 1727, a company official arriving in Pondicherry remarked that 'M. Lenoir did not feel the blue cloth I had brought to dress the garrison was not appropriate because of its colour. He sold it with some profit and asks the Compagnie [des Indes] to send coarse red cloth' instead. At that time, the company officials informed again officials in France that it was so 'extremely hot [in India] that Europeans could barely support even light clothing.' Furthermore, it was obvious the European soldiers and the topasses could better afford the deductions of such clothing from their pay. In March 1728, the Pondicherry council opted to clothe the garrison with blue guigham with red cuffs, but this does not seem to have been permanent although the 'guigam' material, also called 'guigam pinasse' or 'spinasse' was preferred in torrid India. Thereafter, the usual uniform at Pondicherry appears to have been of red serge with blue cuffs sent from France into the 1730s. However, at Mahé on the Malabar coast, the troops posted there had uniforms made of blue 'guingam' with red cuffs.[13]

The uniform issue obviously included breeches, stockings, shoes and hats. Gaiters were also worn although it is uncertain as to when they were introduced. They certainly had been an issue for a while by 1737 when a fight erupted at an inspection due to a soldier reacting violently against a *lieutenant* who commented that his gaiters were not white enough.[14]

After many exchanges of letters, the company's board in Paris ordered the council in Pondicherry on 17 May 1737 to 'henceforth dress the troops with blue 'guingam' with red serge cuffs' as well as sending 1,100 soldier's hats. Two years later, the Paris council specified that it would no longer send serge for the uniforms because stronger 'guigam' material could be made and purchased and India. In 1745 a request was made to make 2,000 soldier's coats of 'guingam' with red cuffs and 2,000 breeches, 8,000 soldier's shirts, 8,000 pairs of shoes and 4,000 pairs of gaiters. Some 200 officer's coats were to be made cut as 'volants' of fine 'guingam' material from Gondelour, the fronts lined with the same 'guingam', the cuffs and small collars for officers

12 *Procés-verbaux de deliberations du Conseil souverain de la Compagnie*, Vol.1, p.306.

13 AC, C2, 74, unsigned memoir, 7 October 1727; *Correspondance du conseil supérieur de Pondichéry et de la Compagnie*, Vol.1, pp.82-83, 307-308; Anon., *Procès-verbaux des délibérations du Conseil supérieur de Pondichéry*, Vol.2, p.165; Alfred Martineau, *Les origines de Mahé de Malabar* (Paris: Champion, 1917), p.198.

14 Édmond Gaudart, *La criminalité dans les comptoirs de l'Inde au XVIIIe siècle* (Pondichéry, 1937), pp.119-120.

An Indian shoemaker making a pair of European shoes assisted by his wife, eighteenth century. Much of the production of such shoes would have been made for the European soldiers posted in India. Their uniforms were also made in India. (Bibliothèque Nationale de France, Paris)

of red 'Camelot' and trimmed with gold or gilded brass buttons. The basic uniform colour remained blue thereafter.[15]

At that time, nearly all European men followed the overwhelming fashion of wearing their hair long and tied in a queue at the back no matter where they might be at home or overseas. Law de Lauriston recommended that European soldiers should always consider wearing wigs in India, especially those who might get in drunken brawls with equally drunk Indians who might grab them by their queue to beat them up badly or even kill them. This could also happen to officers and men in other circumstances such as heated arguments over some matter. He concluded by stating the 'more than one soldier or even officer owe their lives to this artificial hairpiece, which is unknown in most parts of India'.[16]

15 AC, C2, 27, Ordre au Conseil Supérieur de Pondichéry, 17 May 1737; AC, C2, 28, Extrait du régistre général de la Compagnie des Indes, Paris, 14 July 1739; AC, C2, 81, f 10, Mahé de La Bourdonnais to Dupleix, Isle de France, 1 August 1745. According to François Garsault, *L'Art du Tailleur* (Paris: Desaint, Saillant & Nyon, 1769), pp.18-19, the 'volant' was a sort of coat without buttons or buttonholes at the cuffs, no pockets nor pocket flaps and has a collar with a button and a buttonhole. It was an ample coat since it could be put over a 'justaucorps' in France. In India, its ample cut must have made it cooler to wear, especially if made of light weight 'guigam'.

16 Law de Lauriston, *Mémoire*, pp.359-360. He further related an incident involving an officer named Jobard who got into a fiery argument with a ferry master regarding a very long delay in

Uniforms wore down quickly in India. This was essentially due to the lightweight Indian textiles and the lack of care by the soldiers. Regarding their dress, Dupleix commented in a 1753 that in spite of replacing it frequently, the soldier's uniform was often 'in rags' soon thereafter. Some men had even required three issues within six months. A 1760s memoir was severely critical of the uniforms issued. Tricorn hats lost their shape during the rains and their black felt could cause deadly sunstroke under the intensely hot sun of southern India. Forage caps made a better headdress, but were not perfect either. The coat of blue 'guigam' or 'spinace' material was like a filter during rains so the soldier was soon drenched to his bones. When the sun came out, it dried quickly but also shrank so that turnbacks rolled in eventually looking like two ropes hanging down. Since the rest of the coat and other articles of clothing of this material also shrank, the uniform would become too small and just about unwearable. Wool-based cloth seemed the better option since there were cold nights in India, but the sun's heat then became problematic. The soldiers in India were also accused of very negligent care regarding their uniforms, but could they be blamed for the quick degradation of such clothing for which their pay was deducted?[17]

Bussy's Deccan Army 1751-1755

The uniforms described above, varied as they could be, were merely a modest sampling. A peak of sorts was reached by the European troops of Bussy's army campaigning in the Deccan. This force, which travelled several times across central India, was far from Pondicherry and clothed several times by or with the assistance of allied Indian princes. The descriptions below are nearly all from the unsigned journal of a French soldier who was part of that force during those years. All description found are presented below.[18]

At Hyderabad, April 1751

- Kirjean's Company: blue jackets, breeches and caps; red cuffs, lapels and cap turban, the latter having a blue fleur-de-lis on the front.
- Grenadier Company: red jackets, breeches and caps; blue cuffs, lapels and cap turban, the latter having a red fleur-de-lis on the front.

providing a boat to cross the Ganges River. One of the ferry's 'Pion' guards grabbed Jobard's queue and pulled hard at it only to fall down on his back while the other 'Pion' guards were utterly amazed, not understanding what had happened. By then, Jobard had drawn his pistol, was given back his wig with excuses and was quickly taken to a boat. Had he had his own hair, he 'would have been beaten unconscious' or worse.

17 Depréaux, 'Troupes coloniales d'autrefois, Mémoire sur les troupes de l'Inde [c. 1763]', pp.428-429; Martineau, *Dupleix*, Vol.3, pp.58-60

18 Depréaux, 'Les uniformes de la Compagnie des Indes…', pp.163, 167-168, 171-173, 178. There may have been more descriptions, but the third folder of this journal corresponding from January to June 1753 was missing when it entered the Bibliothèque Nationale in Fond Français, Nouvelles acquisitions, 9358.

- [Bussy's] Volunteer Company: blue jackets, breeches and caps; yellow cuffs, lapels and cap turban, the latter having a blue fleur-de-lis on the front.
- Artillery Company: blue coats and breeches; red cuffs and lapels, with hats.

Shirts with white and blue gaiters were also issued.

At Aurengabad, July 1751

Bussy's troops were all clothed with: red coats and breeches; green cuffs and lapels; red caps with green turbans. The *sergents* of the fusilier companies had on their caps a fleurs-de-lis with the motto '*Pericula ludus*' with a cord around it, embroidered in silver on green, the caps' crown having a small silver tuft. *Caporaux* and fusiliers had the same embroidery on their caps, but in white silk.

- Kirjean's Company: its caps had a red cloth grenade.
- Volunteer Company: a white rosette.
- Artillery Company: a bomb [unspecified colour].
- *Caffres* and topasses; a red cloth fleur-de-lis.

All were issued a pair of gaiters. The memorialist further observed that the troops 'looked very good'.

Bussy further reported from Aurengabad on 23 September 1751 that 'our Europeans and *Caffres* were very properly dressed, and I would say richly for our dragoons. Indeed, they have very fine scarlet coats, as do our troops, but with a narrow gold lace, and since we have no hats, all wear caps, but ornamented with a lace'.[19]

At Hyderabad, June 1753

- Dragoons: green coats and breeches; red cuffs, collar and aiguillettes; green caps with the front in sheep's fur and brass buttons.
- [Bussy's Horse] Guards: red coats trimmed with lace, red breeches, green cuffs also trimmed with lace; gold thread aiguillettes; bandoliers of red and green squares edged with a gold lace with gilded brass hooks; hats edged with gold; gilt buttons.
- Artillery Company: green coats and breeches; red cuffs; green and red caps with a red cannonball in front; horizontal pocket flaps on the coats; red buttons.
- [Kirjean's] Volunteer Company: blue coats and breeches; red cuffs and lapels; blue caps with three white laces on the back and the front in sheep's fur; pewter buttons and white aiguillettes.
- 'Étrangers' Company: red coats and breeches; red buttons; yellow cuffs and lapels; red and yellow caps with a red fleur-de-lis in front.
- Topasses: 'Couleur de chair' [basically a pink or buffish-pink hue] coats and breeches; red cuffs, lapels and buttons; 'Couleur de chair' and red caps.

19 AC, C2, Vol.51, Bussy to Pondicherry council, 23 September 1751.

- 'Corps de Troupes' [three fusilier companies]: red coats, breeches and buttons; green cuffs and lapels; red and green caps with a red fleur-de-lis in front. These companies were distinguished by epaulettes: white for the first; green for the second; blue for the third.

All of these units, 'when in battle formation, looked magnificent.'

The Volontaires Portugais Company was seen at Aurengabad, on 11 June 1753: 'dressed in the French fashion, red coat, green cuffs' and lapels.[20]

At Aurengabad, 4 November 1754

- 'Grenadiers à cheval' [Horse Grenadiers]: blue coats; red cuffs and lapels; yellow brass buttons.
- [Bussy's Horse] Guards: red coats; green cuffs with gold lace; gold laced hats; bandoliers of red and green small squares with two gold laces at each side.
- *Caffres*: [fourteen] 'some mounted on elephants, others marching on foot; some had blunderbuss [muskets], others had sabres. They marched before the general [Bussy] when he went out… They wore long red robes and drawers with high hussar style caps garnished with bearskin with very long hair having a large silver fleur-de-lis in front of the cap.'
- 'Corps du Bataillon' [battalion companies]: red jackets and breeches; green cuffs and lapels; red buttons. *Sergents*: red coats without lapels; green cuffs edged with a gold lace.

All the European troops were issued hats. No further data appears on the dress of the Deccan troops in the following years.

Law de Lauriston's Corps in North Central India 1757-1761

In theory, the European troops of this small corps would have been wearing the company's blue uniform with red cuffs when it left the lodge of Cossimbazar, Bengal, in mid-1757. How long this uniform would have lasted during its travels is unknown. Eventually, perhaps in 1758 or 1759, it would have needed new clothing.

From April 1759, it served with the Indian army of the 'Chazada' (Crown Prince Ali Johor) that was marching east towards Bengal. In May 1760, he became the Great Mughal taking the name of Shah Alam II. Law de Lauriston and his corps was attached to the Great Mughal's Indian army until January 1761. As seen above with Bussy's army, Indian princes clothed French corps serving with their armies and red was the predominant colour. An Indian watercolour shows the Great Mughal reviewing a company of European soldiers wearing plain black tricorns, coats without cuffs or collar that are completely red, dark blue breeches and stockings (reconstructed by Patrice

20 Gentil, *Mémoires*, p.60.

Courcelle, see colour plate). Since Law de Lauriston's corps being the only European unit in the Great Mughal's army, it would be the one depicted.[21]

European Cavalry

Governor General's Guards

Governor-General de La Haye's company was seen wearing 'blue cassocks' at Calicut on 18 March 1672. The '24 guards of M. Dupleix' were described as mounted on good horses, well dressed and led by their officers at a parade in 1752. They wore a 'scarlet coat with black cuffs, gold lace border edging. Their captain has gold lace at all seams.' The dress of the Comte de Lally's company would have been, as was the custom, the livery colours of their master, possibly red lined with green with gold buttons and lace.[22]

Commandant Bussy's Horse Guards

See 'Uniforms of Bussy's Deccan Army 1751-1755' above.

Dragoons and Grenadiers à cheval (Horse Grenadiers)

See 'Uniforms of Bussy's Deccan Army 1751-1755', above, and the plate illustrating the 1754 uniform of the Grenadiers à cheval. La Tour's 1756-1761 dragoons were said to have superb uniforms, but no description has emerged.

Hussars

No description found; a basic hussar dress such as a jacket decorated with many buttons and cords with a cap for headdress is possible.

European Artillery

Gunners may not have had uniforms until the mid-1740s and then possibly only in India where distinct companies of artillery were created. Artillerymen on the Coromandel and Orissa coasts would have most likely had the same blue uniforms with red cuffs as infantrymen from the stores at Pondicherry. For Bussy's army in the Deccan, please see 'Uniforms of Bussy's Deccan Army 1751-1755', above, and the plate illustrating its 1751 uniform.

21 Law de Lauriston's *Memoir* did not describe uniforms, but he noted textiles such 'material of all types' be it silk or cloth at Benares and good linen dyed red near Delhi, pp.293, 351; watercolour in Bibliothèque Nationale de France, Paris, Col. Gentil bequest, Manuscrits, Français 24219.

22 Anon., *Relation d'un voyage fait aux Indes orientales*, p.78; Prévost d'Exiles, *Histoire générale des voyages*, Vol.XXXVI, pp.328; BNF, Ms Français, 8971, folio 109, "Relation des principaux événements arrivés aux Indes dans la province du Carnate…de juillet 1749. Jusqu'au 17 Octobre 1752."

Volontaires de Bourbon

The material culture of this unit is, so far, largely unknown. Since they served on foot, they would have been armed as infantry with muskets, bayonets, swords or possibly sabres as they were considered elite troops with infantry accoutrements. Regarding their uniform, it was red according to the confused incident it caused at the 1758 siege of Madras. It may have been red also when they were with Bussy's army during 1752-1755.[23]

Sepoys of the Compagnie des Indes

According to the unsigned and memorandum on the sepoys of circa 1755, quoted above, efforts were made to provide the sepoys with some elements of uniform dress while acknowledging that their basic costume could never be totally changed. The Indian costume of a sepoy consisted of:

> [A] long Mughal style robe, with folds at the lower waist, closed in front [of the chest] and fastened with wide ribbons or cords at left. This robe, which goes down to the heels, folded up in all war operations [or campaigns] is held up by a belt at the waist in which the dagger is also held... The sleeves are narrow and go the middle of the wrist; they wear long drawers that go to their heels and for shoes they have 'babouches' or flat shoes, without heels, that are pointed at the end.[24]

This costume was usually made of white linen or other light fabric, but other colours might be worn; the robe might also fasten on the right side and some also fastened at the centre of the chest. The headwear could be turbans of various shapes, some being scarves tied in folds while others would have material shaped on a form to obtain an elevated and large circle.

This costume was common to all sepoys and most of its elements were similar to the basic male costume in India. It was not a uniform as such and could have many personal features. Furthermore, the origins of the soldiers brought a certain similarity in styles. Mughals would wear their clothing in a certain way, Persians in another, Hindustani Muslims could be distinguished from Rajputs and so on.[25]

Adding arms and accoutrements did not result in distinctive features revealing in which army they served. This became a problem, not only to tell friend from foe, but also to distinguish the sepoys in the service of the

---

23 Martineau, *Bussy*, p.252. The Volontaires de Bourbon in the Deccan should not be confused with the Volontaires de Kerjean, Bussy's army senior company that had blue uniforms in 1751 and 1753 as per Depréaux, 'Les uniformes de la Compagnie des Indes...', pp.163, 172.

24 'Mémoire sur la Milice des Cipayes', p.413.

25 Irvine, *The Army of the Indian Moghuls*, p.183. 'As for uniform, the only sign of it originally was a red turban worn by all in the imperial employ... For the great mass of the army there was usually no uniformity of dress...' There could be 'some few regiments clothed in uniform. For example, as early as Farrukhsiyar's reign, the Surkhposhari (the Red Regiment) is spoken of... And it would seem ...that in Muhammad Shah's time there were some regiments of body-guards clad alike, and known ...from the colour of their coats, red, yellow or black.'

Left: An eighteenth century 'Angarkha' Indian robe or tunic. The 'angarkha' was the main dress for men's wear in India for several centuries. It is seen in countless illustrations by Indian artists and could feature many variations in detail. It was therefore the most common garment of Indian soldiers in the service of princes and sepoys in European forces. It was usually made of white cotton as this example. (Metropolitan Museum of Art, New York, Irene Lewisohn and Alice L. Crowley Bequests, 1976. 149.4)

Right: Back view of a sepoy soldier in the service of the Compagnie des Indes, mid-eighteenth century. Note the French fleur de lys on the heels of the shoes, a detail taken from an original in the Musée de l'Armée. Print after Lucien Rousselot. (Private collection, author's photo)

Compagnie des Indes from those in the armies of allied Indian princes, who were largely undisciplined and often looting inhabitants. When accused, the prince's sepoys routinely replied they were not involved and accused the Compagnie des Indes's sepoys for the depredations. As a result, there was an issue of blue jackets with red cuffs to the company's sepoys, seemingly at Pondicherry. There are no details as to exactly when although it seems to have been during the later 1740s. In any case, when the sepoys saw their pay being deducted for more than what they estimated the jackets were worth, they protested and the scheme was abandoned. Another issue in October 1750 was a supply of blue shirts with drawers to supplement the Indian clothing of sepoys in garrison at the fortress of Gingee. The choice of a blue hue may have been to identify them as in the service of the Compagnie des Indes.[26]

Certainly, a most colourful issue was the clothing provided by the Chevalier de Mouy who commanded a force of 12 companies gathering 1,200 sepoys of the Compagnie des Indes in the province of Nellore, possibly at about 1755. He obtained a supply of red, blue, yellow and green material

26 'Mémoire sur la Milice des Cipayes', p.419; Martineau, *Dupleix*, Vol.3, p.35.

in equal quantities, which he had made into jackets having collars, cuffs and lapels of a contrasting colour as facings. The colours were as follows:

- Yellow jackets with red collars, cuffs and lapels
- Yellow jackets with blue collars, cuffs and lapels
- Yellow jackets with green collars, cuffs and lapels
- Red jackets with blue collars, cuffs and lapels
- Red jackets with yellow collars, cuffs and lapels
- Red jackets with green collars, cuffs and lapels
- Blue jackets with red collars, cuffs and lapels
- Blue jackets with yellow collars, cuffs and lapels
- Blue jackets with green collars, cuffs and lapels
- Green jackets with blue collars, cuffs and lapels
- Green jackets with yellow collars, cuffs and lapels
- Green jackets with red collars, cuffs and lapels

The mixture of colours in this instance was amazing, but not unusual for troops in the service of the European monopoly companies in India. The Nellore sepoys were satisfied since the deduction was fair and, wearing these uniforms, they could not be blamed for rampages they did not commit. Furthermore, French officers perceived that their sepoys became very proud to wear uniforms, an obvious morale boost. By the later 1750s, Law de Lauriston noted that 'they are provided with a uniform' whose colour was given as 'a red jacket' in remarks on his sepoys from Bengal made in March 1758. This also was the main colour used for the uniforms of British sepoys at that time. A uniform colour was probably never officially settled upon due to availability of materiel and because many sepoys still wore their own clothing.[27]

Top: A Compagnie des Indes sepoy's shoe, eighteenth century. The back (invisible) has a fleur-de-lis on the heel. Print from Depréaux's *Uniformes*.... (Author's photo)

Bottom: Pair of Indian metal slippers, eighteenth century. These slippers were meant to protect the wearer's feet in battle. (Musée Guimet, Paris, author's photo)

Caffres

The original costume of these African warriors was simply a square loincloth tied to waist belt. They also wore a 'leather band that hangs down to their feet. This band is about six inches wide and its edges are decorated with small iron

27 'Mémoire sur la Milice des Cipayes', pp.419-420; Law de Lauriston, *Mémoire*..., pp.310, 579; William Y. Carman, *Indian Army Uniforms, Infantry* (London: Morgan-Grampian, 1969), pp.96, 130, 161 for uniforms of British sepoys; mostly red jackets, but also some green.

rings'. They also had a leather cap ornamented in dress occasions with long cock's feathers. Those with Bussy's army are recorded being issued uniforms in July and September 1751 and November 1754. Please see 'Uniforms of Bussy's Deccan Army 1751-1755', above.[28]

Ile de France and Ile de Bourbon European Troops

The early dress of the European companies posted on these islands might have been either of grey-white cloth coming from France or of red serge or blue guigham from India. Clothing from far-away France was rarer. In September 1726, the soldiers were reported as being barefooted, without hats, shirts, drawers and stockings. Obtaining clothing from India was obviously much quicker and simpler. By 1733, guigham waistcoats were routinely mentioned. In 1738, the Paris council officially approved and ordered that the practice of sending uniforms from India to the islands be continued. This implies that red coats with blue cuffs and then blue coats with red cuffs along with blue waistcoats and breeches were the usual uniforms worn up to 1738 and only the blue coats with red cuffs thereafter, just like the troops in India. The troops there had received similar instructions in 1737.[29]

Military supplies listed in 1743 mention gold laced 'half beaver' hats for *sergents*, blue guigham and scarlet serge (presumably for coats and coat cuffs), blue stockings as well as striped guigham waistcoat and breeches likely for undress. Probate inventories of the belongings of deceased soldiers at hospital of Ile de France confirm these trends. In 1749, Jean-François Lebenne, invalid soldier, had his old red coat with blue cuffs and a newer guigham 'Epinasse' coat with red cuffs and gold buttons', a guigham waistcoat and breeches, a wig, a hat and two pairs of new shoes from India. *Sergent* Jean-Baptiste Mery, commanding the troops detached on Rodrigues Island, who passed away on that island, 28 August 1751, had an old coat, 25 white shirts, three pairs of blue breeches, two blue coats, 12 pairs of white stockings, six pairs of blue stockings, a hat laced with gold and a sword with a silver hilt and its belt.[30]

There might be additional features added on certain occasions. Following the capture of Madras in 1746, the contingent of soldiers that had come from Iles de France and Ile de Bourbon put green palm leaves on their hats as a distinction from the Pondicherry soldiers who had taken the lead position in the victory parade.[31]

---

28 Maréchal, *Costumes*, Vol.4, pp.4-5.

29 Lougnon, *L'Ile Bourbon sous la Régence*, p.312; ADR, Co 1222, Reciept of 6 June 1733; AC, C2, 28, Extrait du régistre général de la Compagnie des Indes, Paris, 2 June 1738.

30 ADR, Co 1503, État des Effets délivrés pour le service de la troupe, 1743; APL, 1P, 271, bundle 4 to 7, piece 92, Jean-François Lebenne, invalid soldier, deceased at the hospital of Isle de France, 30 July 1749: 1P, 271b, bundle 8 to 10, piece 48, *Sergent* Jean-Baptiste Mery, 28 August 1751.

31 Gennes,*Mémoire pour le sieur de La Bourdonnais*, p.56. This incident was a manifestation of the rivalry between the companies in India and those of the islands.

During the Seven Years War, some supplies from Europe or India did not reach the islands. By 1760, uniforms were made on locally to clothe the garrison. This consisted of coats, waistcoats, breeches, gaiters, shoes and caps. There were seemingly no hats available, but there was 'Camelot' cloth (obviously red) for the coat cuffs and turbans of the caps. The material for those and other garments would have been blue.[32]

Louisiana –Uniforms of the Crozat and Compagnie des Indes Troops 1716-1732

The uniform of the two companies of 1704 and the dress of two other companies that arrived in 1715 during the Crozat monopoly are basically unknown. The establishment was doubled by four more companies that arrived in 1716. Fortunately, a detailed list describing their uniforms sent that year has survived.[33]

Sergents had a hat edged with silver lace; a coat of white cloth lined with blue serge and blue cuffs edged with a fine silver lace with 26 silver plated buttons; a waistcoat of blue cloth lined with linen with 36 small brass buttons; a pair of breeches of blue light weight cloth lined with linen and with leather pockets; a pair of gaiters was to be issued yearly and a pair of stockings the second year; white shirt; black cravat and shoes.

Drummers wore a hat edged with false gold lace; a coat of blue cloth lined with red serge and red cloth cuffs with 26 brass buttons. The lace was of the 'grande' livery of the king, which was crimson or red with a white chain that edged both sides of a central white strip of lace bearing small crimson or red triangles. This grand lace the royal livery was usually reserved to troops belonging to the king's royal guard. Crozat obviously obtained permission to use it. Waistcoat of red light-weight cloth lined with linen and 36 small brass buttons; breeches of red light-weight cloth lined with linen and with leather pockets; stockings, shirt, cravat and shoes as above. A linen smock issued every second year.

Soldiers had a hat edged with false gold lace; a coat of grey cloth lined with blue serge with blue cloth cuffs and 26 brass buttons; a waistcoat 'as those of the drummers'; a pair of breeches of blue cloth lined with linen and leather pockets. Second and third year's issues 'as those of the drummers'; being smocks, shirts, cravats, stockings and shoes. Gaiters were supposed to have been sent for *sergents*, drummers and soldiers, but did not arrive.

With some exceptions, this dress followed the basic uniform of the Companies franches de la Marine adopted from 1716, the most visible difference being the *sergents'* silver buttons and lace and the soldiers' red waistcoat. The above uniforms were to be worn until about March 1720

32 ADR, Co 1226, État des ouvrages…pour l'habillement [1760].

33 AC, C13A, 4, Habillement pour la Louisiane, 27 July 1716. In this document, headdress is simply called 'hats' would most likely have lace that we have added in the button colour; the colour of cuffs is not given and would have been the colour of the lining; the indication 'as those of the drummers' would indicate red waistcoats for soldiers.

because Crozat had obtained that the 'grand' clothing issue of a coat would last three years (instead of the usual two). The smocks, waistcoat and breeches were to be issued the second and third year with shirts, stockings and shoes yearly, but it was in fact longer. This, excepts for stockings, may have been the only clothing received for troops in Louisiana until June 1721. By then, what the soldiers wore must have been in rags.[34]

The 1721 clothing issued would have been the same as Compagnie des Indes' uniform at Lorient and as described above except for black cravats. White or grey-white coats with blue cuffs and lining were confirmed as worn in Louisiana as were blue waistcoats and breeches. There had been no gaiters in the 1716 shipment, which were esteemed 'very necessary' to save wear of the stockings. At length, they were sent with uniforms by 1724 along with linen smocks. More gaiters arrived in 1728 and 1729 in shipments that included blue waistcoats and blue breeches.[35]

The officer's uniform was the same as the men's as shown by Capitaine de Lauze who had, when he passed away in 1717, a white uniform coat with blue cuffs and brass buttons.[36]

Senegal European Troops

The earliest information on the dress of the French troops in Senegal dates from the Compagnie des Indes administration. From the 1720s, the company's grey-white coat with blue cuffs was the standard uniform. The issue at Lorient to a soldier sailing to Senegal included a coat, a waistcoat, a pair of breeches, a hat, a pair of stockings, two shirts, two cravats, a pair of shoes, a pair of gaiters, a musket with its bayonet, a waist belt and a 'gargoussier' ventral cartridge box. Probate documents of deceased soldiers mention these items. *Sergents* had hats edged with gold. For the trip, a linen waistcoat and a pair of linen breeches were issued.[37]

Once in Senegal, strong linen frocks lined with lighter linen and linen breeches would often been worn as undress; some may have been made at Saint-Louis. In 1756, a new officer, the Chevalier de La Chaise, who was going to Senegal, was advised that the troops' uniform was a 'white coat, blue cuffs, blue waistcoat and breeches' and since the climate there was 'extremely hot' his uniform had to be made with light materials.[38]

34 AC, C13A, 4, Substance et habillement des troupes, 25 December 1715; AC, B, 42, Mémoire due l'habillement [1720]; AG, A1, 2592, Troupes, Postes et Forts in Directors to the Compagnie des Indes, Biloxi, January to June 1721.

35 AC, B, 43, Habillement des 10 Compagnies d'infanterie à la Louisiane, Hôtel de la Compagnie des Indes, Paris, 6 December 1724; État général des dépenses…à la Louisiane, New Orleans, 1724; État général des dépense de la Compagnie des Indes à la Louisiane, 1729; Dumont de Montigny, *Regard sur le monde atlantique*, p.228.

36 Louisiana State Museum, Archives and Manuscripts Division, Probate of deceased *Capitaine* de Lauze, 26 October 1717.

37 AC, D2C, 17, Compagnies detaches au Senegal, 29 May 1727; Lacroix, *Les Français au* Sénégal, pp.93, 107, 114

38 Delcourt, *La France et les établissements français au Sénégal entre 1713 et 1763*, p.242; APL, 1P, 280b, 48, Godeheu to M. Gireux, Lorient, 7 January 1756.

Colours and Standard

Colours

There are no doubts that the European troops of the various French East India companies had colours. Precise information is nevertheless so far very rarely found. Even when it is, matching a unit to a described colour is hypothetical at best. Since about the mid-twentieth century, reconstitutions have often shown a red colour with a white central bar bearing a crowned round shield bearing three gold lilies on blue. Unless this colour can be supported by unquestionable primary sources, it must be considered as totally erroneous.

At the battle of 16 December 1750 near Chettipet, the signal to three nabobs to switch sides was a blue colour with a white cross, recognised as 'the colour of our companies' by a French soldier present in the field. What this meant can be interpreted several ways. For instance, it could mean that were the colours of all European companies or only to some of them. Either way, they were identified as belonging to French European troops.[39]

Although not describing unit colours, the journal of a soldier in Bussy's army did consign in his journal the appearance of the distinctive flags that surmounted the tents of senior officers in the field during February 1754.

Commandant Bussy: a white cornet-type flag with three point bearing three red lilies; the hospital: white field with a blue cross; artillery *Capitaine* Gallard: red field with a white cannon on its carriage at the centre and a white cannonball at its muzzle, white bombs at each corner; infantry grenadier *Capitaine* Gadeville: white field, red cross and a red grenade in each quarter; M. Jainville: white field, red cross and a red lily in each quarter and a white (?) crescent at the centre; Bussy's 'saucar' (banker): white field with a red horse at the centre. The more junior officers 'each had a guidon to mark the emplacement of their marquise' tents.[40]

On 4 November 1754, that same soldier in Bussy's army mentioned that 'the colours were blessed, which were like those of last year. They numbered 13, with three guidons for our horse grenadiers.' Unfortunately, they were not described.[41]

The Indian watercolour depicting French soldiers being reviewed by Great Mughal Shah Allam II in about 1760 shows a rectangular all

Blue colour with a white cross, first half of the eighteenth century. This design may have been used for colours of the Compagnie des Indes troops. At the battle of 16 December 1750 near Chettipet, India, the signal to three nabobs to switch sides was a blue colour with a white cross recognised as 'the colour of our companies' by a French soldier present in the field. It would have been generally similar to this colour carried by the Boulonnois embodied militia. (Du Vivier manuscript. Brunon collection, author's photo)

39 BNF, Ms Français 8971, Relation des principaux événements arrivés aux Indes…, July 1749 to 17 October 1752; BNF, Ms Français 12087, Relation de la victoire remportée sur Nazerzingue…, by an unknown soldier.

40 Depréaux, 'Les uniformes de la Compagnie des Indes…', pp.176-177.

41 Depréaux, 'Les uniformes de la Compagnie des Indes…', p.178.

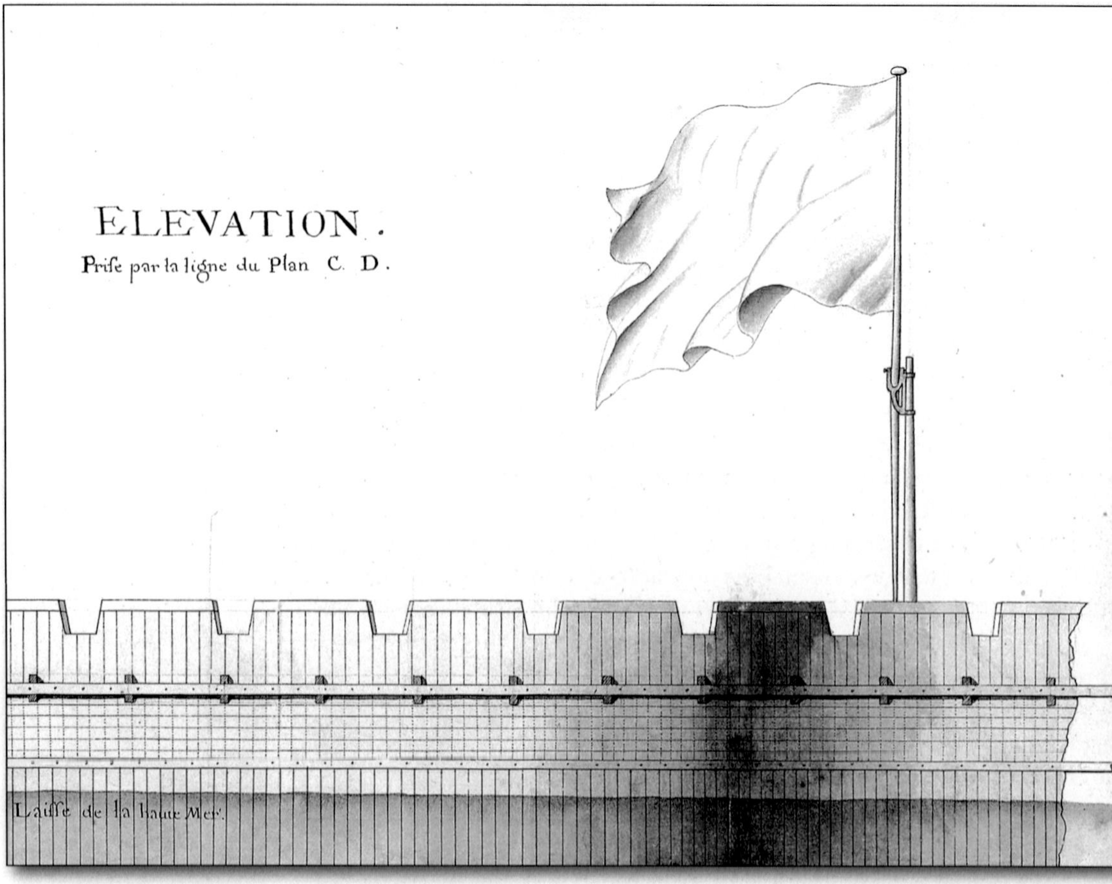

The white standard of France hoisted at the entrance to the Mississippi River, Louisiana, 1723. The battery built there by engineer Le Blond de Latour was at the Gulf Coast. (Archives Nationales Outre-Mer, 04DFC0028A01)

violet colour (without any devises or crosses). Its pointed pole has the scarf tied below the spear emblematic of all colours in the French armed forces; however, its colour appears to be dark red instead of white as in France. This might also represent the cords, in which case they could be in the hues of the colour, but these would appear to be too wide and without its tassels with fringes. It could also be a company colour rather than a unit colour. It is extremely unlikely to be an Indian army colour. These were triangular and coloured red, green and white bearing Asian devises and badges.[42]

Captured colours and flags can be a source for the study of vexillology. In 1836, the British Honourable East India Company turned over all captured colours to the chapel of the Royal Hospital in Chelsea. As well as the presumed older ones being very poorly documented, they were in a terrible conservation state, some with only a few dusty rags remaining when descriptions were attempted in 1841. A few had a white cross typical of eighteenth century French infantry colours, which might be associated with Compagnie des Indes units. Two colours had the white cross with blue quarters, much as the 1750 colour for European companies described above, except for the

42 Irvine, *The Army of the Indian Moghuls*, p.34.

An elephant with a palanquin or 'howdah', mid-eighteenth century. This print after sketches of the Chevalier Gentil shows the elephant partly covered with cloth usually described as red with gold lace and fringes. The triangular flags could be green or white with a gold sun and gold fringes. Gentil was in two parades at Aurengabad in 1753. Print in Langlès' *Monuments anciens et moderne de l'Hindoustan*. (Bibliothèque Nationale de France, Paris)

upper square near the pike being red with a yellow snake thereon, which likely indicates a sepoy unit; the remnants of other colours seemingly much the same. They were said to have been taken at Seringapatam in 1798 or even later from 'French Corps' which seems next to impossible. Their design is typical of the royal army before the French Revolution and of the troops of the Compagnie des Indes in India before 1770. They could have been more likely captured by Indo-British troops during the mid-eighteenth century. Please see the colour plates for our interpretive reconstruction.[43]

Standards

The standard seen over Fort Dauphin in Flacourt's book (see chapter 2) agrees with the August 1664 charter of the Compagnie des Indes orientales. It specified that its ships would 'hoist at their stern the white standard with the arms of France' that would have been the crowned shield with the three gold lilies on a blue field . During the Sun King's reign, the arm of Navarre, gold chains on a red field, were often added. Such a standard 'of the company' was seen on a ship in May 1688 at Pondicherry.[44]

In October 1661, King Louis XIV had ordered that all warships should henceforth hoist a plain white standard. Merchant ships were to have blue

43 W.Y. Carman to author, 4 September 1981. Other Indian colours could be 'plain green, white, red, and white triangle, buff (which might have been white) with a red edge triangle.'

44 Francheville, *Histoire de la Compagnie des Indes…*, p.32; Martin, *Mémoires*, Vol.2 p.546.

flags with a white cross and the royal arms, but there were many variations and exceptions. Thus, the 1719-1770 Compagnie des Indes had the same plain white standard as the king's navy, which was also hoisted in a French overseas territories and well as at all metropolitan seaports.[45]

There were also other standards seen in India during the many great ceremonial parades, see chapter 7.[46]

45 AM, A1, 6, Ordonnance pour les pavilions, 9 October 1661; Chartrand, *Armies and Wars of the Sun King*, Vol.5, p.270 and colour plates.

46 A large triangular flag nicknamed 'Dupleix's standard' measuring 3.1 metres equilateral and dated 1749 is preserved in the Musée de l'Armée in Paris. See Le Diberder, 'Le prix des trous prestigieux. Restauration de la bannière dite pavillon de Dupleix', *Revue des amis du Musée de l'Armée*, No. 84 (1980), pp.33-36.

21

Militias

The organisation of militia was fairly sketchy in all the company's territories except for the Ile de France and Ile de Bourbon. Apart from mustering volunteers in emergencies, a more permanent militia structure does not appear to have been very urgent or even desirable in other territories.

Ile de France and Ile de Bourbon

Although Ile de France had a garrison since its first French settlement in 1721, organising its militia does not seem to have been a priority. Things remained fairly informal until 1735 when the energetic La Bourdonnais arrived at Ile de France on 5 June as Governor-General of the islands. He soon considered its inhabitants to be in a place where 'licentious behaviour and anarchy' reigned and immediately set about to transform and expand the population that indeed went from 172 Europeans and 648 slaves in 1735 to 342 Europeans and 2,612 slaves within five years. La Bourdonnais further organised two companies of militia at Ile de France that may have totalled about 100 men at the most; they were drilled the first Sunday of every month so that they could manoeuvre with the regular troops. They may have numbered about 200 or even 300 with some free Africans in 1748 when the British unsuccessfully attacked Ile de France[1]

The mid-seventeenth century early settlers of Ile de Bourbon were all more or less militiamen since there was no garrison. At length, from 1697, a militia of sorts was organised mainly because of the increasing incursions of escaped slaves who became redoubtable maroons. There were then about 1,600 Europeans and 2,000 Africans, nearly all the latter being slaves from Madagascar and the coast of Africa. The militia was not, at that time, a substantial military organisation; it did however make the men familiar

1 Mahé de La Bourdonnais, 'Mémoire touching les îles de France et de Bourbon' in Pierre Margry (ed.), *Relations et mémoires inédits* (Paris: Challamel aîné, 1867), p.316; H. Bourde de la Rogerie, *Les Bretons aux Iles de France et de Bourbon (Maurice et Réunion) au XVIIe et XVIIIe siècles* (Rennes: Oberthur, 1934), pp.69, 154-155, 160.

with some basic notions of discipline. A company gathered men of Saint-Denis and Sainte-Suzanne while another was at Saint-Paul. On 23 November 1718, Governor de Beauvollier created a militia organisation by ordering all able-bodied settlers from 15 to age 50 in all four administrative quarters of the island to own a flintlock musket, attend drill training as well as perform public works; recalcitrants would be fined. The militia nevertheless proved incapable of repulsing the 1721 pirate raids on the harbours of Saint-Denis and Saint-Paul. At the time, a pirate nicknamed de la Buze even managed to capture briefly the viceroy of Portuguese Goa who had called on the governor of Bourbon on the way to India. Following this embarrassing situation, a regular garrison was posted on the island while the Portuguese sent warships to cruise about Madagascar.[2]

By 1732, the population of Ile de Bourbon was increasing rapidly and consisted of about 2,000 Europeans and 5,500 Africans. The settlers were basically more concerned with agriculture than with seafaring and so the island was rapidly developing as a plantation economy with valuable cash crops of coffee and later sugar. It was during this period that many men on Ile de Bourbon acquired a reputation for their skill at target shooting and exceptional endurance as hunters in the island's mountains.[3]

During his term as Governor-General of the islands, La Bourdonnais addressed the strength and efficiency of the militia. On 21 August 1741, he wrote to the Council of Ile de Bourbon announcing a total reorganisation of the militia 'of the islands' according to the orders given to him by the minister of the Navy Maurepas. This had rather elaborate and unusual measures that divided the militiamen into six classes according to the 'their merits, faculties and especially their zeal' to which one must add their standing and wealth in the islands. All able-bodied men aged from 15 to 60 were obliged to serve in the militia. The various companies were to assemble in their *quartier* (district) every month and have a general muster three times a year. There were penalties and punishments for recalcitrant militiamen.[4]

This was not greeted with unanimous joy in Ile de Bourbon and, by August 1742, its council received a voluminous document signed by a multitude of militiamen asking to be reassigned to another class along with their many opinions about the new organisation. Since the militiamen of Ile de Bourbon formed most of the population of the islands and were also renowned as the most reliable, a proportion of them having become famous for their remarkably good target shooting, the authorities immediately reacted favourably and altered the plan as a result. The number of classes was reduced to four:

2 ADR, Co 6, Sur l'exercise Militaire, 1718 and Ordonnance, 24 September 1719; Georges Azéma, *Histoire de l'Ile de Bourbon* (Paris: Plon, 1862), pp.23-24; Anon., *Histoire abrégée de l'Ile Bourbon ou de La Réunion de puts sa découverte jusqu'en 1880* (Saint-Denis: Gabriel & Gaston Lahuppe, 1880); pp.36-37 Albert Lougnon, *L'Ile de Bourbon pendant la Régence* (Paris: Larose, 1936), pp.85, 208.

3 Henri Cornu, 'Economies et Commandeurs à l'Ile Bourbon au temps de la Compagnie des Indes', *Académie de l'Ile de la Réunion*, Bulletin 1959-60, Vol.19e, p.63.

4 Gennes,*Mémoire pour le sieur de La Bourdonnais*, p.28; ADR, Co, 1231, Extrait d'une lettre de La Bourdonnais au conseil de Bourbon, August 1741.

A settlement at Ile de France, first half of the eighteenth century. The small figure of a European gives some clues as to the aspect of the militiamen. In this case a shirt or plain short waistcoat, breeches and a brimmed hat. Illustration on a manuscript map of Ile de France. (Bibliothèque Nationale de France, Paris)

A plantation or small village at Ile de France, first half of the eighteenth century. Illustration on a manuscript map of Ile de France. The European has a waistcoat, breeches and a somewhat indistinct hat with a brim. The African might have a loincloth. (Bibliothèque Nationale de France, Paris)

1st class: the mounted Gendarmes, 2nd: the Dragoons, 3rd: the *Habitants* (inhabitants) who formed the infantry, and 4th: 'the poor inhabitants, overseers and servants' with a few chosen trusted Africans to help serve the artillery. Each *quartier* had a number of men from each class.

This was satisfactory to most militiamen and, on 20 August 1742, the new organisation was decreed and regulations for weapons, uniforms and equipment were announced for the first three classes.[5]

Gendarmes

The first class was the cavalry Gendarmes, which gathered the wealthiest gentlemen and 'most notable inhabitants', and was patterned after the King's own royal guard Gendarmes in Versailles. They had the first rank in protocol and senior in the militia. Members of this class were to fight mounted or on foot and provide their own good horses, weapons and all have luxurious 'officers' uniforms'. Each gendarme was accompanied by four of his trusted Africans armed with spears, hatchets, scythes, picks and other tools. The Gendarmes had certain privileges such as the right of the line, not being obliged to stand guard and, obviously, were favoured to attend and escort the governor. To become a gendarme trooper was considered prestigious and applications to belong to the corps were considered and seemingly mostly approved by the council.[6]

In late September 1749, a letter to the Superior Council of Ile de Bourbon signed by about two dozen men, who were probably all militia officers, protesting on the privileges granted to the company of Gendarmes in that it set apart the rich from the ordinary inhabitants. Stating that there should be no distinction for all inhabitants, it pointed out that the 'Corps de Gendarmerie' was 'even more useless and only fatigued the poor inhabitant' by making him believe that, because of his poverty, he did not have 'the same rights and prerogatives as the rich.' The Gendarmes, besides having splendid uniforms and horses, were exempt from standing guard and their riding tours of the island could not be compared with real cavalry patrols made by mounted militiamen in cities like Metz and Strasbourg. It concluded that in the future, no one should be exempt from the daily services for the 'security of the island and its inhabitants.' On 1 October, the petition was rejected by the Superior Council pointing out that the exemptions granted to the Gendarmes had been approved by the minister of the Navy and the Compagnie des Indes in France so that the demands were 'contrary to the instructions [given] to the said corps.'[7]

5 ADR, Co, 1231, Declaration des habitants de Bourbon sur les differences classes ou ils désirent entrer, August 1742; ADR, Co, 1232, États des habitants de claque quartier divides en classes, 22 August 1742; ADR, Co, 683, regulation in: Extract des Régistres des deliberations du Conseil d'administration de l'Isle de Bourbon, signed by councillors and La Bourbonnais, 20 August 1742.

6 Crepin, *Mahé de La Bourdonnais*, p.89; ADR, Co, 1233, Requette de Guy Dumesnil, 1742; please see: Michel Hanotaux, *Gendarmes & Chevau-légers de Sa Majesté le Roi* (Paris: Épopée, 2023) for a fine and richly study illustrated of the Gendarmes of the royal guard.

7 ADR, Co, 1234, À Nos seigneurs du Conseil de l'isle de Bourbon and note from council, 1 October 1749.

By the 20 August 1742 regulations, the Gendarmes had a scarlet coat with black velvet cuffs, '28 brandebourgs with tails of gold', gold buttons 'like the brandebourgs', scarlet coat lining, scarlet breeches, beaver felt hat laced with gold set in a saw-tooth pattern and a white plume edging the brim, soft leather gaiters with buckles. They were armed with silver hilted swords, cavalry carbines and pistols, and equipped with buff sword belts edged with gold lace, powder horns with a red silk cord each, Morocco leather 'gargoussier' type cartridge boxes edged with gold lace, buff carbine shoulder belts also holding its bayonet, saddle covered with a crimson velvet seat, scarlet housings edged with a wide and a narrow gold lace. A 1756 document indicates the coat's cuffs colour had changed to superfine blue cloth as well as, possibly, its lining.[8]

Dragoons

The militia dragoons were to serve mounted and on foot. They were the second rank in protocol gathering prosperous men. They provided their own horses and were to be accompanied by two of their trusted Africans armed as above. Each dragoon provided his own uniform. It consisted of a green coat with scarlet cuffs, gilded brass buttons, green breeches, beaver felt hat edged with gold musketeer style lace and leather gaiters with cords. They were armed with the same type of sword as the Gendarmes, a cavalry carbine with its bayonet and pistols, 'gargoussier' of red morocco leather, powder horn with a green cord, saddle with green cloth seat, green housings with a single gold lace.

Habitants

The third class was made up of most men in the islands, neither very rich nor very poor being usually small farmers or artisans. They were to be accompanied by one of their trusted Africans. They also had to provide their own weapons, uniforms and equipment that were much less elaborate than above. The uniform specified consisted of a coat made of blue 'guingan' Indian material having small white squares [checkered] with scarlet cuffs, silver buttons, breeches of the same 'guingan' Indian material as the coat, beaver felt hat edged with gold musketeer style lace. Weapons and equipment consisted of a musket with a sling and a silver-hilted sword like the Gendarmes, a Morocco leather 'gargoussier' and a powder horn with a blue cord.

The fourth class consisted of 'the poor inhabitants, employees and servants.' Africans chosen to assist in the service of artillery were also included. They were not required to have uniforms, and weapons could be issued to them if

---

8 ADR, Co, 1506, Etat des effets…pour l'uniforme de Mssrs. Les officiers et Cadets faisant le service auxdit lieu…1755 et delivré en 1756 – et pour celui de Mssr. Les Gendarmes, St. Denis Ile de Bourbon, 30 June 1757.The effects appear to have been for eight officers and cadets of the Compagnie des Indes troops at Ile de Bourbon that would have had blue uniforms and 58 scarlet clad Gendarmes. Some of the key entries are: eight Beaver hats laced with gold from Paris; 58 id. of half beaver; 72 ells Royal blue 'Camelot'; four ells id. Superfine; four to six id. fine; 58 ells scarlet 'Calmande' superfine; eight gross buttons (rest illegible & torn); 222 ells silk lace of various colours; seven ounces blue thread; eight ounces scarlet thread; seven white [hat] plumes attractive and ample; 116 ells white linen from France.

necessary by the island's governments. A cleric on the way to India described the men of Ile de Bourbon in 1703 as 'wearing nothing else than shirt and pantaloon, in the style of Italian breeches', with a headdress made from a banana tree leaf. They had no shoes or stockings, there being no shoe or stocking makers on the island. The men's 'ordinary' costume was described in 1705 by a Sieur Durot as being 'a shirt, a waistcoat, a coat of taffetas or other light textile. They wear a handkerchief on their head, loosely tied at the back, and a hat, but go out without stocking or shoes, the heat of the country and sand' making their wear difficult. The lack of shoes appears to have much regressed in the following decades.[9]

India

The lodges of the French monopoly companies in India did not have settlement schemes as in other territories in the Indian Ocean islands. There was no vast expanse of uninhabited land; India was a fully populated country and its land was overwhelmingly occupied. The French civilian residents there (and also in Senegal) were mainly employees of the company, merchants or skilled artisans. None of them were especially interested in maintaining a permanent militia structure and it was obviously not considered practical by the local authorities.

Residents could be called to provide some service on special occasions or during periods of threats. This mainly concerned Pondicherry where most lived. In 1740, when the Marathas approached the city, Governor-General Dumas managed to muster up to 1,200 Europeans residents and company employees. When La Bourdonnais arrived at Pondicherry with his fleet in August 1746, Governor-General Dupleix ordered that:

> [A] guard of honour should be formed of Europeans, merchants, officers, soldiers, East Indians, Carnatic sepoys, and others dressed in their best. With this escort, and with flourishes of trumpets, drums, etc., the Governor proceeded to the beach, to await the arrival of M. de la Bourdonnais.[10]

At Chandernagor, a militia was formed from French residents in early 1757 that numbered about 300 men to which were added some 200 sailors from ships stranded in the Hooghly River. Besieged by a greatly superior Indo-British force, the garrison put up a gallant defence from 14 to 23 March when it capitulated. The French civilians in the fort, which also included some 50 women, 'were allowed to go where they pleased'.[11]

At the 1760-1761 siege of Pondicherry, the utterly undiplomatic and abrasive Comte de Lally ordered all European civilians to parade on the

9 Quotations from Albert Lougnon (ed.), *Sous le signe de la tortue* (Paris: Larose, 1958), pp.123-124, 136, 159.

10 H. Castonnet des Fosses, *L'Inde française avant Dupleix* (Paris: Challamel, 1887), p.253; Ananda, *Diary*, Vol.1, p.217.

11 Arthur Broome, *History of the Rise and Progress of the Bengal Army*, p.108.

beach under the city's walls armed and wearing uniforms to make the British believed the regular garrison was huge. The negative reaction of the European civilian population to this order was tremendous. Needless to add that following this incident, the notion of an organised and efficient militia, armed and uniformed, could not be further entertained.[12]

Louisiana

The Louisiana militia was rather peculiar in that it was not really organised until the end of 1729 in the Gulf Coast due to a crisis, 1,100 kilometres north in Illinois, due to increasing settlements. The organisation of each entity mirrored its own social and economic status. One followed the militias of the West Indian plantations and seaborne trade, the other was based on modest farming and trade with indigenous First Nations.

Gulf Coast Volunteers

The eighteenth century Gulf Coast settlements of French Louisiana mainly consisted of the seaports of New Orleans and Mobile. By law, male settlers able to bear arms were liable to militia duty as elsewhere in New France, but a more elaborate organisation was not in place during the first three decades of Gulf Coast Louisiana. Although there were alarms and some fighting with either aboriginal or European opponents, the inhabitant fit to bear arms were not enrolled into a reserve force as other settlers in Canada or in the West Indies. This was probably due to the small population of early Louisiana as well as to the great distances between settlements and, quite possibly, a certain reluctance to be hampered by military obligations. This absence of a permanent militia organisation continued under the rule of monopoly companies including the Compagnie des Indes.

Early accounts nevertheless mention inhabitants being mustered and serving with regular soldiers and being led by regular officers. The first major instance appears to have been when Commandant General (later Governor) Bienville mustered a mixed force of about 166 of the best soldiers he had with 45 volunteers to attack Spanish Pensacola in May 1719, and some volunteers were also present at the defence of Dauphine Island and Mobile as well as the recapture of Pensacola in September of that year. However, Bienville noted did report that the inhabitants entertained 'bad will' about military matters. In 1722-1723, tensions with the Natchez First Nation resulted in some settlers being attached to squads of soldiers in the Natchez area.[13]

12 Fantin-Desodoards (trans.), *Révolutions de l'Inde pendant le dix-huitième siècle ou mémoires de Typoo-Zaeb*, Vol.2, pp.338-339; Voltaire, *Fragments sur* l'Inde, p.122; Hamont, *La fin d'un empire français aux Indes*, pp.255-257.

13 AC, C13A, 5, Bienville to the Navy Council, 20 October 1719; Giraud, *Histoire de la Louisiane française*, Vol.4, pp.292-295. It is interesting to note that, in 1719, a proposal was made to raise in France a six company regiment of militiamen as soldier-artisan settlers for Louisiana that would have worn dark iron grey coats with red cuffs, waistcoat, breeches and stockings, brass buttons, false gold laced hats and black gaiters, but this suggestion was not implemented as per AC, C13C, 1, "Régiment de Milice pour la Louisiane". Another 1719 memoir proposed

When the Natchez warriors attacked and destroyed Fort Rosalie on 28 November 1729, with much of its settlers and garrison being killed, there was no reserve force in Lower Louisiana having a permanent organisation enabling a quick and orderly muster of armed individuals having a certain amount of military knowledge with a chain of command under government authority. An organised militia in Louisiana was now urgently needed, especially in defenceless New Orleans. Governor Périer thus mustered 150 city residents to whom weapons were issued and they were formed into four companies of urban militia. The officers appointed were selected among Superior Council members for *capitaines* and senior employees of the Compagnie des Indes for subalterns. The militia's immediate duty was to stand guard at New Orleans while what troops and volunteers Governor Périer could gather would go up to Natchez.[14]

At about this time was also organised a small group of African slaves belonging to the Compagnie des Indes, who had answered a call to volunteer in the defence of New Orleans on the promise of freedom if they served bravely. They were armed with edged weapons. The panicked population of the capital feared an attack by warriors as part of a general uprising. So did Governor Périer who had heard rumours that the Chaouacha, a small community southwest of the city, conspired to join the uprising. He therefore tasked the African volunteers to eliminate the Chaouachas, which they soon did with discretion and efficiency. This rather questionable and desperate pre-emptive action nevertheless seemed to have shown that Governor Périer was in a fighting stance and would attack rather than wait for an assault, something that must have given heart to the population of New Orleans as well as to allied or at least neutral First Nations.[15]

Militia Organised and Deployed

Shortly thereafter, an elite 'Company of Cadets', here meaning gentlemen, was formed by Governor Périer out of the well-off employees of the Compagnie des Indes in New Orleans. It mirrored the elite uniformed companies of city 'Milice Bourgeoise' in France and the West Indies. It was considered New Orlean's 'colonel's company' as the senior militia company and numbered about 40 men. Its elite status caused some grumbling in other companies. One of the unit's members, Marc-Antoine Caillot, recalled they outfitted themselves with a brilliant uniform of scarlet and white (see colour plate). It is noteworthy to mention that uniforms were procured by these militiamen almost as soon as the Louisiana Militia was first organised on the Gulf Coast. The other militiamen did not have uniforms as yet, but while their officers

that the Compagnie des Indes was obliged to organise a militia and issue each man a musket with its bayonet and a cartridge box as well as attend drill every Sunday, as per AC, C13A, 5. Louisiane 1719, proposed article No. 14, but nothing was done.

14 AC, C13A, 12, Périer to Minister, 18 May 1730; AC, C13C, 1, memoir on 'La colonie de la Louisiane', c. 1730. Périer was actually titled commandant general at the time and governor from 1730. There is no precise date as to the organisation of the four militia companies, but it would certainly have been during the first weeks of December 1729.

15 McConnell, *Negro Troops of antebellum Louisiana*, pp.6-7; AC, C13A, 12, Périer to Le Pelletier, 18 March 1730.

also wore their civilian clothing, they also wore gilded gorgets, the badge of commissioned rank in most armies. They also had to have swords, an obligation for officers because they had gentlemen's status.[16]

Now that a distinct force of militia with its own commanders had been organised, its legal framework was needed. Although Gulf Coast Louisiana was administratively a component of New France, it was in practice all but independent from the authority of its Governor-General at far away Quebec City. It was not only a question of distance and time, the lower part of Louisiana was a very different type of colony to Canada. It had much more in common with the plantation society of the French West Indies with which it had frequent links. Thus, administrators in New Orleans took a Caribbean model: the royal ordinance concerning the militia of the French windward island issued since 1 September 1727. On 18 February 1730, the Superior Council at New Orleans registered this royal ordinance thus making it the militia law of Louisiana. Its main dispositions were as follows.

The militia was to be organised in companies, each led by a *capitaine*, a *lieutenant* and an *enseigne* for infantry and a *cornet* for cavalry, the *capitaines* having royal commissions and subalterns holding letters of appointment. *Capitaines* were exempted from paying taxes for 12 slaves, *lieutenants* eight slaves and *enseignes* and *cornets* six slaves. The militia staff consisted of *majors* and *aide-majors*. All inhabitants fit to bear arms were to be registered as militiamen on pain of fines. When serving with regular troops, the militia units marched after the regular troops and were at the left of the line. Militia officers were subordinate to regular officers except those who had been regular *capitaines* who had authority over regular subalterns. Local governors could issue instructions to improve the militia's service and cancel officer's commissions if necessary. Militia officers were obliged to apply all government orders, be they royal or local, that regarded the 'discipline and police of the inhabitants'. All governors and military commandants, but also civil administrators were enjoined to apply the ordinance to be obeyed by all regular and militia officers and inhabitants of the colony. On the whole, it was estimated there were about 400 to 500 men able to bear arms.[17]

The notion of a general uprising by the First Nations hostile to the French was partly vindicated in early January 1730 when, north of Natchez, the Yazoo (or Yazou) warriors overcame the French settlement there including its Fort St Pierre killing its small garrison and any settlers they found. Meanwhile,

16 Marc-Antoine Caillot, *A Company Man. The Remarkable French-Atlantic Voyage of a Clerk of the Company of the Indies: A Memoir by Marc-Antoine Caillot* (edited with introduction by Erin M. Greewald, trans. Teri F. Chalmers) (New-Orleans: Historic New Orleans Collection, 2013), pp.130-132. The original is Memoir Ms 2005, Sieur Caillot, 'Relation du voyage de Louisiane…' preserved at the Historic New Orleans Collection. Diderot and d'Alembert, *Encyclopédie ou dictionnaire raisonné des sciences* (Reprint of the first edition of 1751-1780, Stuttgart: Frommann, 1966), tome XVI, p.442; Garsault, *L'Art du taillieur*, p.19; Suzanne & André Gousse, *Costume in New France from 1740 to 1760: A Visual Dictionary* (Chambly: La Fleur de Lyse, 1997), p.36 for *volant*, p.33 for *surtout* and p.24 for *justaucorps*.

17 Library and Archives Canada, MG 18, H24, Ordonnance concernant les Milices des Isles du Vent, 1 October 1727, copy registered on 18 February 1730 by the Louisiana Superior Council at New Orleans. AC, C13C, 1, A memoir on Louisiana, undated but 1730. This estimate did not include the Illinois and may not have included Mobile and its area.

Governor Périer had basic fortifications built around New Orleans that must have kept many militiamen and their slaves busy, but they certainly felt more secure as these works progressed. Militiamen would have also certainly stood guard over these ramparts. Much closer to New Orleans was the German Coast, home to about 170 German settlers, some of whom were killed while defending themselves against hostile warriors. The community's leader was Charles Frederick D'Arensbourg, who had been an officer in the Swedish army, and he mobilised the settlers into a militia corps.[18]

By mid-January 1730, the Chevalier de Loubois, an experienced officer, led a mixed force of about 200 regulars, volunteers of the New Orleans and German Coast militia and also 15 free Africans that had been issued with weapons including muskets. There were also more Africans, most likely slaves, tasked with pioneer and logistics duties. The expedition was joined by about 600 allied warriors, mostly Choctaws. In February, it attacked the Natchez at their fortified village, from which they eventually fled. It was remarked that the armed Africans 'had fought bravely and if weapons could have been issued to all other [Africans], they could have taken the place of soldiers [who 'served very badly at this siege'], and we could have overcome the besieged.' Their prowess in battle was not forgotten. The New Orleans and German Coast militiamen, commanded by Messers D'Arembourg and de Laye, also did very well. They willingly did all the work and all else 'that we had ordered them to do.' Of the militiamen, Governor Périer remarked that they would become very good soldiers as soon as they had been trained.[19]

Reinforcements later arrived from France and, in January 1731, another expedition against the Natchez that included regular troops, cadets from the Compagnie des Indes employees, 150 militiamen under *Capitaine* de Bénac, commander of the militia, some African volunteers and about 150 allied warriors that besieged and destroyed another Natchez fortified village at the end of the month. There were more skirmishes thereafter and the French post at Natchitoches was attacked in October 1731, but the garrison included armed settlers/militiamen resulting in the withdrawal of the attackers by 5 November. This last engagement basically was the end of the hostilities.[20]

---

18 AC, D2C, 50, muster of troops in New Orleans, 1730; Reihhart Kondert, 'Les Allemands en Louisiane de 1721 à 1732', *Revue d'histoire de l'Amérique française*, Vol.33, No. 1 (June 1979), pp.58–59, 61. The notion of a wide-ranging plot for a general uprising is discussed in Arnaud Balvay, La *Révolte des Natchez* (Paris: Félin, 2008).

19 Pierre-François-Xavier de Charlevoix, *Histoire et description générale de la Nouvelle-France* (Paris: Giffart, 1744), Vol.4, pp.264-269; McConnell, *Negro Troops*, p.7; Baillardel and Prioult, *Le Chevalier de Prade*l, p.72; Fort Rosalie (or Natchez) was rebuilt as an earthwork with a strong garrison of three officers and 90 regulars of the Compagnie des Indes troops.

20 Charlevoix, *Histoire et description*, Vol.4, pp.293; Lous R. Nardini, *My Historic Natchitoches, Louisiana, and its environment* (Natchitoches: Sel-Published, 1963), pp.44-46, 49-50. Nardini confuses militiamen with regular soldiers. The commander mentioned he could only arm 16 men, who may have been inhabitants. For the full story of the Gulf Coast Militia, please see: René Chartrand, 'The French Louisiana Gulf Coast Militia 1729-1769', *MC&H*, Vol.73, No. 3 (Fall 2019), pp.197-212.

Illinois or Upper Louisiana Militia

In the eighteenth century, New France was made up Canada, Isle Royale and Louisiana. Upper Louisiana, commonly called 'Les Illinois', was settled mainly by Canadians who ventured to that area from the early eighteenth century. Until 1717, it was administratively part of Canada and was then transferred to be the upper part of Louisiana. It was not a plantation-based society; its settlers were, much as in Canada, more concerned with trade with the First Nations and with family farming. In 1723, there were about 340 settlers in the pioneer villages of Kaskaskia, Cahokia and Fort de Chartres. The commandant of the garrison at the fort was a de-facto lieutenant-governor with a local Provincial Council established in 1716. The militia was officially created from 1723 at Kaskaskia when a company was organised there under the authority of the Illinois Provincial Council. Its organisation was based on the Canadian militia, since most of the settlers in Illinois would have been militiamen in Canada.[21]

On 3 April 1669, Louis XIV ordered Governor-General Courcelles to 'divide' his subjects in Canada into companies 'with regard for their proximity, and, after having divided them in this way, to select captains, lieutenants and ensigns to command them . . . to issue orders that they assemble once a month to practise handling weapons.' This was an obligation for all men able to bear arms from 16 to 60 years of age. Care was to be taken, the king added, that the militiamen 'always be well armed and always have the powder, lead and fuses necessary to use their weapons when needed.' The majority of the Canadian population lived on their own farms so that the militia was organised in conjunction with the local village's parish. Apart from military concern, a local Canadian militia company could be called upon to organise public works, make censuses, see to the application of certain regulations such as those for fire prevention or land management. The *capitaine* was generally a successful and popular local personality who was relatively well educated as usually were the other officers. They had no pay, but did have some tax exemptions. They had no uniforms and needed none; many of the militiamen who lived in the countryside were renowned for their good target shooting with their hunting muskets, which much resembled trade muskets for the indigenous First Nations.[22]

A minority were young men from farms who went off to trade and paddle canoes in the far-off wilderness travelling to the very edges of the known world to Europeans in North America, beyond the Great Lakes and westward on the Great Plains via rivers such as the Missouri, becoming *coureurs des bois* and *voyageurs* for several months or years or for life. As

---

21 Margaret Kimball Brown and Lawrie Cena Dean, *The French Colony in the Mid-Mississippi Valley* (Carbondale, IL: American Kestrel Books, 1995), p.18; Gregory M. Franzwa, *The Story of Old St. Genevieve* (Patrice Press: St. Louis, 1967), p.42-43. The Canadian Militia was organised from 1669 following instructions from King Louis XIV.

22 AC, C11A, Vol.125, Louis XIV to Courcelles, 3 April 1669; Brown and Dean, *The French Colony in the Mid-Mississippi Valley*, pp.11, 18; André Gousse, 'Le temps des capitaines de milice', *Cahiers de la Seigneurie de Chambly*, No. 42 (September 2018), pp.6-18; René Chartrand, *Canadian Military Heritage Vol.1 1000-1754* (Montréal: Art-Global & Dept. of National Defence, 1993), pp.73-75, 90-91

early as 1681, it was estimated that some 500 to 800 young men in Canada had vanished into the western wilderness. Their close relations living within indigenous communities made them outstanding masters of wilderness warfare by mixing indigenous tactics with European organisation; they were nevertheless militiamen and some of them would volunteer to become part of raiding parties. This was therefore the type of militia that was organised in the Illinois Country with more companies added as time passed and the population rose. By 1731, there were some 400 settlers in Illinois and rising rapidly. To these could be added many dozens, perhaps even more, wilderness traders who did not write reports or appear in censuses. Nevertheless, some of them appear to have been fighting shoulder to shoulder with the First Nations' warriors against Villasur and his Spaniards.[23]

The Compagnie des Indes stewardship of Louisiana ended from July 1731 in favour of the royal government.

23 Louis Armand de Lom d'Arce baron de La Hontan, *Voyages du Baron de La Hontan dans l'Amérique septentrionale* (Amsterdam: L'Honoré, 1705), Vol.1, pp.134, 171-173, 257, 347, 370; L. Le Jeune, *Dictionnaire général…du Canada* (Ottawa: Université d'Ottawa, 1931) Vol.1, pp.442-443; Georges-Hébert Germain, *Les Coureurs des bois* (Montréal: Libre-Expression, 2003), p.59 and also well illustrated with notable and accurate costume illustrations by the late authority and artist Francis Back.

Conclusions

The number of troops of the several East India companies show a tremendous evolution from a few hundred men in the seventeenth century to a multiethnic and multicultural army from the 1740s. This type of information is rather scarce before the first quarter of the eighteenth century. The numbers presented below cannot be hyper-precise, but they do reveal important trends, notably because of the increasingly high proportion of non-European soldiers in the service of the company from the 1740s.

During the 1720s, the number of soldiers standing guard at Lorient and overseas became somewhat clearer. In round numbers, it was: 1,500 Europeans, 250 Indians and Africans. Total: 1,750.[1]

Numbers increased substantially during the 1740s and this was largely due to increasing military activities in India. The Indian topasses were now considerably outnumbered by the sepoys while African *Caffres* arrived at Pondicherry: 1,550 Europeans, 5,300 Indians and Africans. Total: 6,750.[2]

A decade later, in the mid-1750s, many more Europeans had been sent to India while the numbers of sepoy had more than doubled by 1755-1756: 4,280 Europeans, 11,600 Indians and Africans. Total: 15,880.[3]

The ratio of Europeans compared to Indians and Africans was much higher in the 1720s. Six out of seven soldiers were European. By the 1740s, the ratio was inverted with, basically, up to four or five Indian and African soldiers to one European. With several thousand European recruits arriving in India in the early 1750s, the ratio then became about one European to three Indian and African soldiers.[4]

From the 1740s, when only India is considered, the Indian and African *Caffre* soldiers overwhelmed the French soldiers there at ratios of eight or

1 1720s – Europeans: Louisiana 425; India 375; Senegal 150; Iles de France 450; Lorient 100. Indians (topasses only): 150; Africans in Senegal: 100.

2 1740s – Europeans: India 600; Senegal 150; Iles de France & Bourbon 500; Lorient 300. Indians: 4,800; African *Caffres* in India: 400; Africans in Senegal: 100.

3 1755-1756 – Europeans: India 3,400; Senegal 280; Iles de France & Bourbon 300; Lorient 300. Indians: 11,000 (sepoys); African *Caffres* in India: 350; Africans in Senegal: 250.

4 If one adds 300 to 500 Pions (armed constabulary) in India, the totals come to over 2,000 in the 1720s, 7,000 in the 1740s and 16,000 in the 1750s.

nine to one, which shows an absolute trust and confidence by the French governors Dumas and Dupleix in their non-European troops. The French thus appear to be the first of the European East India companies to undertake large-scale recruitment and training of numerous sepoy contingents to the same level of European armament and training as French soldiers.

In effect, a multi-ethnic force featuring a large majority of Asians was created. Its successes again the huge Indian princely armies from 1746 showed geo-strategist Dupleix that relatively modest-sized Indo-French formations could lead to considerable influence in India and even direct control of a substantial part of it. Its main tool would be the valorous and European trained sepoys with a core of French soldiers and commanders. For the Compagnie des Indes, revenues from those territories ensured that the expanding Indo-French army would have the means to honour its expenses and turn in a good profit. The company's shareholders should have been delighted, but in the short term, the dividends were disappointing and the enthusiasm for more overseas ventures was rather low in mid-eighteenth century France.

Although not even listed in published registers of the French metropolitan army, the nearly 7,000 troops of the Compagnie des Indes in the 1740s had risen to some 16,000 men in the mid-1750s. This total, compared to some 157,347 of the royal metropolitan army in 1756-1757 'not including the Militia and the Invalids' amounted to about one soldier of the Compagnie des Indes for 10 or 11 royal army soldiers. Up to then, the company's army was not a negligible factor, but could it be sustained?[5]

The answer is no. As recounted above in a litany of regrettable strategic steps such as abandoning the Deccan and Bengal, the company's army could only regress from lack of a sufficient financial base from lost land revenues. As defeats compounded in the final years, desertion became endemic; historians noted mostly the French deserters, but obviously great masses of sepoys had also vanished by late 1760. Sepoys were the essential factor; the numerous might of the company's army. Their departure meant the end of French India.

The arrival of French royal troops in India during 1758 did not improve matters. Apart from serious command flaws and tensions between metropolitan and the company's troops, the Régiments de Lorraine and Lally could not be said to have been awe-inspiring examples of soldierly discipline and steady valour in the field while weakened by widespread desertion. The company's European soldiers were not much better when brigaded with metropolitan troops, but otherwise usually proved resilient even when increasingly faced with overwhelming odds. British accounts are the best sources in these aspects.

5 TNA, WO 93/2, Memorial of the Force of France by Land and the Service on which it is employed in the Year 1757. Adding the royal (embodied) militia and invalids put the army at 197,000 men. We have used this more realistic assessment of the actual strength of the French army by a French spy (the original document is in French and translated) for the British. Printed French registers had unrealistic figures even before the war such as 395,382 in the 1748 *État général des troupes de France*, p.216 and 441,758 in the 1753 *État général des troupes françoises*, p.334.

'La Belle d'Inde' – Madame Catherine Grand, later Princess de Talleyrand, 1783. This superb portrait by Élizabeth Vigée-Lebrun depicts, next to Dupleix, possibly the best known person from French India in metropolitan France, then and now. Catherine Noël Verlée (1762-1834) was born in India, her father being a Compagnie des Indes harbourmaster at Chandernagor in Bengal. After a first marriage, she arrived in Paris in 1782. Gifted with great beauty and wit, she was an immediate social and fashion business success. In 1802, she married Charles-Maurice de Talleyrand, the outstanding diplomat and politician of the Napoleonic era. The merciless Paris wits nicknamed her 'La Belle d'Inde', a play on words because, in France, 'dinde' means the fowl turkey. (Metropolitan Museum of Art, New York)

By the later 1750s, the French troops in India were clearly outnumbered by the arrival of British royal regiments joining the Honourable East India Company's European infantry regiments and artillery companies. The British in India had employed modest numbers of European and topas soldiers since the seventeenth century. Undoubtedly inspired by the mid-eighteenth century French example regarding an imperial dream of dominating India, the British enlisted large numbers of sepoy 'native infantry' battalions from the mid-1750s. Contrary to France, the emphasis with increased overseas ventures was popular in Great Britain, which saw its progress on the world's oceans and far-distant shores.[6]

Lack of naval support from France was dramatic. D'Aché proved as inept at sea as Lally on land in his reluctance to engage the British navy's squadrons or support land operations. However, was he given the tools to 'do the job' with only one royal ship-of-line, the rest of his squadron being large Compagnie des Indes merchant ships armed for war? These were very good ships, but they were not warships. British naval commanders and sailors were all of the Royal Navy serving in purpose-built warships and they eventually outnumbered the French gaining total control of the Indian coastline. With that, French India was doomed.

6 TNA, WO 379/1, Distribution of His Majesty's Land Forces (by year); TNA, WO 380/16, Notes on regiments: 39th (Aldercron's) Foot, 12 companies (936 NCOs & privates) to India 1754-1758; 79th (Draper's) Foot, 12 companies (1,322 NCOs & privates) to India 1759-1760; 84th (Coote's) Foot (900 NCOs & privates) to India 1759; 96th (Monson's) Foot, 9 companies (990 NCOs & privates) to India 1761, Randolph Jones, 'Portuguese Soldiers in Seventeenth Century Ceylon: their dress, weapons, and flags', *Arquebusier*, Vol.26, No. 1 (2002); Capt. Williams, *An Historical Account of the Rise and Progress of the Bengal Native Infantry, from its first formation in 1757, to 1796* (London: Murray, 1817), pp.3-6; W.Y. Carman, *Indian Army Uniforms: Infantry* (London: Morgan-Grampian, 1969), pp.96, 130, 161. When adding the Royal Artillery detachments, the Honourable East India Company's troops, the number of Europeans was about 7,500 with possibly 20,000 sepoys by 1760-1761.

Elsewhere, with the 1756 declaration of the Seven Years War, many decades of neglect of the once powerful French navy and army now took its toll. The last remnants of France as the pre-eminent European and world power built up by the Sun King Louis XIV were shattered in the laissez faire attitudes during the reign of Louis XV. The army was revealed to be outclassed in nearly all aspects except bravery when crushed at Rossbach in 1757 by Prussia's King Frederick II, still hailed as a near-genius tactician. Henceforth, the outstandingly efficient Prussian army was the influential military model. The French navy was practically helpless from 1756 with only 33 ships-of-the-line to confront Britain's 88 ships-of-the-line. Following various defeats and the disastrous November 1759 battle off Quiberon won by Sir Edward Hawke against a hapless Comte de Conflans, the French Navy could only align 14 ships-of-the-line (three in the Indian Ocean) against the Royal Navy's 111 (15 in the Indian Ocean). In America, Québec and Guadeloupe had been taken in 1759, the 'Year of Victories' for the British, with Senegal and Gorée falling the previous year, but not without a fight by the company's tiny garrisons.[7]

Amidst all these disasters, the talented, efficient and wily Duc de Choiseul cumulated France's ministries of war, foreign affairs and the navy from January 1761. While he energetically set about reorganising the army and rebuilding the navy during the following decade, he was also emblematic of the widespread apathy of the French public for ambitious overseas ventures. In a report to the king, he wrote that Corsica would be more useful to France than Canada. The influential Voltaire felt the same way. Vast overseas territories were no longer desired; Great Britain could have them. The national focus was henceforth mainly aimed at European affairs.[8]

For all that, the Compagnie de Indes and its troops and navy did not entirely disappear in 1761 because commercial interests in Asia were still important following the return of Pondicherry and a few lodges in India to France after the war. The last garrisons at Lorient and India were reorganised into royal troops in 1772-1773.

So ended the last remnants of the French East India companies' amazing military forces. They had a remarkable and amazing heritage made by its French, Indian and African soldiers, in almost unthinkable battlefield successes that had far-reaching consequences in Asia that led to European domination.

7 Dull, *The French Navy in the Seven Year's War*, pp.161-162, 263-265, 275-277.

8 Jean-Pierre Guiicciardi (ed.), *Mémoires du Duc de Choiseul* (Paris: Mercure de France, 1987), p.210.

Colour Plate Commentaries

(i) Fusilier, Garrisons of Lorient, Louisiana and Senegal, 1720s – early 1730s

The company's troops in France, Louisiana and Senegal were issued with the same basic uniform, which was almost identical to that worn by French marines. It consisted of a grey-white cloth coat with blue cuffs and lining, a blue waistcoat, blue breeches and stockings, 36 large brass buttons for the coat, 36 small brass buttons for the waistcoat and a hat edged with false gold lace. Cravats could be black or white. In the warm climates of Louisiana and Senegal, linen gaiters were issued as well as linen smocks and breeches. The soldier's sword was identical to the ones used by metropolitan army and marines; the company bought military infantry muskets at Saint-Étienne that would have been the Model 1717. The leather cover of 'gargoussier' ventral cartridge box probably had a plain cover flap. A powder horn with brass fittings was slung over the left shoulder by a narrow buff belt. The waist belt was of buff leather with a brass buckle.

(ii) Fusilier, Compagnie des Indes troops, India, Ile de France and Ile de Bourbon, mid-1720s to mid-1730s

The usual uniform of troops in India and the French Indian Ocean islands of Ile de France and Ile de Bourbon appears to have been red coats with blue cuffs although there were exceptions with surplus lemon yellow material being made into uniforms at Pondicherry in 1721 and blue coats with red cuffs for soldiers posted at Mahé in 1728. On the whole, red appears to have been predominant in India and the islands until the Compagnie des Indes ordered blue 'guigam' in 1737. Buttons were of brass and the hat lace yellow.

(iii) Company of Gentlemen Cadets, New Orleans Militia, Louisiana, December 1729

This rather privileged company gathering the well-off employees of the Compagnie des Indes was the only one that procured a uniform for itself when the militia was organised from November 1729 following the Natchez uprising. This uniform is the earliest known for a militia unit, not only in Louisiana, but in all of New France. It consisted of a scarlet *volant* type coat, a white waistcoat, white breeches and white silk stockings, a hat edged with silver lace upon which was also a white cockade. The buttons were most likely of white metal, probably silver. The rather mysterious *volant* was a simpler coat than the usual *justaucorps* coat. The *Encyclopedie* defined the *volant* as type of *surtout* coat that was lightweight with fewer pleats and partially lined. *L'Art du tailleur* considered the *surtout* was like a *justaucorps*, but with buttons going down from the neck no further than the waist with only three buttons at the skirts' back slit. It further described the *volant* as 'a kind of *justaucorps*' that '1…has no buttonholes on the sleeves; 2, no pocket flaps nor pockets; 3, it overlaps in the centre back; 4, it sometimes has a collar with one button and buttonhole…' Although the government's arsenal issued arms and equipment, there was a shortage of weapons. The cadets might have been armed with Model 1717 infantry muskets or more luxurious brass-mounted privately owned muskets as well as wear their own swords. Although this unit was a somewhat Bourgeois militia unit, many of its member took part in the campaigns against the Natchez in 1730-1731 and the Chickasaws in 1736.

(iv) Sepoy Fusilier, Compagnie des Indes troops, Coastal India, late 1740s.

While most sepoys in French service were seemingly not uniformed, some were. The earliest attempt appears to have been at Pondicherry sometime in the later 1740s when authorities felt they sepoys have some uniform dress so that they could be easily identified. The issue consisted of a blue 'gilet' (a short waistcoat-like short jacket) with red cuffs, the standard hues of the French troops in Asia at the time. Their clothing was otherwise the white linen garments worn by Indian men in general. These uniformed sepoys would have been armed, like other sepoys in the French service, with Model 1728 musket with bayonets and their own Indian Talwar type sabres and Katar style daggers. Their accoutrements would have been similar to their French comrades, the 'gargoussier' cartridge box on the waist sword belt and the powder horn with its narrow buff sling. Some, or perhaps all, of the sepoys that garrisoned Pondicherry during the failed British siege of 1748, may have worn these jackets. However, due to the rather stingy officials who charged the sepoys more than what the jackets were worth, they rightly refused to wear another issue. When deductions were made fairly, sepoys were pleased to wear uniforms.

(v) Fusilier, European Companies, Compagnie des Indes troops, Coastal India, circa 1750-1761

From May 1737, the basic uniform for troops in India was officially condoned by the Compagnie des Indes as being made of Indian 'guigam' light material dyed blue with red serge cuffs. The coats had brass buttons and were not lined. Waistcoats do not seem to have been issued; they are not mentioned. Blue 'guigam' breeches, linen shirts, cravats, shoes and gaiters, hats edged with yellow or false gold lace. From the late 1740s, red collars were added and the coat skirts were turned back while cravats could also be black. The 'giberne' cartridge box with its buff leather shoulder belt gradually replaced the one worn on the waist belt. The Model 1728 musket was probably the most seen although some of the company's 1751 contract model, nearly identical except for brass furnishings might have reached India by the mid-1750s. The figure shows a fusilier on campaign in the field with open coat on a warm day.

(vi) Sepoy Fusilier, Compagnie des Indes troops. Nellore District, India, circa 1750-1755

Of the uniformed sepoys in French service, some 1,200 of them divided into 12 companies stationed in the Nellore District had remarkably varied and highly colourful European style uniform jackets, each company having its own distinctive hues. This plate shows one of the three companies wearing yellow jackets, its facings being red. We show the buttons as cloth covered in the facing colour. The remainder of their dress was Indian-style and usually of white linen or cotton. Several styles might be worn and the type of turban shown is the then increasingly popular style with a rigid frame within.

(vii) *Enseigne* with colour, European Companies, Compagnie des Indes troops, India, circa 1750

At the defeat of Nasir Jang's army near Chettipet 16 December 1750, a French soldier described the colour 'of our companies' as blue with a white cross. Until now, a contemporary primary source had seemingly not been found describing the colour of the Compagnie des Indes' European infantry in India or elsewhere. It is likely this was the colour model for all European infantry in the company's service. The *enseigne* wears the officers' uniform for troops in India and at the Ile de France and Ile de Bourbon, a dark blue coat with scarlet cuffs and gilded buttons, blue waistcoat edged with gold lace, blue breeches, white gaiters, gilded gorget and gold-laced hat.

(viii) *Enseigne* with colour, Sepoy Companies, Compagnie des Indes troops, India, circa 1750

Indian troops could have the typical Mughal style triangular flags, but records also mention colours with a white cross and blue quarters except for the upper left one being red with a yellow snake, this last said to be typical of sepoy colours. The design was otherwise very typical of French colours. Most sepoys wore Indian costume, including their officers who would have had a more luxurious version. There was no officially prescribed uniform as such and all aspects of the dress, weapons and equipment of sepoy officers could vary greatly.

(ix) Artilleryman, Bussy's Deccan Army, Compagnie des Indes troops, India, April 1751

The various French East India companies always employed artillery specialists as cadres for serving guns in its ships and at its overseas territories. Artillerymen grouped into distinct companies only appeared in India during the 1740s as circumstances dictated. They most likely wore the company's standard blue coat with red cuffs for all its troops in Pondicherry, but actual descriptions have only been found for the gunners of Bussy's army in the Deccan. Our figure shows the blue coat with red cuffs issued at Hyderabad in April 1751. However, for the July 1751 issue at Aurengabad, they had red coats and changed again to green coats June 1753. This variety was typical in Bussy's army as its clothing depended on what allied princes could supply.

(x) *Caffre* fusilier, Bussy's Deccan Army, Compagnie des Indes troops, India, July 1751

Many hundreds of African *Caffre* warriors, by reputation very brave and merciless, became soldiers for the company in India during the 1740s and 1750s. They were trained, armed and issued clothing by La Bourdonnais who brought them to India in 1746. Their appearance seems to have been unrecorded until 32 *Caffres* were attached to Bussy's army that went into the Deccan in 1751 were described. Their uniform issued at Aurengabad in July consisted of a red coat with green cuffs and lapels, red breeches, red caps with green turban and a red fleur-de-lis thereon.

(xi) Grenadier, Company of Grenadiers à cheval, Bussy's Deccan Army, Compagnie des Indes troops, India, November 1754

This unit was most likely an upgrade of the dragoons of Bussy's army to the prestigious title of Grenadiers à cheval (Horse Grenadiers). Only the royal guard in France had a unit of Grenadiers à cheval, none were amongst the line cavalry, nor the dragoon regiments. As dragoons in 1753, the unit had red coats in 1751, green coats and fur-trimmed caps (see colour illustration of a plate by Rousselot) in 1753, but as Grenadiers à cheval, they were seen on 4 November 1754 wearing blue coats with red cuffs and lapels trimmed with yellow brass buttons, with tricorns hats as headdress. The dragoon-type leather gaiters worn in France could easily have been made in India and we show those – they could have small buckles or cords to fasten their sides. Weapons would have consisted of either the infantry Model1728 musket or the 1751 Compagnie des Indes grenadier musket, cavalry/naval pistols ,and sabres that could have been those for mounted troops with two branches or infantry grenadier's sabres. In effect, whatever was available in India. That would also be true for saddlery. This unit in India had distinguished services and was amongst the last to capitulate at Gingee in 1761.

(xii) Fusilier, Law de Lauriston's Compagnie des Indes corps in north-central India, circa 1759-1761

This plate is an interpretive reconstruction of the figures of French soldiers seen in an Indian painting showing them being reviewed by Great Mughal Shah Alam II, possibly in 1760. While details are vague, the French-style coat is shown as completely red. No facing colour, no collar, no cuffs and no turned back skirts are shown, nor any buttons for the enlisted men. These probably were red cloth-covered buttons as hooks and eyes seem much less likely. The breeches and stockings are shown as very dark blue. Black tricorns without edging lace. The dark brown accoutrements were very likely made in India. The cartridge box with a plain cover is suspended by a brown shoulder belt shown slung over the right shoulder (rather than the left as universally worn). This would likely be because no swords are shown for the enlisted men (but are shown for officers). This Indian-made uniform may have been taken into wear from about April 1759 when the corps served with the Mughal army until January 1761.

Appendix I

Soldier's Clothing Documents 1746-1751

Material necessary to make a soldier's uniform at Lorient, 9 July 1746
For a coat:
1 ell 3/4 white cloth, 2 ells 1/2 blue serge for lining, 3 dozen large brass buttons, 1/6 ell of blue cloth for the cuffs.
For a waistcoat and pair of breeches:
3 ells of blue tricot cloth, 2 ells of raw linen for lining the waistcoat and breches, 3 dozen small brass buttons.[1]

Sale of goods, Lorient, 13 June 1749
1 white cloth soldier's coat with blue cuffs, 1 pair of blue cloth breeches, 2 pairs of blue wool stockings.[2]

Jean-François Lebenne, invalid soldier, deceased at the hospital of Ile de France, 30 July 1749.
A 'Epinasse' coat with red cuffs and gold buttons, a red coat with blue cuffs, a wig, a hat, a 'guingam' waistcoat and breeches, two pairs of new shoes from India.[3]

The red coat belonging to this veteran soldier may have dated from the 1720s or 1730s while the 'Epinasse' and 'guingam' items would have been blue dating from the 1740s.

Clothing of *Sergent* Jean-Baptiste Mery, commanding the troops [detached] on Rodrigue Island, deceased on that island, 28 August 1751.
This document reveals an unusually high number of shirts, stockings, caps and breeches. It may indicate that the *sergent*'s lodging was also used to store extra clothing for the detachment on remote Rodrigues Island.

1 APL, 1P, 4, f 36, Façon d'habit de Soldat, 9 July 1746.
2 APL, 1P, 271, bundle 8 to 10, piece 55.
3 APL, 1P, 271, bundle 4 to 7, piece 92.

Sword with silver hilt and its belt, a gold hat lace, a silver hat lace, a used hat, a wool cap, white brandebourg lace, 5 pairs of shoes, 5 white cravats, an old coat, a waistcoat of stripped 'guingam', 25 white shirts […], 3 pairs of blue breeches, 1 pair id. of stripped 'guingam', 2 blue coats, 12 pairs of white stockings, 5 drawers of red 'guingam', id. of Gondelour, 4 blue shirts, 20 white [presumably night or forage] caps, 6 pairs of blue stockings.[4]

4 APL, 1P, 271b, bundle 8 to 10, piece 48.

Appendix II

Celebration at the Palace of the Government of India, Pondicherry, 9 October 1752

Pomp and circumstance certainly were massive and popular with Indian princes. As seen from the description below, such events could also be given in grand style by Governor General Dupleix during the peak of the Compagnie des Indes' power and influence.[1]

On 9 October [1752], the birth of the Duc de Bourgogne was celebrated with much magnificence. Work to prepare a fireworks [spectacle] representing the temple of fidelity had been going on in the last three months; an order in council [called] for a general illumination of the city. The previous day, all the officers and their ladies had been invited on behalf of Mr. Dupleix to attend the Te Deum, then at the diner and a ball from three in the afternoon. The festivities began at the sound of the clock's bell [followed by those of the] Jesuits, the Capucins and of the foreign missions that did not stop until the end of the Te Deum, and at the sound of the Negara, or Indian war music, which is a privilege of the governors of Pondicherry due to their quality as nabobs and monseldar. It consists of a dozen players of hautbois and trumpets that are very loud, accompanied by copper tam-tams and kettledrums of enormous size...

At five in the evening, M. and Mme. Dupleix went to the citadel's church, proceeded by sepoys on foot and mounted, elephants, peons, dressed Caffres, and chouquedars with their silver rods, and accompanied by 24 horse guards. It can be said that this march had airs of grandeur... There is no sovereign in India that marches with more splendour... The Te Deum was sung to the sound of the city's cannons and from the [ships in the] harbour. All then went to the new government palace in the citadel to see the fireworks that faced the back of this building on the main square.

---

1 BNF, Ms Français 8971, Recueil de pièces sur l'Inde, Unsigned 'Relation des principaux événements arrives aux Indes dans la province de Carnate et le long de la côte Coromandel enter les françois et les Anglais depuis le mois de Juillet 1749. Jusqu'au 17 Octobre 1752...'

It is impossible to imagine anything so beautiful [as this building] which is so well decorated in this country, it surprises all who see it. It is built in the Italian taste, with columns all around, which are necessary for more coolness. No one would believe these columns to be [an imitation] of marble, when seeing their whiteness and polish; everything is done with infinite taste, and ornamented with very well executed figures [statues], the apartments are large and well ventilated, the floors and the ceilings are all different, some being made with the finest woods and others with porcelain tiles; gold, silver and wall paintings are everywhere.'

Quantities of refreshments were offered while waiting for nighttime to see the fireworks, which were well executed; there were many emblems and mottos regarding the government, the citadel with the private houses being also well illuminated. At about eight, everyone went to the old government house, which is where M. Dupleix resides until the new one, that will cost no less then 200,000 'pagodes', is finished. M. Dupleix opened the ball [by dancing] with Mme. Dupleix; it can be said that this assembly, [was] made up of over 50 ladies magnificently dressed and covered with jewels, especially Mme. Dupleix and her daughter. All the men too were also superbly dressed, suffocating in the heat under the weight of the richest laces and textiles.

The death of Nazer jang had many inheritors in Pondicherry; there reigns since then an air of opulence with almost everyone. At ten, M. and Mme. Dupleix and almost everyone sat at a table with 50 covers for the ladies who were served by the gentlemen; there was another table of 60 covers for them and one of 20 at which was Rajaset, son of Sandersact, and the Indian nobles who were served [with food to their] taste. The other [guests] were served with as much delicacies and profusion the most exquisite and rare wines [to be found] in India. Toasts to the health of the king and of the royal family and that of M. and Mme. Dupleix that were drunk to the sound of the citadel's and the ships' cannons. We rose from the tables at midnight and the ball continued; many came with masks, and it ended at seven in the morning. This festivity cost 25,000 rupees to the company.

Appendix III

Compagnies Franches de la Marine Detachments in Land Operations

As mentioned in the text of this book and seen in some of its illustrations, the French king's navy occasionally detached some of its marines to support the troops of the French East India companies. Usually known as Compagnies franches de la Marine (Independent companies of the navy), they were considered elite royal troops forming a very large corps that had two components: 1) up to a hundred companies based in France that provided marines for warships; 2) various numbers of companies serving as regular garrisons in the several French territories in America. In 1691, the corps had 10,300 officers and men based in France and 2,538 in America for a total of 12,738; in 1755, there were 10,300 officers and men in France and 8,216 in America whose total came to 18,516.[1]

The detachments encountered in India, Africa and Louisiana belonged to the establishment of shipboard marines based in France.

1687-1689 – 12 companies in Siam (Thailand).
1689-1693 – Detachments served as the garrison of Pondicherry amounting to two companies in 1693 when captured by the Dutch.
1699-c.1701 – Detachments served at Pondicherry.
1699-1704 – Detachment served as the garrison at Biloxi, Louisiana.
1701-c.1702 – Detachment at the post of Assini on the Guinea Coast of Africa; repulsed a Dutch attack in November 1702. Assini abandoned in 1705.
1719 – Detachment of shipboard marines participated in the defence of Dauphine Island, Louisiana and the capture of Pensacola, Spanish Florida.

1 René Chartrand, *Compagnies franches de la Marine* (Versailles: La Compagnie d'Élite/Épopées, 2022), p. 24. All variations in the establishments of all companies of all French territories in Amrica are also given from 1674 to 1769.

1748 – *Capitaine* Le Marchand, *Lieutenant* Le Vayer (both wounded) and at least 100 marines served at the 1748 defence of Pondicherry.[2]

1751 – A detachment of 100 marines joined Bussy's corps at Aurangabad.

1752 – A company of 80 men of the navy was attached to Law's army besieging Trichinopoly during the autumn of 1752. They were specifically to serve the artillery.[3]

1758-1761 – the Chevalier de Poüet organised a temporary battalion of marines in Pondicherry recruited from sick or wounded sailors that had not been able to board ships before their departure as well as enlisting various adventurers in the city. The battalion, which was sometimes called 'Volontaires de la Marine', was in many actions such as the failed 1758 siege of Madras, the 1760 Battle of Wandewash and the 1760-1761 siege of Pondicherry. The marines in the garrison of Pondicherry mustered 295 men including 17 officers on 15 January 1761.[4]

2 'Relation du siege de Pondichéry', *Gazette*, 1749, pp. 244, 248.

3 BNF, Ms Français, 8971, 'Rclation dcs principaux événements arrivés aux Indes dans la province du Carnate…de juillet 1749. Jusqu'au 17 Octobre 1752.'

4 One of these was René Madec who had served previously in the regular army in France and was soon promoted to sergeant as he could train the sailors in military drill and manoeuvres. René Madec, pp. 69-70; Duval d'Eprémesnil, *Mémoire,* pp. 308, 317, 342; 'State of the French Forces…at Pondicherry', 15 January 1761, *The Daily Advertiser*, London, 22 July 1761.

Appendix IV

Shipments of Troops from Lorient 1756-1757 and 1760

The abstracts of documents below are from the Archives du Port de Lorient. Troops were shipped mostly to India during 1756 and 1757, notably officers and enlisted men of the Régiments de Lorraine and Lally along with artillery detachments from the royal army officers. Many only reached India in 1758. These records concern some 93 officers and 1,712 men went to the East Indies. Of these, two officers and 223 enlisted men belonged to the troops of the Compagnie des Indes. The metropolitan unit shipped in 1760 was the Régiment de Cambrésis that remained at Ile de France until 1763.

These Lorient records concerned only troops that sailed on ships belonging to the Compagnie des Indes' fleet. We are extremely grateful to Geneviève Beauchêne, archivist and paleographer, for transcribing and communicating these unpublished documents to our attention.[1]

28 janvier 1756. Départ [departure] du vaisseau *Duc de Béthune* pour le Sénégal et l'Ile de France.
Passager [passenger] pour l'Ile de France:
un lieutenant d'artillerie, M. Jabre Dréau

13 mars 1756. Départ du vaisseau *Duc d'Orléans* pour l'Inde.
Passagers [passengers]:
troupes de la Compagnie [des Indes], 90 hommes [men]

13 mars 1756. Départ du vaisseau *Duc de Berry* pour l'inde.
Passagers:
troupes de la Compagnie [des Indes], 69 hommes

13 mars 1756. Départ du vaisseau *Seychelles* pour l'Inde.
Passagers:

1 APL, Armements au long cours. Rôles des bureaux, 2P9, III (1756), 2P10, I (1757), 2P10, IV (1760).

un capitaine des *troupes de la C[ompagn]ie [des Indes]*, M. de Vervaine et son domestique noir [black servant], Valentin
troupes de la Compagnie [des Indes]: 64 hommes

The reinforcements of metropolitan royal troops to India left France in two divisions. The first division was led by *Maréchal de Camp* de Soupire consisting of the ships *Comte de Provence, Duc de Bourgogne, Saint-Louis, Silphide, la Reine* and *Compagnie des Indes*, plus a merchant ship from Nantes. It sailed from Lorient on 28-30 December 1756 and arrived at Pondicherry on 8 September 1757. The second division led by *Chef d'Escadree* d'Aché with the Comte de Lally sailed from France on 3 May 1757 consisting of the *Zodiaque* (a 74-gun royal warship), the *Bien-Aimé, Vengeur, Centaure, Dauphin, Condé, Moras, Diligente, Penelope, Pacifique, Saint-Luc* and *Émeraude*. It sailed from Brest on 3 May 1757 and arrived at Pondicherry on 28 April 1758.[2]

28 décembre 1756. Départ du vaisseau *Comte de Provence* [58 guns] pour l'Inde.
Passagers:
M. de Soupire, Maréchal de Camp
M. le chevalier d'Estrée. Aide de Camp
M. Lauson, Aide de Camp
un secrétaire et un dessinateur géographe
Lorraine Infanterie:
M. de Carrière, commandant de bataillon
M. Guillermain, capitaine de grenadiers
M. de Saint Amant, capitaine d'Infanterie
M. de Mouzière, capitaine aide-major
un lieutenant et un lieutenant en second de grenadiers
un lieutenant et un lieutenant en second d'infanterie
C[ompagn]ie de grenadiers de Guillermain, 60. hommes
C[ompagn]ie de saint Amant, 57 hommes
détachement de la C[ompagn]ie de Tasservile, 13 hommes
Corps Royal d'artillerie et du génie:
M. de l'Isle Salin, capitaine commandant
M. de Fontenay, capitaine
un lieutenant et un lieutenant en second
détachement du Bataillon de La Motte, 25 hommes
détachement du bataillon de Soucy, 25 hommes
[11 officers, 180 men]

28 décembre 1756. Départ du vaisseau *Duc de Bourgogne* [54 guns] pour l'Inde.
Passagers:
M. Luchev, commissaire des guerres [commissariat]

2 Saint-Yves, 'L'expédition de l'Inde. Les Instructions du gouvernement de Louis XV au comte d'Aché', pp. 294-300. Brest was the assembly point of the 2nd division and some ships first sailed in March and April 1757 from Lorient to join it.

Lorraine Infanterie:
M. de Verdière, colonel
M. de Tillecourt, second commandant de bataillon
M. de Brucaud, capitaine aide-major
cinq capitaines d'infanterie
cinq lieutenants
cing lieutenants en second
C[ompagn]ie de Sécatic, 56 hommes
C[ompagn]ie d'Hatoze, 56 hommes
C[ompagn]ie de Ducrest, 56 hommes
C[ompagn]ie de Trudaine, 56 hommes
C[ompagn]ie de Tasserville, 17 hommes
[18 officers, 241 men]

30 décembre 1756. Départ du vaisseau *Saint-Louis* [54 guns] pour l'Inde.
Passagers:
Lorraine infanterie:
cinq capitaines d'infanterie
cinq lieutenants d'infanterie
cinq lieutenants en second d'infanterie
C[ompagn]ie de Tondut, 57 hommes
C[ompagn]ie de Ginestoux, 55 hommes
C[ompagn]ie du Gouyon, 56 hommes
C[ompagn]ie de Saverny, 57 hommes
détachement de la C[ompagn]ie de Folnay, 25 hommes
[15 officers, 250 men]

30 décembre 1756. Départ du vaisseau *la Reine* [20 guns] pour l'Inde.
Passagers:
Lorraine Infanterie:
deux capitaines d'infanterie
deux lieutenants d'infanterie
deux lieutenants en second d'infanterie
C[ompagn]ie de Ganay, 57 hommes
C[ompagn]ie de Poignat, 56 hommes
détachement de la C[ompagn]ie de Tasserville, 17 hommes
[6 officers, 130 men]

30 décembre 1756. Départ de la frégate *la Sylphide* [30 guns] pour l'Inde.
Passagers:
Lorraine Infanterie:
un capitaine de grenadiers
un capitaine d'infanterie
un lieutenant de grenadiers
un lieutenant d'infanterie
un lieutenant en second de grenadiers
un lieutenant en second d'infanterie
C[ompagn]ie de grenadiers, 59 hommes

C[ompagn]ie de Viart, 51 hommes
détachement de la C[ompagn]ie de Folnay, 14 hommes
[6 officiers, 124 hommes]

30 décembre 1756. Départ du vaisseau *Compagnie des Indes* [20 guns] pour l'Inde.
Passagers:
Lorraine infanterie:
deux capitaines d'infanterie
deux lieutenants d'infanterie
deux lieutenants en second d'infanterie
C[ompagn]ie de Chaffoy, 57 hommes
C[ompagn]ie de Montauger, 56 hommes
détachement de la C[ompagn]ie de Folnay, 17 hommes
[6 officiers, 130 hommes]
6 mars 1757. Départ du vaisseau *Le Vengeur* [54 guns] pour les iles de France et de Bourbon.
Passagers pour l'Inde:
M. de Lally, Brigadier
M. Boussiev, ingénieur géographe
Lally Infanterie:
M. de Morvez, capitaine
M. de Beaumont, capitaine
M. Freagh, capitaine
M. Magauby, capitaine
M. de Romainville, lieutenant
M. Collaghan, lieutenant
M. Macarty, lieutenant
M. Darcy, lieutenant
M. Fussey, lieutenant
C[ompagn]ie de Morvez, 55 hommes
C[ompagn]ie de Freagh, 55 hommes
Corps Royal d'Artillerie et du Génie:
M. de Précourt, major
M. Derveux, capitaine
M. de Triaire, lieutenant
Détachement: 30 men
[14 officers, 140 men]

6 mars 1757. Départ du vaisseau *Dauphin* pour l'Inde.
Passagers:
un lieutenant des *troupes de la C[ompagn]ie* [des Indes]
Lally infanterie:
un capitaine
quatre lieutenants
C[ompagn]ie de Groghigan, 54 hommes
C[ompagn]ie de Nagli, 52 hommes
[5 officers, 106 men]

8 avril 1757. Départ du vaisseau *Le Bien Aimé* [58 guns] pour l'Inde.
Passagers:
M. Dubois, intendant
M. Guyard, secrétaire
Lally Infanterie:
M. Kennedy, colonel
M. de Breteuil, colonel
M. de Crillon, colonel
M. d'Heguerty, capitaine de grenadiers,
M. Sheldon, capitaine,
M. de Blumkest, capitaine
M. Reveru, capitaine
M. Kelly, lieutenant
M. Launew, lieutenant
M. Meoghev, chirurgien major [surgeon major]
C[ompagn]ie de grenadiers d'Heguerty, 48 hommes
C[ompagn]ie de Sheldon, 53 hommes
Corps Royal d'Artillerie et du Génie
Détachement du bataillon de Soucy, 23 hommes
Détachement du bataillon de la Motte, 20 hommes
Troupes de la Compagnie [des Indes]:
Détachement de la C[ompagn]ie des dragons de La Tour, 44 hommes
[10 officiers, 188 hommes]

Apprehending a British attack on Ile de France, the single battalion Régiment de Cambrésis of the royal army sailed for the island on 26-27 March 1760 arriving on 11-12 July. Its sick soldiers were sent to recuperate at Ile de Bourbon in late August. The British did not attack the islands and the regiment went back to France in 1763.[3]

26 mars 1760. Départ du vaisseau *Comte d'Artois* pour l'Ile de France.
Passagers:
Cambrésis Infanterie:
Chevalier de La Galissonière, colonel
[with staff officers and seven companies, 334 officers and men]

26 mars 1760. Départ du vaisseau *Berryer* pour l'Ile de France.
Passagers:
Cambrésis Infanterie:
[four companies, 171 officers and men]

27 mars 1760. Départ du vaisseau *Massiac* pour l'Ile de France.
Passagers:
Cambrésis Infanterie:
[six companies]

---

3 ADR, Co, 202, Directeurs de la Compagnie des Indes to Conseil de l'Ile de France to Conseil de Bourbon, 14 February 1760; Co, 204, same to same, 14 March 1760; Co, 519, Conseil de l'Ile de France to Conseil de l'Ile de Bourbon, 29 August 1760.

Select Annotated Bibliography

Main Manuscript Primary Sources

Archives Nationales Outre-Mer, France, Colonies (AC), series A (orders), B (ministerial correspondence), C1 (Far East), C2 (India), C11A (Canada), C13 A and C13C (Louisiana), D2C (Troop records), E (Personnel Records), F1A (Finances), F3 (Moreau de Saint-Méry Collection), Dépot des Fortifications des Colonies (DFC)

Archives Nationales, France, Marine, series A1 (orders), B3 (campaigns), G (armaments).

Service historique des Armées, France, Archives de la Guerre (AG), series A1.

Archives du port de Lorient (APL), series 1P.

Archives départementales de la Réunion (ADR), series Co.

Archives du port de Rochefort (AR), series 1E.

Bibliothèque Nationale de France (BNF). As given in footnotes.

The National Archives, UK, (TNA), War Office (WO).

Printed Primary Sources

Anon., *Procès-verbaux des délibérations du Conseil souverain de la Compagnie des Indes* (Pondichéry: Société de l'histoire de l'Inde française, 1911-1914) 3 volumes. Essential.

Depréaux, Albert, 'Les uniformes de l'Armée de la Compagnie des Indes d'après un journal inédit de la campagne du Décan 1751-1755', *Revue de l'histoire des colonies françaises*, No. 54, Vol. XIV (1926). Oustanding source on material culture, uniforms in particular, from a contemporary journal. Also quite useful on the Deccan campaigns.

Dumont de Montigny, Jean-François-Benjamin, *Mémoires historiques sur la Louisiane* (Paris: Bauche, 1753) and *Regard sur le monde atlantique* (Québec: Septentrion, 2008) which is the publication of his full manuscript memoirs with drawings and maps persevered at the Newberry Library (Chicago), Ayer MS 257.

Dupleix, Joseph François, *Réponse du sieur Dupleix à la lettre du sieur Godeheu* (Paris: Cellot, 1763). Letter with many supporting documents written by Dupleix when he sailed back to France in 1754-1755 refuting the charges by Godeheu. Essential.

Duval d'Eprémesnil, Jean-Jacques, *Mémoire à consulter et consultation, pour le sieur Duval Dumanoir, & M. Duval d'Espremenil, avocat du roi au Châtelet ; héritiers du feû sieur Duval de Leyrit, gouverneur de Pondichéry. Avec les lettres que les sieurs Duval de Leyrit & de Lally se sont écrites dans l'Inde, pour servir de pièces justificatives* (Paris: Lambert, 1766). A memoir by the son of the deceased governor of Pondicherry supported by a voluminous correspondence between Lally, Governor Duval de Leyrit and the council of Pondicherry. It was damning for Lally who was unfortunate that the memoir's author was, besides being the late governor's son, one of the best lawyers and prosecutors in France at the Châtelet high court. Essential.

Gentil, Jean-Baptise-Joseph, *Mémoires sur l'Indoustan, ou empire Mongol* (Paris: Petit, 1822). Gentil (1726-1799) served in India in the Compagnie des Indes's troops from 1752, notably with Bussy, and with Indian princes from 1761 until 1775. He was a keen observer of military and political events in these essential and descriptive memoirs.

Gennes, Pierre de, *Mémoire pour le sieur de La Bourdonnais, avec pièces justificatives* (Paris: Delaguette, 1750). Essential.

Hill, S.C. (ed.), *Bengal in 1756-1757. A Selection off Public and Private Papers Dealing with the Affairs of the British in Bengal during the Reign of Siraj-Uddaula* (London: Government of India and John Murray, 1905), Vol.3. Valuable selection of primary sources.

Law de Lauriston, Jean (ed. Alfred Martineau), *Mémoire sur quelques affaires de l'Empire mogol, 1756-1761* (Paris: Société de l'Histoire des Colonies françaises, 1913). One of the most important documents on the French in India divided in three parts, the first is on the 1757-1761 campaigns of Lauriston's column, the second describes in detail its travels and the third has a glossary.

Martineau, Alfred (ed.), *Correspondance du conseil supérieur de Pondichéry et de la Compagnie*, (Pondicherry: Société de l'histoire de l'Inde française, 1920-1930) 6 volumes. Essential.

Martineau, Alfred (ed.), *Mémoires de Francois Martin. fondateur de Pondichéry 1665-1696*. Paris: Société de l'Histoire des colonies françaises, 1931), 2 volumes. Essential.

Orme, Robert, *A History of the Military Transactions of the British Nation in Indostan from MDCCXLV [1745]* (London: Nourse, 1775) Vol. 1 and 2 (1778). A most valuable source because Orme (1728-1801) was in India at the time of the events related and became the historian of the Honourable East India Company.

Vinson, Julien (trans. and ed.), *Les Français dans l'inde : Le journal d'Anandarangappoullé 1736-1748* (Paris: Leroux, 1894). More extensive version published in English as: *The Private Diary of Ananda Ranga Pillai, Dubas to Joseph François Dupleix*, translated from the Tamil by J. F. Price and K. Rangachari, from 1736 to 1761 in 12 volumes, (Madras: Government Press, 1904-1928). Valuable source from the perspective of the translator to Dupleix. Nevertheless to be considered with caution when he often reports rumours. The entries concerning events he actually saw are reliable.[1]

Voltaire, *Fragments sur l'Inde, sur le Général Lalli, et sur le comte de Morangiés* (Unknown Publisher, 1773). This great French philosopher, historian and polemist wrote this remarkably incisive account of the last years of French India; he obviously met some of the veterans and had access to certain state papers. The book has no publisher nor city given, but it may have been Geneva. Voltaire had his French residence close to that city in Switzerland where he would abscond if irate French authorities sought to arrest and jail him.

1 An example is the murder at Gingee of officer Charles Saubinet which he reports on 1 February 1756. Yet Saubinet signs a letter on 18 September 1756 and is clearly alive the following years as late as 1765.

Printed Studies

Boudriot, Jean *Compagnie des Indes 1720-1770* (Paris: Self-Published, 1983). Although essentially a study concerning the company's ships and navy, it also delves upon the various areas where it had lodges. Very well illustrated with a wealth the author's line drawings, contemporary prints and reproduced documents. Highly recommended.

Chassaigne, Marc, *Le Comte de Lally* (Paris: Société de l'histoire des colonies françaises, 1938), p. 33. Essential.

Fortescue, J.W., *A History of the British Army* (London: Macmillan, 1899), Vol. 2 and Vol. 3 (1902). Essential classics offering much data as well as a British perspective.

Giraud, Marcel, *Histoire de la Louisiane française* (Paris: Presses universitaires de France, 1966), Vol. 3 and 4. Especially useful for the Compagnie des Indes period of governing Louisiana.

Hanotaux, Gabriel, and Martneau, Alfred (eds), *Histoire des colonies françaises et de l'expansion de la France dans le Monde*, (Paris: Plon, 1932), Vol. 5 and 6. Very useful general outlooks.

Haudrère, Philipe *La compagnie française des Indes au XVIIIe siècle 1719-1795* (Paris: Librarie de l'Inde, 1989), four volumes. Essential and outstanding work. Covers all aspects of the company's holdings in India and everywhere else; some parts and appendices on military organisation, lifestyle the troops, list of officers, etc.

Irvine, William, *The Army of the Indian Moghuls: Its Organisation and Administration* (London: Luzac, 1903). Essential work, very detailed and taken from Indian and European primary sources.

Hill, S.C., *Three Frenchmen in Bengal or the Commercial Ruin of the French Settlements in 1757* (London: Longmans, Green, 1903). Good source on the French in Bengal.

Kaepelin, Paul, *La Compagnie des Indes orientales et François Martin* (Paris: Challamel, 1908). Detailed in business transactions, less in military matters, but essential being very well sourced.

Malleson, G.B., *History of the French In India* (London: Allen, 1893). Still a useful British classic, partly outdated by the more recent publications, notably by Kaepelin, Martineau and Haudrère's studies. Malleson's other works (cited in our chapters) are also recommended.

Martineau, Alfred, *Dupleix et l'Inde française 1749-1754* (Paris: Société d'éditions géographiques, maritimes et coloniale, 1922-1928), 4 volumes; *Bussy et l'Inde française 1720-1785* (Paris: Société de l'histoire des colonies française, 1935); *Les origines de Mahé de Malabar* (Paris: Champion, 1917). Absolutely essential.

Nicolle, David, *Mughul India 1505-1761* (London: Osprey, MAA 263, 1993).

Richmond, Herbert W., *The Navy in the War of 1739-48* (Cambridge: University Press, 1920), Vol. 3.

Rodger, N.A.M., *The Command of the Sea* (London: Penguin/National Maritime Museum, 2004). Essential for the Royal Navy.

Stone, George Cameron, *A Glossary of the Construction, Decoration and Use of Arms and Armour in all countries and at all times* (Portland, Maine, USA: Southworth Press, 1934). Still the most comprehensive work on the topic. Especially notable for Asian weapons.

Vaissière, P. de, *Dupleix* (Paris: Plon, 1931).

From Reason to Revolution – Warfare 1721-1815

http://www.helion.co.uk/series/from-reason-to-revolution-1721-1815.php

The 'From Reason to Revolution' series covers the period of military history 1721–1815, an era in which fortress-based strategy and linear battles gave way to the nation-in-arms and the beginnings of total war.

This era saw the evolution and growth of light troops of all arms, and of increasingly flexible command systems to cope with the growing armies fielded by nations able to mobilise far greater proportions of their manpower than ever before. Many of these developments were fired by the great political upheavals of the era, with revolutions in America and France bringing about social change which in turn fed back into the military sphere as whole nations readied themselves for war. Only in the closing years of the period, as the reactionary powers began to regain the upper hand, did a military synthesis of the best of the old and the new become possible.

The series will examine the military and naval history of the period in a greater degree of detail than has hitherto been attempted, and has a very wide brief, with the intention of covering all aspects from the battles, campaigns, logistics, and tactics, to the personalities, armies, uniforms, and equipment.

Submissions

The publishers would be pleased to receive submissions for this series. Please email reasontorevolution@ helion.co.uk, or write to Helion & Company Limited, Unit 8 Amherst Business Centre, Budbrooke Road, Warwick, CV34 5WE.

Titles

1 *Lobositz to Leuthen: Horace St Paul and the Campaigns of the Austrian Army in the Seven Years War 1756-57* (Neil Cogswell)
2 *Glories to Useless Heroism: The Seven Years War in North America from the French journals of Comte Maurés de Malartic, 1755-1760* (William Raffle (ed.))
3 *Reminiscences 1808-1815 Under Wellington: The Peninsular and Waterloo Memoirs of William Hay* (Andrew Bamford (ed.))
4 *Far Distant Ships: The Royal Navy and the Blockade of Brest 1793-1815* (Quintin Barry)
5 *Godoy's Army: Spanish Regiments and Uniforms from the Estado Militar of 1800* (Charles Esdaile and Alan Perry)
6 *On Gladsmuir Shall the Battle Be! The Battle of Prestonpans 1745* (Arran Johnston)
7 *The French Army of the Orient 1798-1801: Napoleon's Beloved 'Egyptians'* (Yves Martin)
8 *The Autobiography, or Narrative of a Soldier: The Peninsular War Memoirs of William Brown of the 45th Foot* (Steve Brown (ed.))
9 Recollections *from the Ranks: Three Russian Soldiers' Autobiographies from the Napoleonic Wars* (Darrin Boland)
10 *By Fire and Bayonet: Grey's West Indies Campaign of 1794* (Steve Brown)
11 *Olmütz to Torgau: Horace St Paul and the Campaigns of the Austrian Army in the Seven Years War 1758-60* (Neil Cogswell)
12 *Murat's Army: The Army of the Kingdom of Naples 1806-1815* (Digby Smith)
13 *The Veteran or 40 Years' Service in the British Army: The Scurrilous Recollections of Paymaster John Harley 47th Foot – 1798-1838* (Gareth Glover (ed.))
14 *Narrative of the Eventful Life of Thomas Jackson: Militiaman and Coldstream Sergeant, 1803-15* (Eamonn O'Keeffe (ed.))
15 *For Orange and the States: The Army of the Dutch Republic 1713-1772 Part I: Infantry* (Marc Geerdinck-Schaftenaar)
16 *Men Who Are Determined to be Free: The American Assault on Stony Point, 15 July 1779* (David C. Bonk)
17 *Next to Wellington: General Sir George Murray: The Story of a Scottish Soldier and Statesman, Wellington's Quartermaster General* (John Harding-Edgar)
18 *Between Scylla and Charybdis: The Army of Elector Friedrich August of Saxony 1733-1763 Part I: Staff and Cavalry* (Marco Pagan)
19 *The Secret Expedition: The Anglo-Russian Invasion of Holland 1799* (Geert van Uythoven)
20 *'We Are Accustomed to do our Duty': German Auxiliaries with the British Army 1793-95* (Paul Demet)
21 *With the Guards in Flanders: The Diary of Captain Roger Morris 1793-95* (Peter Harington (ed.))

22 *The British Army in Egypt 1801: An Underrated Army Comes of Age* (Carole Divall)
23 *Better is the Proud Plaid: The Clothing, Weapons, and Accoutrements of the Jacobites in the '45* (Jenn Scott)
24 *The Lilies and the Thistle: French Troops in the Jacobite '45* (Andrew Bamford)
25 *A Light Infantryman With Wellington: The Letters of Captain George Ulrich Barlow 52nd and 69th Foot 1808-15* (Gareth Glover (ed.))
26 *Swiss Regiments in the Service of France 1798-1815: Uniforms, Organisation, Campaigns* (Stephen Ede-Borrett)
27 *For Orange and the States! The Army of the Dutch Republic 1713-1772: Part II: Cavalry and Specialist Troops* (Marc Geerdinck-Schaftenaar)
28 *Fashioning Regulation, Regulating Fashion: Uniforms and Dress of the British Army 1800-1815 Volume I* (Ben Townsend)
29 *Riflemen: The History of the 5th Battalion 60th (Royal American) Regiment, 1797-1818* (Robert Griffith)
30 *The Key to Lisbon: The Third French Invasion of Portugal, 1810-11* (Kenton White)
31 *Command and Leadership: Proceedings of the 2018 Helion & Company 'From Reason to Revolution' Conference* (Andrew Bamford (ed.))
32 *Waterloo After the Glory: Hospital Sketches and Reports on the Wounded After the Battle* (Michael Crumplin and Gareth Glover)
33 *Fluxes, Fevers, and Fighting Men: War and Disease in Ancien Regime Europe 1648-1789* (Pádraig Lenihan)
34 *'They Were Good Soldiers': African-Americans Serving in the Continental Army, 1775-1783* (John U. Rees)
35 *A Redcoat in America: The Diaries of Lieutenant William Bamford, 1757-1765 and 1776* (John B. Hattendorf (ed.))
36 *Between Scylla and Charybdis: The Army of Friedrich August II of Saxony, 1733-1763: Part II: Infantry and Artillery* (Marco Pagan)
37 *Québec Under Siege: French Eye-Witness Accounts from the Campaign of 1759* (Charles A. Mayhood (ed.))
38 *King George's Hangman: Henry Hawley and the Battle of Falkirk 1746* (Jonathan D. Oates)
39 *Zweybrücken in Command: The Reichsarmee in the Campaign of 1758* (Neil Cogswell)
40 *So Bloody a Day: The 16th Light Dragoons in the Waterloo Campaign* (David J. Blackmore)
41 *Northern Tars in Southern Waters: The Russian Fleet in the Mediterranean 1806-1810* (Vladimir Bogdanovich Bronevskiy / Darrin Boland)
42 *Royal Navy Officers of the Seven Years War: A Biographical Dictionary of Commissioned Officers 1748-1763* (Cy Harrison)
43 *All at Sea: Naval Support for the British Army During the American Revolutionary War* (John Dillon)
44 *Glory is Fleeting: New Scholarship on the Napoleonic Wars* (Andrew Bamford (ed.))
45 *Fashioning Regulation, Regulating Fashion: Uniforms and Dress of the British Army 1800-1815 Vol. II* (Ben Townsend)
46 *Revenge in the Name of Honour: The Royal Navy's Quest for Vengeance in the Single Ship Actions of the War of 1812* (Nicholas James Kaizer)
47 *They Fought With Extraordinary Bravery: The III German (Saxon) Army Corps in the Southern Netherlands 1814* (Geert van Uythoven)
48 *The Danish Army of the Napoleonic Wars 1801-1814, Organisation, Uniforms & Equipment: Volume 1: High Command, Line and Light Infantry* (David Wilson)
49 *Neither Up Nor Down: The British Army and the Flanders Campaign 1793-1895* (Phillip Ball)
50 *Guerra Fantástica: The Portuguese Army and the Seven Years War* (António Barrento)
51 *From Across the Sea: North Americans in Nelson's Navy* (Sean M. Heuvel and John A. Rodgaard)
52 *Rebellious Scots to Crush: The Military Response to the Jacobite '45* (Andrew Bamford (ed.))
53 *The Army of George II 1727-1760: The Soldiers who Forged an Empire* (Peter Brown)
54 *Wellington at Bay: The Battle of Villamuriel, 25 October 1812* (Garry David Wills)
55 *Life in the Red Coat: The British Soldier 1721-1815* (Andrew Bamford (ed.))
56 *Wellington's Favourite Engineer. John Burgoyne: Operations, Engineering, and the Making of a Field Marshal* (Mark S. Thompson)
57 *Scharnhorst: The Formative Years, 1755-1801* (Charles Edward White)
58 *At the Point of the Bayonet: The Peninsular War Battles of Arroyomolinos and Almaraz 1811-1812* (Robert Griffith)
59 *Sieges of the '45: Siege Warfare during the Jacobite Rebellion of 1745-1746* (Jonathan D. Oates)
60 *Austrian Cavalry of the Revolutionary and Napoleonic Wars, 1792–1815* (Enrico Acerbi, András K. Molnár)
61 *The Danish Army of the Napoleonic Wars 1801-1814, Organisation, Uniforms & Equipment: Volume 2: Cavalry and Artillery* (David Wilson)
62 *Napoleon's Stolen Army: How the Royal Navy Rescued a Spanish Army in the Baltic* (John Marsden)

63 *Crisis at the Chesapeake: The Royal Navy and the Struggle for America 1775-1783* (Quintin Barry)
64 *Bullocks, Grain, and Good Madeira: The Maratha and Jat Campaigns 1803-1806 and the emergence of the Indian Army* (Joshua Provan)
65 *Sir James McGrigor: The Adventurous Life of Wellington's Chief Medical Officer* (Tom Scotland)
66 *Fashioning Regulation, Regulating Fashion: Uniforms and Dress of the British Army 1800-1815 Volume I* (Ben Townsend) (paperback edition)
67 *Fashioning Regulation, Regulating Fashion: Uniforms and Dress of the British Army 1800-1815 Volume II* (Ben Townsend) (paperback edition)
68 *The Secret Expedition: The Anglo-Russian Invasion of Holland 1799* (Geert van Uythoven) (paperback edition)
69 *The Sea is My Element: The Eventful Life of Admiral Sir Pulteney Malcolm 1768-1838* (Paul Martinovich)
70 *The Sword and the Spirit: Proceedings of the first 'War & Peace in the Age of Napoleon' Conference* (Zack White (ed.))
71 *Lobositz to Leuthen: Horace St Paul and the Campaigns of the Austrian Army in the Seven Years War 1756-57* (Neil Cogswell) (paperback edition)
72 *For God and King. A History of the Damas Legion 1793-1798: A Case Study of the Military Emigration during the French Revolution* (Hughes de Bazouges and Alistair Nichols)
73 *'Their Infantry and Guns Will Astonish You': The Army of Hindustan and European Mercenaries in Maratha service 1780-1803* (Andy Copestake)
74 *Like A Brazen Wall: The Battle of Minden, 1759, and its Place in the Seven Years War* (Ewan Carmichael)
75 *Wellington and the Lines of Torres Vedras: The Defence of Lisbon during the Peninsular War* (Mark Thompson)
76 *French Light Infantry 1784-1815: From the Chasseurs of Louis XVI to Napoleon's Grande Armée* (Terry Crowdy)
77 *Riflemen: The History of the 5th Battalion 60th (Royal American) Regiment, 1797-1818* (Robert Griffith) (paperback edition)
78 *Hastenbeck 1757: The French Army and the Opening Campaign of the Seven Years War* (Olivier Lapray)
79 *Napoleonic French Military Uniforms: As Depicted by Horace and Carle Vernet and Eugène Lami* (Guy Dempsey (trans. and ed.))
80 *These Distinguished Corps: British Grenadier and Light Infantry Battalions in the American Revolution* (Don N. Hagist)
81 *Rebellion, Invasion, and Occupation: The British Army in Ireland, 1793 -1815* (Wayne Stack)
82 *You Have to Die in Piedmont! The Battle of Assietta, 19 July 1747. The War of the Austrian Succession in the Alps* (Giovanni Cerino Badone)
83 *A Very Fine Regiment: the 47th Foot in the American War of Independence, 1773–1783* (Paul Knight)
84 *By Fire and Bayonet: Grey's West Indies Campaign of 1794* (Steve Brown) (paperback edition)
85 *No Want of Courage: The British Army in Flanders, 1793-1795* (R.N.W. Thomas)
86 *Far Distant Ships: The Royal Navy and the Blockade of Brest 1793-1815* (Quintin Barry) (paperback edition)
87 *Armies and Enemies of Napoleon 1789-1815: Proceedings of the 2021 Helion and Company 'From Reason to Revolution' Conference* (Robert Griffith (ed.))
88 *The Battle of Rossbach 1757: New Perspectives on the Battle and Campaign* (Alexander Querengässer (ed.))
89 *Waterloo After the Glory: Hospital Sketches and Reports on the Wounded After the Battle* (Michael Crumplin and Gareth Glover) (paperback edition)
90 *From Ushant to Gibraltar: The Channel Fleet 1778-1783* (Quintin Barry)
91 *'The Soldiers are Dressed in Red': The Quiberon Expedition of 1795 and the Counter-Revolution in Brittany* (Alistair Nichols)
92 *The Army of the Kingdom of Italy 1805-1814: Uniforms, Organisation, Campaigns* (Stephen Ede-Borrett)
93 *The Ottoman Army of the Napoleonic Wars 1798-1815: A Struggle for Survival from Egypt to the Balkans* (Bruno Mugnai)
94 *The Changing Face of Old Regime Warfare: Essays in Honour of Christopher Duffy* (Alexander S. Burns (ed.))
94 *The Changing Face of Old Regime Warfare: Essays in Honour of Christopher Duffy* (Alexander S. Burns (ed.)
95 *The Danish Army of the Napoleonic Wars 1801-1814, Organisation, Uniforms & Equipment: Volume 3: Norwegian Troops and Militia* (David Wilson)
96 *1805 – Tsar Alexander's First War with Napoleon* (Alexander Ivanovich Mikhailovsky-Danilevsky, trans. Peter G.A. Phillips)
97 *'More Furies then Men': The Irish Brigade in the service of France 1690-1792* (Pierre-Louis Coudray)
98 *'We Are Accustomed to do our Duty': German Auxiliaries with the British Army 1793-95* (Paul Demet) (paperback edition)

99 *Ladies, Wives and Women: British Army Wives in the Revolutionary and Napoleonic Wars 1793-1815* (David Clammer)

100 *The Garde Nationale 1789-1815: France's Forgotten Armed Forces* (Pierre-Baptiste Guillemot)

101 *Confronting Napoleon: Levin von Bennigsen's Memoir of the Campaign in Poland, 1806-1807, Volume I Pultusk to Eylau* (Alexander Mikaberidze and Paul Strietelmeier (trans. and ed.))

102 *Olmütz to Torgau: Horace St Paul and the Campaigns of the Austrian Army in the Seven Years War 1758-60* (Neil Cogswell) (paperback edition)

103 *Fit to Command: British Regimental Leadership in the Revolutionary & Napoleonic Wars* (Steve Brown)

104 *Wellington's Unsung Heroes: The Fifth Division in the Peninsular War, 1810-1814* (Carole Divall)

105 *1806-1807 – Tsar Alexander's Second War with Napoleon* (Alexander Ivanovich Mikhailovsky-Danilevsky, trans. Peter G.A. Phillips)

106 *The Pattern: The 33rd Regiment in the American Revolution, 1770-1783* (Robbie MacNiven)

107 *To Conquer and to Keep: Suchet and the War for Eastern Spain, 1809-1814, Volume 1 1809-1811* (Yuhan Kim)

108 *To Conquer and to Keep: Suchet and the War for Eastern Spain, 1809-1814, Volume 2 1811-1814* (Yuhan Kim)

109 *The Tagus Campaign of 1809: An Alliance in Jeopardy* (John Marsden)

110 *The War of the Bavarian Succession, 1778-1779: Prussian Military Power in Decline?* (Alexander Querengässer)

111 *Anson: Naval Commander and Statesman* (Anthony Bruce)

112 *Atlas of the Battles and Campaigns of the American Revolution, 1775-1783* (David Bonk and George Anderson)

113 *A Fine Corps and will Serve Faithfully: The Swiss Regiment de Roll in the British Army 1794-1816* (Alistair Nichols)

114 *Next to Wellington: General Sir George Murray: The Story of a Scottish Soldier and Statesman, Wellington's Quartermaster General* (John Harding-Edgar) (paperback edition)

115 *King George's Army: British Regiments and the Men who Led Them 1793-1815, Volume 1* (Steve Brown)

116 *Great Britain and the Defence of the Low Countries, 1744-1748: Armies, Politics and Diplomacy* (Alastair Massie)

117 *Kesselsdorf 1745: Decision in the Fight for Silesia* (Alexander Querengässer)

118 *The Key to Lisbon: The Third French Invasion of Portugal, 1810-11* (Kenton White) (paperback edition)

119 *Not So Easy, Lads: Wearing the Red Coat 1786–1797* (Vivien Roworth)

120 *Waging War in America: Operational Challenges of Five Armies* (Don N. Hagist (ed.)

121 *Sailors, Ships and Sea Fights: Proceedings of the 2022 'From Reason to Revolution 1721–1815' Naval Warfare in the Age of Sail Conference* (Nicholas James Kaizer (ed.))

122 *Light Troops in the Seven Years War: Irregular Warfare in Europe and North America 1755–1763* (James R. McIntyre)

123 *Every Hazard and Fatigue: The Siege of Pensacola 1781* (Joshua Provan)

124 *Armies and Wars of the French East India Companies 1664-1770: European, Asian and African Soldiers in India, Africa, the Far East and Louisiana* (René Chartrand)

125 *Suffren Versus Hughes: War in the Indian Ocean 1781-1783* (Quintin Barry)

126 *The Russian Patriotic War of 1812: The Russian Official History* Vol.1 (Modest Ivanovich Bogdanovich, trans. Peter G.A. Phillips)

127 *The King and His Fortresses: Frederick the Great and Prussian Permanent Fortifications 1740-1786* (Grzegorz Podruczny)